THE HOUSE OF AUSTRIA

C·A·MACARTNEY

THE HOUSE OF AUSTRIA

THE LATER PHASE
1790–1918

AT THE UNIVERSITY PRESS

Edinburgh

©

C. A. Macartney 1978
Edinburgh University Press
22 George Square, Edinburgh

ISBN 0 85224 338 3 (Hardbound)
      0 85224 351 0 (Paperback)

Printed in Great Britain by
R. & R. Clark Ltd
Edinburgh

PREFACE

This book was first planned as a shorter and more manageable version of my *Habsburg Empire*, first issued under another imprint in 1969 and reissued, with some corrections, in 1971. As it now eventually emerges, it does not quite answer to that description. The task of compression necessitated a great deal of radical rewriting; further, much material has appeared, or has been brought to my notice, since the manuscript of its predecessor left my hands in 1967. I have tried to take account of this, and also to correct errors that had disfigured the first work. Should Providence grant me the years, and some publishers the grace, I hope to incorporate these improvements, and others still, in a third version of the larger work, which it will then be more fitting to describe as an expansion of this one. Pending the coming, which at best cannot be very soon, of that day, I make bold to suggest to any readers of this volume desirous of finding further details on any point mentioned in it, to seek them in its larger brother or in one of the works listed in the bibliography (which does not, however, mention publications later than 1968).

Purists may cavil at my title, objecting that the rulers of the Monarchy dropped the title 'Maison d'Autriche' early in the period covered by my narrative. But the problem of how to style the Monarchy was one to which neither historians nor even chefs de protocole ever found a watertight solution, at least, one which did not spring a leak in a few years, and the most obvious and popular approximations have been heavily overpre-empted. My title at least reduces the risk to anyone ordering it by post of getting someone else's book on the Monarchy sent to him in error – and, of course, vice versa.

C.A.MACARTNEY

CONTENTS

CONTENTS

One

THE TURNING-POINT OF
1790

The rule of the Habsburgs in Central Europe lasted a little under six and a half centuries. Broadly and on balance (each of the processes was, of course, interrupted by standstills and reverses), the first five were a period of territorial expansion and growth of titular dignity abroad, and at home, of centralization and consolidation of the Monarchic power. In the later period territorial losses outnumbered gains, the titular dignity had to be shared with other dynasties, and at home, the Crown was driven onto the defensive, sometimes into retreat, by popular forces, national and social. The turning-point in the central Monarchy (it had come a couple of months earlier in the Netherlands) can without extravagance be dated to a day: 28 January 1790, the day on which Joseph II, who had pushed absolutism and centralization further than any of his predecessors, signed a Rescript revoking most of the measures which he had imposed in Hungary since succeeding to the undivided rule over the Habsburg dominions on the death of his mother ten years earlier. He died only a month later, leaving his brother Leopold, who succeeded him, confronted with positions which were clearly not tenable *in toto*, and had, moreover, been produced through policies of which Leopold himself disapproved. It is with Leopold's efforts to save from these what he thought worthy of retention, while withdrawing the rest, that this narrative begins; but it will not be wholly intelligible without some description of the situation which the new ruler found facing him.

Although Joseph's undivided rule had begun only in 1780, his mother had made him co-Regent with herself fourteen years earlier, and he had been German King and Holy Roman Emperor a year longer still. He was thus not new to the business of government, but his mother had allowed him little final responsibility, or opportunity to translate into practice his idea of what the Government of a State should be.

It should, as he saw it, be an enlightened absolutism; enlightened, because it was the Monarch's duty to promote the welfare of his subjects; absolute, because it was for him alone to say in what that welfare consisted, and how it should be achieved. The authority must be his alone, and the executants of it obedient exclusively to his orders; no other instance was entitled to command any part of that obedience, and any instance, or any condition, incompatible with the realization of the objective, was to be swept aside or eliminated.

The Monarchy as Maria Theresa had left it was neither absolute enough for Joseph's taste, nor enlightened enough. The Monarch's authority in it was, indeed, already unrestricted in many fields. He was solely competent for its foreign policy (conducted for him by the head of his *Haus- Hof- und Staatskanzlei*, 'Family, Court and State Chancellery'), and supreme head of its armed forces, which were in charge of another central organ, the *Hofkriegsrat* (Court War Chancellery), and now consisted of a standing army 164,000 strong, 143,000 of them raised by conscription from the Hereditary Lands[1] (outside the Tirol), the Bohemian Lands, and Galicia, and 21,000 by 'voluntary enlistment' from Hungary, plus a militia contingent from the Tirol and another from the Military Frontier.[2] All Hungarian nobles were liable for military service if the 'insurrectio' (*levée en masse*) was proclaimed. At his sole disposal were also the revenues, administered by a third central service, the *Hofkammer* (Camera), derived by the Crown from its properties and from certain other sources, among them most forms of indirect taxation, including the yields of customs and excise duties, and the yields from, or royalties on, the mines of precious metals.

Outside these fields, however, the Monarch's constitutional authority was less absolute. Practically every Land possessed rights and privileges which he had bound himself on accession to respect, and nearly all of them, 'institutions of self-government', usually consisting of Estates, composed of representatives of its nobles, meeting periodically in Diet (*Landtag*),[3] who, before the centralizing reforms of Maria Theresa's reign, had administered autonomously – subject to the ultimate control exercised by the Monarch through his secretariats, the Court Chancelleries – most of their Lands' internal affairs, exercising their own authority through the manorial lords who were the direct masters of the unfree populations of their manors. The Monarch's authority had therefore been limited in its field, and in respect of the unfree populations, while ultimately supreme, only mediate in his exercise of it; even where he did issue orders affecting them, he addressed these to the manorial lords, who were responsible for the execution of them.

In the Western Lands, however, the division of the pie had become very much that of the owl and the panther. The powers of the Estates had never been extensive in the Hereditary Lands. In the Bohemian, they had once been very large, but had been reduced to the Hereditary level by Ferdinand II's *Vernewerte Landesordnungen* of 1627 and 1628, and they had been whittled away later in both groups.

Each of the three[4] Court Chancelleries, dealing with internal affairs, now maintained in each Land under its jurisdiction an office whose president saw to the execution in his Land of his Chancellery's orders.[5] As the bureaucratic machine extended its grip over more and more fields of human life, each, whether virgin or previously controlled by the Estates, was assigned to the local *Gubernia*, which also took over from the Estates and made into branches of their own the offices of the 'Circles' (*Kreise*) into which the larger Lands had been divided. For economy's sake, the manorial lords were left to exercise the administrative and judicial authority of the first instance in their manors, but the sphere of their competence was limited, and their exercise of the functions left to them closely supervised by the Circle officials. The one important right still nominally retained by the Estates was that of voting, or refusing to vote, the Land's *contributio*, or share of the costs – which since the introduction of the standing army had far exceeded the resources of the Camera – of the central services of the Monarchy, and that right had become in fact only nominal: the bill was presented to them decennially in advance, and they were taught better than to query it. Otherwise, their functions, where not purely decorative, did not go much beyond the administration of a few local funds.

The position in Transylvania was not very different. Its Diet, once a responsible assemblage of its 'Three Nations',[6] had been so packed with nominees of the *Gubernium* or members of it sitting on the Diet *ex officio*, as to make it a mere mouthpiece of that body.

It was only in the Kingdom of Hungary that the Monarch's powers were still subject to limitations extensive both on paper, and in practice. The Hungarian nobles had retained important rights, including the treasured one of exemption from all taxation, which had been lost by their opposite numbers in the Western Lands,[7] and a powerful and often intractable machinery for defending them. The Hungarian Diet, which under the law had to be convoked every three years, was bi-cameral, and the consent of both its 'Tables' had to be given before any new law was enacted, or any existing one altered. The 'Upper Table', or House of Magnates, which was composed, apart from various oddments, of the chief dignitaries of the realm, higher administrative officials appointed by the Crown, higher prelates, and adult male members of 'magnate' families, usually accepted with little demur the Crown's wishes; but the core of the Lower Table consisted of two representatives sent to it by each of Hungary's fifty-two Counties and four Free Districts, and most of these country squires were, not without reason, suspicious of any proposal coming from Vienna, and unwilling to accept it except at a price.

Hungary possessed a further line of defence in its Counties. Each

of these had at its head a Lord Lieutenant (Föispán) appointed by
the Crown, but his deputy, the Alispán, and all the County's other
functionaries, were members of the local nobility, elected triennially
by their peers, and it was an autonomous institution, self-governing
in many fields, and even when putting into effect orders received from
above, doing so in virtue of its autonomous rights. It was not entitled
to take an autonomous decision which ran contrary to the law of the
land, nor to disregard any lawful order, but it was its right to refuse
to execute any demand which lacked legal sanction.

The position of the Monarch *vis-à-vis* the Land's 'institutions of
self-government' was weaker in Hungary than in Austria also in
another respect. The head of the Hungarian *Gubernium*, there called
the *Consilium Locumtenentiale*, was the Palatine, who was not
simply the King's nominee and executant of his will. He was elected
by the Diet from a short-list presented to it by the King, and his
function, apart from acting for the King in his absence from the
country, was to represent the King *vis-à-vis* the 'nation' and *vice
versa*, mediating between the two when the necessity arose.

The issue most frequently in dispute between the Monarch and the
nation related to the size of Hungary's *contributio* in terms of cash,
supplies, and also, since the size of Hungary's contingent to the
armed forces still depended on a vote from the Diet, manpower. The
consents of the Diets of the Austrian Lands to the corresponding demands, where still necessary (they were no longer needed for the
manpower), had, as we have seen, become a formality, but in Hungary
the Diets which Maria Theresa tried to persuade to accept the
reforms (which would have involved some taxation of noble land) resisted so stubbornly that she dropped the attempt, and she succeeded
in getting from them only small increases, in any kind, in the *contributio*, which left it proportionately far below that being paid by any
Austrian Land.

Joseph, and also his like-minded advisers, resented this position
bitterly, partly on account of its practical effects in terms of a smaller
army and a less well-filled public purse (this deficiency could be, and
was, largely made good by various indirect means), but also because
of its incompatibility with the principle of absolute monarchic
authority.

There were many other respects in which Joseph felt his mother's reforms, nearly all of which had been carried through in the first years
of her reign – in her later years she had tended to rest on her laurels –
to have been incomplete. Spiritual and cultural life, as she left them,
still wore the blinkers of the Counter-Reformation. A personal piety
which amounted to bigotry had not deterred her from asserting

her monarchic rights against challenges to them from the Vatican, but she had not attacked the constitutional and material power-positions of the Catholic Church in her dominions. Non-Catholic Christians were not even allowed, except by special permission, to reside in the Hereditary and Bohemian Lands, except Silesia and, within limitations, Lower Austria. In Hungary, and still more, Transylvania, they were 'tolerated' and allowed to profess their faith, but under burdensome disabilities. Jews were subject to humiliating discrimination, and excluded from many callings. The properties of the Catholic Chapters and of the numerous monasteries and convents covered vast areas. Maria Theresa had insisted on her supreme authority over the educational system, which she had greatly modernized and laicized, but the influence over it of the Catholic Church was still very strong.

Her new bureaucracy was still only half a bureaucracy, the old aristocracy set to perform a new role, and doing so with only half a heart. It was, moreover, cumbersome and inefficient; in many respects producing less satisfactory results than those of the old system, which, although crude and summary, had at least been based on local knowledge. The Empress had done much to better the lot of the unfree peasants, limiting the days of 'robot'[8] which could be legally exacted from them, forbidding abuses and illegal exactions, and establishing a control over the working of the Manorial Courts. But she had not abolished the *nexus subditelae*, so that the unfree man was still the 'subject' of his manorial lord, his personal freedom still incomplete, his protection against exactions and extortions still tenuous in the backward areas into which the arm of law did not easily reach, and his holding still almost the sole source of non-Cameral revenue in Hungary, while even in the Western Lands a noble's demesne land was taxed at only half the rate paid by the 'rustical' peasant-cultivator.

Economic conditions, while varying enormously from Land to Land, were still very backward in some parts of the Monarchy. Its most advanced parts, in this respect, were its Western outliers of the Netherlands and the Milanese, whose economy was that of the Western Europe to which they belonged geographically. In the central Monarchy, Vienna, which had blossomed like a rose since the retreat of the Turks had carried the frontier away from near-eyeshot of it, was now the largest and most splendid city of Central Europe. But Vienna was a special case: it owed its magnificence less to the enterprise of its own citizens than to the historical fortune that had made it the residence of Europe's most august dynasty. In the generations before 1780 industry had made rapid progress in some of the Hereditary and Bohemian Lands. Old-established industries such as

Styrian iron and Bohemian glass had reawakened to new life, and
many industries had been established: some in and round Vienna
itself, to meet the needs of the army and the growing appetite of the
Court and its entourage for luxury goods, others in Bohemia and
Moravia, where the textile and woollen industries, in particular, had
been developed intensively with the help of protective tariffs, subsidies and the like, to make good the loss of Silesia, formerly the most
highly industrialized Land of the Central Monarchy.

These Lands also contained several not inconsiderable towns, and
their agriculture was modern and productive. But the Alpine Lands
were still little more than a tangle of mountain valleys, their natural
resources lying fallow for want of transport, the towns in them few
and small. The parts of Hungary recently recovered from the Turks
had not yet been fully reclaimed for cultivation, or even habitation:
they could still hardly show a town deserving of the name, hardly
even a skilled craftsman; in many parts of them the populations lived
in wretched shacks, barely weather-proof, subsisting by cattle-
breeding or the raising of a few meagre crops by the most primitive
of methods. Eastern Galicia, where the Tatar slave-raids were still
almost a living memory, was in no better case. Living standards in
Western Hungary were higher; those of some of its great lords, mag-
nificent, but here, too, the economy was almost entirely agricultural,
since the industrialists of the Bohemian Lands had prevented the
facilities enjoyed by them from being extended to Hungary by the
argument that the lighter taxation borne by them would enable the
Hungarian entrepreneurs to undercut their Austrian competitors.
Later, the customs barrier between Hungary and the West had been
heightened and so manipulated as to place even Hungarian agriculture at a disadvantage against the Austrian.

There were hardly any bright spots in the financial situation.
When Maria Theresa ascended the throne, she had found just 70,000
gulden in her treasury, little coming into it, after generation on generation of her spendthrift forebears had depleted the Cameral resources by sales (almost always disadvantageous) of State properties
and farming out (again too cheap) of regalia, many Lands in arrears
with their *contributio*, and a public debt of 100,000,000 gulden,
including £320,000 advanced by the Bank of England. The outlay
incurred by her during her reign had not been small, although her
wars had been largely financed by allies. Her great servant, Haugwitz, had then brought in the arrears from the *contributiones* and
raised the yield from them, and her husband, a shrewd financier, had
by various devices reduced the burden of the State debt, both internal
and foreign-owned, so that in 1775 the budget was actually balanced.
The equilibrium was, however, upset again by the war of 1777, and

the subsequent budgets showed renewed deficits, which were met by the issue of currency notes called *Bankozettel*.

That war had been Joseph's own enterprise, and in engaging in it he had shown his dissent from his mother's policies also in the international field. Enormous as had been the improvement in the Monarchy's international position since the dark days of 1741, there were in 1780 two potential sources of danger to it: the advancing power of Russia, and the unslaked ambition of Frederick of Prussia. Maria Theresa was not blind to either threat, but thought both best met by a defensive and non-provocative policy; in this field, too, she preferred to rest on the laurels won by her in her youth in defence of her legitimate rights. Joseph, ambitious and a militarist by temperament—he was the first of his line to appear habitually in uniform—favoured a forward policy which would give the Monarchy added strength to defend its positions, and he had no objection to advancing beyond them, for his spirit lusted after aggrandisement for aggrandisement's sake. Her action in stopping the war was to him another proof that under her the Monarchy was not being ruled as it ought to be.

The national composition of the Monarchy to which Joseph succeeded in 1780 was extraordinarily complex. As the statistics and map at the end of this volume show, it contained eleven major nationalities, not counting innumerable smaller fragments, or the special cases of the Jews and gypsies. None of these constituted an absolute majority in the Monarchy as a whole, nor even in its central core of the Austro-Bohemian and Hungarian Lands, and Galicia, although some constituted such majorities in each of the big groups of Lands and in individual Lands. Further, it was only very rarely that the ethnic boundaries of the main areas of settlement of nationalities coincided with the political boundaries of the units of which the Monarchy was the aggregate in the sense that even a Land, not to speak of a group of Lands, was ethnically homogeneous. Nearly every Land, even when the majority of its population belonged to the same nationality, contained minorities, sometimes very large and important ones, belonging to other nationalities, and conversely, it was exceptional for all, or nearly all, the members of one nationality to inhabit only one Land. The map and the figures show also that the main location of some of the ethnic groups was central, their chief areas of settlement lying near the political and administrative heart of the Monarchy, while others were distant and peripheral. Important aspects of the national position which do not emerge at all from the graphical representations were the nature of the relationship in which each nationality stood towards the dynasty, and the very big differences in the social, material and economic levels on which each of them stood.

The crude racialist picture often drawn by the enemies of the Monarchy, portraying it as consisting of an oligarchy of 'master races' lording it over a larger number of 'subject races' is, indeed, totally false for the period with which this work is concerned. A certain master-subject relationship based on ethnic origin had existed at earlier dates in certain parts of the Monarchy, but even where that had once existed, later centuries had blurred, where they had not entirely obliterated, the old ethnic criterion. The inter-national hierarchy which had evolved during those centuries took no account of ethnic origin in theory, and only occasionally in practice. On the one hand, the great majorities of the earlier so-called master races had sunk into the ranks of the unprivileged masses; on the other, the privileged classes now contained large numbers of men whose efforts, or those of their forebears, had lifted them out of servitude. It was, however, a fact that the effects of long cohabitation, supervening on the earlier relationship, had produced a hierarchy of national cultures in the sense that some peoples of the Monarchy could show a national culture with a social spectrum that extended upwards through the professional and bourgeois classes into a lower and higher nobility, while others stopped short on the peasant or near-peasant level, their own higher classes, or aspirants to such status, having discarded their original national criteria, and with them, their national self-consciousnesses, in favour of those of a more 'advanced' neighbour.

This process had gone on, under different conditions and with different results, in each of the three main groups of Lands of the central Monarchy—even, to some extent, in each Land—before their unification under Habsburg rule, and differently again after it. In the old Alpine Lands the arriving Germans had quickly reduced the Slovenes to the peasant level: here not only the nobility, but even the bourgeoisie, outside the remote Italian fringe, was purely German. Up to the seventeenth century the Czechs had possessed a proud and powerful aristocracy, but the religious wars had brought them down to a level not much above that of the Slovenes. A few families of their old aristocracy had survived the wars, but had adopted the political outlook of their new class-fellows, which may be described as one of strongly provincial, but not Czech, *Habsburgtreue*. In the whole Austro-German-Bohemian group of Lands the German element had been the leading one economically, culturally and socially, even before Maria Theresa's administrative and educational centralization, and this had both strengthened and institutionalized their leadership, leaving not only the aristocracy, but all the middle classes of all these Lands, outside the Italian fringe, German-speaking, and most of them, since national consciousness usually quickly followed language, also German-minded.

The Hungarian nobles in 1780 still traced their political ancestry back in a direct line to the original Magyar conquerors of the country. The continuity which they defended was one of political status, not necessarily of lineage, and the original stock had been repeatedly replenished with newcomers, often of non-Magyar origin. The recruits, or their sons, had, however, almost invariably adopted the language and *mores* of the older members of the class, so that while here, too, the Magyars no longer constituted a 'ruling race', since the great majority of the people were no more privileged than the Slovaks or Ruthenes of the country, the politically and socially dominant element in the country was the Magyar. The bourgeois class were, indeed, mainly non-Magyar (chiefly German or Serb), but they were systematically excluded from political influence.

There were Croat nobles, but they did not represent a Croat national culture; many of them did not even speak the language. The Serbs of the Frontier formed a *corpus separatum* not to be fitted into any general pattern. There were Roumanians among the nobles of the Transylvanian Counties, but the majority of the Roumanians there, whose religion was Orthodox, were unfree men and came nearer than any other people of the Monarchy to deserving the description of a 'subject race'.

In Galicia the old Ruthene nobility had Polonized almost to a man after their homelands had passed under Polish rule in 1349. The Ruthenes were almost entirely a peasant people.

In 1780 even the central Monarchy was still too little of a political unity for any one of its peoples to have achieved a 'master' position outside its own group of Lands. But to an eye viewing it as a whole, the Germans stood out as easily the leading single ethnic element in it. They were the strongest of them numerically—and in this respect our figures do not tell the whole story, since as masters of the leading State of the German Reich the Habsburgs could always draw on other members of the Empire if their own stock of native-born soldiers or civil servants ran short. Socially, economically and culturally, they were the most advanced of them all (except the peripheral Italians). While not enjoying political representation outside their own group of Lands, except in Transylvania, they were to be found in considerable numbers in most of them, and in many played an important economic and cultural role. Their main area of settlement lay at the heart of the Monarchy, and included its capital, the seat of the dynasty, its association with which reached back to the foundation of the Monarchy itself, while the Poles were still only a conquered people, and the Magyars half-reluctant partners to an uneasy truce. Maria Theresa herself, and also Joseph, felt themselves to be Germans by personal nationality. All these things worked together to produce a quite special personal relationship between the dynasty and its German subjects.

We should finally recall that the Monarchy's own frontiers were not ethnic. Almost everywhere they cut across lines of ethnic settlement. There were Germans inside the Monarchy, Germans outside it, and so too with Italians, Poles, Ruthene-Ukrainians, Roumanians, Serbs, Croats, even Slovenes. In each case, moreover, except those of the Croats and Slovenes, and in their cases only if they were so counted, and not as Yugoslavs, the numbers of the nationality living adjacent to the frontiers of the Monarchy, but outside them, exceeded those living inside it.

The Monarchy to which Joseph now succeeded thus contained all the ingredients out of which, when the activating element of the new nationalism was poured over them, emerged the 'national problem' which largely dominated the political life of the Monarchy, and in the end, brought about its disintegration.

Pushed to its extreme, the new nationalism queried the very basis of the Monarchy's existence. For the title in virtue of which Joseph succeeded to his Empire was that of legitimacy, as conferred by the formal acceptance by the other Powers of the validity of the claims which his ancestors had put forward to sovereignty over the dominions of which it was composed; and the factor of ethnic congruity had played no part, either in their assertion of those claims, or the acceptance of them by the other Powers. The new nationalism, on the contrary, maintained that by natural law the legitimate State was that which contained all the members of a nationality, and that its function was to satisfy and, as it were, incorporate the satisfaction of, their national aspirations.

It was only when the Monarchy was nearing its last hour, and in a quite abnormal international situation, that this extreme claim was ever put forward, and then only partially admitted. But long before that the peoples of the Monarchy had begun to demand a measure of political satisfaction inside it for their national aspirations. These demands, while not attacking the existence of the Monarchy, did call in question the ideological foundations of the authority of its rulers, which, resting as they did on its subjects' duty of allegiance to their legitimate Prince, regarded it as an a-national structure in which the nationality of its citizens was simply a personal attribute, like their ages or sex, from which no sort of political right could derive. Even where completely loyal, demands of the new nationalism thus raised an issue of principle between its proponents and their Monarch. But while this did not make the Monarchs unwilling to give pragmatic satisfaction to reasonable requests for national desiderata, it was extraordinarily difficult to see how this could be done in the complex situation described above. What pattern could be found to satisfy the divergent aspirations of so many peoples, so different and so differently placed?

The Monarchy never found a definitive answer to either aspect of its national problem. It maintained to the last the a-national character of its central services, but it proved quite unable to depoliticize the national feelings of its peoples, who for their part continued to regard the a-national State as an insufficient answer to their aspirations. Still less did it prove possible to elimitate the conflicts between the different national claims. These were still waged, and with increasing acerbity, when the Monarchy's last hour struck.

But in 1780 no one could well have foreseen what a place the national problem would soon be occupying in the history of the Monarchy. An observer not looking closely below the surface might easily have supposed that no such problem existed, outside the special case of Galicia. No protests against the centralization and Germanization of the political system in the West had come from the Bohemian Estates, and none against the Germanization of the educational system from either Czechs or Slovenes : both peoples had rather welcomed it as opening to their sons the door to advancement. The Germans themselves had not treated the priority conferred on their national culture in any spirit of self-regarding nationalism. When they introduced non-Germans to the German language and way of life, they did so simply as a means of promoting the consolidation of the State, and there does not seem to have been in them any feeling (as there never was in any of their rulers) that a non-German by birth, once he was linguistically qualified, was a less desirable recruit to the services and professions than a German born.

The national surface was equally unruffled in Hungary. Maria Theresa accepted the Magyar quality of the Hungarian 'nation' as a fact which need not affect its political relationship with the dynasty. She did not attempt to extend her measures of Germanization across the Leitha. The Diets of her reign – there had, indeed, been only three of them – had concerned themselves at length with political, military and economic questions, but the 'national' issues which dominate many of their successors do not figure on their agenda.

The Magyars themselves, not feeling their Magyardom endangered, felt no need to assert it aggressively, or to press it on others ; not even to cultivate it among their own members. Their own historians describe the period as the most slumbrous, in this respect, in all the country's history. The magnates were already half denationalized. Maria Theresa welcomed them in Vienna and loaded them with favours there, and although her object was simply the political one of securing their loyalty, the effect was that they learned there to use in

their own homes the French or German languages current in the polite society of the capital to the extent of forgetting their own, and to
look down their noses at their bog-trotting country cousins. And lack
of pride or even interest in their nation's past was not confined to the
cosmopolitan grandees. The squireens at home spoke Magyar among
themselves or with their peasants, but it was to Vienna or Paris that
they looked for 'culture'. On the other side, the aspiring non-Magyars
of the day subscribed as unreluctantly as their predecessors to the
convention that 'to be a noble was to be a Magyar' (the converse pro-
position, of course, did not hold good) and accepted as willingly the
assimilation which was the price of advancement. When the burghers
of the German towns of Hungary, the Transylvanian Saxons and, for
that matter, the Serbs of the Military Frontier, asserted their national
identities, this was not in any spirit of modern nationalism.

There was no trace among the Croats, either, of any national revivals. The only real precursor of the later national movements was
an unexpected one enough, the people concerned being among the
most backward of the whole Monarchy. As long before as 1732 a
Roumanian Uniate Bishop, known impartially as 'Micu' or 'Klein'
(both words mean 'small') had started a campaign for political rights
for his people, backing his case with appeals to 'historic rights', that
is, to the alleged historic priority over Magyars, Germans or Slavs
of the Roumanians in Transylvania, as descendants of the Roman
colonists of Dacia, or alternatively, of Romanized Dacians. This
claim, which after him was maintained by a handful of disciples
known as the 'Transylvanian Triad', was never thereafter dropped by
his countrymen. It was still being asserted with passion in 1978.

The quietude of the national picture in 1780 was, however, that of
February fields before the sprouting of the corn in them, and if it was
the *Zeitgeist* that had carried the seed into the Monarchy, Maria
Theresa had herself largely drawn the furrows to receive it through
her educational reforms. If the schooling received by a Czech or Slovene boy was in German, it was still schooling, and a child who had
been taught to think in German learned to think in his mother-tongue
also. In Hungary the seed did not even lie so deep. Some years earlier,
a real Magyar national-cultural revival had set in, again owing much
to the Court, for many of its pioneers, including the best-known of
them, György Bessenyey, had studied in Vienna at the famous There-
sianum, or served in the same city in the Royal Hungarian bodyguard. Enthusiasm for their gospel was spreading among the middle
nobility, the country's real leaders, more widely than was suspected
by the Queen or by her aulic advisers.

Not merely contemptuous as Joseph was of the feelings of others, but positively blind to them, he saw in the multi-national composition of his Monarchy chiefly another impediment, the result of its linguistic diversity, to the efficient administration of it, and included the remedying of this administrative weakness in the list of the changes to which he set his hand as soon as his mother's eyes were closed. The pages which follow sketch briefly the main results of his activities during the ten years which elapsed before his own death. Since our object is not to write a history of his reign, but to show what was the situation which he bequeathed to his successor, this sketch is presented not chronologically, but by subject. We begin with his political and administrative innovations, including under this head, since he himself saw it in purely administrative terms, his treatment of the national problem.

On accession, Joseph cleared the way for his proposed measures in this field by refusing to submit himself to coronation in Hungary, with its obligatory oath to observe the national liberties. Later, he refused also to sign the 'Joyeuse Entrée' in the Netherlands. He demonstrated his contempt for traditional rights and forms by having the symbols of them, the Bohemian Crown, the Ducal Hat of Lower Austria, and finally, the Holy Crown of Hungary itself, taken from their homes and lodged in the Imperial Treasury in Vienna.

In the administrative reorganization which followed, Joseph retained the great top-level division of the Monarchy into the Austrian Lands (including Galicia), the Lands of the Hungarian Crown, the Netherlands and the Milanese, and, strangely, even enlarged the competence of the Hungarian Court Chancellery, both by extending it to Transylvania, whose separate Chancellery was abolished, and by giving it charge of the Cameral agenda for all the Hungarian Lands. In both the Austrian and the Hungarian groups of Lands, however, the administrative sub-units were reshaped. In Austria, six enlarged *Gubernia* replaced the thirteen smaller ones. Hungary-Croatia was divided into ten new Districts, the delimitation of which ignored the historic frontier between the two Kingdoms, each under a Royal Commissioner; and Transylvania was similarly redivided into ten sub-units which ignored the limits of the old Saxon and Szekel districts.

Practically all traces of self-government disappeared in both these groups of Lands. In the Austrian, the Estates lost almost the last of such remnants of authority as Maria Theresa had left them. In Hungary, the Föispáns disappeared. The Alispáns were appointed by, and responsible to, the Crown. The County *Congregationes* met once a year, to little purpose, since their autonomy had been taken from them.

Two Rescripts of 1787 introduced analogous political systems in the Netherlands. German was made the sole language of all official business in Hungary, as from the date of the communication (4 May 1784), in the central offices, as from one year after it in the Counties, and on the lowest levels, after three. Officials not acquainted with the language after that date would be dismissed. Knowledge of German was to be a condition of admission to the Diet.

Similar orders were issued in respect of Bohemia, the Littoral and Galicia (where, indeed, it proved so difficult to find enough German speakers that Latin had to be reinstated provisionally). Only the Netherlands and the Milanese were spared. German was made the sole language of instruction in all higher and secondary schools, except that intending priests might study Latin in the high schools. The primary schools, too, were Germanized, except that religion might be taught in the pupils' mother tongue. Again, the Netherlands and the Milanese were spared.

Joseph's answer to protests was that he was not conducting a campaign against non-German languages, but acting in the interests of efficiency, German being the language most widely used in his dominions (among which he counted the Reich) and also that used on all higher cultural levels. This was true enough, but it is fairly certain that Joseph, who was the most German-minded Habsburg to ascend the throne for 300 years, would have Germanized all his subjects if he had had the time and the power.

All these structural and administrative changes proved, as we shall see, short-lived, as did, in Hungary, the loss of its constitutional rights of self-government, on both the national and the local levels, while in the Netherlands the dictatorship hardly got beyond the blue-print stage. But, as in the religious field, some of the effects of the enactments outlived the measures themselves. The replacement of the old self-government by bureaucratic rule had, indeed, begun forty years earlier, but it was only under Joseph that the peoples of the Monarchy learned beyond all unteaching to regard bureaucratic rule, directed from a lofty and invisible centre, as the normal and indeed the right form of government, and if Hungary at the time resisted the application of the system, it constructed a similar although less elaborate one centred on Budapest when it recovered its internal autonomy.

It was also under Joseph that the bureaucracy itself emerged as a distinct class and social factor, with a distinctive outlook which earned it the right to share with that of the Church the name of Josephinianism. Even Maria Theresa's administrators had still been largely local nobles, or their employees, who tended to identify themselves with their own local or class interests, or those of their employers.

Joseph's bureaucracy was a central service, like the army, owing its allegiance wholly to the Crown, and thus completely centralist in its political outlook. Both *qua* centralists and *qua* servants of the auto-cracy, they were hostile to the old federalists, which an increasing number of them also disliked on social grounds; for Joseph brought many more non-nobles into his service, and facilitated their promo-tion by insisting on the criterion of merit.

All these factors, which may have been reinforced by the circum-stance that so many of the bureaucrats were Germans, made them particularly hostile to Hungary. The numerous attempts made by Austria's Monarchs to extend total centralization to Hungary found no stronger supporters than in the Josephinian bureaucracy, and the social class to which they belonged.

The class had, indeed, its own problems. Joseph paid them meagre salaries, which they were not allowed to supplement by the accep-tance of *douceurs*, however traditional and harmless, or by taking second employments, and he made the latter resort impossible by consistently overworking them. They were allowed little initiative; although he himself complained of being overburdened with trivi-alities, everything had to be sent up to him. They were also subjected to a galling and even intimidating supervision, which took from them the taste to exercise such initiative as the system would have allowed them. This was exercised in part by secret 'conduitlisten', sent in annually by the superior of each official, partly by the police, which was reorganized on the initiative of the ambitious Governor of Lower Austria, von Pergen. First in Lower Austria, later in all Lands, the force was divided into 'criminal' and secret branches, the former charged with the detection of ordinary crime, the latter with duties which, beginning with the supervision of the work of other govern-ment departments, were then extended to watching the activities of foreigners and other suspicious elements. To enable it to perform these duties, its permanent staffs were enlarged, and it was allowed to employ outside informers, who were rewarded if their 'denunciations' proved well founded.

The secret police was also given the duty of reporting on public opinion, to the expression of which Joseph allowed remarkable free-dom, up to the last months of his reign. The publication of works which were immoral, or calculated to bring religion into disrepute, was forbidden, but little else. Free criticism was permitted of all pub-lic affairs, and even of the person of the Monarch himself.

The one field in which Joseph admitted any limitation on his own will was that of religion. He professed himself a good Catholic, ad-mitted the supreme authority of the Holy See *in puris spiritualibus*, and habitually maintained that the purpose of his enactments was to

defend the Faith against abuses and distortions. But his definition of
pura spiritualia was extremely narrow. He personally laid down the
exact forms to be used in Church services, and the number of candles
to be used at each. He stopped loopholes left by his mother through
which the voice of the Vatican might have filtered – the direct correspondence between Austrian bishops and Rome was prohibited – and
replaced the episcopal and monastic seminaries, which he described
as 'nests of the fanatical hydra of ultra-montanism', by eight State-
controlled 'General Seminaries' as the sole training-grounds for intending priests. Some of his measures could easily have been regarded
as detrimental even to the spiritual authority of Rome. A 'Toleration
Patent', issued in October 1781, while leaving Catholicism the 'dominant religion' of the State, and treating smaller Confessions with extreme harshness, allowed the Calvinist, Lutheran and Orthodox
Churches to build their own places of worship and schools, to own
land, practise crafts and hold posts in the army and civil service,
without being required to take an oath or attend a religious ceremony
contrary to their consciences. Another series of Patents, issued, with
variants, in different Lands, relieved Jews of the obligation to wear a
distinctive dress and of many other restrictions. They were still debarred from some careers, but could now enter many professions, including that of medicine. Another series, which actually brought the
Pope to Vienna to register a protest (he got no comfort from Joseph,
and was treated by the Chancellor, Kaunitz, with studied discour-
tesy) resulted in the dissolution of over 600 monasteries and nun-
neries. Many of their properties were sold, and the proceeds, after
some provision had been made for the dispossessed victims, paid into
a fund which, under the 'Livings Patent' of 1785, was used for found-
ing new parochial livings.

Marriage, although it still had to be contracted in front of a priest,
became a purely civil contract, the validity of which derived exclusively from the law of the land.

It may be remarked that while several of Joseph's measures in this
field were repealed by his successor, the spirit which they inculcated
was one of his most enduring legacies to posterity, which, as we shall
see, witnessed prolonged and embittered conflicts between the devoted adherents of Rome and the partisans of the local Erastianism
which was habitually, and with justice, called 'Josephinianism'.

Joseph's peasant legislation was, contrary to later legend, not revolutionary, for he, like his mother, maintained the *nexus subditelae;* but three big Patents of 1781 made it less burdensome.
The 'Serfdom Patent' (*Leibeigenschaftspatent*) extended to the other
Lands the condition of 'moderate hereditary subjection' already attained by the Hereditary Lands by abolishing the restrictions on the

peasants' personal freedom which had survived elsewhere. The 'Sub-jects' Patent' (*Untertanspatent*) of September 1781 made it really possible for the 'subject' to obtain legal redress against illegal de-mands made of him by his lord (or his lord's agent), and the Penal Patent (*Strafpatent*) of the same date further limited the penalties which a Patrimonial Court was entitled to impose. A number of minor reforms followed, and Joseph also tried (without much effect) to make the lords follow the example which he set on his own lands, of introducing emphyteutic tenures and to encourage the buying in of holdings and commutation of dues and services against cash rents. Meanwhile, he had been working out a plan to raise the whole *contri-butio* from a single land tax, to be levied equally on all land through-out the Monarchy at a rate of 12.22 per cent of its assessed value. The rustical peasant was in addition to pay his lord a further 17.78 per cent in lieu of all seigneural dues and servitudes, and out of the remaining 70 per cent also his communal dues. It was calculated that these, with his expenditure on seed, replacement of live-stock and worn-out tools, etc., would amount to 20 per cent, leaving him 50 per cent for his own maintenance and that of his family. As first announ-ced, in February 1789, this measure was to come into force on 11 November 1789; but the date was subsequently postponed to 10 February 1790, so that it had not yet come into effective operation when he died.

We can only touch fleetingly on a few of Joseph's other activities, which were innumerable, for there was no aspect of his subjects' lives which escaped his attention. The judicial system, which now became entirely independent of the administrative, was completely recast: the jurisdiction of the State Courts was extended to cover almost all cases above the Patrimonial Court level, and all separate jurisdic-tions, except the military, abolished. Maria Theresa's criminal code was amended, and an entirely new civil code, the 'Bürgerliches Gesetzbuch', introduced. Like his mother, Joseph was in favour of schooling for the masses, and many new elementary schools were founded under his auspices. Like her, he thought it superfluous for the common man to receive further education, except in so far as it served to produce efficient civil servants, or in specialist subjects such as medicine. Even his mother's famous creation, the Theresi-anum, was abolished. In his economic policy, Joseph built further on the foundations laid by his mother. A new tariff, promulgated in 1781, prohibited the importation of no less than 200 articles, except under licence, and then subject to an *ad valorem* duty of 60 per cent. The construction of factory enterprises in Bohemia and Lower Aus-tria was pressed on, probably with more attention to the shop-windows than to the foundations; the discrimination against Hungary

was maintained and even extended: it was made practically impossible for Hungary to obtain from abroad any raw materials or manufactured articles except those produced in Austria, which entered
Hungary duty-free, while Hungarian cattle and wheat entering Austria paid a higher duty than the same articles from other countries;
and it was made almost impossible for her to export her products
elsewhere.

Many of Joseph's innovations were, naturally, bitterly resented by
the victims of them, and their victims' sympathizers, the more so for
the manner in which they were introduced; for Joseph was not
simply unmindful of the feelings of others, but took a positively sadistic pleasure in wounding them. With tact and decent manners he
could have secured at least grudging acceptance of much which his
gratuitous offensiveness made intolerable. As it was, discontent
against his regime was soon running high among his subjects. But
he might yet have mastered it but for the disastrous consequences of
his ambitious military and foreign policies. One of the first acts of his
reign was to order the strength of the standing army to be raised to
225,000. This was already one of the most generally unpopular of all
his enactments. Prospective conscripts combined with their landlords
to evade it, and the figure could be reached only by the extension of
conscription to Hungary and the Tirol.

But he wanted not only to have an army, but to use it. As early as
May 1781 he concluded an alliance with Catherine of Russia. His
purpose was defensive: to safeguard his rear against Prussia while he
strengthened his position in the West. But here, too, his besetting
fault of disregarding the feelings of others led to one failure after
another. His denunciation of the Barriers Treaty, and other moves in
the Netherlands, provoked great resentment in Holland and also estranged France, and his pursuit of his great objective, the exchange
of the Netherlands against Bavaria, together with a tactless assertion
of his Imperial rights, frightened the German Princes into forming a
loose alliance under the leadership of Prussia, whose ambitious Aus-
trophobe Minister, Hertzberg, saw in the situation a possibility for a
further advance still if embarrassment came to Austria from any
other quarter. This situation arose when war between Russia and the
Porte broke out again in 1787. The provocation had all come from
Russia, but it was Turkey which, egged on by Prussia, declared war,
so that Austria was bound under the treaty to help Russia. But she
need only have contributed a modest auxiliary corps. Instead Joseph,
inspired by what evil genius his chroniclers can only guess, sent
down a great force of 250,000 men, which was too large even to de-
ploy effectively and much too large to keep supplied. It won some
initial successes, eventually taking Belgrade, but for the most part be-

came embogged in the marish plains of South Hungary, where a third of its numbers went down with the ague. Meanwhile Catherine left the Austrians to take the brunt of the fighting, while Prussia concluded an alliance with England and Holland, sent a force to the Galician frontier and established secret contact with the Hungarian malcontents.

Discontent was soon running very high indeed, in almost every Land of the Monarchy, and among every class of its population; for – the visitations of the recruiting sergeant apart – the war created shortages and had sent prices soaring. There was widespread unrest among the peasants, who had expected total liberation. There was even an effervescence in Vienna and some other centres of modern left-wing radicalism which found Joseph's regime insufficiently radical and even questioned his cardinal assumption of the absolute Monarch's absolute authority.

Joseph, although already mortally sick, faced the storm with incredible courage, or obstinacy. To meet the unrest from the lower classes, he reintroduced a strict censorship, and reorganized and strengthened the police: while the enforcement of regulations was left to the local authorities, upper services, especially the secret police, were made a separate service with the status of a *Hofstelle* (Department of State), under the charge of von Pergen, reporting directly to the Emperor.

These measures, if they strengthened the despotic character of the regime, were yet effective. But the 'Right-wing' opposition was more formidable. In the Netherlands, where Joseph had chosen just these years to introduce his most far-reaching innovations, he at first refused absolutely to listen to the vehement protests which came from the Estates there, but the situation got beyond his control, and in mid-November he withdrew the most objectionable of his enactments. It was too late. On 25 November 1789 the Estates of Flanders declared him forfeit of the throne, and Belgium proclaimed its independence on 10 January 1790.

By this time the situation in Hungary was hardly less critical. In the absence of a Diet, Joseph had been forced to address his demands for men and supplies to the Counties, which, under strong pressure, voted them, but sabotaged the execution of the measures, while protesting most vigorously against the illegality of the procedure. The *Consilium* and even the Court Chancellery supported them and strongly urged Joseph to repeal his unlawful enactments, convoke the Diet, submit himself to coronation, and take the oath to the constitution. Driven against the wall, Joseph yielded here also. On 28 January, in a letter which protested how good his intentions had been, he revoked all his enactments relating to Hungary, except the

Toleration, Livings and Peasant Patents. He promised to convoke a Diet when his health should allow it, and ordered the return of the Holy Crown to Hungary.

On 18 February the venerated symbol was escorted back to Pressburg, amid scenes of indescribable jubilation. But Joseph was not destined ever to wear it. He died two days later.

Two

LEOPOLD II

When Joseph knew himself to be dying, he had sent for his brother and prospective successor, Leopold, to share his burden. The call had been unwelcome to Leopold. For twenty-five years he had governed the family secundogeniture of Tuscany with a wise moderation, and he was reluctant to leave the tranquillity of the Grand Duchy for the storm-centre of Vienna. Like his brother, Leopold had absorbed the doctrines of the contemporary Enlightenment, and largely from the same teachers; but the conclusions he had drawn from them were not the same as Joseph's. He was convinced that the storms which his brother had conjured up could be appeased only by methods totally different from Joseph's. In a letter written by him to his sister, Marie Christine, wife of the Governor-General of the Austrian Netherlands, on 14 June 1789, when the conflict there was reaching explosion-point, he had expressed belief in Montesquieu's doctrine of the division of powers, and of the 'contract between sovereign and people' which entitled the latter to disobey the former if he violated the contract, and had even welcomed the French Revolution as setting 'an example which all sovereigns and governments of Europe would be forced, willy-nilly, to obey', and something from which 'infinite happiness would result everywhere'. The letter was obviously not meant only for its recipient's eyes, but Leopold was certainly sincere in his beliefs that it was 'useless to try to impose even good on the peoples if they were not convinced of its utility' and that constitutional government was preferable to dictatorship, from the points of view of sovereign and subjects alike. He was absolutely unwilling to share the government with Joseph, lest foreign Courts and the Monarchy's own peoples should deduce that he endorsed his brother's principles and methods, and therefore delayed his coming until the news of Joseph's death reached him. Then, perforce, he started north, arriving in Vienna on 12 March.

The most urgent of the problems confronting him was that posed by the dual, and interconnected, threats of rebellion in Hungary and invasion by Prussia. This he attacked immediately. Only a fortnight after his arrival, he wrote to the King of Prussia protesting his own pacific intentions and his innocence of any wish to upset the balance in Germany. Difficult negotiations followed, but he was able to conclude on 27 July 1790 the 'Convention of Reichenbach', under which he promised to make peace with the Porte on the basis of the *status quo ante bellum*, while Prussia agreed that Austria's authority should be restored in Belgium, subject to an amnesty and the restoration of the former constitution, which should be jointly guaranteed by Prussia and the Maritime Powers. The armistice with Turkey was then signed at Giurgevo on 23 December, and a definitive peace – under which Austria lost most of what she had gained in the war, including Belgrade – at Sistovo on 4 August 1791; while a peace treaty between Russia and Turkey, which brought the frontier between them to the Dniester, was signed at Jassy on 9 January 1792.

The Agreement of Reichenbach was denounced by Kaunitz and the extreme Austrian Prussophobes as a retreat before Prussian pressure, and Leopold himself so described it in correspondence with Catherine. Yet he indubitably gained far more than he lost by concluding it. Nearly all the positions from which he retreated were in any case untenable. If he lost the friendship of Russia, and the rivalry between Austria and Prussia was only put into cold storage – and that not for long – yet he gained in the west an invaluable breathing-space during which he enjoyed the titular leadership of Germany (his coronation as Emperor took place on 9 October) and in December was able, although again not for long, to reassert the sovereignty of his House in Belgium, which Austrian troops reoccupied in December. He was quit of an exhausting, expensive and unpopular war, and had gained another important advantage, because after signing the Convention Prussia dropped her support of the disaffected elements in Galicia and Hungary.

Already on his journey northwards Leopold had been met in every provincial centre by deputations paying their respects, but also presenting lists of wishes and grievances. More petitions awaited him in Vienna. Those from Hungary called for immediate attention, for if he was to be crowned, as was obviously and urgently necessary, agreement would have to be reached on the terms on which the coronation should take place. This was no mere formality, for some elements in Hungary were asserting that Joseph's disregard of the constitution had rendered invalid the contracts of 1683, 1715 and 1741 between Crown and nation, and were demanding a new election, to be accompanied by an entirely new codification of the relationship. Leopold convoked a 'Coronation Diet' for June, but before he could be crowned the terms of the Coronation Diploma had to be agreed. Leopold was adamant on the right of himself, and after him his heirs-at-law, to succeed to the throne, but showed himself ready to make reasonable concessions, and in fact gave some immediate tokens of goodwill which, together with the news, which had filtered through, of his negotiations with Prussia, brought about the dropping of the demand for an election, and the Diet met according to programme. This was only the first step, for many Counties still sent in, through their representatives, very far-reaching demands. But hot heads were cooled by the news of the Convention of Reichenbach and by rumours that the King of Prussia had given away the names of his foreign correspondents. Leopold played another trump card when, in September, he allowed the Serbs of Hungary to hold a 'Diet' which asked for their constitution in a separate 'national' organization, with its own territorial basis. The coronation duly took place on 15 November, Leopold having, as he had stipulated, signed a Diploma in the same terms as Maria Theresa. But the negotiations continued into the next year, when they terminated in a series of important Laws.

The Diet recognized Leopold's hereditary right and that of his heirs to the throne, and the King's right to 'govern' the country. But Leopold gave a solemn pledge, which was embodied in a Law (Law X of 1790), that in spite of the links which, under the Pragmatic Sanction, existed between it and the King's other dominions, Hungary, with its *partes adnexae*, constituted 'a free Realm, independent in all the forms of its government (including all its administration), not subject to any other Land or people, and possessed of its own form of State and Constitution'. It could therefore be ruled and governed only by its own lawfully crowned King, only in accordance with its own laws and customs, and 'not after the pattern of other provinces'. He agreed that the right to enact, interpret and repeal legislation resided jointly with the King and the Estates in session. Neither he nor his successors would rule by Patent or Rescript. The successor to the throne was bound to submit hinself for coronation within six months of accession. The Diet had to be convoked triennially. While foreign affairs and defence remained Monarchic services, the consent of the Diet was necessary for demands for taxes or recruits. The central structure of the Government, including the Hungarian Court Chancellery, was left untouched, but the Palatine had to reside in the country.

For the rest, Leopold refused to agree to the union with Transylvania, and he did not accept the Serbs' separatist demands, but gave them a Court Chancellery of their own. Laws were passed enacting the substance of the three Patents which Joseph had not retracted, but with some modifications. Protestants got freedom of worship in Hungary and Croatia, and in inner Hungary, even full equality with Catholics. The Greek Orthodox Church became 'established'. Maria Theresa's 'urbarium' was provisionally legalized and other laws legalized the substance of Joseph's main peasant Patents of 1781, although not his later enactments in that field. The nobles automatically recovered their exemption from taxation, and the proposed land survey was cancelled. Economic legislation, in general, reverted to the 1780 position.

Many of these decisions were recognized as provisional; six committees were to be set up to work out proposals in a large number of fields.

Transylvania got its old constitution restored, and its Court Chancellery. Leopold passed to the Diet a petition, entitled *Supplex Libellus Valachorum*, which he had received from the Roumanian leaders, protesting their people's claim to historic priority and asking that their nobles should be constituted a fourth 'nation'. This the Three Nations, whose feelings towards the Roumanians, never friendly, had been exacerbated in 1784 by the dreadful Jacquerie of the 'Horia Rebellion', rejected out of hand. All that the Roumanians got was the equality to which the Orthodox Church was promoted here also.

The constitutional position in the western Lands was easily dealt with. Nearly all of them had asked for the restitution of historic rights, and the Bohemian extremists had been hardly less extravagant than the Hungarians. They demanded return to the *status quo ante* the *Vernewerte Landesordnung*, including the right to elect their Monarch. But it was not necessary to take them seriously. Leopold had himself crowned in Prague on 12 August 1791, and ended by declaring 1764 the datum line for the constitutional position in all the western Lands. As all Maria Theresa's main reforms had been completed by that date, this meant that the centralization and *de facto* absolutism which she had by that time established, were maintained, but not Joseph's aggravations of it, The Tirol had some ancient liberties restored, including its exemption from taxation, and in Styria the bourgeoisie got more representation on the Estates, and the peasants one voice in them.

For the rest, Leopold rubbed the rough edges off his brother's innovations, but refused to repeal those which he thought beneficial. He abolished the general seminaries and reinstated some monasteries, but maintained the Toleration and Livings Patents and refused to allow the Holy See to recover any more of its influence over the Austrian Church, affirming the principle that the clergy were servants of the State, not entitled to speak except on purely religious questions. He promised to consider changing Joseph's marriage law, but did not get down to doing so. He suspended the extremely harsh punishments in Joseph's Penal Code, and set up a new Commission to work out a new Code. Another Commission was to work out a new educational system, allowing much more initiative and self-government to the teachers. The censorship was made more stringent, but the police were put back under the *Hofkanzlei*, and a large part of Joseph's extensive apparatus of secret police liquidated, Leopold contenting himself with his own small band of confidants.

In spite of strong protests from the Estates, Leopold refused to withdraw his mother's peasant enactments, or, with minor exceptions, those of his brother, but he did suspend the introduction of the great Patent of 1789/90, while reserving his right to reissue it after it had been reconsidered. The system of direct taxation was thus back on its pre-1789 footing, and with it, the rustical peasants' obligations to their lords.

Some import restrictions were removed, but Leopold had not got fairly down to the field of economic policy when he died.

There are indications that Leopold meant, when the time was ripe, to go much further towards introducing a more genuinely representative system under which the Estates, remodelled to allow more representation to the burghers and the peasants, whose conditions were also to be improved further, would really have shared the responsibility of government with the Crown. He had, with the help of secret confidants, worked out preliminary ideas for these changes in two selected areas, Hungary and, oddly, Styria. But he was a very secretive man, and we have only tantalizing glimpses of these plans, which had hardly even reached the blue-print stage when he died. All he had hitherto accomplished was thus only an emergency operation of pacification, which left behind it a great number of loose ends. As far as it had gone, however, it had been eminently successful. The return of peace and the demobilization of the army, with the consequent relaxation of the financial stringency, had sent a sense of relief through the whole country. The Estates, if not satisfied, had been appeased, and even the peasants placated; the unrest which had still been running high among them in the summer of 1791 had died away by the end of the year.

Unhappily, this pacification had not extended to the country's foreign relations, where the situation had deteriorated again in 1791. It had, indeed, proved possible for Austria to sign treaties with Prussia (provisional, 25 July 1791, and definitive, 7 February 1792) embodying a rather loose agreement for co-operation in Poland, and also a guarantee by each party to help the other with 20,000 men against any attack[1] or in the event of internal unrest. But there had been mounting friction between the Empire and France which had changed Leopold's earlier favourable view of the French Revolution. On 1 July 1791 he had invited all the sovereigns of Europe to inform France that they regarded Louis's cause as their own, and on 27 August, he and Frederick William had jointly issued the 'Declaration of Pillnitz' describing conditions in France as a matter of common interest to all sovereigns, and expressing the hope that they would collaborate effectively to establish an order which took account both of the rights of sovereigns and the welfare of the French people. The declaration was cautiously worded: its authors were prepared to mobilize to achieve its objects, but only if other States participated. This reservation took most of the reality out of the threat, but it inflamed feeling in France against both the foreign interference and its own dynasty, which had seemed ready to profit by that interference. From that moment war between Austria and France had become an increasingly imminent certainty.

This was the position when, on 1 March 1792, Leopold died with tragic suddenness, after only a few days' illness.

Three

FRANCIS II (I)

The death of Leopold put an end to what had been, for good or ill, the most dynamic epoch of Austrian history, and opened an era which, on the contrary, was static almost beyond precedent. The willed immobility was, moreover, far longer-lived than the previous activity; for while Joseph's and Leopold's reigns had between them covered only a dozen years, Francis himself occupied the throne for thirty-three, and his dead hand continued to hold the reins of government for another thirteen, so that March 1848 found Austria in all respects which government ingenuity could contrive in the condition in which Francis found it in March 1792.

This was due in part to Francis's personal qualities, partly to the situation which confronted him on his accession.

Francis was not at all a stupid man: he was even shrewd above the average, and endowed with a disconcerting power of drawing from a situation the conclusions which were correct by his own premises. Neither was he in any respect a bad man. His private life was irreproachable, and as ruler he conscientiously sought his subjects' good, being convinced that God had laid this duty on him when He set him over them. He did not wantonly oppress them, nor waste their substance on luxurious living – his Court was modest to the point of parsimony – nor on search for the aggrandisement of himself or his House. None of his numerous wars were, in his eyes, waged for any other object than the defence of his rights, and of the order decreed by God. But to add to his youth and inexperience – he was only just twenty-four years old when he succeeded to the throne – he was mentally near-sighted and unimaginative, and also timid and suspicious, shrinking instinctively from the unknown and unfamiliar, and entirely lacking in Joseph's social vision, imaginative power and restless impatience with the imperfect. He could never have been a reformer for reform's sake. There was only one direction in which he would have preferred change, for he was as convinced as his uncle of the rightness, theoretical as well as pragmatic, of monarchic absolutism – it has well been said of him that for him absolutism was not simply a means to an end, but an end in itself – and had he been in a position to do so, he would certainly have stripped the Estates of his dominions of such vestiges of power as they had managed to salvage from his predecessors' forays. But he was clear-sighted enough to appreciate that only Leopold's cautious compromises had banished the hornet's nest which Joseph's impetuosity had brought about the family's ears. Leopold's concessions had been largely necessitated by the danger of the international situation, and this was now more threatening still, for on 27 March, thus less than four weeks since Leopold had closed his eyes, Louis had sent Francis an ultimatum calling on Austria to dissolve all alliances contracted without the foreknowledge of France, and to withdraw her troops from the Franco-German frontier. A month later, this demand having been rejected, Louis had told the *Assemblée* that France was at war with 'the King of Bohemia and Hungary'. In this situation it would have been quite impossible for Francis, in common prudence, to provoke those classes among his subjects who traditionally constituted the strongest force in each of his Lands, and on whose goodwill the integrity of his dominions, and even his own throne, might be supposed to depend. His first step had of necessity to be to seek a composition with those forces, if such could be reached, and the quest for this occupied the first weeks of his reign.

Fortunately for him, it was not too difficult, for the Estates of all his Lands were themselves deeply anxious for a settlement with the Crown which should definitively banish the threat of revolution, from outside and below, infiltrating from France, or, even more disquieting, from inside and above, should the unquiet ghost of Joseph not prove to have been well and truly laid. Given assurance of the Crown's conservative intentions, they were entirely willing to accept the reality of central political control that lay behind Leopold's recognition of their shadow-existences, and to serve the Crown as junior partners in the common cause. The only part-exception was Hungary, where final agreement between the Crown and the Diet had not yet been reached, and there was a possibility that the Diet might take advantage of the situation to put forward extremist demands. There were in fact anxious moments while the terms for the Coronation Diet were being negotiated, but in the end both sides compromised. The Diet produced only a short list of demands, only one of them of the first importance: that the Illyrian Court Chancellery should be abolished (the rest were chiefly for more instruction in Magyar in the secondary schools). Francis accepted these demands, and the coronation took place on 6 June. In return the Diet, while denying any legal obligation, voted a handsome contribution in men and kind towards the war, and cheerfully postponed what should have been the biggest item on its agenda, the consideration of the reports of the Committees set up by its predecessor. Prague gave even less trouble: here no considerations of substance were even asked, and the coronation took place on 8 August. That in Frankfurt had already taken place, again without difficulty and without any attempt by the Electors to extend the Electoral Capitulations, on 14 July.

Internal peace had thus been established, on the basis of what amounted to a freezing of the political *status quo*. It was an emergency operation which, as has been said, was really necessitated by the emergency situation. The tragedy for Austria was that the quieter times, which would have allowed a constructive revision of its terms, were slow to arrive, and by the time they did so, resistance to any change whatever, unless in the direction of more unqualified absolutism, had become with Francis a fixed and immutable principle.

He was now able to turn his chief attention to the war with France: and while this work is primarily concerned with conditions and developments inside the Monarchy, it is necessary for the understanding of these to remember that for the next twenty-three years Austria was never truly at peace: during nearly half of them she was actively at war, and during most of the rest either salving the wounds received during the last campaign or preparing for the next. The wars further brought her many territorial changes and altered her position in Germany. The essential facts of the first thirteen of these years are as follows:

Austria's first war with France lasted almost exactly five years. Then, having been deserted by Russia and the smaller German States, she had to sign the preliminary Peace of Leoben (18 April 1797), and on 17/18 October, the definitive Peace of Campo Formio. Under this she ceded Belgium definitively to France and secretly promised to support the cession to her of most German territory west of the Rhine, She also lost the Milanese, incorporated in a 'Cis-Alpine Republic' extending as far east as the Adige (Etsch), acquiring in compensation Venice east of the Adige, with the Markgravate of Istria and Dalmatia. Meanwhile, in 1793, Prussia and Russia had combined to effect between them the Second Partition of Poland, out of which Austria had come out empty-handed; but Thugut, who had taken over the conduct of foreign affairs from Cobenzl, made a secret agreement with Russia, and under the third and total Partition of 1795 secured for Austria an area then collectively termed West Galicia and comprising Lublin, Cholm, Cracow and Sandomir.

Thugut undisguisedly treated the Peace of Campo Formio as only an armistice, and after he had reached new agreements with Russia and Britain, as well as Naples and Portugal, Austria redeclared war on France in March 1799. Her armies won early successes, as they had in the previous war, but in 1800 Bonaparte, having made his peace with Russia, drove them out of Italy and penetrated far into the Austrian homelands. On 2 February 1801 Francis had to accept the Peace of Lunéville. This brought Austria no direct losses – even the addition of the episcopal territories of Trent and Brixen – but the family secundogenitures of Tuscany and Modena disappeared, and her influence in Germany was greatly weakened by the reduction, under the remodelling of Germany, of the power of her traditional supporters, the Catholic Princes.

Exhausted, impoverished and war-weary as his peoples were, Francis dismissed Thugut in favour of more pacifically minded advisers (the consortium Colloredo – Cobenzl) and remained neutral when war recommenced between France and Britain in May 1803, but changed his policy again, and on 9 August 1805 Austria joined the coalition with Britain and Russia. The hostilities opened in September, and this time the disaster was speedy and overwhelming. The bulk of Austria's main army was lost when its commander, Mack, surrendered at Ulm on 20 October. Napoleon then advanced swiftly down the Danube, occupied Vienna, and on 2 December inflicted a most bloody defeat on the largest remaining Austrian army, together with its Russian allies, at Austerlitz. On 26 December Francis had to sign the terrible Peace of Pressburg under which, while acquiring Salzburg, Austria lost her recent acquisitions from Venice, which went to the new Kingdom of Italy; Tirol and Vorarlberg to Bavaria, and her surviving possessions in West Germany to Baden and Württemberg. She had to pay an indemnity of forty million francs. Other articles of the treaty declared Bavaria, Württemberg and Baden to be sovereign States, and on 6 August, when Napoleon created the 'Confederation of the Rhine' under his own protection, Francis further renounced the title of Holy Roman Emperor and released all Estates from their obligations to the holder of it. He remained an 'Emperor', and thus equal in dignity to the rulers of Russia and France, for in August 1804 he had, anticipating this demotion, assumed the title of Hereditary Emperor of Austria (the move had no other significance).

At this point we may return to pick up the threads of internal developments in the Monarchy since 1792.

Francis's first move after his father's death had been to appoint his former tutor, Count Franz Colloredo, head of his *Kabinett*, or private secretariat, with the rank, previously unknown, of *Kabinettsminister*. Colloredo was to be his constant adviser and act for him in his absence. The appointment was important for the spirit in which the Monarchy's government was thereafter carried out. Colloredo, through whose office all roads to the throne from any quarter, except that of the Imperial family itself, led for several years, was honourable, unselfish and devoted to his former pupil, but he was a man of mediocre abilities with a strongly clerical and ultra-conservative outlook (according to some writers, several of Francis's chief phobias against such ideas as constitutionalism and enlightenment had been directly inculcated into him by his ex-tutor and mentor). Virtually all high appointments were made on his recommendation, which was almost always given in favour of a member of the high aristocracy, resulting in a system which has been described as 'one of aristocratic bureaucracy, or if you will, bureaucratic aristocracy'[1] absolutist and centralist in its institutions, aristocratic and ultra-conservative in its direction of them. The middle ranks of the services, indeed, still contained a considerable number of old Josephinians, for no purge was carried through.

Actually, the new appointments made during these first years were very few. Except that he reinstated the police as an independent *Hofstelle* under Joseph's old Chief of Police, von Pergen, and created the new post of *Kabinettsminister*, Francis did not alter the basic structure of the machine: the *Hofstellen* and *Hofkanzleien* (Court Chancelleries) were left untouched. On the top-most level, the practice at first was that the Ministers of Foreign Affairs, War and Police, and at times, that of Finance, reported directly to the Emperor, via his *Kabinettsminister*: reports from the Court Chancelleries went first through the *Staatsrat* (Council of State).[2] Since this system allowed no minister any opportunity of learning what his colleagues were doing, the Archduke Charles persuaded his brother in 1801 to institute a '*Staats- und Konferenzministerium*', composed of all 'real' ministers, with assessors for special questions, which was to meet regularly under the presidency of Francis himself, to discuss problems affecting more than one department. But no one except Charles himself wanted his activities co-ordinated. The sessions of the ministry grew rarer and rarer until its abolition, described below, in 1808.

After he had sent Colloredo to the Foreign Ministry, Francis had not renewed the post of *Kabinettsminister*, so that although the reports sent up to him went first to his *Kabinett*, they were not officially screened or sorted there. All business ranking as top-level came up to him personally and his was the only hand in which all threads ran together. If he wished for advice, he sought it where he would, perhaps from the minister concerned, perhaps from some member of his *Kabinett*, perhaps from some quite independent quarter. The level at which any question could be settled without further reference was determined by the so-called '*Dienstrèglement*', a sort of body of administrative case-law, which had grown up throughout the decades in highly arbitrary fashion; it sometimes allowed a department to take autonomously decisions which were not only themselves of the highest importance, but also vitally affected the work of other departments, while at other times questions of absurd triviality had to climb the entire bureaucratic ladder as far as the *Staatsrat* or the Crown itself. At once too suspicious and too conscientious to delegate authority, Francis never had the *Dienstrèglement* amended, and insisted on having submitted to him a mass of documentation which no man on earth could have mastered, so that it sometimes accumulated on his writing-table unexpedited, often even unread, for years, or perhaps for ever.

The more sensible and more outspoken members of Francis's entourage complained often enough of the inefficiency of this system, but they never succeeded in getting it altered; and it may be noted that these criticisms were always directed exclusively against the cumbrous working of the machinery, never against the principle of monarchic absolutism: the constitutional fault found by some of them was never that it was too absolutist in Austria, but that it was not absolutist enough in Hungary.

Meanwhile, the end which Francis was setting himself to achieve through this apparatus had become more and more wholly that of stabilization of existing conditions, to the exclusion of change from any side, or in any direction. The very fact that he regarded the war with France as an ideological one, waged in defence of the existing legitimate order against revolution, would already have sufficed to prejudice him most strongly against innovations, even if his preoccupations had left him time to think them up. His mind and spirit had meanwhile been hardened, first by the execution, in January 1793, of Louis of France and his consort (Francis's own aunt), and a year later, by the discovery in his own dominions of two 'Jacobin' conspiracies, one in Vienna, the other in Hungary. The Viennese 'conspiracy', while reflecting a real discontent with the war, was a childish enough affair of a few romantics who did little more than plant a 'tree of liberty' and dance round it singing tipsy catches in praise of freedom. Its Hungarian counterpart, the leading figure in which was a certain Abbé Martinovics, a former secret agent of Leopold's, was more widespread and reflected a more general discontent, but little more formidable, since hardly any two of its participants had the same idea of what it was meant to achieve. Both were easily discovered and the leading figures in them punished with extreme barbarity, and Francis then settled down to make his system watertight.

Political immobility was easily achieved in the Hereditary Lands by the simple method of making the meetings of the Estates pure formalities: here the effective rule was, as Joseph's had been, purely

bureaucratic. But while Joseph had used his bureaucracy to introduce social and economic innovations, Francis used his to prevent
them. On the land he refused to repeal his predecessors' reforms in
favour of the peasants (a step which would have strengthened the
power of the Estates *vis-à-vis* the bureaucracy), but he also refused
to carry them any further. Any further change in the landlord–
peasant relationship was made dependent on the consent of both
parties and, in some cases, also on official sanction (which was often
refused), so that generally speaking, the position remained as Leopold had left it. The Manorial Courts were similarly left intact, with
minor and local modifications. Replacement of them would, indeed,
have further extended the authority of the Crown, but here financial
considerations came into play. The Manorial Courts cost the State
far less than would have their equivalents of salaried magistrates.
The Government's policy towards industry was not altogether con-
sistent, for there were among Francis's advisers some mercantilists
who wanted it developed, and here and there a licence was granted
to found a new enterprise or enlarge an existing one. Another school,
however, warned against the social danger which would result from
the growth of an industrial proletariat, and the landowners complained constantly of shortage of labour on their estates. On balance,
the policy prevailed of discouraging all but small local enterprises,
so that in this field too, Austria, while not positively retreating, lagged
ever further behind her advancing neighbours.

But Francis's pursuit of stability went further than this. With his
real gift for going to the heart of a problem, he saw that conditions
and institutions would remain stable only if the wish to change them
was absent. First the twig must be bent. Rather surprisingly he did
not share the widely current view that it was safer for the poor to be
unlettered. On the contrary, he wished that every child in his dominions should receive an adequate elementary education, and that sufficient further instruction should be available to provide the State with
as many efficient servants as it needed, including the teachers whose
task it would be to produce the next generation of 'high-minded,
religious and patriotic citizens'. A *Ratio Educationis* for the western
Lands issued in 1806 (its Hungarian counterpart followed in 1808)
divided the responsibility for lower-grade education between the
State and the Catholic Church. Education remained a State service,
and the State was responsible for the teachers' salaries (which, incidentally, were so meagre as largely to frustrate Francis's intentions)
and the upkeep of the buildings, while the Church was responsible
for the general supervision of the system, including the conduct of
the teachers, and teaching posts were given for preference to persons
in Holy Orders. The teaching in the lowest grades, outside the 'Three

Rs' was largely religious instruction, supplemented in the higher classes by instruction in practical subjects, civics, and similar disciplines.

The minds of adult *subjecta* were guarded against corruption primarily through the censorship, which in 1801 was transferred to the police and made more rigorous. Any utterance of nature to disturb, or even to question, the public order was strictly forbidden; in 1803 journalists were forbidden to print anything whatever on domestic affairs beyond what was appearing in the *Wiener Diarium* (the official gazette) or ministerial hand-outs, or any foreign news not passed by the censor. Reading rooms and circulating libraries were forbidden, also literary reviews, which might contain extracts from forbidden books. Even mottoes on fans, snuff-boxes, musical instruments and toys had to pass the purity test. A 'recensoring Commission' went through all books published between 1780 and 1792; in two years it condemned 2,500 of them.

The watch over the subject's private life was chiefly the province of the secret police. Neither Joseph nor Leopold had employed anything like the number of spies, of all walks of life, who reported to von Pergen's agents, nor had their net been thrown nearly so wide. While no class was exempt from surveillance, special attention was paid to the middle classes, in whom Colloredo and others of Francis's advisers had from their observation of the French Revolution diagnosed the chief fermenting agency. To be an 'intellectual' was to be an automatic suspect, and since the security of the State depended on the loyalty of its servants, both civil and military (and the defeats suffered by Austria's generals had been so constant and so conspicuous that Francis was not satisfied with the normal explanation of incompetence, but smelled treason), these were kept under the closest supervision.

A great drive was carried through against the secret societies, which were regarded, not without reason (the 'Jacobins' of the 1794 trials had nearly all been freemasons), as foci of subversion and carriers of infection. It became really dangerous to be a mason, and in 1801 all public servants, not excluding Archdukes, were required to sign a declaration that they did not belong to such an association. Presently the ban was extended to become nearly all-embracing. The formation even of charitable associations required special permission, and learned societies were forbidden, except those devoted to the promotion of agriculture. Permission had to be obtained even for a dance employing an orchestra of more than two instruments.

It is easily possible to form an exaggerated idea of the malevolence of these services. Their purpose was rather prophylactic than punitive. The Austria of the day knew no concentration camps. It was rare for anyone to be arrested and detained without trial on political grounds. A man might have his doings and sayings reported for years, and yet live quite unmolested, and sentences for political offences were, with the notable exception of those passed on the 'Jacobins', usually light, at least by modern standards.

But in their own way, the measures were devastatingly effective. Not only did the production of literature, except the lightest trash, stop almost completely, but with it perished also the taste for reading. Still less, of course, was any 'subject' tempted to indulge in the highly dangerous pursuit of independent thought.

Most of the peoples to whom this 'system' was applied bore it with the most complete philosophy. There was a good deal of grumbling against the wars, especially those of 1799–1801, but the cause of it was discontent with rising prices, shortages and the activities of the press gangs. It was directed against the 'war party' at the Court, not against Francis personally, for he was held to be a man of peace. Similarly, the great popularity enjoyed by the Archduke Charles was due less to the fact that, unlike most Austrian generals, when he fought battles, he sometimes won them, than to the general knowledge that he was against fighting them at all, at any rate with armies not properly equipped and supplied. The discontent, such as it was, was not political. The aristocracy continued willingly to accept the *de facto* dictatorship so long as it remained conservative. We hear hardly anything of peasant unrest during the war years: a series of good harvests, coinciding with an era of high prices for agricultural produce, seemed to them ample compensation for the continuance of the *robot* and the Manorial Courts. As for the 'intellectuals', while a few lively spirits left the country altogether, the great majority wore their muzzles with perfect grace.

Outside the central bloc of Austro-Bohemian Lands, Austria's rule in the Venetian provinces was, during the few years that it lasted, unpopular, but there again, the causes of the discontent were economic – high prices and unemployment – and it did not take dangerous forms. The Poles were having the worst of both worlds. The efforts at constructive reform undertaken by Joseph had died away under Francis, since Vienna was reluctant to invest money, even if it had any, in a province its hold over which seemed so insecure. But it needed every penny, and every soldier, that it could get, and Galicia was made to contribute its full quota of recruits, while taxation, direct, and indirect, including the salt tax, which hit the peasants very hard, was far higher than it had been before the Partition. Meanwhile, a hierarchy of Estates had been set up, but they were never convoked: the province was still administered from Vienna, by German or Czech officials, and largely in the German language. The

Poles naturally resented these concomitants of Austrian rule, and
even more, the very fact of it. But they still found it preferable to the
rule of Orthodox Russia or Protestant Prussia, and the malcontents
seldom got beyond ineffectual plottings or minor demonstrations,
easily repressed.

Hungary presented a more serious problem. Apart from the feeling, widespread in Court circles, that it was wrong on principle that
constitutional institutions should exist anywhere in the Monarchy,
and the still more general feeling that anything that a Hungarian wanted must *ipso facto* be nefarious, both the *Hofkriegsrat* and the *Hofkammer* complained unremittingly that so long as the Hungarian
Diet retained the right to limit Hungary's *contributio* in both kinds,
Austria was fighting her wars with one hand tied behind her back.
Francis's own initial confidence in Hungary's good behaviour had
been badly shaken by the Martinovics conspiracy, but fortunately
for him, the revelations had also confirmed the anxiety of the Hungarian Conservatives to keep on good terms with the Court, while the
attendant arrests had intimidated the radicals. Consequently, the
Diet which Francis duly convoked in 1796 was in a chastened mood.
It voted the substantial *contributio* in cash and kind asked of it,
agreed to raise the strength of the Hungarian standing army to
52,000 men, and consented to a further postponement of the consideration of the Committee reports, asking in return only minor
concessions.

In 1799 Francis evaded the possibility of new arguments with the
Diet by the simple, although unconstitutional, device of leaving it
unconvoked; but after the Peace of Lunéville neither side was prepared to see this procedure repeated. The Archduke Charles, who
was engaged in big plans for reorganizing the army, which included
the replacement of the former service for life by one of eight to ten
years, followed by a term with the reserves, pleaded that it was essential for this system to be extended to Hungary, coupled with the introduction of conscription there. The *Hofkammer* was insistent on the
need for a larger *contributio*. Now, again, a strong party wanted
compulsion applied, but the Palatine, the Archduke Joseph,[3] who so
often during his long tenure of office was to render invaluable service
as mediator between Crown and nation, persuaded his brother to put
the demands to a Diet, and this was convoked in 1802. The result
was an uneasy compromise that left neither side satisfied. The Diet
voted only 700,000 gulden in cash, in place of the two millions asked
of it, and while agreeing that the strength of the contingent to the
standing army should be raised to 64,000 for a provisional period of
three years, refused to allow the introduction of conscription, or of
certain forms of taxation out of which the higher *contributio* could

have been paid. Francis, for his part, closed the Diet as soon as he had got his half-loaf, without giving a hearing to the long list of *postulata* which had been prepared for his consideration, and had included besides the usual requests for more extensive use of the Hungarian language in the public services and education, also a demand for revision of the inequitable fiscal relationship with Austria.[4]

The course of the Diet of 1805 was little happier. Intimidated by the advance of the French armies, it agreed at the last moment to offer a larger contingent of troops, and to call out the *insurrectio*, but the swift ending of the hostilities deprived these concessions of their value. Again, Francis had granted in return only the minor concession that some official correspondence *might* be conducted in Magyar. The atmosphere had been poisoned by the fact that when the French troops reached the Hungarian frontier, the officer commanding the *insurrectio* had, misunderstanding his instructions, informed their commander that Hungary was declaring herself neutral.

If the Diets accepted for so many years the repeated disregard of their wishes and their rights, this was chiefly because the big and medium land-owners, whose voices were those which counted, were doing very well out of a situation which created an almost unlimited demand for wheat and oats for the armies, at prices not depressed by the competition of 'Odessa wheat'.[5] Many of them were accumulating substantial fortunes out of the high prices, while paying off their debts in the depreciating currency. In this situation the demand for industrial protection also lost much of its urgency: its place was taken largely by demands for outlets and markets for agricultural produce. These classes also appreciated to the full Francis's conservative attitude towards the landlord–peasant relationship, which allowed them to exploit the labour of their peasants to the full, while the magnates were relatively indifferent about the use of the national language, which many of themselves did not speak.

But if the position was fairly satisfactory for the dominant classes, it was a satisfaction bought at the expense of the true long-term interests of the country; it was not without reason that a later generation of Hungarians counted these years, and the decade that followed them, 'lost to their country'. And the successes that the Diets did achieve, in keeping Hungary's contribution in terms either of manpower or of money, to the needs of the Monarchy, to figures which on any basis of calculation were disproportionately low, aggravated immeasurably the difficulties of the Departments whose task it was to keep the Monarchy a going concern.

For manpower and money were the two commodities of which the Monarchy was during all these years in unremitting and crippling short supply. For economy's sake, Leopold had not made good the wastage of manpower incurred in Joseph's disastrous campaign, and at the beginning of 1792 the Monarchy had had only 225,000 men with the colours. After that, the large and constantly growing number of persons able to claim exemption made it extraordinarily hard to obtain the quota of conscripts from the Lands liable to conscription. The army's ranks were filled largely by recruiting from the smaller German States, and even so its numbers seldom reached the prescribed war strength.

Leopold had also called in a proportion of the paper money which Joseph had issued to pay for his campaigns, but twenty-eight million *Bankozettel* were still in circulation when he died, and although Francis's Government obtained a few foreign subsidies for its French wars, and raised other sums by internal loans, some voluntary, others forced, it was soon driven to resort again to the printing press. Up to 1796 the *Bankozettel* were everywhere accepted at their face value, but after that year, while the Government continued to make its payments in them, and to accept them from the tax-payer, they were quoted in private transactions, both at home and abroad, at a discount which by 1804 had risen to 125 : 100. Meanwhile the cost of living had nearly trebled between 1801 and 1805. While some classes of the population, including most primary producers, were doing well out of the situation, others, such as State employees and rentiers, were being reduced to dire straits.

After the disaster of Austerlitz, Charles again begged his brother most urgently to place the conduct of affairs in the hands of younger and more competent men and, up to a point, Francis listened to him. Foreign affairs were entrusted to Count Philipp Stadion, an 'Imperial Knight' from the Rhineland, who had, however, passed his career in the Austrian service. Charles himself was given the exceptional title of 'Generalissimus', which left him solely competent for all military questions. Others whom Francis now drew increasingly into his councils were two more of his brothers, the Archdukes John and Rainer.

Charles made good use of his powers : he straightened out various administrative tangles, dismissed twenty-five generals, humanized discipline and secured acceptance for his plan of keeping only part of the standing army permanently with the colours, the rest being organized as reserves. He also persuaded Francis to accept the idea of a second reserve, or militia, for home defence in case of invasion ; the Archduke John was to work out the plans.

Less progress was made in other fields. Stadion's aim was to rally the German States against Napoleon under Austrian leadership, and he hoped to achieve this by an appeal to German national feeling, which was, moreover, to be strengthened by representing Austria as the champion, not only of national feeling, but of far-reaching social and political reform. In 1806 and 1807 Francis was unwilling to accept such advanced ideas. Some administrative reforms were introduced in various fields, but none of these went very deep, and none succeeded in touching the weakest point of all, the financial situation, which went from bad to worse, with the circulation of *Bankozettel* rising to nearly 450 million gulden and the discount rate to 175. The Finance Minister, Zichy, cheerfully admitted his inability to cope with the position, and a special Commission failed to agree on the remedy. They were agreed only on one point: it was hopeless to expect any real improvement in this respect, or any full implementation of Charles's reforms, unless Hungary – now a considerably larger part of the Monarchy than before the treaty – could be induced to shoulder a larger share of the burden. In an attempt to achieve this Francis convoked a Diet in April 1807, and he asked it for an increased *contributio*, a single extraordinary contribution towards the cost of rearmament, and the introduction of conscription to keep the Hungarian regiments up to strength.

Unfortunately the concessions which he offered in return were minimal, and the Diet consequently displayed an obstinacy which earned it the soubriquet of 'the Accursed'. It demanded something like budgetary control over any monies voted by it, was adamant on the conscription issue, and pressed strongly for consideration of its *postulata*, especially in the economic field. In the end it voted a 'voluntary gift' from each noble of one-sixth of his rents and one-hundredth of his other income and agreed to the conscription of 12,000 men, but not more. This was to be in return for consideration of its *gravamina*, which Francis promised to give, but instead of doing so, he closed the Diet again (in December), leaving his promise unfulfilled. The indignation in Hungary rose to fever pitch.

It was an unhappy situation both at home and abroad, for with Prussia crushed at Jena and Russia come to terms with France at Tilsit, Britain had been left to face Napoleon alone except for her small allies, Portugal and Sweden. In spite of this, a party at Court, headed by Stadion, had begun pressing for war, and in January 1808, this party received a powerful reinforcement in the person of the new Empress, the vivacious Maria Ludovica d'Este, whom Francis in that month took for his third wife, after another conspicuously short widowerhood.[6] How far Francis's new bride was really responsible for his change of heart cannot be said with certainty, but it is a fact that after the wedding, preparations for war were taken in hand seriously. In June a Patent appeared establishing a *Landwehr*, or people's militia, in which service was compulsory for all males in the Hereditary Lands between the ages of eighteen and forty-five who were not already serving with the colours or reserves, or belonging to an exempted category. The *Staats- und Konferenzministerium* was abolished, and the *Staatsrat* reinstated and given a new and more energetic President in the person of Count Zinzendorf, who was empowered to hold regular meetings which might be attended by the Ministers of Foreign Affairs and War. Francis himself was to preside over these meetings; in his absence the Archduke Rainer was to deputize for him. Zichy was replaced at the head of the Finance Commission by the far more competent Count O'Donnell.

Then, on 31 August, Francis convoked another Hungarian Diet under the pretext of having his bride crowned. This time strong pressure was brought to bear at the elections, and the elected members were placated with a cornucopia of *douceurs*, including a Danae's rain of orders and decorations. It was not in vain. The Diet earned itself the name of 'the Handsome' by agreeing that the strength of the standing army should be raised if necessary, by a further 20,000 men, and the King given authority in advance for three years to call out the *insurrectio*.

Meanwhile a horde of publicists, some native, others, such as Gentz and the brothers Schlegel, imported, were set to whipping up German national feeling in the Monarchy and the German States, which they did in articles and pamphlets, the nationalist and even democratic tone of which ordinarily would have made Francis faint. Even intellectual freedom was represented as 'the first condition of all culture', and Austria as its champion.

It was characteristic of the mental outlook not only of the Rhinelander Stadion, but of all his team, that this campaign should have treated the non-German peoples of the Monarchy as *quantités négligeables*: the only heed paid to them was that some of the leaflets were translated into Czech and Slovene, without modification of their German appeal. They replied by treating the campaign with great indifference. In Vienna and the German Austrian Lands, on the other hand, enthusiasm reached a really high pitch. National dresses were worn and songs sung, and volunteers from exempted classes offered their services to the *Landwehr*. The mood, fed by most misleading reports from the minor German capitals, St Petersburg and Paris (Metternich, Ambassador there, was responsible for the last-named) was one of almost boundless optimism. As to finance, Stadion himself admitted that Austria could not afford a war, but, he said, she would be still less able to afford one later. A considerable number of Francis's advisers, including the Archdukes Charles, Rainer and Joseph, were still against war, Charles arguing that the army was exhausted and the reorganizing of it still incomplete, but a Council on 9 February 1809 decided in favour of war, and seeing that this was to be waged with or without him, Charles gave up his opposition. On 9 April Austria declared war. Charles led one army across the Inn, while another, under John, entered Italy and a third penetrated the Tirol, where the local militia, led by Andreas Hofer, rose to help them.

All the optimistic calculations proved to have been wrong. France remained united, the Czar did not move, the German Princes refused to accept Austria's leadership; Bavaria and Württemberg even sent large contingents to help Napoleon. Outside Austria's frontiers only the Tirolean peasants fought for her. Napoleon cut the Austrian armies of the Danube in two and on 10 May reached Vienna, which surrendered after a couple of days. Charles gave battle at Aspern, with a success which, however, he inexplicably failed to follow up. John's armies were beaten in the race for home by those of Beauharnais, and the *insurrectio*, which should have joined him in Hungary, proved to be of little help; the men fought bravely enough, but the *Hofkammer* had failed to provide them with arms, or even uniforms. The combined armies were heavily defeated at Györ on 14 June. Charles, after sending fruitless messages to John to join him, gave battle again at Wagram on 6 July, only to be defeated with heavy losses. On the 11th/12th he signed an armistice with Napoleon.

The ensuing peace, signed at Vienna on 14 October, was even harder than its predecessor of Pressburg. Austria lost the entire Littoral, with its big hinterland, this going to form a 'Kingdom of Illyria' under French rule; her Polish acquisitions under the Third Partition, which went to form a 'Grand Duchy of Warsaw', and areas in the west to Bavaria. She was required to pay a heavy indemnity, to reduce her army to 150,000 men, and to join the Continental Blockade.

The Tiroleans fought on bravely, and at first with some success, but in the end the big battalions prevailed. Hofer was taken in chains to Mantua and shot.

The reception of the news by the Viennese of this humiliating peace was less edifying. 'What a crush on the streets', wrote a contemporary; 'What joy! People embraced and kissed one another. Everything proved with what longing the day of deliverance had been awaited.'

Now Francis changed his advisers again. Stadion had already resigned and Metternich, who had been *de facto* in charge of foreign affairs since the armistice, took over the portfolio formally in October. Charles was dismissed abruptly and ungraciously after Wagram, and was pursued thereafter by Francis with a dislike and distrust that were deepened by a suspicion (which seems to have been quite unfounded, although Napoleon would have liked to see the change made), that he had aspired to the throne. Rainer, too, lost his position as adviser on internal affairs. John's positive disgrace came only three years later, when it was alleged (again, probably without foundation) that he had been plotting to have himself proclaimed 'King of Rhaetia'. Of Francis's 'Cabinet of Brothers' there survived only Joseph, whose standing in Hungary made him indispensable.

In so far as anyone now possessed Francis's ear, it was Metternich, who quickly came to occupy a position of outstanding importance in Francis's councils. In foreign affairs he called the tune almost completely, if only, as he himself admitted, by implanting his own views in Francis's mind. His influence in domestic affairs was more intermittent, but also very great. He was indeed justified in claiming, as he did when the claim became popular, that he had not 'invented the system': he had found it already there when he came to the Ballhausplatz. But he approved whole-heartedly of its principles, and made himself its second father by his constant endorsement of it.

The immediate line of Austria's foreign policy was in any case marked out by the international situation. She had, as Metternich at once told Francis, no choice but to seek Napoleon's favour, whatever the cost. The price, which was Metternich's suggestion (although Napoleon seems to have hinted that it would be acceptable), was the hand of Francis's eldest daughter and favourite child, Marie Louise; the marriage was celebrated on 2 April 1810. It did not, indeed, bring Austria the rewards which Metternich seems to have expected, for Napoleon made the return of the Illyrian provinces conditional on an alliance with Russia. This would have involved the cession of Galicia, and when in 1812 the alliance was after all concluded, and Austria should have received substantial rewards for a relatively modest contribution to the compaign against Russia, the campaign went badly and the rewards did not materialize. The chief immediate effects of the *revirement* were at home. The appeal to national and popular feeling, which had proved such a dismal failure, was dropped like a hot potato and the political and social freeze reestablished.

In one direction only the peace-terms of 1809 brought a real change. The Continental Blockade left Austria without the imports from England with which she had previously covered a considerable part of her requirements of manufactured goods. The return of peace at home created a large demand for those products, and the demobilized soldiers provided abundant manpower. Under pressure from the interests involved, the *Hofkammer* largely changed its attitude towards industry. While the old restrictions were maintained for the *Polizeigewerbe* (small enterprises working for the local market), almost complete freedom was introduced for the larger *Kommerzialgewerbe*. The ban on the importation of machinery was lifted and a host of new factories came into being, especially in Bohemia and Moravia. The largest contingent was those which produced cotton and woollen goods, in which English domination had been most complete; but these years saw also the beginnings, in the same provinces, of a sugar-beet industry to make good the lack of cane-sugar.

The financial position, however, continued its downward slide. The war had brought fresh burdens to the exchequer, the indemnity, another, the territorial losses, yet another. More and more *Bankozettel* had to be printed, and the course of them sank remorselessly. At the beginning of 1811 the circulation had reached 1,060 millions and the course stood at over 1,200.

Just before this date O'Donnell had died. Francis had replaced him by Count Joseph Wallis, *Oberstburggraf* (Governor) of Prague, a man of no financial expertise, but of brutal energy. On 15 March there appeared under Wallis's name a Patent calling in all *Bankozettel* and small coins. These were to be exchanged against 'redemption notes' (*Einlösungsscheine*) at the rate of one new to five old, of the same face value. All taxation, direct and indirect, was to be paid in the new currency, in which the Government was to pay its own salaries, pensions and so on. The interest on State loans was, however, to be cut by half. The Government promised never to allow the issue of future paper money to exceed the new figure of 212 million *Einlösungsscheine*. For private debts contracted since the currency began to fall, a scale (the *Wiener Scala*) was introduced, converting them at a rate calculated on the value of the *Bankozettel* as quoted at Augsburg in the month in which they were contracted. This operation certainly brought justice to some classes of society, but it inflicted grievous hardship on others, including many landowners, large and small, and many of the new entrepreneurs. It remained a hideous memory among the people, who persisted in describing it as a State bankruptcy for four shillings in the pound.

The Patent also produced the severest clash to date with Hungary. On the Palatine's strong advice, Francis had not promulgated it there, as Metternich had advised him to do, but he had convoked the Diet, told its members that it was to be applicable there, and invited them to take steps to apply it, and also to raise the *contributio* by a hundred per cent. The Diet resisted so bitterly that in May 1812 Francis dissolved it and introduced a Patent 'provisionally' pending the convocation of the next Diet, in practice, that is, indefinitely.

And after all the Patent did not achieve its purpose. Prices, after

remaining stable for a while at the new nominal level, rose again
sharply. The small military operation which Austria was required to
undertake in 1812 was paid for out of taxation, but in 1813 the
weakening of Napoleon's position after his disaster in Russia was so
apparent that the war party in Vienna began to rearm in preparation
for intervention on the side of France's enemies. The cost of these
preparations already forced the Government to break its word and to
make another issue of paper money, beautified with the name of
Anticipationsscheine, and when Austria declared war, as she did on
11 August 1813, even these proved insufficient, although the Austrian army was conspicuously and miserably the worst equipped of
any in the field. The end of the campaign found Austria among the
victors, but the old story of soaring prices and a tumbling currency
had repeated itself. In 1815, during the Hundred Days, the amount
in circulation of the *Wiener Währung* (Viennese currency), as the
Einlösungs- and *Anticipationsscheine* were collectively called, was
over 675 million gulden, and it was being quoted at nearly 350.

Four

THE SYSTEM AT ITS ZENITH
1815–30

But Austria's fortunes were on the upgrade at last. When peace returned to her in 1815, it was with a different countenance from that which she had worn during her fleeting visits of earlier years. Under the peace settlement Austria emerged with all the territory she had lost since 1792 except the Netherlands and the Vorlande, and almost all the acquisitions made at any time since that date, except West Galicia, where she retained only a right of co-supervision with Russia and Prussia in Cracow, now a Free City. She dominated Italy through her own possessions of Lombardy and Venetia, through family connections (the secundo- and tertio-genitures in Tuscany and Modena had been restored, and Marie Louise given Parma, Piacenza and Guastalla for life) and through her influence over the other Courts. The solution of the German question reached in May 1820 when the *Bund* was constituted as a federation of thirty-five 'sovereign Princes' and four Free Cities, under Austrian Presidency, gave the Emperor of Austria more influence in Germany than the Holy Roman Emperor had enjoyed for generations: it would have been no greater had Francis reassumed, as he could have done, the old title (which might have involved him in conflicts with Prussia). And if the Czar's 'Holy Alliance' never looked like being more than the 'verbiage', which was how Metternich himself described it, the Quadruple Alliance set up a 'Concert of Europe', which he confidently believed would play a tune both called and conducted by himself.

Finally Austria was booked to receive an indemnity of 150 million francs, an agreeable change from the obligation of paying one with which she had ended previous wars – and instead of having to support a foreign army on her soil, she was keeping 30,000 men on that of France.

The shadow side of the picture was in its material aspects; the near-total financial exhaustion to which the wars had brought the Monarchy and the devastating economic conditions which accompanied the ending of them. The harvests of 1815 and 1816 were so catastrophic that people perished in their thousands of starvation and its attendant diseases, while prices rose fantastically. An ensuing series of good harvests put an end to this distress. On the other hand

the reappearance of Odessa wheat brought a precipitous fall in agricultural prices that ruined many producers large and small, especially in Hungary and Galicia. Manufacturers suffered just as heavily
when England began to throw her accumulated stocks on the market,
often at dumping prices, ruining completely many industries which
had sprung up during the Continental Blockade, and survivors were
forced to reduce output drastically and lay off many hands.

In both these fields a slow improvement followed this nadir, although many years were to pass before it was more than partial in
either. The economic recovery was a gradual process which was not
marked by any single outstanding development. The financial position,
however, did witness such a development. Stadion, who in 1814 had
been made a sort of financial overlord, succeeded in 1817, after a
couple of false starts, in bringing into being with the help of foreign
capital a 'Privileged National Bank', empowered to issue its own
notes, which it then exchanged against the 'Wiener Währung' at
the rate of 100:250, a shade higher than that at which the latter
was then being quoted. It proved possible to hold the exchange at
this rate, and the Bank's notes gradually replaced the old paper, and
the Government was able to use them, and metal, which now re-
emerged, interchangeably, and even to resume full nominal payment of
its own debt.

Stadion succeeded also in raising revenue very substantially (from
50 million gulden in 1814 to 94 in 1817 and 110 by 1830), while
expenditure was trimmed severely. In spite of this, financial equilibrium was not achieved. Every year closed with a budgetary deficit,
ranging from 50 m.g. downward. To meet these the Government's
regular resource was to borrow, by internal or external loans. Both
types were usually raised through a small ring of banking-houses
among which that of Rothschild soon towered pre-eminent. The
Rothschilds rendered Austria extraordinary service in 1823, when
they persuaded the British Government to write off almost the whole
debt of over £28 million then owed it by Austria, and themselves
always arranged that Austria should get the money she wanted. But
they made her pay through the nose – sometimes 7 – 9 per cent – for
the accommodation, and her debt to them soon became an extremely
heavy item in her debit balance. They also exacted political rewards
for their services. Salomon Rothschild's influence strongly affected
many of Metternich's decisions.

Austria's financial difficulties were a major reason for the forced
restraint which characterized her foreign policy during these years.
The biggest economies were made, perforce, in the defence budget,
which Francis personally ordered to be kept to 40 (later 45) m.g. per
annum. This figure was always slightly exceeded, but still involved

reducing the peace-time strength of the army by suspending recruiting, neglecting training, and leaving equipment unmodernized. These economies were bitterly opposed by Metternich, with whose ambition to see Austria guardian in chief of the European order they were obviously incompatible. But the necessity was ineluctable, and under its compulsion the guardianship reduced itself to putting back on their thrones a few thoroughly undeserving Italian princelets. Another result of the stringency, an unanticipated and most embarrassing one, to which we shall return, was to strengthen considerably the bargaining power of the Hungarian Diet.

In some of Francis's dominions, international obligations, or considerations of expediency, imposed the introduction of constitutional forms. Thus the Congress had laid on the Partitioning Powers the obligation to grant their Polish subjects certain 'national institutions', and this ruling could be the less easily ignored because the Czar Alexander had given Congress Poland a relatively liberal constitution. Galicia was accordingly promoted to the status of a Kingdom, under a Viceroy with a regular system of Estates. The German *Bundesakte* laid down that every 'State of the Bund' must have a 'Constitution of Estates'; accordingly, Estates were set up in Salzburg, and those of some other Alpine Lands remodelled. Finally, Lombardy and Venetia were combined into another Kingdom, again under a Viceroy (the Archduke Rainer) with a 'Congregations-General' composed of representatives of the land-owners and the larger towns, while Lombardy and Venetia each received 'Provincial Congregations'. The language of administration, the Courts and education was Italian, and the services staffed, so far as considerations of security allowed, with Italians, natives either of the Provinces, or of the Trentino.

Lombardy-Venetia and Galicia were given their own Chancelleries, which, however, unlike the Hungarian, were not separate services, but with the *Vereinigte Hofkanzlei*, formed sections of a great Ministry of the Interior, under an *Oberster Hofkanzler* (Supreme Court Chancellor). When this arrangement was made, the *Staatsrat* was made into a general supervisory body to control the work of all departments except the Ministry of Foreign Affairs and the Hungarian Chancellery; it was composed of four sections, each under a *Realminister* and dealing respectively with justice, internal administration, finance and defence. 'Beside and above' this (the relationship was never more exactly defined) stood a '*Staats- und Konferenzrat*', composed of past and present *Realminister* and other members nominated by the Crown, sometimes for life, sometimes for limited periods. The first President of this body was Count Zichy; after his death in 1826, the post was given to Prince (as he had been

created in 1813) Metternich, who in 1821 was also made formal
head of the *Haus- Hof- und Staatskanzlei* and in 1824 received the
title, not borne by any servant of the Crown since Kaunitz died, of
Chancellor of State.

None of these arrangements, however, altered the character of the
regime. The Galician Estates, although they now met regularly, and
the Lombard-Venetian Congregations General, had no more powers
than those of the German-Bohemian Lands, that is to say, none. It
was still Francis, and he alone, who took the final decision on any
subject whatever, in his unfettered discretion and on the basis of
whatever advice he chose. If Metternich, whom he consulted almost
daily, seemed to exercise a large influence over these decisions, it was
because Metternich, as he himself admitted, advised the course to
which Francis already inclined. The other weaknesses of the 'system'
remained unremedied. Metternich found that the Presidency of the
Konferenzrat, which met no oftener than had its predecessor of 1801,
did not even afford him any insight into the work of the departments
other than his own, much less any control over them. Files on every
sort of subject, important or trivial, still accumulated unread in
Francis's study.

Observers of the 'system' noted only two respects in which its
character or emphasis seemed to alter a little. According to some, the
influence in it of the aristocracy diminished as Francis took the reins
more firmly into his own hands, in favour of that of centralizing
bureaucracy in which the *Beamtenadel* was more strongly represented. Secondly, the Roman Catholic Church regained a good deal of
the influence which it had lost since the death of Maria Theresa.
Francis, although personally pious, held strictly to the Josephinian
concept of the relationship between Church and State. Tentative
negotiations with the Holy See for a Concordat, although supported
by Metternich, broke down on Francis's steady refusal to yield
ground in this respect, and acceptance by a cleric of the role of servant of the State still led to preferment more quickly than did piety.
Most influential churchmen of the day, especially those connected
with the teaching professions, adapted themselves to this fact of life.
But in April 1816, Francis became a widower once again, and in
October of the same year took as his fourth wife the ultra-devout
Bavarian Princess, Carolina Augusta, under whose influence, and
that of Metternich, whose sympathies were turning in the same
direction, a 'Pious Party' appeared at the Court, changing its atmosphere perceptibly.

In general, however, the happy outcome of the Congress of Vienna
had confirmed Francis in the belief that he had been right all along.
Time and again, during the preceding twenty-five years, he had

listened to advisers who had wheedled him into this or that innovation, and every time he had done so he had lost a war, and usually
a province. Since 1810 he had gone his own way, and had emerged
triumphant, all the lost ground recovered, and twenty-five years
weathered, twenty-one of them without serious internal political
trouble.

It was in any case his honest belief that not only all that was good
for the 'subjects', but all that, if right-minded, they could, and did,
want, was material well-being and good laws. The former condition,
temporarily absent, would return in due course; the latter had been
fulfilled in 1811 – 12 with the issue, following the new Penal Code, of
the new 'General Civil Code'. For the rest, what was needed was not
further concessions to the wrong-headed, but even stricter adherence
to what experience had proved to be the correct course.

Consequently, the social and political freeze was maintained
strictly, and the maintenance of stability developed into a still finer
art. The charge of the police and censorship passed in 1815 from
the relatively liberal-minded von Hagen to Count Sedlnitzky, who
was, indeed, not the terrorist as which he figures in the pamphlet
literature of 1848 – he was not so much sadistic, as over-timid – but
under his regime the criteria of what could be published, said or even
thought with safety were made still narrower. A second police service
was directly under the control of Metternich. This operated chiefly
outside the Monarchy, and it was probably the reports of Metternich's agents abroad, with the glosses put on them by him, that were
chiefly responsible for the intensification of the anti-intellectual drive
that set in after 1815. Not without reason, Francis regarded most of
his own peoples, Hungarians, Poles and Italians excepted, as basically innocent, provided that they were not corrupted by contagion
from abroad. But the outside world, particularly Germany, was rife
with 'Liberalism', and when German youths indulged in indiscreet
demonstrations, and suspicious symptoms of infection appeared in
several universities of German-Austria, a grand inquisition set in
which cost many Professors, including the famous Bolzano, their
chairs. Regulations were tightened up, first in the teaching profession,
then outside it; the army of police spies multiplied still further, and
the list of activities in which a 'subject' could indulge without police
supervision dwindled monthly.

These were not conditions conducive to vigorous intellectual or
artistic life, at least in the capital, where activities were doubly
subdued; by official control, and also by financial stringency, or
perhaps it should rather be said, by the new official attitude towards
it. In Francis's day the convention ruled that bills had to be paid, and
the very buildings of his day reflected his staid and upright person-

ality in an architecture that was economical, unpretentious and domestic.

It is, however, an exaggeration to represent the period, even in Vienna, as devoid of any cultural achievements whatever. Beethoven had not yet fallen silent, and Schubert was in his brief prime. Grillparzer, a notable literary figure by the standards of any country or age, was able to get his plays produced (not always, indeed, without difficulty). And for some of the non-German peoples of the Monarchy, the period was almost a cultural springtime.

In the West, the national culture which made the biggest advance was the Czech,[1] which enjoyed the extraordinary advantage of aristocratic patronage and financial support, for soon after the return of peace, a group of Bohemian magnates, headed by Count Kaspar Sternberg, left without occupation, and irked by the bureaucratic centralism of the administrative system, took up the cause of the local culture, both Czech and German, and founded a number of institutions for the furtherance of it. The preliminary work of standardizing, purifying and enriching the Czech language had already been carried through by the pioneers, Dobrovský and Jungmann, and the harvest of their work was now reaped by a generation of romantics, Jan Kollár, author of an extraordinary heroic epic, *Slavy Dcera* (*The Daughter of Slava*), Paul Josef Šafařik, who compiled a History of the Slav Languages, and the most famous of all, František Palacký, author of a monumental 'History of Bohemia'.[2] The Czech language found another important helper in a man to whom we shall return, Count Franz Antal Kolowrat-Liebsteinsky, a Bohemian magnate of very strong Czechophile sentiments, who in 1810 had been given the post of Governor of Bohemia, in which capacity he secured more place for the Czech language in the *Gymnasia* of Bohemia, and also ordered that in future preference in appointments to the administrative services should be given *ceteris paribus* to candidates knowing that language. Since most secondary instruction was still in German, Bohemia still looked, to a superficial observer, like a German province with a Czech peasantry, but the tide was already nearing its turn, and in the next generation the advance of the Czech element would become obvious, and irresistible.

The seeds of a Slovene national revival had been sown by the French authorities in the 'Kingdom of Illyria', who had meant to make a Slovene State of it, and had drawn up the blue-prints for an advanced system of education in the 'local language'. The returning Austrians had restored the *status quo ante*, in which virtually all such instruction as the population had received had been in German, but a sprinkling of younger Slovenes had retained their awareness that they were not Germans, and had, after much debate among themselves, found an agreed answer to the first question by deciding that the Slovene language was to be developed as a distinct one, not, as some had wanted, identified with Croat – an all-important decision from which, it is fair to say, there had followed the development of the Slovenes as a distinct people. They had not got much further than this, for there was no nationally-minded Slovene aristocracy to do for them what the Bohemian magnates were doing for the Czechs; the only patron in high places of the Slovene culture was the Archduke John, who after his enforced retirement to Graz had founded there an institution for the local culture which was the counterpart – actually, the prototype – of the Royal Bohemian Society in Prague. But the foundations of the later development had been laid.

There were even shy stirrings of national-cultural aspirations among the Ruthenes, who, however, had not yet been able to answer definitively the first question of their linguistic, and hence their national, identity and whatever answer they gave annoyed someone. When they said that the language which they spoke was Ukrainian, the Russian Government, which was denying the very existence of a Ukrainian language or people, protested to the Austrian Government, accusing it of fostering subversion among the Czar's subjects. When they suggested that it was Russian, it was the Austrian Government that was alarmed. The Poles denied that it was anything more than a mere dialect of Polish. In the end the Government, following the line of least resistance, had allowed all secondary education in Galicia, where not given in German, to be entirely Polonized, with only a little instruction in the local dialect in the primary schools, such as they were.

There were some similar stirrings across the Leitha, where, however, the position showed many variants. Among some of the peoples of the Lands of the Hungarian Crown it was one of near-complete standstill. Klein-Micu and his colleagues had not yet found successors among the local Roumanians. Both the Orthodox and the Uniate Bishops were good administrators, and under their regimes the numbers and quality of the schools of both Confessions increased, and with them, the numbers of potential national leaders of the future, but not of the present: most of the more active-minded young Roumanians emerging from the schools, if not themselves taking Holy Orders, emigrated to the Danubian Principalities, in which they came almost to monopolize the teaching professions, thereby, indeed, preparing the ground for the later movement for unification of the Roumanian people on both sides of the Carpathians. For the Serbs, Hungary was at that time playing host to a very vigorous Serbian cultural movement, for the total absence of any sort of intellectual life in the Principality drove its ambitious young men abroad.

Their chief meeting-place was the University of Pest, where a group
of them founded a literary society, the *Matica Srbska*. This then
moved to Újvidék (Novi Sad), which won for itself the name of
the 'Serbian Athens', as the chief centre of the Serbian national culture of the day. But the seed scattered from Újvidék fell almost exclusively in the Principality. The Serbian Archbishop of Karlóca,
Stratimirović, was an ultra-conservative, who imposed on his
people, so far as he was able, a complete cultural standstill, while the
Serb communities outside his jurisdiction were already beginning to
succumb to the decay which overtook them fully in later decades,
their members either Magyarizing, or emigrating to Serbia. The
Croat nobles of the day had still no thought for anything except the
defence of their antique constitutional privileges, and clung fanati-
cally to the Latin language in which these documents were enshrined.
A journalist who obtained a licence to publish a paper in the Croat
language had to give up the project because he could find no sub-
scribers. Among the non-Magyars of the Lands of the Holy Crown
only the Slovaks made a little progress, and that was a story of doubtful stirrings, perplexed by the same preliminary riddle as was tor-
menting the Slovenes and Ruthenes. Round the turn of the century
the cause of Czecho-Slovak linguistic unity had been taken up by a
group of Slovak Protestants, to whom the idea came naturally because the Bible used by them was a Czech one, introduced into Hungary by the Hussites. The growth of this movement inspired a Slovak
Catholic priest named Bernolak to start, with the assistance of the
Archbishop-Primate, Rudnay, himself a Slovak, a counter-movement
for developing the western dialect of Slovak as an independent language, precisely in order to save the Slovaks from the 'Hussite
tongue', and consequent infection with Protestantism. Each party
founded circles and institutions in order to keep the other out, so
that the very fact of the dispute contributed to the awakening of a
Slovak national consciousness, without, indeed, reaching final agreement on just what a Slovak was.

Much the most vigorous of the national-cultural revivals across
the Leitha was that of the Magyars themselves. This was, of course,
no product of the restoration years. As we have seen, its beginnings
reached back to the age of Maria Theresa, and its vigorous self-
assertion was an aspect of the national revolt against Joseph II's
policies of centralization and Germanization. It was, however, only
now that it was really getting into its stride. A group of linguists,
among whom Ferencz Kazinczy was the most prominent, had
completed the great task of purifying the language, freeing it from
foreign corruptions, rationalizing its grammar and enriching its
vocabulary, and the linguistic 'renewal' was now being followed by

the first burgeonings of a literature which was still crude, but already producing works of something more than promise, the appearance of which was being hailed by the nation with justified pride.

The test which a censor was supposed to apply to a work was whether it was politically safe. The products of the new national revivals, especially those of the non-suspect peoples, were, if they passed this test, actually to be encouraged, as taking men's minds off politics. This reasoning was, of course, quite fallacious. In the first place, many of the works approved by the censors were not non-political at all: the *Slavy Dcera*, for example, is simply a hymn of hate depicting the sufferings of the Czechs at the hands of their German and Magyar oppressors. But even where the direct political implication was not apparent, the appearance of any successful literary product heightened the national pride of the people in whose tongue it was composed and thus brought nearer the day in which it would claim a voice in the conduct of the Monarchy's political affairs. It is, however, true that none of these products preached active subversion, and politically, the surface of affairs in the Monarchy during these years presented a picture of almost unruffled calm. No single political trial of an Austrian subject took place in the Hereditary Lands during the last twenty years of Francis's reign, and the tranquillity in most other parts of the Monarchy was hardly less complete. In Galicia the Poles, their early hopes disappointed and the revival of them not yet come, submitted passively to their condition and even showed some disposition to make the best of it. When, in 1826, Prince Lichnowsky was sent to Lemberg as Viceroy, with the specific and avowed mission of winning their good will, the response with which he met was not altogether negative. In Lombardy several persons, some of them members of the highest aristocracy, were arrested in 1820 for conspiratorial activities, and barbarous sentences passed on them. But their objective had not been simply to free Lombardy from Austrian rule. This might have resulted as a by-product had they been successful, but the chief targets of the Carbonari and other societies to which they belonged had been the regimes in Naples, Piedmont and the Romagna. Extensive repressive measures followed the arrests, and while these were naturally unpopular, they were effective, and there were no further symptoms of unrest.

The only challenge to the regime came from Hungary, and there the issue involved was unconnected with the new nationalism. When the Crown had wanted money and recruits from Hungary in 1813 and 1815, it had found ways of obtaining them without going through the constitutional procedure of getting them voted by a Diet, and the Hungarians, while murmuring against the illegalities, had submitted to them. But when the Crown repeated the procedure in 1820, the protests were very vehement, and when, in 1822, it made fresh demands, among them, for a *contributio* of five and a quarter million gulden to be paid in silver, or if in *Einlösungsscheine* at the new rate, thus thirteen and a half million gulden, many Counties refused to pay, and their resistance was so unmanageable that after two years of struggling, Francis decided to convoke the Diet, which would at least be one body, not fifty-two, and one in which one of its two Benches might be expected to support him.

The Diet, when it met in 1825, thereafter remaining in session for two full years, contained a considerable number of members describing themselves as 'Oppositional'. It did not, however, deserve in every respect the adjective of 'Reform' afterwards bestowed on it. Like every Diet, it asked for wider use of the Magyar language in public life, and the debates on this issue were made memorable by the gesture of a young aristocrat, Count István Széchenyi, who volunteered to devote a year's income from his estates to the foundation of a Hungarian Academy. But not one of the instructions with which the fifty-two Counties had, according to practice, armed their representatives suggested reform of the peasants' conditions, and the one speaker who raised the question at a session was shouted down by his colleagues. In this respect there was no difference between the attitudes of the sympathizers with the Government, and the Opposition. The latter saw their task, almost exclusively, as that of defending Hungary's immemorial (and highly unreformed) constitution against the encroachments of Vienna. In this respect, however, they did score a certain success: they extracted from Francis a sort of apology for his past conduct, an acknowledgment that legislation imposed without the Diet's consent was illegal, and a promise to convoke another Diet in 1830, for full consideration of the nation's *postulata* and to be presented in the form of revised editions of the Committee Reports of 1792. Modest as these results were, they did constitute a certain victory – the only one of the period in the whole Monarchy – for the principle of constitutionalism against absolutism, and they made possible the fuller developments described on later pages.

THE SYSTEM ON THE WANE
1830-5

Most historians put the beginning of the *Vormärz* – the years in which the revolutions of March 1848 were gestating – at Francis's death in 1835. Five years earlier might be a truer date. The 'Concert of Europe' had, of course, never followed the movements of Metternich's baton anything like so obediently as he had hoped, and it had not been long before Britain was right out of the orchestra and France's membership of it hardly more than nominal. The three Eastern Powers, however, had continued to form a Conservative group, although in this, Austria was steadily losing ground to Prussia in Germany with the expansion of the *Zollverein*, and the uneasy friendship which still tied her to Russia hid many conflicts of interest. But then came the terrible year of 1830 with the July Revolution in Paris and its concomitants in Belgium, Poland and Italy. Metternich collapsed at his writing-table when the news from Paris reached him, moaning that his life's work had been destroyed. He recovered his poise, and afterwards conducted a series of masterly salvage operations. He 'restored order' in Italy, reinstating Austria as the ruler, direct or indirect, of most of the peninsula, and at München-grätz, in 1833, he re-established solidarity with Russia and Prussia on the principle of mutual support against revolution, smoothing over the differences which had arisen between Austria and Russia over Poland and Turkey, and extracting from Czar Nicolas a promise to stand by Francis's son, Ferdinand, when he should succeed to the throne.

But these had truly been salvage operations, carried through against dangers that did not look like decreasing, and many were asking whether the Monarchy would not soon find itself confronted with similar threats at home, and if so, how it should meet them. For Francis the answer was simple. His abhorrence of change had by now become almost pathological. 'I want no change,' he told the *Hofkanzler*, von Pillersdorf, in 1831. 'Let the laws be applied justly. Justice is all in all.' When Pillersdorf suggested that change was sometimes necessary, Francis replied: 'This is no time for reforms. The people are like men who have been severely wounded. One must not keep touching and irritating their wounds.' And Metternich regularly backed him with his old parrot-cry that 'this was no time for innovations'.

But Francis himself was not the man he had been. He had been badly ill in 1826, and, when he recovered, much of his old industry and determination had gone. In 1829 he set up a 'Standing Inner Conference', to which he entrusted all the top-level business of the State, except the exercise of Royal prerogatives, such as acts of grace, and the final decision in matters of the very highest importance.

And the spirit in which this body worked was not a completely faithful replica of Francis's. Of its three members, one was Metternich, whose outlook was of course, the same as Francis's own. The second, Count Nádasdy, the President of the *Hofkammer*, is not recorded as holding any pronounced views on any subject whatever. But the third member did not quite fit into the picture.

This was that Count Kolowrat whom we have met on a previous page as patron of Czech culture in his capacity of Governor of Bohemia. In 1826 Francis had called him to Vienna and entrusted him with various jobs, all of which he performed with such efficiency as to emerge as head of both the political and the financial sections of the *Staatsrat*, and thus *de facto* Minister both of the Interior and of Finance. Under his auspices the State budget for 1830 had closed with the smallest deficit within living memory, and his estimates for 1831 had actually provided for a surplus, which was not, indeed, realized owing to the military expenditure demanded by Metternich to meet the international situation.

Popular opinion classified Kolowrat as a 'Liberal'. He himself disclaimed the description; his principles, as he once told Metternich, were as conservative as the Chancellor's own, and there was, in fact, nothing revolutionary in his conduct of his portfolios. But he did disagree with Metternich's nostrums of 'a forest of bayonets and a rigid adherence to the *status quo*', which, in his view, 'only exhausted the government's resources and provoked the middle classes into allying themselves with the masses against the aristocracy'. Precisely the maintenance of the existing social order required that any available money should be spent 'on promoting the material well-being of the masses, bringing them well-being as a reward for their industry'. The very presence in the top-most councils of State of a man holding these views, a man, moreover, who notoriously detested Metternich, made the continuance *ad infinitum* of the 'system' appear less axiomatic.

Apart from the Inner Conference, Francis was now leaning chiefly on his youngest brother, the Archduke Ludwig, who was, indeed, by all accounts the least talented of them all, but the only one left who was not, like Joseph and Rainer, indispensable elsewhere, or, like Charles and John, in disgrace.

Inside the Monarchy, meanwhile, the danger-year of 1830 was

passing over well enough. Of all the Principalities of Italy, Lombardy-Venetia had remained the most tranquil. The Polish revolutionaries had left Galicia out of their plans, in the hope of buying diplomatic support from Austria. There had been enough emotional disturbances to make Francis replace Lobkowitz by the more imposing figure of the Archduke Ferdinand d'Este, to whom, since he was a notoriously easy-going man, there was attached a stronghanded military *ad latus*, who tightened up security precautions, but did not find it necessary to take any drastic measures. The stirrings of new life in the German-Austrian and Bohemian Lands did not go beyond a few demonstrations, a little coffee-house talk, and the appearance of a few mildly pink literary effusions. The obvious danger spot was Hungary, where sympathy for Poland was being expressed so clamorously that many of Francis's counsellors advised him against fulfilling his promise to convoke the Diet. But Metternich needed men and money for his proposed military operations, and both the Palatine and the Hungarian Chancellor, Reviczky, advised that it would be safer to convoke the Diet, than to postpone it again. Convocation would also make it possible to kill a second bird with the same stone. Francis's eldest son, Ferdinand, was clearly incapable of becoming an effective ruler. He was physically frail, an epileptic and mentally, simple almost to the verge of idiocy. He had long been pronounced unfit to marry, and although he was eventually given a bride, it was known that he could never become a father. His younger brother, Franz Karl, was no genius, but a man of average capacities, and the wife whom he had married in 1828, Sophie of Bavaria, was expecting to become a mother (in the event she was delivered, in August, of a boy, Francis Joseph), and some wished to see Franz Karl declared his father's heir. But natural affection, and respect for the principle of legitimacy, made Francis unwilling to pass Ferdinand over. He took the decision to give the succession to Ferdinand, and arranged to make this irrevocable by having him crowned King of Hungary.

The Diet was, accordingly, convoked for October, but only to experience a repetition of Francis's old trick. He presented it with two *propositiones:* to crown Ferdinand, and to vote 50,000 men and a cash subsidy for the campaigns. The Diet fulfilled the former request, having consented, not without murmuring, to an unchanged Coronation Diploma. When it came to the next point, the magnates, who were as anxious as Metternich himself to see the fires of revolution stamped out, were ready to vote the men immediately. The Lower Table wanted to exact a price, but ended by giving in in return for a single concession, that knowledge of the Magyar language was to be compulsory for all State employees and lawyers '*intra limites*

regni' (i.e. excluding Croatia) and a promise that their more extensive *postulata* should be given a full hearing at another, special,
Diet to meet the next July. Then they allowed themselves to be sent
home.

But, in 1831, Francis again evaded keeping his promise, this time
pleading danger of infection, since a devastating outbreak of cholera,
carried from Russia across Galicia, was ravaging the country, where
it carried off nearly 250,000 victims – one in twenty five of the entire
population. Thus another year passed before the Diet met, and in the
intervening period, its mood changed greatly. This was due partly to
the epidemic itself, and its concomitants. The ravages of the plague
had been worst in the north of the country, where the population was
at once the most backward, and the most oppressed. Rumours had
run round there that the authorities, the landlords, and the Jews, had
been conspiring to reduce the population by poisoning the wells, and
there had been a Jacquerie in which nobles and their bailiffs, Jews
and priests had been massacred on a scale which had shattered the
common complacent belief that all was well between the landlords
and their peasants. Many, of course, simply called for severe repressive measures, which were in fact carried through; but others believed the truer answer to lie in remedying the peasants' grievances.
But both parties agreed that the problem could not be ignored. And
just before this, Count István Széchenyi, the man who in 1825 had
inspired the foundation of the Hungarian Academy, had published
his book '*Hitel*' (Credit).

Hitel is an astonishing work, and Széchenyi an astonishing
figure. The scion of one of Hungary's great families which combined
a tradition of loyalty to the Crown with one of devotion to their
people – his father had been the founder of the great library in Pest
that still bears his name – he had passed his early manhood as an
Imperial officer. When the wars ended, he had sent in his papers, and
had travelled widely in Western Europe, especially England. He had
been shocked by the contrast between the wealth, progress and civic
liberty which he saw there, and the poverty, backwardness and
degradation of his own country, and in *Hitel* he had the hardihood to
declare that the causes which left Hungary what he called 'the great
fallow-land' were none other than the cherished privileges of its
nobles. These were detrimental to themselves. Their exemption from
taxation prevented the accumulation of capital for the construction of
communications, for lack of which the harvests rotted ungathered on
the ground; the 'aviticitas'[1] made it impossible for them to borrow
money on their estates for necessary improvements; the *robot* which
they exacted from their 'subjects' brought in only one third of the
day's work of a hired free labourer. He added with unsparing frank-

ness that the remedy lay with the nobles themselves, whose sloth, selfishness and complacency produced and tolerated these evils.

Naturally, *Hitel* met with a mixed reception. The traditionalist squires denounced its author as an unpractised dilettante, a fouler of his own nest, a traitor, a red revolutionary. But to others, the book and a sequel to it, *Világ* (Light) came as a revelation, an inspiration, and an enormous encouragement. When in December 1832 the Diet afterwards known as the 'Long' met at last, Széchenyi had few disciples in the House of Magnates, except an old Transylvanian friend, Baron Miklós Wesselényi, whose ownership of an estate in Hungary entitled him to sit in Pozsony as well as Kolozsvár. But the Lower Table contained a considerable number of reformers, including one Ferencz Deák, a country squire from Zala, who was to prove a host in himself. The agenda made it possible for the reformers to raise almost any point they wished, in the guise of a proposed amendment to one of the Committee reports, and they pressed for a large number of reforms, some of them radical by the standards of the day, ranging from reform of the conditions of the peasants to abolition of the *aviticitas*, removal of unequal restrictions on the Protestants, and amendment, by negotiation with the Austrian Estates, of the tariff relationship between Hungary and Austria. But they were still heavily outnumbered by the combined forces of the Crown, the magnates, and the Conservatives on the Lower Bench, and by the end of 1834 the Crown had given way only a short distance on a few issues,[2] and on others, including that of the tariff, it had not given way at all.

So far, then, the proceedings had constituted another victory for the forces of immobility, but in the wider field, they were losing ground heavily. By this time, Széchenyi's criticisms of the constitution were finding very wide acceptance, and Széchenyi himself was becoming a back number. To the younger generation of Hungarian intellectuals, taught by the writings (which easily penetrated the slipshod censorship) of contemporary French political philosophers to regard liberty as the panacea against all evils, Széchenyi's programme of measured reform from above appeared as positive reaction. The young *jurati* who attended the Diet in unprecedented numbers[3] made this clear in their rowdy accompaniments to its proceedings, and chance provided a channel through which a version of the modern creed could be heard in Hungary. This was the voice of Lajos Kossuth.

A little older than the *jurati* – he had been born in 1802 – Kossuth was still young enough to share their faith in the supreme virtue of liberty, and the circumstances of his birth and upbringing – he was the son of technically 'noble' but impecunious parents from the tra-

ditionally anti-Habsburg North-East of Hungary, Lutherans at that –
had bred in him the conviction that of all forms of liberty, national
liberty was the most important. He agreed with Széchenyi on the
backwardness of Hungary, but attributed it primarily to the domination then being illegally exercised over her in many ways by the
Austrian regime – he was not at the time against the Austrian
connection as such – and believed the first necessity to be to restore
the relationship to one which accorded with Hungary's historic
rights. But, unlike some of the politicians who later invoked his
name, he did not make this view an excuse for present inactivity: he
rather maintained that internal reform, besides being desirable in
itself, would also bring national liberty nearer: the emancipation of
the peasants, for example, itself a postulate of liberty, would also
multiply twenty-fold the forces fighting for the national cause, and
one great service that he rendered to his country was that by making
radical social reforms a national postulate, he won over to their cause
many who would otherwise have rejected them. It is true that this
linking of the issues stiffened further the resistance of the Court and
its supporters to reforms to which they might otherwise have agreed.

Kossuth lacked Széchenyi's assets of birth, wealth, and influential
connections: also, it must be admitted, of knowledge of the world.
But in other respects he outdistanced him easily. 'The Count's'
literary style was involved, his delivery halting, even his command of
the Magyar language imperfect. Kossuth was a superb orator and a
brilliant writer, with an extraordinary gift for enlisting the sympathies of his audience for whatever cause he was pleading. His thesis,
moreover, was more popular than the other man's: it is pleasanter to
hear your tribulations ascribed to the wickedness of others, than to
your own wickedness and sloth.

Kossuth's chance came to him in an odd way, The favour of a
patroness had enabled him to attend the Diet as proxy for an absen-
tee magnate. This position did not give him a vote in the Diet's proceedings, but a friend commissioned him to produce a record of
them. He used this to produce what was less a record, than a series
of brilliant propagandist pleas for the cause of reform. Copied out
by hand by enthusiastic *jurati*, the 'reports' circulated throughout
Hungary, and were read avidly. Soon Kossuth's disciples numbered
their thousands, and his was the most popular name in the country.

Simultaneously with the Kingdom, Transylvania burst into political activity. This was largely the single-handed work of Wesselényi,
whose lineage and background resembled those of Széchenyi, but his
temperament was rather akin to Kossuth's. In 1831 he took advantage of an attempt by the *Gubernium* to impress recruits without the
sanction of the Diet to let loose a crisis as result of which a Diet was

really convoked in 1834. It was, indeed, a packed body and was dissolved after only a few weeks, after which the constitution was suspended and the Archduke Ferdinand d'Este put in as Royal Commissioner with plenipotentiary powers.

Simultaneously with this again, the political atmosphere in Croatia underwent a sudden and sensational transformation. The pioneers of this were not the local nobles, who were slow to free themselves from their legalistic fixation, but young *honoratiores* and students, who were no social revolutionaries – their minds were too full of higher things to bother about peasants' grievances – but were also not interested in the maintenance of noble privileges. The object of their concern was their people as a whole, and their goal, the cultivation of everything that was 'national' – language, customs, traditions, and the satisfaction of the political ambitions which the thought of the day regarded as the due of a nation. Their movement was total also in its disregard of political boundaries: what mattered was that a man should be a Croat, irrespective of whether his home was civilian Croatia, the Frontier, Dalmatia, or for that matter, Bosnia.

That the immediate expression of this attitude was something different from the common run of megalomaniac territorial claims was again due to a personal factor. The accepted *spiritus rector* of the little band, and also the only one of them of a publicistic turn of mind, was a young man named Ljudevit Gaj. Gaj had attended several Universities, among them that of Pest. There he had come under the influence of Kollár, who had inspired him with a vision of a great 'Illyrian' nation *in posse*, comprising Croats, Serbs, Slovenes and Bulgars. Gaj set himself to weld these four peoples into a nation *in esse* and began by trying to give them a common tongue. The results were, up to a point, considerable. There were at the time three chief forms of spoken Croat. Gaj succeeded in getting his own people to adopt as their standard written form that variant which was that spoken in Southern Dalmatia and the Herzegovina, and which the Serbian linguistic reformer of the day, Vuk Karadžić, was persuading his people to adopt for standard Serb. Standard Serb and standard Croat thus became one language as spoken, although not as written, since the Orthodox Popes refused to accept the Latin alphabet, and Gaj, on his side, refused to renounce it for their Cyrillic. The Slovenes refused, as we have said elsewhere, to alter their language, as did the Bulgarians.

Still less was Gaj able to persuade the Slovenes, not to speak of the Bulgars, or even many of his own people, to exchange their particularist national consciousness for an 'Illyrian' one, or even to accept the latter as an outer bracket, but he gained a few disciples, among them the important figure of Count Janko Drašković, one of the most prominent Croats of the day. In 1833 Gaj also saw Kolowrat, to whom he explained how useful 'Illyrianism' would be, primarily in stiffening the Croats and Slovenes against the Magyars, but also in 'influencing in favour of attachment to Austria the Slav peoples across the Austrian frontiers, and weakening Russia's influence over them.' He got a licence to publish a paper, the *Novine Hrvatska* (Croat News), which began with a great flourish of Illyrianism. This seems still to have found few adherents, but meanwhile particularist Croat national feeling had been growing apace. In the following year the demand for the use of it in Croat public life became as tempestuous as the parallel demand for the use of Magyar across the Drave, while the hymns of hate against the Magyars with which Gaj filled his columns far exceeded in virulence anything from the other side.

Six

THE *VORMÄRZ*

On 25 February 1835 Francis was seized with a sharp fever, and on 2 March he died. From his death-bed he had addressed two letters to his successor. One, which had been composed for him by Metternich, although Francis had made one addition to it, enjoined Ferdinand 'not to displace the bases of the structure of the State, to rule and not to alter', to follow the principles which had guided Francis himself, to take the advice of the Archduke Ludwig in important domestic (*innere*) matters (this had been Francis's addition) and to bestow on Metternich 'his most faithful servant and friend' the confidence which he, Francis, had so long reposed in him, and to take no decision on public affairs or questions of personnel without consulting him. The second letter, dictated by the Court Chaplain, Wagner, in substance adjured Ferdinand to continue the work of purifying the Church from Josephinian unorthodoxes. Here, too, Francis was to be guided by Metternich and Wagner.

Metternich's enemies naturally revolted against this shameless jumping of the gun, and a prolonged squabble for power ensued which ended in the establishment of a Council of Regency disguised under the name of *Staatskonferenz*, the nominal permanent members of which were Ferdinand, Ludwig, Franz Karl, Metternich and Kolowrat. Of these Ferdinand was a figurehead pure and simple, and Franz Karl, who was there to keep the place warm for his son, Ferdinand's presumptive successor, not much more. The chief function of Ludwig, who presided in the absence, which was almost invariable, of the Emperor, was to keep the peace, where he could, between the other two, the real controllers of policy, whose spheres of competence were, or should have been, divided: Metternich being in charge of foreign affairs, while Kolowrat, as President of the *Staats- und Konferenzrat*, was overlord of every other department, including finance and, after 1840 (till when it had been independent), defence. When, as sometimes happened, the head of one of the multiple ministries, chancelleries and so forth who, with sundry 'advisers' constituted the *Staats- und Konferenzrat*, was invited to report to the *Staatskonferenz*, he still did so as Kolowrat's lieutenant.

The Archduke Ludwig was already a super-Conservative, who also held it his duty to obey Francis's dying instructions to the best of his ability, while on the rare occasions on which either Metternich or Kolowrat wanted to 'alter' anything, the other did his best, out of jealousy, to block the move. Consequently, the single direction in which any change in the 'system' was perceptible was that the 'Pious Party' made some further advances under the now convinced patronage of Metternich and the influences of the Archduchess Sophie and of the talented tutor to her sons, the later Cardinal, Joseph Othmar von Rauscher. Renewed negotiations for a Concordat broke down again, but the Society of Jesus was readmitted to all parts of the Monarchy (before, it had been allowed only into Galicia), and a community of Protestants who had managed to survive in the Tirol were expelled from their homes. Otherwise, surface immobility was maintained so completely that historians are apt to dismiss the *Vormärz* cursorily as years in which nothing changed. This is a mistake, for under the surface new forces, economic, social and *in posse* political, were swirling round the bases of the pillars on which the 'system' rested, and gathering the strength which would soon bring it down in ruins.

Basic to all the developments was the increase of the Monarchy's population. Almost static during the war years 1792 – 1815, it had begun to rise very rapidly after the conclusion of peace, and in 1843 stood at some 37.5 million – 17.5 in the western Lands, 15.6 in the Lands of the Hungarian Crown and 4.8 in Lombardy-Venetia, an over-all increase of about 40 per cent since 1792. The global figure covered, indeed, wide variations: the increase had been relatively slow in the Alpine Lands, but very fast in Bohemia, Galicia, and central and southern Hungary.

The population was still mainly rural, and mainly agricultural. In 1845 80 per cent of the total were still living in villages or scattered farms, and 73–4 per cent still derived their livelihoods from agriculture, forestry or fisheries. In both respects, however, the picture was changing, with increasing rapidity. As the industrial depression lifted, the wider opportunities of earning a livelihood otherwise than off the land, combined with the pressure of population on it, had set off a drift into the towns, especially the larger centres. Vienna had now a population of nearly 400,000, Milan, nearly 150,000, Prague, over 100,000, Venice, little short of it, Pest, 80,000, or 40,000 more including Buda, across the river, Trieste and Lemberg, 50,000 each, Graz, 40,000.

A shift was going on also out of agriculture into other occupations, especially industry. This, again, was recent and local, and again, accelerating.

The development of industry in Hungary had, as we have seen,

been deliberately held back by the *Hofkammer*, with such success
that the whole Kingdom and Croatia together could in 1848 muster
only 23,000 factory hands, 78,000 handworkers, and 35,000 miners.
The purpose of this policy had been to facilitate the growth of
industry in the western Lands, where it had further been protected
against competition from outside by an elaborate system of tariffs
and import prohibitions. But there, too, progress had been impeded
by governmental policy. It was true that even during Francis's last
years, the advocates of economic liberalism had been gaining ground
in Vienna, and after his death, virtually all official restrictions on the
foundation of new enterprises, at least those ranking as *Kommerzialgewerbe*, had been lifted, but the effects of this changed attitude had
been largely nullified by the rigid restriction of the note issue imposed
on the National Bank by the Government, the Government's own
repeated applications to the money market, producing an unending
stream of State obligations, and its insistence that its own demands
for any credit available must have priority. The Government's scale
of priorities had set the tone for the general public, and not only the
big majority of small private savers, but also the religious and other
foundations which constituted the only other source of non-exorbitant
credit, preferred to put their savings into State papers rather than risk
them in private enterprise. Consequently, up to about 1835, there had
been little real growth in industry even in the Hereditary Lands; the
most important industries there were still the old-established ones of
leather-working, furniture and brewing round Vienna, Bohemian
glass, Styrian iron, and the silk-weaving of the Lombard plain.

But the twenty years of peace had, after all, brought with them a
certain accumulation of domestic capital, and in the late 1830s this
appears to have been reinforced by a sudden influx from abroad,
probably emanating from the House of Rothschild. The cotton
industry of Lower Austria, and even more, that of Bohemia, made a
sudden and phenomenal spurt. Within a few years the number of
enterprises in the industry doubled, while the import of cotton-yarn
multiplied eightfold between 1835 and 1842, and that of raw cotton,
threefold.

These were just the years when Austria's steam-driven railways
began to operate. A line from Vienna to Brünn was opened in 1839,
and after this, the network expanded rapidly, the lines in the north
being constructed chiefly under the auspices of the Rothschilds, while
their rival, Sina, secured a concession for a line from Vienna to
Buda-Pest and another to Trieste. The railways not only provided
employment for a considerable labour force (it had been decided to
use home products for them), but by linking the capital with the coal-
and iron-fields of northern Bohemia and Silesia, made possible the

later development of a heavy industry, hitherto retarded by its dependence for power on waterpower or timber, as well as by the impossibility of carrying its products away from their sources. In these years the Monarchy's production of coal rose almost threefold and that of iron, about fivefold. The new industries were of the highly mechanized factory type, as opposed to the old-fashioned home-work, performed by hand. In 1846 a total of about 16.73 per cent of the population of the Monarchy was occupied in industry and mining. As a global figure, this was still small enough, particularly since it included a big proportion of artisans; but it must be remembered that not only Hungary-Croatia and Transylvania, but also Galicia-Bukovina and Dalmatia contributed virtually nothing towards it. In Lower Austria, Styria and Bohemia workers in these employments now constituted a substantial proportion of the population: one quarter of the population of German Bohemia did spinning, this being the sole employment of half of them.

Trade, communications and the professions were also taking their share of the growing millions.

On the land, the pattern of agriculture itself was changing. With bigger markets for their products, and easier access to them, more producers, large and small, were going over to production for profit. Besides the old staple crops of cereals, vegetables, wine, tobacco and horned cattle, sheep-farming for wool had become important, especially in Hungary, and industrial crops such as flax and sugar-beet were being grown in the Bohemian Lands and Galicia. The exploitation of the forests for timber was becoming more systematic.

The biggest change here, however, was the increased density of the population. The towns were taking only a fraction of the new millions; many more of them still remained on their farms. In some parts of the Monarchy, notably central and southern Hungary, the growth was absorbed by bringing new areas under cultivation, and while most of the reclaimed land was incorporated in large estates, it was not uncommon for the owners to lease parts of them to 'contractualist' peasants, or even to dedicate them as urbarial land. In the older-inhabited Lands the denser population had had to be accommodated by subdivision of the peasant holdings. Here whole *sessiones* were now a rarity, and even half-holdings not very common; the most usual size was a quarter, the minimum that entitled its occupant to rank as a 'peasant'; and in most of the western Lands, as also in northern Hungary and Transylvania, this class was already outnumbered by the small- and dwarf-holders, and by the cottagers and totally landless men.

These economic developments were lending to the social structure of the population a new complexity. To the traditional component elements of the Court and its servants, the rural landlord and the peasant-cultivator, there had to be added, on the one hand, considerable urban and rural proletariats, and on the other, in certain centres, substantial bourgeoisies of prosperous manufacturers and traders, with their concomitant professional men and artists.

It was above all the last-named classes – more precisely, their Viennese members (who constituted far the largest fraction of them) whose lives, and particularly their amusements, bulk most largely in the pages of foreign travellers, and on which the panegyrists of Austria's 'good old days' love best to dwell. The Viennese culture of the day, called the *Biedermeyer* after a popular manufacturer of furniture, had, indeed, a grace and charm of its own. There was little great wealth, but a sufficiently widespread modest well-being to permit the return of the traditional atmosphere of Viennese life. It was no age of giants: the best painter of the day, Schwind, emigrated, and Waldmüller went unrecognized. The popular musicians of the day, Strauss and Lanner, were turners of valse tunes, and the best-known writers, authors of comedies. but the comedies were very witty, and the valse tunes more than catching, and while most of the members of the Viennese society of the day did indeed find their chief pleasure in light music, wine and society gossip, a minority of them performed serious work in several fields. To take only one example, the medical faculty of Vienna University, recovered from a long torpor, produced in Rokitansky and Skoda two figures of European calibre.

The much-publicized gaiety of Viennese life in the *Vormärz* should not, however, blind us to the fact that for a considerable part of the population of the Monarchy the period was one of much material hardship, and for not a few, of naked destitution.

It is difficult to generalize about the level of industrial wages, and figures would mean little without more knowledge than we possess of their purchasing power. In the older-established industries they seem to have been very tolerable. The Scotsman, Turnbull, who travelled through Upper Austria and Styria in 1838, found that the wage of a worker there was sufficient to enable him 'to eat, drink and smoke to his heart's content', especially as he usually got his cottage with an acre of allotment thrown in. His wages compared not unfavourably with the salary of a lower-grade civil servant or small professional man. He was also not made 'to feel the enormous value of time'. But, Turnbull writes, the industrial revolution had not yet reached those parts. It was already reaching Bohemia, where the population was also far denser, and was bringing with it, in the new factories there and in Lower Austria, every social evil. Wages were a pittance, especially in the cotton factories, and worst of all for the women and children, who were employed very extensively. A child's working day was usually 12½ hours, with a 1½ hours' break at midday. Hours for adults were entirely unregulated; the average working day for an adult was 13–16 in a factory, or 12 in a mine. There was no legal Sunday rest (there were, it is true, many public holidays). Housing conditions were deplorable, especially in the big cities. Worst of all was the unemployment, especially rife in the cotton industry, where the introduction of labour-saving machinery in the early 1840s had thrown scores of thousands out of work; and this class was particularly hard hit, for while the older, semi-patriarchal enterprises, including the woollen-mills of Moravia, usually tried to see their workers through hard times, the entrepreneurs in the new cotton-mills, many of which were undercapitalized and unable to withstand even a small falling-off in the market, simply turned their workers off when a crisis arrived.

It is even more unsafe to generalize about conditions on the land. A quarter-session sounds meagre, but the tenure of it often carried with it common rights sufficient to enable its holder to live comfortably enough. Where, as was largely the case in the Alpine and Bohemian Lands, a peasant had commuted his dues for a cash payment, the depreciation of the currency had made this burden a very light one, and travellers in these Lands often remarked on the prosperous and well-fed appearance of the local peasants. In these Lands, too, the arm of the law was reasonably effective in preventing injustice or oppression by the landlord or his agent. Contrary to the universal belief west of the Leitha, the same conditions prevailed in some parts of Hungary, although there there were big variations, which coincided with curious exactitude with the differences in the ethnic composition of the population. The German communities, many of which were of recent origin, and often 'free', were usually prosperous, the Magyar, reasonably so. But the Slovaks and Ruthenes of northern Hungary, with the Vlachs of Transylvania and the Poles and Ruthenes of Galicia, often led the most miserable existences, mercilessly harassed and exploited by conscienceless masters, before whose exactions, which often went far beyond what was allowed by law, they were helpless. They aggravated their own misery by their phenomenal consumption of raw spirit. Below the *sessionati* peasants, all too many dwarf-holders, and more still cottagers and landless men, were living perilously near the starvation line, as shown by the fact that deaths from diseases of under-nourishment were very common; in some areas, almost endemic. And a bad harvest, or some such natural disaster as a big flooding, could often plunge the entire population of the area affected into complete destitution.

In the years with which we are now dealing, the authorities seem not to have regarded the condition of the really destitute classes as presenting any problem. If a harvest failed badly, there might be some distribution of relief, perhaps a remission of taxation. For the industrial unemployed, the remedy was, again, relief, and perhaps the organization of public works. For the rest, the Austrian authorities, like those of most European States of the day, regarded the proletariat chiefly as potential revolutionaries, to be kept under close police surveillance. The one social class which, *qua* class, was almost everywhere giving practical expression to its grievances, was the relatively prosperous one of the *sessionati* peasants. Contemporary writers in almost every Land record mournfully, in almost the same terms, the 'stubborn' attitude of its peasants. Rents arrived late, dues in kind were of inferior quality, bailiffs' orders were sabotaged, and in the performance of their *robot* the peasants had developed the techniques of slow motion and passive resistance to a pitch of virtuosity against which the bailiffs were powerless where their unrestricted use of the whip was gone. Széchenyi's calculation that the day's work of one hired free man was worth three days of *robot* was a fairly common estimate; some writers put the figure substantially higher.

The peasant question, however, was *sui generis*. Outside it there were stirrings, which were political rather than social, among important sections of the middle classes. One of these had a special character: this was the criticism of the 'system' that was being voiced with great openness by influential members of the Viennese middle classes (that the malcontents included some born aristocrats does not affect the essentially 'bourgeois' character of their ideology). This group stood apart because neither its inspiration nor its objectives were connected with the new nationalism. The philosophy of these men was a curious, and often somewhat illogical, blend of Liberalism and Josephinianism. They assumed the continuance of the existing State, but wanted the 'system' replaced by a 'modern' one, free from censorship and petty police control, shorn of feudal trappings, efficient and economical, and above all, placing the control of the public purse in the hands of the tax-payer. These reforms were to be made secure by effective representative constitutional institutions.

Some of them were primarily Liberals, others primarily Josephinians, but so long as the State was neither free nor efficient, the two groups could combine without noticing the differences between them, and together, they constituted a force to which their position at the heart of the Monarchy's economic, social and intellectual life lent an importance out of all proportion to their numbers. They met and aired their views in a number of 'circles', the most important of which were the *Niederösterreichischer Gewerbeverein* (chiefly an association of business men), the 'Concordia' (literary and artistic) and most important of all, the *juridisch-politischer Leseverein* (Reading Club), a large association, whose heterogeneous membership included many of the men who played leading roles in 1848. Frowned on by Metternich, it was patronized, largely for that reason, by Kolowrat, and left quite unmolested by the police.

In the other Lands of the Monarchy constitutional and even social aspirations usually appeared as elements in, or functions of, the national movements that were gathering strength in almost all of them, although not everywhere with equal strength, still less, with equal obtrusiveness. Lombardy still seemed tranquil enough, and the passivity of Venice was a byword among Italian patriots. Galicia was calm on the surface : a qualified observer described the period as 'the quarter-century of conspiracy' and the Polish nobles as 'one vast band of conspirators', but the conspiracies were clandestine, and did not involve preparation for early action. The unsuspicious old Arch-duke regularly reported to Vienna that all was well.

Two main schools of thought were emerging among the Ruthenes. The 'Old Ruthenes' or 'St Georgeites', so called because their leader, Mgr. Jachymowicz, was Vicar-General of the Metropolitan Church of St George in Lemberg, and most of his disciple priests attached to the Church, taught that the Ruthenes were indeed a distinct people, speaking a distinct language. The 'Young Ruthenes', headed by Mgr. Szaszkiewicz, Provost of Přemysl Cathedral, held that the Galician Ruthenes were ethnically and linguistically indistinguish-able from the Ukrainian inhabitants of Czarist Russia. The St Georgeites, having their headquarters in Lemberg, were in closer touch with the *Gubernium* there, but they were a group of intellec-tuals without roots among the people, to whom the language which they tried to popularize – a concoction called 'Jasice' that consisted of local, Russian and Polish borrowings imposed on an Old Slavonic basis – was quite unintelligible to the common man, whereas the Young Ruthenes were encouraging and developing something that really existed. Finally, the famous Russian pan-Slavist, Pogodin, had enlisted the support of the Czarist Government for a campaign to convince the Ruthenes that they were really Great Russians.

A small Slovene national movement was developing under the inspiration of a journalist of the curiously un-Slovene name of Bleiweiss (actually, a corruption of Blavec), but it had not yet made much impact on the Slovene people, or on the authorities.

In Bohemia (the word is operative for the developments were not paralleled in Moravia) things were much livelier. Here two vigorous movements were developing, each national in a sense, but not in the same sense. A new generation of young Czech national enthusiasts calling themselves *Vlastenci* (patriots), and belonging chiefly to the *honoratior* class, represented the future. So far, they were asking only for the equal use, with German, of the Czech language, now a fully developed instrument, in public life and education; but that would obviously only be the first step. At the same time, the pressure of centralizing bureaucratic rule was generating in the Bohemian Estates its reaction, which was not Czech nationalist in the modern sense of the term – few members of the Estates spoke more than a few words of Czech, or wanted to speak more – and certainly not socially progressive, for all of them except a small 'liberal' group headed by Count Albert Deym were extreme social reactionaries, but a political demand that the Lands of the Bohemian Crown should be given the same degree of independence from Vienna as was enjoyed by their Hungarian counterparts. According to them, the *Vernewerte Landesordnung* of 1627 was still the public law of the land, and all innovations since that date, illegal.

In the late 1830s the Estates caught the *Oberstburggraf*, Count Chotek, out in a technical irregularity and opened a campaign that developed into an acrid feud between them and the *Hofkanzlei*, which was acutely embarrassing to the latter. They were, however, unable to enforce any immediate change in the system, nor had they yet found, or even sought, any common ground with the *Vlastenci*.

The biggest turbulence, as in the preceding period, was in the Lands of the Hungarian Crown. Metternich had taken charge of Hungarian affairs in the *Staatskonferenz* (Kolowrat, for once, yielding them to him easily, since he found the Hungarian Chancellor, Reviczky, too temperamental for his taste), and he quickly showed the iron fist. As soon as the Long Diet rose, which was on 2 May 1836, he had Reviczky replaced by Count Fidél Pálffy, a Hungarian citizen but an extreme exponent of aulic policy who did not even speak Magyar, and the other key offices filled with men of like kidney. Several young *jurati* were arrested; then came the turns of Wesselényi and Kossuth, neither of whom was any more protected by parliamentary immunity. Kossuth, who had been carrying on his reportage in a new form, was sentenced to four years' imprisonment for incitement and Wesselényi, to three.

The sentences, particularly that on Wesselényi, whose exploits in saving life during floods which had devastated Pest had made him a popular hero, were highly unpopular. Metternich could not escape having another Diet convoked in 1839, because he needed from it a vote of men and money in view of the dangerous international situation, but the elections for it boded ill for him. They returned a considerably increased number of oppositional members to the Lower Bench, and

among the magnates, some thirty-five aristocrats, led by Count Lajos
Batthyány, constituted themselves a 'Liberal Opposition'. A prolonged deadlock over an issue of free speech followed the opening of
the Diet in June. It was broken eventually by a transaction devised
by Deák, now the acknowledged leader of the Liberals in the Diet.
The political prisoners were released, and Pálffy replaced by the
somewhat less unpopular Count Antal Majláth; in turn the Diet
voted 38,000 men, to be recruited by conscription. Afterwards the
Government gave way on several other points. The laws passed
included one giving a peasant the right to buy in his holding, another
allowing Jews to settle in Royal Free Boroughs (although not in the
Cameral mining towns), a third regulating, on surprisingly advanced
lines, child labour in industry, and a fourth making the Magyar
language the sole official language for addresses to the Crown and
for correspondence to and from the Consilium and the Camera,
and between Hungarian instances (including ecclesiastical) in the
Kingdom. Knowledge of the language was even made a condition of
appointment to a cure of souls even in non-Magyar districts.

These concessions, however, still left the Opposition unsatisfied,
and Metternich soon found particular cause to regret one of them.
When Kossuth emerged from prison, more bellicose than ever for
his experiences, an admirer gave him the editorship of a journal, the
Pesti Hirlap. He turned this opportunity to extraordinary advantage.
Many still looked askance at him. Széchenyi could perhaps hardly
be counted any more as 'oppositional', for on many questions he
stood nearer to the Party of Considered Reform (see p. 76n3) than to
the Liberals; he and Kossuth were now attacking one another in
barbed pamphlets which did little to enhance the reputation of either
man. But Deák distrusted Kossuth's wisdom and disliked his provocative tone, and another group now becoming important, the so-
called 'Centralists',[1] thought some of his enthusiasms, particularly
the nebulous devotion which he lavished on the County system, so
detrimental that in 1844 they bought the *Hirlap* and terminated his
editorship of it. But the wider public was more susceptible to the
emotional appeal that Kossuth exercised superbly in periods to which
his incarceration lent an oracular authority, and his three years of
editorial activity can fairly be said to have established beyond eradi-
cation in the popular mind his identification of reform in any
direction with opposition to Vienna, and the consequent priority of
the political issue.

During these years, then, the Hungarian Opposition gained ground
with headlong rapidity; but so did the opposition to the Opposition.
For a time Vienna, on Kolowrat's instigation, had continued to load
Gaj with conspicuous marks of favour, but in 1840 his 'Illyrianism'

elicited protests from the Porte, whose favour was important to Metternich at that juncture. Further, as the Hungarian Serbs grew more nationally conscious, they became, not more Austrophile, but more Russophile; the pull was operating the wrong way. Gaj himself visited Russia and took money from Russian agents. In 1842 the *Staatskonferenz* forbade the use of the word 'Illyrian'. But the Rescript conveying the prohibition contained assurances of sympathy towards the Croat people, and a promise that their 'public rights' would be defended. It was therefore no discouragement to the Croat nationalists, whom in 1841 Count Drašković had organized in a political party, first styling itself 'Illyrian', with a programme, drawn up for it by Drašković, which called for the creation of a Great Croatia, to include, besides Croatia itself, the Slavonian Counties, Dalmatia, Fiume, and ultimately, Bosnia and the Slovene Lands of Austria, united in a sub-State directly under Vienna. The opposition to the 'Illyrians', as everyone continued to call them — although in 1842 they changed their official title, in obedience to Vienna's ruling, to 'National' — was carried on by a congerie of elements generally known by the equally inappropriate name of 'Magyarones',[2] who although easily outnumbered among the medium Croat nobles, were able for some years to hold their own fairly well, since besides the half-Magyarized magnates who with their followers constituted their main strength, they traditionally enjoyed the support of Croatia's two communities of 'sandalled nobles'.

Meanwhile, the rejection of Gaj's brand of Illyrianism by the Serbs of Hungary, who in 1842 had acquired a new and very bellicose Metropolitan, by name Joseph Rajačić, by no means meant that they were turning towards Hungary. After the accession of Alexander Karageorgević to the throne of Serbia in 1842, the Principality's new Minister of the Interior, Garašanin, even began making cautious propaganda among them in favour of a rival brand of Illyrianism, to be dominated by Belgrade.

These years saw also the first serious clash between the Magyars and the non-Magyar 'nationalities' of the Kingdom (Hungarian usage always designated the non-Magyars by this term). The emotion inspiring the early Magyar linguistic and literary pioneers had been simply the laudable one of pride in their own people and its past, and if this had lent strength to the demands made by successive Diets after 1792 for wider use of the Magyar language in public affairs, it should be remembered that those demands were addressed exclusively to Vienna, and at first aimed only at changing the system under which the nation's public business was transacted in a language not its own. It should also be remembered that at that time political life in Hungary was the preserve of its nobles, the vast majority of whom, except some of the denationalized magnates, were linguistically Magyars. The inconvenience to which the few excep- tions would have been subjected by the substitution of Magyar for Latin − one foreign language for another − would have been minis- cule compared with the greater convenience brought to the majority, and no one seems to have suggested the contrary. Neither had those wishing to enter public life raised any objection to the demand that adequate place should be given to the language in secondary and higher education, and the Magyars on their side did not object when Slovaks and Serbs who did not aspire to these careers founded their own schools. As for the peasants, no one troubled about them; poli- tical nulls as they were, it did not matter what language they spoke.

But the demand that the Magyar language should be given its due place in public life led on imperceptibly to ever wider definitions of the words 'due' and 'public' and hence to the feeling (and this was encouraged by the romantic poets of the literary revival, who loved to dwell on the achievements of the first conquering Magyars) that the Magyar language and culture were the only ones befitting a patriotic Hungarian. And by this time national feeling was awakening also among the 'nationalities'. It was far from universal. There were plenty of them who were positively eager to turn themselves into Magyars; plenty more who would have been quite willing to accept a structurally Magyar State, but also many who felt that they had the same natural right as the Magyars themselves to use their own national language, cultivate their national attributes and take pride in their national pasts.

But the logical sequel to the assertion of equal natural rights would have been the assertion of equal political rights: that is, the demand that Hungary should not be a Magyar national State, but a multi- national one, in practice as well as principle. Magyar opinion, even its moderate elements, refused to admit this conclusion, both as con- trary to its own immemorial tradition, and as potentially dangerous to the integrity of the Hungarian State. Vienna's open patronage of the Croats and Serbs lent real colour to this fear, and suspicious noses sniffed treason also in the 'pan-Slav' utterances of some Slovak leaders.

There were many moderates, Széchenyi among them, who main- tained that tolerance and understanding would still reconcile the Nationalities to life even in a State the top-level structure of which was Magyar. But the hotheads, whose numbers included Kossuth, opened a campaign in 1842 to the effect that the only true salvation lay in eliminating completely all non-Magyar feeling in the entire population (it was a tragic outcome of the very broadening and de- mocratization of the reformers' political outlook that it now seemed necessary to extend Magyarization also to the peasants). The Magyar chauvinists pressed this demand with injurious outcries against those unwilling to accept it which at once justified and stimulated the very feelings which they hoped to repress, and the vicious circle came into being which was destined later to encompass the ruin of Hungary.

The first open clash came when in 1840 a certain Count Károlyi Zay was elected Superintendent of the Hungarian Lutheran Church, to which many Slovaks belonged. Zay celebrated his election by announcing that it was 'the sacred duty' of 'everyone who fights for freedom and common sense, every loyal subject of the House of Austria' to Magyarize. A deputation of Slovak pastors went to Vienna and secured the cancellation of the unwisest of Zay's proposals, among which had been that they should fuse their own Confession with the Calvinist, and one outcome of Zay's campaign was, typically, the opposite of that wished by him, for the Slovaks then agreed between themselves what should be the 'authorized version' of their national language, and began issuing in it a newspaper for the voicing of their national aspirations.

In the elections for the 1843 Diet the reformers committed the tactical error of making the chief plank in their programme the extension of taxation for the *cassa domestica* to noble land. The Government mobilized the 'sandalled nobles', to whom the reform would have dealt a crippling blow, and thanks to their tumultuous interventions the elections brought the reformers only small gains. The scales in the Diet being very equally balanced, neither side gained much advantage, but the Opposition secured the defeat of a Government proposal to abolish the internal customs line between Hungary and Austria. This measure was desired by the big agrarian interests, even though it would have entailed the taxation of noble land and the introduction of the Austrian indirect taxation, including the excise on tobacco. But the economic unification would clearly also have strengthened the political unity of the Monarchy, and the nationalists opposed it for that reason. Instead, an association was founded, under Kossuth's auspices, for the protection and encouragement of Hungarian industry.

The session also witnessed the worst clash to date with the Croats. A Croat deputy addressed the House in his own language. The Magyars lost their tempers, and adopted a motion to make Magyar not only the sole language of administration and all education in the Kingdom, but also that of the legislature and of all communications with the central authorities, and between Hungarian and Croat instances. Unlike any previous linguistic legislation this directly affected the Croats, and although it was not altogether unreasonable to ask of the handful of Croat deputies that they should address the four hundred or so Magyar deputies in the latter's own language, the Croats cried to high heaven. Metternich mediated a compromise on the parliamentary question, and the Crown agreed that all secondary and higher instruction in the Kingdom of Hungary should be in Magyar, while elementary instruction was to be made the subject of a later enactment.

Outside their victory on the tariff question, the Opposition had not gained much ground, but the proceedings had been so turbulent as to leave Metternich convinced that Hungary was 'only a step away from the Hell of revolution'. He did not dare suspend the constitution, but he agreed a programme with Count György Apponyi, the young and energetic newly-chosen leader of a group of magnates styling themselves the 'Progressive Conservatives'.[3] The Diet was to be made into an orderly and effective body by reform of its procedure, and the Föispáns were to see to it by every means that their Counties, in which they were to reside, sent right-minded deputies to it. 'Administrators' were to be sent into Counties where the Föispáns refused to undertake this task, or proved unequal to it. The customs union with Austria was to be carried through, and there was to be a big programme of public works, especially on communications, to be carried through with Austrian help, both governmental and private.

As soon as the Diet rose, which was in November 1844, Apponyi was appointed Vice-Chancellor, under Majláth, whom he succeeded soon after as Chancellor. Other appointments included that of Széchenyi, for whom a Department of Communications was created in the Consilium. Administrators were put into eighteen Counties (the other Föispáns toed the line). At first the prospects looked bright, for the economic programme made a wide appeal, especially since Kossuth's 'Buy Hungarian' appeal had been a rather ignominious failure. But its authoritarian side, with the prospect of closer association with, and presumably dependence on, Vienna, was widely resented, so that the outlook was not yet set fair.

In Croatia the Illyrian Party had, by a rather dubious manœuvre, compassed the disfranchisement of the sandalled nobles and was now in command of the Sabor, with a programme which for practical purposes was simply one of hostility to Hungary. The Serbs were demanding another national congress. In Transylvania Magyar nationalist feeling was mounting apace, and expressing itself in two demands: one, which had almost completely ousted the old particularist feeling, for union with Hungary, the other, for further Magyarization of the Grand Principality itself by linguistic legislation similar to that in Hungary. The Crown, which in 1844 had appointed as Chancellor Baron Samuel Jósika, a member of Apponyi's group and a man of aulic sympathies and a strong hand, refused such demands, but as in the Kingdom, they evoked strong reactions among the non-Magyars. The Saxons rallied under a new leader to resist the 'Union', the idea of which was opposed as strongly by the Roumanians, among whom a more vigorous national feeling, encouraged by their kinsfolk in the Danubian Principalities (now virtually independent of the Porte) was spreading through the younger generation.

Austria's foreign relations showed a similar picture of surface calm half-masking real decline. By now France had joined Britain right out of earshot of the Concert. Frederick William III of Prussia loyally acknowledged Austria's leading position in Germany up to his death in 1840, as did his successor, Frederick William IV, after him. Nearly all the Italian Princes, Charles Albert of Savoy not excepted, gratefully accepted the Austrian support to which, as they knew well, they owed their thrones. But the continued extension and consolidation of the *Zollverein* was inexorably levering Prussia into the *de facto* hegemony in Germany, while in 1841 the *Staatskonferenz*, owing partly to objections from the Bohemian industrialists, partly to difficulties over the position of Hungary, missed an opportunity of placing Austria at the head of a rival grouping. In both Germany and Italy the currents of nationalism and liberalism were steadily eating away the undersurface of the ice on which Austria's position rested. No similar threats came from Russia, but Austria's relationship even with Russia was clouded in the 1840s by the failure of negotiations for a dynastic marriage, and the Czar himself returned from a visit to Vienna with highly unfavourable impressions, most candidly expressed, of the stability of the Monarchy and the competence of its rulers. For that matter, the growing feeling among the Liberals in the Monarchy that Austria had sunk into the position of the Czar's European outpost and police agent was a considerable factor in their dislike of Metternich's 'system'.

The history of Austria's finances was, simply, the old one. The ministers who, under Kolowrat, struggled with the problem (Peter Eichhoff from 1835 to 1840 and Kübeck after him), were unable or unwilling to increase revenue from taxation perceptibly. They cut expenditure where they could, but every budgetary year still ended with a deficit, small up to 1841, but considerable after that year, when the State took over the financing of the railway construction. As before, their only nostrum was to borrow, and they devoted most of their efforts to keeping the national credit so good that the loans could be floated on reasonable terms. They were not so usurious as those of twenty years earlier, but a steadily increasing proportion of the State revenue nevertheless went on the interest and amortization of them. It was calculated that in the 1840s the State debt had more than trebled in twenty-five years and the service on it multiplied tenfold, not counting lottery loans, and in 1847 the interest was forty-five million gulden plus six million for amortization, almost as much as the total yield of direct taxation and little less than the cost of the defence services. The latter was kept down to fifty million gulden a year, but to achieve this, the nominal peace strength of the army at the beginning of 1847 was only a little over 400,000 (war strength, 630,000) and the number of men actually with the colours only about 275,000. The equipment had been little modernized since 1815.

The morale of the forces was little better than their equipment. The term of service was reduced again in 1845, to eight years, but most of the conscripts were still men whom local authorities found undesirable and gladly handed over to the recruiting sergeant when he came round.

Seven

BEFORE THE STORM

The two years 1846 and 1847, usually counted as the last of the *Vormärz*, in fact possess their own distinctive character. Between them and their predecessors there is a marked psychological difference. The complacent confidence of the masters and beneficiaries of the 'system' in its rightness and its durability, the no more than half-reluctant acceptance of it by its critics and victims – both are gone. In their place comes an expectation of imminent change which is regarded with hopeful anticipation by some, with anxious foreboding by others, but of which all are conscious.

The transformation was wrought largely by a single event, the origins of which lay outside the Monarchy. Since 1840 the Polish 'National Committee' in Paris had included peasant emancipation in its programme. Agents toured the Polish countryside, spreading the news among the peasants, and sent back such sanguine reports of its effect on them that the Committee decided to initiate a revolt, in which the peasants were to join in return for liberty and land. The revolt was to embrace the territories of all three Partitioning Powers, to begin in Poznań, Cracow and West Galicia. Zero day was fixed for 21 February 1846. '

The secret of course, leaked out. Russia and Prussia took due precautions, but in Galicia the old Archduke refused to take the reports seriously. Then, on 17 February, the *Kreishauptmann* (District Governor) of Tarnow, Freiherr von Breinl, received a message from Cracow that the revolt was about to break out there (the day having been advanced) and in Tarnow. A stream of peasants came to Breinl's office, all saying that they had been told to assemble that night, armed with scythes and flails, march on Tarnow, and 'massacre the Germans'. The accounts of what ensued do not agree. Breinl swore afterwards that he had told the peasants that they must obey only their lawful masters, namely, the Austrian authorities; the Polish version is that he told them to attack their lords, and even set a price on rebels' heads. Whatever the truth, a Jacquerie to which 1,458 Polish nobles fell victim took place round Tarnow and elsewhere in West Galicia. Order was soon restored there; in Cracow, where the insurgents formed a 'government' which drove out the weak Austrian garrison, it took a few days longer before Russian and

Prussian troops entered the city, but then the Poles themselves called the enterprise off.

One result of this ill-starred adventure was that on 6 November Austria, having secured the consent of Russia and Prussia, annexed the Free City. The annexation brought her little joy, for her partners' consent had been given only reluctantly, while Palmerston denounced it as a breach of the Acts of the Congress of Vienna. Austria's international credit, already weakened by the alleged massacres, the Polish version of which was generally believed, sank further still. She had also saddled herself with a new, numerically small but intelligent and highly intransigent contingent of Polish subjects.

The *Staatskonferenz* recalled the Archduke, and sent out in his stead a commissioner, Count Rudolph Stadion, to restore order, but it was in a quandary how to deal with the peasants, who believed, rightly or wrongly, that they had been promised reward for their loyalty, and clamoured to receive it. The *Konferenz* felt that they had to be appeased, but did not want to appear to be condoning massacre. A few half-hearted concessions failed to placate the peasants, particularly when disastrous floods on the Vistula ruined the homes and fields of great numbers of them. Count Francis Stadion, who had meanwhile replaced his brother, advised further concessions, combined with the formation of a paramilitary defence force and other security measures, but weeks of waiting saw neither reforms nor defence measures put into force and both the peasants and the nobles of Galicia seething with discontent, with no one able to suggest how to placate the one without alienating the other irretrievably.

Meanwhile the peasant unrest had spread to other Lands, in several of which the peasants were refusing *robot* and threatening worse things yet. Several *Gubernia* pressed the *Staatskonferenz* for prophylactic measures, but that body could nerve itself only to another Patent, which had little effect beyond convincing the peasants that the Government would not help them, whereas if they insisted, they would be able to enforce their own liberation without paying for it at all. It is safe to say that the larger revolution of March 1848 only forestalled a separate peasant rising (unless the Government yielded the whole way) in much of the Monarchy.

This crisis also coincided with a major social crisis in other fields. Already in 1846 there had been harvest failures and disastrous floodings in many Lands. There was starvation in the afflicted areas and prices of foodstuffs soared elsewhere. In 1847 the harvests were worse still, shortages and actual starvation still more rampant and, on top of this, many industries were hit by a crisis of overproduction resulting in mass unemployment, which in its turn produced rioting and machine-wrecking. The worst troubles were in the cotton-mills of

Bohemia, whence starving multitudes streamed into Vienna.

The general awareness of imminent social danger lent to all the familiar national and constitutional movements a new element of hectic urgency. The Estates of Lower Austria sent the *Staatskon-ferenz* a memorandum insisting on their right to approach the Crown with petitions, representations and complaints. Those of Bohemia engaged in another acrimonious dispute with the *Hofkanzlei* when it demanded an increased land tax, while the popular movement there was given an extraordinary stimulus through the genius of a brilliant young journalist, Karel Havliček, who, appointed editor of the largest Czech paper, the *Pražke Noviný*, filled its columns with what purported to be descriptions of Ireland under English rule, but were recognizable attacks on Viennese rule in Bohemia. The Czech radicals grouped themselves in a 'Repeal' movement, strongly Left-wing in social respects, and this was now supported by Deym's Liberal group in the Diet. In Transylvania the conflict grew more acute still between the Magyars on one side, and on the other, the Saxons and Roumanians, who had found a vigorous defender in their new Vicar-General (later Bishop) Mgr. Şaguna.

In the Kingdom of Hungary, Apponyi was already running into difficulties, for Kübeck had largely discredited his economic policy by confining the promised financial help for it to a derisory trickle, and the Viennese financiers refused to open their money-bags without Government backing. Apponyi himself felt that his programme needed to be made more popular, and when on top of this the intimidating news from Galicia arrived, increasing unrest in Hungary, he organized his followers in a 'Government Party' (the first formal 'Party' in Hungarian history), and persuaded them to accept a revised programme which conceded several of the Opposition's demands, including taxation of noble land, abolition of the *aviticitas*, and further measures in favour of the peasants. The other side, combining in its turn in a 'United Opposition' (although its unity was distinctly nominal) replied with an 'Oppositional Declaration' put together by Deák, which constituted a sort of highest common factor of the special wishes of all its constituent groups. It declared that its authors accepted Law x of 1790, but demanded the cessation of all features of the system as then practised, including the Administrator system, which violated that law, and also called for universal equality before the law, complete and compulsory redemption, against compensation for the landlords, of all peasant servitudes, a genuine national ministry exercising control over the budget, and many other reforms. The tariff issue was to be settled through negotiation with the Austrian Estates.

The elections for the Diet, held in the autumn of 1847, found the parties represented on the Lower Table almost exactly equal in numbers, and when the non-controversial business of electing a new Palatine had been got through (old Joseph had died; the Diet elected his son, Stephen, to succeed him) battle was immediately joined. Many of the Government's 'propositions', now in the form of draft Bills, went so far in meeting the Opposition as to endanger its unity seriously. Kossuth, now sitting in his own right (as deputy for Pest County) tried to reunite it by proposing a 'gravaminal representation' to the Crown against the appointment of Administrators. This was a key issue. The Government went so far as to promise that the system should be regarded as an emergency measure only, and the Lower Table accepted this, but only after much debate, and by a single vote, so that the Government could not regard its position as safe.

More dangerous still was the position in Lombardy-Venetia, where, after the long doldrums, demonstrations against Austrian rule suddenly became fashionable. These were openly encouraged from Turin, and Austrian influence seemed to be shaken throughout the peninsula. Radetzky, commanding the Austrian garrison, had at his disposal only 60,000 men, one third of them Italians, and Vienna sent down only driblets in reply to his appeals for reinforcements. At his urgent request, the Crown, in November 1847, sent him authorization to proclaim martial law, if he found it absolutely necessary, but he was not to use the power except in extraordinary emergency.

Meanwhile, owing to expenditure on the railways, on public relief, and on emergency precautions in Galicia, the budgetary deficit was larger than ever. Fears, and among the Left, hopes, that another 'State bankruptcy' was round the corner, became widespread.

Eight

THE YEAR OF REVOLUTION
1848

In the opening weeks of 1848 revolution had already broken out in Sicily, and Piedmont seemed on the brink of attacking Lombardy, but it was only the abdication of Louis Philippe of France that triggered off revolution in the Monarchy. The news reached Vienna on 29 February, and produced the immediate, although prosaic, effect that the population, expecting Metternich to react by organizing a campaign against revolutionary France, besieged the banks and savings-banks to change their paper-money into silver, forcing some institutions to close their doors. It may be remarked here that Metternich in fact spent the ensuing days in precisely the activities which the popular genius attributed to him, but in vain. Palmerston rejected his proposals flatly; the Czar, while approving the operation in principle, thought Austria too weak to take charge of it; Prussia was willing to support Austria in immediate action, but her emissary, Radowitz, demanded as price a reformation of the constitution of the *Bund* which would have transferred the leadership of it to Prussia. The conversations were going on when the plans were swept away by other developments in the *Bund*, and in the Monarchy.

There one man had perceived how to draw political advantage out of financial panic. That man was Kossuth. Addressing the Lower Table on 3 March, and putting his finger unerringly on the weak spot, he denounced in ringing terms 'the pestilential air that breathes on us from the charnel-house of Vienna', from which Hungary could not be safeguarded until she controlled her own finances. He proposed that the Diet submit to the Crown an Address, a draft of which he laid before it. This, broadly, called for fulfilment of the Opposition's social programme, and insisted that the execution of it must be entrusted to a responsible Hungarian Government, 'independent of any foreign intervention'.

In the excited atmosphere no one dared oppose him, and the Lower Table adopted his draft Address unamended. But an Address had to come from both Tables. Apponyi was in Vienna, where he was urging the *Staats- und Konferenzrat* to dissolve the Diet and allow him to 'make' a new one. But Metternich had wanted the Palatine consulted, and he, when he arrived, had said that the other chief dignitaries of the realm must also be consulted. They, too, were called

to Vienna, and their absence from Pozsony was used as an excuse
not to convoke the magnates. Accordingly, an odd pause followed.
Kossuth wanted the Lower Table to send in the Address without
waiting for the magnates, but the Table hesitated. It spent its time
drafting Bills in the sense of the proposed Address, beginning with
one on peasant liberation, while Kossuth strengthened his hand by
arranging for pressure to be put on the Diet by a group of radicals in
Pest, known as the 'Young Hungary', whose *spiritus rector* was the
poet, Sándor Petöfi. They duly produced a 'Twelve Point Programme'
entitled 'What does the Hungarian People want?' which repeated
some of the points in the Address, and added some new ones to them.

Meanwhile, reports of Kossuth's speech had reached Vienna,
where, combined with further news from Paris and Germany (where
by this time half the States were demanding constitutions and demon-
strating for German unity) they put heart into the Liberals and
constitutionalists, who were further encouraged by rumours that the
Archduchess Sophie was on their side. These were in reality totally
unfounded, but the Archduke John was in Vienna, and was urging
his brother to make concessions. In the first days of March several
bodies petitioned the Court for redress of various grievances, while
the *Leseverein* drew up a long memorandum (the work of Bach),
which it forwarded to the Lower Austrian Estates, who were due to
meet on the 13th.

On the 12th the students of Vienna drew up their own petition, for
freedom of the Press, instruction and religion, and general popular
representation. Two professors delivered it in their name to the
Archduke Ludwig, whose reply to it, as to all other representations,
appeared entirely negative. On that day the *Konferenz* had itself
worked out a plan to invite the Estates 'of all Lands whose Estates
rested on old, hitherto unmodified, constitutional Charters' to meet
and consult with a Committee appointed by the Crown on 'possible
measures appropriate to the requirements of the moment', but the
news of this proposal had not reached the public, which would
certainly have dismissed it as totally inadequate.

On the 13th the streets of the Innere Stadt early filled with crowds
which, the day being a Monday (which most workmen habitually
took off), included a number of rough elements from the factory
suburbs, clearly bent on mischief. When the members of the Estates
reached their assembly hall in the Herrengasse, they found the streets
round it thronged. Next arrived a body of students, marching in
formation from the Aula. They forced their way into the courtyard
of the Landhaus, where a young doctor named Adolph Fischhof
addressed them in support of the students' demands. Another student
arrived waving printed copies of a translation of Kossuth's speech in

Pozsony. This was read aloud amid tumultuous cheers. Feeble attempts by members of the Estates to suggest half-remedies were brushed aside, and eventually a deputation of their numbers willy-nilly carried to the Hofburg the demands of the crowd for a constitution and the dismissal of Metternich.

This deputation again looked like proving fruitless, for the Archduke Ludwig said that he could make no concessions impairing the Emperor's sovereignty without his consent, and Metternich, brought over under escort from the Ballhausplatz, saw no need for anything more than the proposed Conference of Estates. But while the arguments went on, the situation in the streets was getting out of hand. Trouble had not been expected, and few precautions had been taken. Most of the few troops in Vienna had been kept in their barracks outside the glacis. Now they were brought in, and after attempts had been made to disperse the crowds, a detachment opened fire, killing four demonstrators. The shots, instead of restoring order, precipitated the reverse, and ugly affrays, in which more people perished, took place both in the Innere Stadt and in the factory suburbs.

The emergence of the submerged tenth introduced a new element into the situation. The bourgeoisie were as hostile to the proletariat as the Court itself. The burgomaster of Vienna, Czapka, appeared asking that the 'Civic Guard', a small and largely decorative force of which he was the titular commander, should be expanded into a full-scale National Guard, adequately armed. He would keep order with this, but the troops must be withdrawn. This was an awkward request, for it showed that fear of the workers was not going to frighten the bourgeoisie into unconditional submission to the Court. Still less reassuring was a clamour which now arose from the students that they too should be armed and allowed to form an 'Academic Legion'.

Up to the late afternoon, the 'party of resistance' at the Court was still in the ascendant. It was felt by all that the Archduke Albrecht, who had been in command of the garrison, must, in the interest of the dynasty's popularity, be taken out of action, but F.M.L. Windisch-Graetz, the military commander in Bohemia, a man generally regarded as the embodiment of ruthless reaction, happened to be in Vienna on private business. Asked whether he could guarantee to 'restore order' if given plenipotentiary powers, civil and military, to do so, he accepted. But while he was making his leisurely personal preparations, further representations came in, including an ultimatum from the Civic Guard promising to restore order provided that the troops were withdrawn, the students armed, and Metternich dismissed, by 9 p.m.

The Archduke yielded step by step. The arming of the students was promised, then the withdrawal of the troops; the change-over began immediately. Finally, Metternich was induced to resign (he left Vienna the following day to start an a laborious journey to England). Sedlnitzky, too, was dismissed, and Apponyi resigned his office.

Enormous jubilation greeted the news of Metternich's fall. Streets were illuminated and crowds assembled in front of the Hofburg to cheer the Emperor. But the Archduke was still determined to keep his concessions to the minimum. Next day proclamations appeared authorizing the formation of a National Guard and abolishing the censorship. But no other concessions were announced, and rumour ran round that Windisch-Graetz, who so far had made no use of his plenipotentiary powers, was planning some bloody action. He was in fact preparing to proclaim a state of siege, but the Court was weakening. Late that night Archduke Franz Karl called a Conference of State, and persuaded its members that it would be wiser 'to volunteer a constitution and then stand fast against further political demands'. The sequel was the publication the next morning of an announcement that the Estates of the 'German-Austrian and Slavonic Realms' were to be called together to advise the Crown on 'legislative and administrative questions' (the word 'constitution' was not mentioned). This, again, was shrugged off as a gesture, and the disorder grew. At last, at 5 p.m., another proclamation appeared adding to the words of its predecessor that the burghers were to receive increased representation at the proposed Conference, the purpose of which was to advise on 'the constitution which We have resolved to grant'. This time it was enough. The demonstrators dispersed, with loyal cheers for Ferdinand. The First Viennese Revolution was over.

The *Staatskonferenz* spent the 16th and 17th largely on the negotiations with Hungary described below; but the West, too, had to be provided with some sort of administration to carry on until the proposed 'constitution' was ready. It was decided that this must take the form of a 'responsible ministry' and this was hurriedly scraped together. Kolowrat accepted, reluctantly, the post of Minister President; Count Ludwig Ficquelmont, President of the *Hofkriegsrat*, was given Metternich's old portfolio; Pillersdorf, from the *Vereinigte Hofkanzlei*, the Interior; Count Ludwig Taaffe, from the *Oberste Justizstelle*, Justice, Philipp, Frh. von Krausz, from the *Gubernium* of Galicia, Finance (Kübeck having refused the appointment), Franz, Frh. von Sommaruga, Education, F.M.L. Peter Zanini, War. Several of these appointments proved, indeed, short-lived. Kolowrat, Taaffe and Zanini all resigned after a couple of weeks, their portfolios being taken over again 'provisionally', by Ficquelmont,

Sommaruga and Count Baillet de Latour respectively. On 4 April, meanwhile, the *Staatskonferenz* and the *Staats- und Konferenzrat* were abolished, the Archduke Ludwig now retiring finally into private life. The Archduke Franz Karl was made a sort of unofficial substitute for Ferdinand; minutes of the ministerial conference were to be submitted to him and their decisions reconsidered if he objected to them.

On 3 April Windisch-Graetz's special commission was terminated and he returned to Bohemia.

It was indeed very much of a provisional arrangement: a certain concession to the revolution, but no product of it. The 'new' men were all old servants of the Crown, continuing their service under a new name: old wine, even old bottles, only new labels. Few of them were even at all liberal in their personal politics. Pillersdorf, Krausz and Sommaruga came fairly near to that description, as did Zanini during his brief tenure of office, but Ficquelmont, a career officer with some diplomatic experience, was generally reputed to be a friend and admirer of Metternich's, while Latour was heart and soul a man of the old regime. The same words apply to the staffs of the old Chancelleries and *Hofstellen*, now become ministries, not to speak of the corps of officers. The transference of power to the people's representatives had yet to come.

The members of the ministry were, as poor Pillersdorf ruefully remarks, entirely inexperienced in any form of government except the bureaucratic, and none of them had previously exchanged political ideas with any other. And they were immediately beset from every quarter with the most acute problems, with each of which they had to deal simultaneously, and each largely in conjunction with every other. Unfortunately for the historian, the limitations of his tools compel him to describe them one by one. It will be simplest to begin with those which soonest deviated into their own orbits.

When the news of Metternich's fall reached Lombardy and Venetia tumult broke out in all the main cities there. It was most clamorous in Milan, where there was street fighting, and in the next few days the little garrison lost nearly one third of its numbers in casualties and desertions. On the night of the 22/23rd Radetzky withdrew the survivors. The Milanese formed a provisional government. Venice had capitulated on the 21st without a shot fired. The insurgents proclaimed a republic with Daniel Manin President. About one third of the land forces and three quarters of the naval declared for Italy. The smaller cities rose in succession.

On the 23rd Charles Albert of Savoy crossed the frontier, announcing his sympathy with 'the heroic struggle of the people of Lombardy and Venetia'. Meanwhile Papal troops were assembling at Bologna,

the Duke of Modena had fled, Leopold of Tuscany had declared for
Italy, and even Ferdinand of Naples was bullied into sending an
expeditionary force northward. All Radetzky could do was to con-
centrate the remains of his army, reduced by the desertion of most
of its Italian units to about 50,000, in the Quadrilateral, whence he
appealed urgently to Vienna for reinforcements. Unless and until
these arrived, he could not hope to take the offensive.

When, in the early hours of the 14th, the news of Metternich's and
Apponyi's fall reached Pozsony, the Palatine renounced further
resistance and convoked the magnates for that afternoon. They, too,
accepted the inevitable. The Address was revised and enlarged,
mainly by taking in many of the 'Young Hungary's' demands, and it
was resolved that a deputation, headed by the Palatine, should lay it
before the Court. The deputation, a large and tumultuous one,
arrived in Vienna on the afternoon of the 15th, its appearance
enhancing the intoxication of joy into which their own successes
were plunging the Viennese. The Address was debated the next day
by a small *ad hoc* Committee consisting of the Archdukes Ludwig
and Franz Karl, Windisch-Graetz, the Transylvanian Chancellor,
Jósika, and a few others. Most of them were for rejecting it outright,
but the Palatine threatened to resign if no concessions were made,
and the Committee, fearing that Hungary might rebel or secede, composed a Rescript in which Ferdinand declared himself willing to
appoint 'a responsible ministry independent in the sense of the
national laws' for the conduct of Hungary's internal affairs. The
Palatine, who was given plenipotentiary powers to represent the King
in executive matters and 'in the sense of the laws', was to propose suitable persons for ministers, to see to it that the laws defining the competences of the ministries took proper account of the links established
by the Pragmatic Sanction, and to submit the proposed laws, with
the rest of the Diet's work, to the Crown for its approval.

The Rescript was handed next day to the Palatine, who appointed
Batthyány 'provisional' Minister President. The deputation then returned to Pozsony, where it arrived to find the situation even more
disorderly than they had left it two days before. Pest was in uproar, and wild rumours were coursing that Petőfi was marching on
Pozsony at the head of an army of peasants armed with scythes and
flails, such as had done such dreadful execution in Galicia. Heartened or intimidated, as the case might be, by the news, the Diet
declared itself a Constituent in permanent session, and in the next
days rushed through a long list of draft laws of nature to transform
the political and social face of the country.

The *nexus subditelae* was abolished, and with it the Manorial
Courts. All citizens were free, and all equal before the law, The

urbarial peasants received their holdings in freehold, and gratis : the compensation to be paid to the landlords was left 'to the honour of the nation'. The nobles' exemption from taxation disappeared, as did the *aviticitas*. The Lower Table was to be transformed into a representative body elected on a franchise to be enacted by the next Diet ; a provisional franchise on which that body was itself to be elected, formed one of the laws. There was to be freedom of instruction. The pre-publication censorship was abolished and the Press declared 'free', although severe penalties attached to many offences, including, besides offences against public decency and libels on individuals, attacks on the dynasty and the integrity and institutions of the State and the conduct of its servants (very wide political use was made afterwards of these provisions). All 'received' Confessions were to enjoy complete freedom and reciprocity. A National Guard was to be set up. The *Partium*[1] were incorporated unconditionally : Transylvania, if its Diet voted to that effect.

The key constitutional law (Law III) laid down that the King, or in his absence, the Palatine, exercised his executive powers exclusively through a 'responsible ministry' under a Minister President appointed by him (on whose proposal the other ministers were appointed) which was to be competent 'for all questions which hitherto fell, or ought to have fallen, within the competence of the Hungarian Court Chancellery, the *Consilium*, the Camera (including the mines), and in general, all civil, Church, fiscal, military, and in general, all questions of defence'. No enactment was valid unless countersigned by a minister with seat (except the minister *a latere*) in Buda-Pest. The departmental ministers were a minister *a latere* to the Crown, with the function of representing Hungary 'through interventions' and 'with responsibility' to Hungary 'in all questions of common interest to the Fatherland and the Hereditary Lands', and Ministers of the Interior, National Finance, Public Works and Communications, Agriculture, Commerce and Industry, Cults and Education, Justice and Defence.

The draft laws, which admittedly left gaps to be filled in by the next Diet, were ready by the 22nd, by which date Batthyány had composed his Cabinet list, a Ministry of all the talents whose members included Prince Pál Esterházy (*a latere*), B. Szemere (Interior), Kossuth (Finance), Széchenyi (Communications), Deák (Justice) and Eötvös (Education). The Minister Designate for Defence, Col. Mészáros, was serving in Italy ; in his absence, Batthyány acted for him.

On the 23rd the Palatine took the proposals to Vienna, where they were very ill received. The Court would have liked best to reject them altogether and subject the contumelious country to military occu-

pation, but since there were no troops available, they were driven to
fight a diplomatic action which proved a slow retreat. Under strong
pressure they ended by accepting unaltered the Laws dealing with
pure Hungarian *interna*. But they fought tenaciously against allowing
Hungary any voice in the Monarchy's foreign policy – if that was
what the terms of reference of the minister *a latere* meant (the point
was never quite decided) – defence, or disposal of the cameral
resources, arguing that the appointment of these three ministers,
with the Law as it stood, would reduce the link between Hungary and
the rest of the Monarchy to that of a Personal Union. The wrangling
went on, with both sides growing more impatient, until, on 31 March,
Franz Karl took over the negotiations from his uncle. The Court
then virtually threw in its hand. A new Rescript accepted Law III *in
toto*, with the addition that 'the employment of the Hungarian forces
outside the frontiers, and the appointment to military offices' while
remaining royal prerogatives, were made subject to the counter-
signature of the minister *a latere*. It was agreed that Hungary, now
being in control of her own cameral resources, should make adequate
provision out of them for the upkeep of the Court and other
expenditure previously met from this source.

A provisional formula was found for one hotly-disputed issue, the
status of the Military Frontier. The Court conceded that the area in
question belonged to Hungary, but the Hungarians gave a formal
assurance that they 'would exercise their lawful authority in it in such
fashion that its military organization remained intact, pending a
future legal settlement'. No agreement, however, could be found on
another point: at the last moment, the Court asked for an assurance
that Hungary would take over a quarter of the national debt, paying
an annual contribution towards it. The Hungarian ministers agreed
to submit the request to the next Diet, but all of them, including
Széchenyi and Deák, were agreed that it was unacceptable.

When such agreement as could be achieved had been reached,
Ferdinand, accompanied by Franz Karl and Francis Joseph, jour-
neyed to Pozsony, and on 11 April formally sanctioned the corpus
of legislation, thereafter known as the 'April Laws', passed by the
Diet of 1847/8, which he then declared closed.

In Vienna, the unrest subsided very quickly after 15 March. The
bourgeoisie wanted no more than they had received, or been
promised: no expensive foreign adventures, fewer soldiers at home,
control over the public purse, freedom to grumble, protection against
the workers. The last-named had been driven back into their rook-
eries, and many arrests made, but the Government abolished, or
reduced, several taxes which bore particularly heavily on the poorer
classes, the employers themselves reduced hours of work, employ-

ment was good (partly thanks to the machine-wrecking) and public works were organized for those still unable to find employment, so that in this field too April was a quiet month.

Only the students and a handful of Left-wing 'intellectuals' remained in their self-cast role of watch-dogs over the new public liberties. They carried this out with gusto. On the 14th all para-military forces had been put under the command of one man, F.M.L. Count Hoyos. The Civic Guard retained its autonomy, but the Academic Legion was to be part of the National Guard, although a separate unit inside it. The Civic Guard carried out its few duties in orderly fashion enough, but the National Guard was a shambles from the first. Hoyos, an elderly man with little military experience, was quite unable to introduce order into it, and it came to consist of a large number of 'companies', each under officers elected by itself, of most various sympathies. The Academic Legion formed itself into a compact body some 5,000 strong, not all of them students, and not all even Austrian subjects, whose nominal commander, Count Colloredo-Mannsfeld, had little control over them; the orders which they followed were issued by a 'Students' Committee', elected from among their own numbers and all militants. When, on 1 April, Pillersdorf issued a Press Law, by no means an illiberal one, they made such a fuss because they had not been consulted that he weakly withdrew it. They organized rowdy demonstrations outside the houses of unpopular ministers; it was their behaviour that caused Kolowrat and Taaffe to resign (Zanini's resignation was due to conflicts with his own department), and they poured out a spate of inconceivably vulgar lampoons against the aristocracy, the bureau-cracy, the Church and their other pet Guy Fawkeses.

In the Alpine Lands, the smell of revolution evaporated even faster. The bourgeoisie were chiefly anxious for the safety of their own persons and property; the demand for a National Guard came high on every list of desiderata submitted to Vienna, none of which asked for more political reforms than increased representation in the *Landtage* for the burghers and peasants. The students of Graz University aped their colleagues in Vienna, but were too few to con-stitute even much of a nuisance value. The workers were too few to cause much social unrest, and the peasants did not need to do so. A Rescript of 28 March had endorsed the principle of the abolition of the '*robot* system', against compensation for the landlords, the details to be worked out within a year, and the peasants, knowing that the *robot* would soon disappear, simply stopped performing it, and no one tried to make them do it. There was some national unrest in the Trentino, although not in the other Italian areas. Some Slovene leaders petitioned for the constitution of a single Slovene Land, to include, besides Carniola and southern Styria, also southern Carinthia and the Littoral. The German majorities in the Lands of mixed population, while not objecting to some administrative decentralization, and wider use of local languages in non-German areas, opposed any changes in their historic boundaries, but even these disagreements remained a sort of family tiff, the grumblings of which hardly reached Vienna.

But outside the Alpine Lands, the picture was different. When the news from Vienna reached Galicia, which was not until the 18th, there were excited demonstrations in Lemberg, and a deputation waited on Stadion with a long list of demands which amounted to the constitution of Galicia as a near-autonomous kingdom under an exclusively Polish administration. Stadion granted a few minor demands, including one for the formation of a National Guard in Lemberg (but not elsewhere), but said that the rest must be presented to the Emperor. A deputation composed mainly of Polish nobles, with some artisans and a few Jews, but no Ruthenes (whom the Poles ignored completely) set out for Vienna, while at home, a 'Central National Council' was set up under a seven-man directorate. In Vienna the deputation met another from Cracow, carrying another petition with substantially the same demands. The two missions conflated their lists, but the Government, partly out of consideration for the susceptibilities of Russia, kept them waiting for their answer, and this when it came amounted only to an assurance that Ferdinand would 'carefully consider all measures conducive to the welfare of his loyal subjects'. Meanwhile, Stadion's confident bearing and fear of how the Ruthenes were going to act, had cooled heads in Lemberg, while in Cracow a 'Burghers' Committee' that regarded itself as the local representative of the Polish Émigré Committee was waiting for news from Paris, where plans were being hatched for extracting from Prussia an independent territory which could be made into a base for an attack on Russia. So long as this possibility existed, the Poles did not want to precipitate a crisis in Galicia, which relapsed temporarily into a condition of suspended animation.

In the Bukovina the local Roumanians set up a National Committee and National Guard and duly sent in a petition for the separation of the province from Galicia, followed by another which asked for the unification of all Roumanian-speaking territories, including Moldavia, Wallachia and Transylvania, in a single 'Roumania' under Habsburg sovereignty. No notice was taken of either of these documents; the National Guard was dissolved and Czernowitz put under martial law.

The *Landtage* of Bohemia and Moravia were not in session on the

crucial days, but unofficial Prague preceded unofficial Vienna. A
certain Dr Kampelik, a Left-wing member of the Repeal Association,
invited sympathizers to meet in the 'Wenzelsbad' tavern on 4 March.
The meeting, which was attended by both Czechs and Germans,
drew up a petition which consisted mostly of demands for social
reform, but it was revised by a friend of Palacký's named Brauner,
who added to it political demands; a single Diet for Bohemia,
Moravia and Silesia, complete equality for the Czech and German
languages in schools and public offices, and all appointments to be
restricted to natives of the Kingdom. A Committee under the
presidency of another lawyer, named Pinkas, revised this again,
expanding further the national demands and watering down the
social ones, and this draft came before another meeting, which took
place only on 15 March. By this time the news of Metternich's fall
had reached Prague, and the Governor, Count Rudolph Stadion, had
already announced the concessions agreed in Vienna on that day.
Since many of those present thought Pinkas's production too weak,
it was decided to take both his draft and Brauner's, with a separate
petition from the students, to Vienna. The answer, composed by
Pillersdorf, was to the effect that most of the demands had already
been granted, and others would be soon. Any constitutional reforms,
and any revision of the relationship between Bohemia, Moravia and
Silesia, could be effected only through the Estates, for the convocation of which the Patent of 15 March had provided.

When this answer reached Prague, it caused bitter disappointment,
for very sanguine expectations had prevailed there. The 'Wenzelsbad
Committee', which by now had swollen into a large and confident
body in which the Left-wing element was strongly represented, while
the German had disappeared from it almost completely, composed
yet another petition which demanded *inter alia* complete equality
for the Czech and German nationalities, guaranteed by a new
Fundamental Law, and the 'indissoluble unification' in respect of
their internal affairs of the three Lands, with a single Diet, a responsible ministry for internal affairs and the necessary central administrative authorities. This was to be enacted by the King of Bohemia
jure majestatis. A number of leading figures, including Stadion
himself, put their signatures to this.

This document achieved results. The reply to it, after having passed
through various hands, including those of Pillersdorf, appeared on
8 April in the form of a Rescript addressed by Ferdinand to Pillersdorf.
This repeated that the administrative unification of the three Lands
would have to be negotiated 'at the next Reichstag'. But it announced
many immediate concessions, including the establishment in Prague
of a 'responsible central administration for the Kingdom of Bohemia,

with extended competence' and an enlarged Diet. The German and Czech languages were to be, in principle, on a footing of complete equality in public life and education, and all persons holding administrative or judicial posts in Bohemia would in the future have to be conversant with both languages. The *Vernewerte Landesordnung* was the basis of Bohemia's relationship with the Crown; in other words, the centralization introduced by Haugwitz was repudiated.

Pillersdorf maintained afterwards that all these concessions were 'provisional' and none would be legally valid unless and until confirmed by the Reichstag. But none of them were so described, and the 'Bohemian Charter', as the Czechs afterwards called the Rescript, awakened endless jubilation among the Czech nationalists and corresponding consternation elsewhere. The Diets of Moravia and Silesia, when they met, sent in caveats against it, and the local Germans were soon sending in counterpetitions against extending the use of the Czech language to German districts.

With this the Bohemian question became a part, and a particularly intractable one, of Austria's German question, by now in full spate.

This question was one completely *sui generis*. For Metternich, the wave of Liberal and national enthusiasm which had swept over south and west Germany in the early days of March had been simply another revolutionary movement to be suppressed, and no one from Austria had attended the Heidelberg Committee which had organized the Frankfurt *Vorparlament*, and practically no one that body's opening sessions. But the antics of the King of Prussia had forced Ficquelmont to take some action, lest Prussia place herself at the head of the new Germany. Anton Ritter von Schmerling, one of Austria's most competent and most Germanically-minded administrators, was sent to the headquarters of the *Bund* to represent Austria on the Committee which the federal Diet had appointed to consider a reform of the federal constitution; and meanwhile German-Austria itself had caught the infection. The most acutely infected were the students, most of whom were sporting black, red and gold cockades and button-holes, but it was not only they who were fired by the vision of the progressive and enlightened Germany that was to emerge from the deliberations of the *Vorparlament*. Many other progressives also looked forward to seeing Austria take her place in the new Germany, introducing its ideas and reforms into her own system. They held, indeed, various views on the form which the new Germany should take: some saw it as a confederation each member of which would retain its own sovereignty, others as a federation; but even the latter assumed that the capital of this would be Vienna, and its head, a Habsburg. And while many of the federalists would not have minded seeing Austria renounce her rule over her Polish and Italian possessions, perhaps even over Hungary, it was axiomatic for all of them that the Bohemian and Slovene Lands, which had belonged to the old Reich, would have to come into the new formation.

The *Vorparlament*, having decided on 2 April to set up a Committee of Fifty to frame the future German constitution, sent invitations to three Viennese, two Tiroleans and Palacký, from Bohemia, to serve on it. It was to this invitation that Palacký sent his famous reply that he 'was not a German, but a Bohemian of Slavonic stock'. The labours of the *Vorparlament*, if they succeeded, could only weaken Austria irremediably, and that would be disastrous, for 'if it were not that Austria had long existed, it would be necessary, in the interest of humanity itself, to create her' as, he suggested, the necessary and only practicable barrier against Russia. It was a bid, which was backed by the Slovenes, to get the Crown to rest its power on its Slavonic subjects. But Vienna was not yet ripe for Austro-Slavism. It let the five Austrians go to Frankfurt, and finally ac-quiesced in the Committee's decision, which the federal Diet itself accepted, to hold elections for a Constituent Assembly, although one lacking legal power to enforce its decisions; making, indeed, a strong reservation that Austria would never sacrifice her independence or her integrity to another body. The elections were held in April/May, whereafter the elected delegates set out for Frankfurt, there to under-take the task which one of their colleagues described as 'trying to kiss a girl with your back turned to her'.

Meanwhile, Count Montecuccoli, *Landmarschall* and head of the Estates of Lower Austria, had, apparently on his own initiative, sent invitations to all the 'Austrian' Lands to send representatives to Vienna for the promised discussions on a constitution. All except Bohemia and Galicia accepted, and quickly decided that a full-dress constitution, with a Parliament, would be necessary. Pillersdorf accordingly compiled a draft, taking as models the two most Liberal constitutions of the day, those of Belgium and Baden, and adding some paragraphs to meet the special conditions of Austria. This, after revision by various hands, was issued as an *octroi* on 25 April. It retained the existing Lands, whose *Landtage* were to 'take account of provincial interests', but the key position was to be held by a bi-cameral Parliament consisting of a Senate composed of members, some hereditary, some nominated by the Crown, some elected, and a Lower House elected on a franchise to be issued later. The powers of the Crown towards it were limited, and it contained an extensive list of civic liberties which included the phrase 'all peoples of the Monarchy are guaranteed the inviolability of their nationality and language'.

It was neither an incompetent piece of work, nor an illiberal one, but it found more critics than admirers. The Polish deputation, which was still in Vienna waiting for the answer to its petition, protested against its disregard of their demands. The Czechs took exception to its general centralist tone, and in particular, to its failure to acknowledge the 'Bohemian Charter'. The same centralism pleased the Germans, but their ultra-centralists, who were now beginning to raise their heads, objected to the exclusion of Hungary and Lombardo-Venetia, while the Viennese radicals found it too conservative, and objected to any constitution, even one which was admittedly only a draft, and even invited amendments, being issued as an *octroi*: it should have been born of the deliberations of a Constituent Assembly. The rowdy scenes of March were re-enacted, with demonstrations against unpopular ministers, of whom Ficquelmont resigned under threat of actual violence. On 10 May the radicals, grown impatient at the delays in fulfilling their demands, formed a blanket 'Political Central Committee of the whole National Guard', which in fact danced to the students' piping. The next day an Imperial Rescript announced the convocation of the Reichstag for 26 June, and published the franchise for it. This was not liberal enough for the Central Committee, which protested against it. Hoyos then ordered the members of the National Guard not to take part in the work of the Committee, and when they objected, suggested that the Committee should 'dissolve itself'. Instead, some units of the Guard, the students, and other elements, in a mass meeting on 15 May, demanded the revocation of Hoyos's orders and the withdrawal of the draft constitution and franchise. The Government dared not refuse, and Rescripts appeared granting the demands; further, after the 18th the National Guard was to share with the military sentry duty at the Palace itself.

These concessions constituted the biggest victories yet achieved for the *vox populi*, but they provoked a counter-move which, while looking to be another retreat by the Court, marked in effect the turning of the tide. Ferdinand's wife and sister-in-law, convinced that the National Guard were plotting to break into the Palace and murder them all, decided to put Ferdinand and themselves in safety. On the 17th the Emperor and Empress drove out, as though to take the air, but their carriage instead drove through the night and the next day, arriving on the 19th in Innsbruck, where they were joined a few hours later by Franz Karl, his wife and their two younger children (Francis Joseph was with Radetzky in Italy). From their place of safety they sent back a defiant message denouncing the 'anarchical faction' whose activities had compelled their flight.

When the news reached Vienna, it produced there a rapid succession of moves and counter-moves. Jubilant radicals hailed it as

Austria's 'flight to Varennes', which would have the same end as its prototype; but it provoked deep consternation among the more sober elements, with effects which included another run on the banks. For a few days, the 'party of Order' seemed to hold the upper hand. The Central Committee transformed itself into a 'Central Association for the Preservation of Law and Order' under Montecuccoli, and all the paramilitary associations promised to place themselves under the orders of the commander of the garrison, F.M.L. Auersperg, should disorder break out. Posters were put up threatening the proclamation of martial law, should that prove necessary. On the 24th the university was closed, and the next day Colloredo-Mannsfeld invited the Academic Legion to dissolve itself, and when they refused, declared it dissolved as an autonomous body.

But then the tide turned again. The students barricaded themselves in the Aula. Again workmen flocked to their help, and many units of the National Guard took their side. As on 13 March, the Government called in the military, and as then, this further inflamed spirits. The Government, helpless, yielded all along the line. It recalled the troops, retracted the dissolution of the Legion, reaffirmed the concessions of 15 May and sanctioned the formation of a new 'Committee of Security' – on which the students were represented – to which it delegated official responsibility for the maintenance of public order and security.

The Committee, which now became the real rulers of Vienna, contained among its eleven members several who were sober and responsible, not least its president, Fischhof. But it also contained extremists, and the next days were another period of turbulence. Warrants were issued for the arrest of 'enemies of the people', including Montecuccoli, and bands of hooligans roamed the streets, molesting the well-to-do, many of whom fled the city. The difficulties of the capital were now aggravated by another financial and economic crisis. Imports were held back, owing to lack of confidence, the gulden fell, prices rose, demand fell off. Then a radical student whom a self-constituted 'Workers' Committee' had made its president persuaded the Central Committee to institute public works, paying at the top rate for unskilled labour. A great army of local unemployed, reinforced by masterless men from Bohemia, and including many very rough elements, invaded the capital and often simply terrorized the authorities into paying them the dole, without working for it. This undermined the credit of the Committee of Security, even in Vienna, while the effect elsewhere of the whole developments was to enhance the provincials' chronic dislike of the capital and to produce a great upsurge of affection for the Emperor and resentment against his persecutors. It soon became fashionable to question, not only

15 May, but 25 April and even 15 March, and to identify the Government itself with the forces which were in reality its captors, branding them as revolutionaries. These unfortunate men had in reality resigned *en bloc;* and were now carrying on only 'provisionally' pending the appointment of their successors. But until these could be found – and the search was difficult – they had to try to make the April constitution work, and they could not leave Vienna. All Pillersdorf could do was to send Frh. von Doblhoff, who had become a minister in May, down to Innsbruck to represent the Government there. His services were soon in demand, for everyone who on any ground objected to the present situation was besieging Innsbruck for remedies. Most of the requests could be, and were, rejected, but one, while it ended to the profit of the ultimate victors, did so only after a series of fluctuations which sent the graph of Czech national aspirations rising to a peak before the abrupt fall in which it ended.

On 5 April Rudolph Stadion had been relieved of the Presidency of the Bohemian *Gubernium* in favour of Count Leo Thun, a Bohemian aristocrat of extreme federalist and clerical sympathies and unquenchable unsnubbableness. Thun took over his duties only after three weeks, during which Bohemia was in practice governed by a 'National Committee' which was largely the Wenzelbad Committee reinforced by some of the recognized national leaders – Palacký, his son-in-law, Rieger, Havliček and others – who had held aloof from it during its first, not yet respectable, days. Arrived in Prague, Thun promptly declared that he would recognize no concessions extracted from the Emperor by force, and announced elections, on a franchise prepared by the National Committee, for a Diet, which was to meet on 7 June, before the Reichstag met in Vienna. He then appointed a 'Provisional National Government', consisting of two high aristocrats, four Czechs and two Germans, to organize the 'responsible central administration' promised in the 'Bohemian Charter'. He then sent Count Nostić and Rieger to Innsbruck to obtain the Court's sanctions for these moves. Windisch-Graetz, now back in Prague, wrote to the Court endorsing the request and asking to be given plenipotentiary powers to take immediate action, when he should think fit, 'to preserve the safety of the Emperor's throne and the welfare of the Monarchy as a whole'.

On this occasion the Government managed to assert itself. Windisch-Graetz's request for powers for himself was refused. Thun was given permission to hold the elections, but only after those for the Reichstag, which would decide on the constitutional question, and he was ordered to dissolve the Council of Government. And shortly after, events occurred which brought further disaster to the Czechs' national hopes.

Palacký had conceived the idea of countering Frankfurt by a Slav Congress, to open in Prague on 1 June. Invitations to send representatives had gone to all the Slav peoples of the Monarchy, and to some outside it.

The Congress was meant as a parallel move to Thun's activities, and a part of the bid to the Crown to rest its authority on a basis of 'Austro-Slavism'. Things did not, however, work out according to plan. The attendance proved more radical than had been expected, and while the Austrian Slavs put forward plans for remoulding the Monarchy nearer to their hearts' desire, the non-Austrians, especially the Poles, produced a series of resolutions attacking in succession the Governments of Prussia, Saxony, Hungary and the Porte, and in general, indulged in radical language highly alarming to the Austrian Court. Further, the week of the Congress coincided, fortuitously, with the culmination of a long-drawn-out crisis in the Prague cotton mills, many of which were closing down owing to the failure of supplies to arrive. There were street demonstrations in which the workers were supported by sympathetic students. Windisch-Graetz seized the opportunity to proclaim the existence of a great revolutionary plot. He took 'military precautions' which were answered by counter-activities. On Whit Monday, 12 June, there were collisions between troops and crowds. On the 15th Windisch-Graetz threatened to bombard the city unless it surrendered unconditionally, and although it did so the next day, he had a state of siege proclaimed in Bohemia. Courts were set up to try disturbers of the peace, and the meeting of the Diet was postponed indefinitely.

With this the teeth of another national movement were drawn. The Bohemian aristocrats withdrew from their short-lived alliance with the intellectuals, who for their part reconciled themselves with the idea of attending the Reichstag. Socially, most of them, indeed, stood fairly far to the Left, but they were so much more interested in the national question than in the social that there was no danger of their ganging up with the Austrian Left (which had, moreover, displayed indecent joy at Windisch-Graetz's success). It was rather to be expected that they would adopt the course, which in fact they followed, of supporting the Government in the hope of being rewarded with national concessions.

The Bohemian crisis had also perceptible effects on feeling among the Austrian Germans. If Thun's and Palacký's bids had come off, there would certainly have been a formidable upsurge among them of 'black-red-gold' disaffection. The danger past, they were prepared to rally again behind the Austrian Government, but many of them were no longer content that it should be *deutschsprächig* in its forms, but a-national in its spirit. It should, far more than previously, be *deutschbewusst* and *deutschgesinnt*.

The Polish National Government's preparations for starting a revolution based on Poznań had presently alarmed the Prussian authorities, who had clamped down on them. The Poles thereupon shifted their attention to Galicia, where they hatched plans for a new *coup*. On 25 April national councils (*Radas*) in Cracow and Lemberg (the former a new body, composed largely of newcomers who had been refused admission to Poznán) were to proclaim simultaneously that they had taken over the government of Galicia, accompanying this with an announcement that the peasants' servitudes were to be abolished as from 3 May. The Austrian authorities, however, got wind of the plan and took precautionary measures. Street fighting really broke out in Cracow on the 25th, but was quelled within twenty-four hours, and in Lemberg the Poles were forestalled. Stadion dissolved the *Rada* and, with the permission of Vienna, issued a proclamation that the peasants' servitudes would be abolished in Galicia as from 15 May. A group of Ruthenes, headed by Mgr. Jachymowicz, who had already petitioned the *Gubernium* for facilities for the use of their language in East Galicia, asked for permission to form their own *Rada*. The ministerial Council, with relief, granted the request and at last gave the Poles waiting in Vienna their answer: some of their requests had already been met, the more far-reaching ones must be rejected. With these moves the situation in Galicia went off the boil, although not off the simmer.

The turn in Italy was equally encouraging. Latour had been hurrying reinforcements down to Radetzky, who on 5/6 May had won a victory over the Piedmontese outside Santa Lucia, which, although the forces engaged were small, and although his position was still precarious, was so important strategically that it has been described as the turning-point in the history of Austria in 1848. There remained the big political danger; negotiations for fusion were going on between Turin, Milan and Venice, and it seemed likely that the first two, at least, would soon reach agreement. Meanwhile much Liberal, and also much financial, opinion in Vienna itself had from the first advocated letting the provinces go, and as early as 20 April Pillersdorf himself had suggested to a ministerial Council that Austria should recognize the independence of Lombardy. His colleagues had rejected this as 'premature', but on 24 May the Government sent an emissary to London to ask Britain to mediate peace on the basis that Lombardy should be released, while Venetia remained within the Monarchy with a statute of self-government. Palmerston refused to mediate except on the basis of total cession of both provinces and the Trentino. Count Casati, head of the Provisional Government in Milan, also rejected the offer and first Lombardy, then Venetia announced their adherence to Piedmont.

Ficquelmont's successor, Wessenberg, nevertheless ordered that the negotiations should proceed, and sent Radetzky instructions to offer Charles Albert an armistice while they went on. But meanwhile further reinforcements had been reaching Radetzky, enabling him to retake Vicenza. He saw a chance of victory, so put Wessenberg's letter in his pocket and sent Windisch-Graetz's brother-in-law, Prince Felix Schwarzenberg, who was serving under him, to Innsbruck with urgent representations that Lombardy could be saved if he received further reinforcements. A ministerial announcement in fact appeared on 1 July that the war in Italy would be prosecuted, and its issue decided in the field.

In Frankfurt a few rather hot-headed speeches were made at first, but the danger that anything might really be done dwindled as the talking got under way, and almost vanished for Austria when, on 29 June, the assemblage elected the Archduke John 'Imperial Vicar' (*Reichsverweser*) of the New Germany and later chose Schmerling to be Minister of the Interior (afterwards Minister President) of its Government.

Meanwhile, Vienna, also, had simmered down, and with the general situation thus easing, the Government felt that Ferdinand could safely return to his capital, and begged him most earnestly to do so. His mentors still hesitated, but agreed that the Archduke John should go in his place. John, who arrived in Vienna on 24 June, showed himself an able, tactful and popular mediator. He reassured the Left by promising that popular rights and liberties would be respected, and proceeded next to negotiate the formation of a new Government. The Committee of Security had suddenly decided that Pillersdorf, who had not, as they wished, dismissed Windisch-Graetz and Thun, was a reactionary, too. He had himself already resigned, and the Archduke let him go. He offered the succession to Doblhoff, who declined it, preferring the Interior, and the Archduke gave it to Wessenberg, who retained the portfolio of Foreign Affairs. At the request of the Court, Latour and Krausz, too, were kept on. The other ministers, the most important of whom were Doblhoff himself and Bach (Justice), were all men of the *Leseverein* type, now re-emerging, upper middle-class Liberal Josephinians, centralists and Germanic-minded, as Doblhoff showed when he did dismiss Thun (nobody dared touch Windisch-Graetz).

The Committee of Security accepted them without perceptible murmurs.

At the turn of June/July the elections for the Reichstag were held, with characteristic results. The Czechs, having once decided to go to Vienna, sent their best men there. The Italians and Slovenes also sent leaders. The Galician 'elections' produced an incongruous mixture of Polish nobles and Polish, Ruthene and Roumanian peasants, many of whom had little idea why they were there. The Germans had made no attempt to organize nationally for the elections, and their lists contained representatives of every imaginable local interest and social stratification from Tirolean ultra-clericals to Viennese pinks. Most of the deputies were a little to the Right or a little to the Left of centre. There were few pronounced reactionaries, or revolutionaries. Peasants, mostly comfortably situated farmers, constituted the largest single occupational group, followed by 'intellectuals' of various brands.

The debut of the Reichstag was not particularly edifying. It was only on 10 July that a quorum could be assembled, even for preliminary business. Then a long wrangle followed before the deputies decided, without prejudice to principle, or to any later decision, to conduct their debates in German. At last it could get down to work, and at its third session, its youngest member, a Silesian peasant's son named Kudlich, proposed the immediate abolition of the *nexus subditelae*, with all rights and duties deriving therefrom, without prejudice to the question whether or how compensation was to be paid to the landlords. Argument on this last question occupied several weeks until on 9 September the Reichstag accepted the solution described in chapter 9. Meanwhile, on 31 July the Reichstag had appointed a 'Constitutional Committee' consisting of three members from each Land (this was a victory for the Germans) which in turn appointed a Committee of Three to draw up a Charter of Fundamental Rights, and a Committee of Five to attack the real problem, the structural one. Otherwise, the deputies of the different nationalities, especially the Germans and the Czechs, spent much of their time in being rude to one another, the rest, in passing or rejecting resolutions on current affairs, or draft laws. The new ministers at first treated the Reichstag with flattering deference, but as the weeks went on they appeared before it less and less frequently, pointing out that it was not a regular legislature: the Crown, acting through the ministers, was still alone competent to take substantive decisions. Bach even told the assemblage that its decision of 9 September was not yet a law; it had still to be sanctioned by the Crown. The atmosphere was, however, now cordial enough to allow the Emperor to return, amid heartfelt rejoicings from the loyal Viennese, on 12 August.

And yet the doom of constitutional life in Austria had already been sealed by the very event that had emboldened the Imperial family to venture back from Innsbruck. On 25 July Radetzky had won a resounding victory over the Italians at Custozza. In a few days after that he drove them clean out of Lombardy. On 8 August Charles Albert signed an armistice at Vigevano. Venice still held out, but a small force sufficed to contain it. The whole balance of forces inside the Monarchy was changed, for the troops which had been engaged in Italy, or kept in reserve for possible use there, were now available for 'restoring order' in the interior of the Monarchy.

Windisch-Graetz wanted himself to begin this operation immediately, and again asked the Court for plenipotentiary powers. In August he received a top-secret authorization, of which even Latour was not informed, to assume command in case of emergency of all the Monarchy's armed forces outside Italy, with plenipotentiary powers also in the civilian field. No stretch of imagination could construe the situation in Vienna, at that juncture, as constituting an emergency, but Windisch-Graetz had a friend of his, Prince Lobkowitz, appointed Adjutant-General to Ferdinand, with instructions that if any further concessions were demanded, or if the Emperor's safety was endangered, he was to be taken for safety to Olmütz.

The programme for the future which he then outlined to the Empress included the abdication of Ferdinand in favour of his nephew, Francis Joseph. The Empress had long wanted this move, which Windisch-Graetz was determined to carry out at the proper moment: not because the Emperor was unfit to govern – Windisch-Graetz would not have objected to a rubber stamp – but because he had sanctioned the April Laws, and some concessions in Austria, and showed an inconvenient disposition to regard himself as bound by his word, But Windisch-Graetz decided that the time was still not ripe for the change. But while Austria might be allowed rope for a little longer, this was to be denied to Hungary.

In that country the social effervescence that had accompanied the political struggles of the early spring had died away very quickly in the towns: the students played no role comparable to that of their Viennese colleagues, and a few industrial strikes were only on shop level. Unrest on the land, on the other hand, had been fairly widespread. The near-half of the rural population that had not benefited materially under the land reform resented their exclusion bitterly, and even the urbarial peasants were aggrieved at some of the terms of the law, as applied. There had been innumerable refusals of rent or its equivalent, others of forcible occupation of land, and not a few, of actual violence. The Government had been obliged to send commissioners into many areas, and even, on 12 June, to proclaim a general 'state of emergency'.

So far, however, as purely social issues were concerned, the crisis had passed by mid-summer, although the peasants as a class still showed a distressing lack of enthusiasm for the national cause.

But many other quarters were bitterly hostile to the new Hungary. From the windows of Vienna's corridors of power, the April Laws appeared simply as concessions to panic, to be withdrawn at the first possible moment. Meanwhile, the gaps and ambiguities in the laws offered many opportunities to make those concessions ineffective. Pillersdorf writes frankly that since none of the Austrian ministers had been notified of the transference of any of their powers, they continued to act as though no transference had taken place. No trouble came at first over foreign affairs, for Esterházy, an old career diplomat who had accepted his appointment only at the request of the Court, hardly seems to have regarded himself, or to have been regarded by the Austrian ministers, as concerned with the Monarchy's international problems. But the *Hofkammer* went on quietly pocketing the yields of the cameral resources in Hungary, and the *regalia*, so that Kossuth found his cupboard practically bare (the yield of the new taxes having not yet come in), and all emergency measures which he took brought protests from either the *Hofkammer* or the National Bank. As for the military, Zanini instructed the regular units stationed in Hungary, the personnel of which numbered about 18,000, most of them Germans or Czechs, to take their orders from the Hungarian Minister of Defence, but it proved impossible to reach the envisaged agreement on the status of the Military Frontier. When Latour succeeded Zanini, he claimed that the control of this was one of the Monarch's 'reserved rights', to be exercised by him through the central (in practice, Austrian) Ministry of War, and acted thereafter on that assumption. The question was very important for both sides, since almost the whole front-line forces of the Frontiersmen, twenty-two regiments, were in Italy, where they formed an important part of Radetzky's army.

Many of the magnates were in Vienna, using all their influence at the Court against their country's new regime. The attitude of the 'Nationalities' was not uniform. Many history-books describe the April Laws as trampling further on the non-Magyars, and them, as rising unitedly against the tyranny. Neither statement is correct. The Laws hardly touched the national question, as such, at all, and a considerable proportion of the Nationalities gave the new Hungary the reception which the Magyars had optimistically expected from all of them, joining the Magyars in their rejoicing over the political and social reforms. The most important exceptions in the centre and north of the old Inner Hungary were among the Slovaks, in some of whose homes dangerous unrest prevailed in the spring. Most of this

was, as it had been in 1830, probably rather social than national in
origin, but some Slovak leaders produced a programme which asked in
substance for the transformation of Hungary into a 'nationalities
State' with an autonomous territory for themselves. Some others
were coquetting with the idea of Czecho-Slovak unity, and were
finding encouragement in some Czech quarters.

The Hungarians put these movements down ruthlessly but effectively, and they also won the first round in Transylvania. The meeting
of the Diet which was to vote on the union had been fixed for 1 June,
and the Roumanians held mass meetings in their national centre,
Balázsfalva, on 24 April and 15 May, to protest against it. They
were, however, too weakly represented in Kolozsvár to prevent the
measure (for which the Saxons voted out of prudence) from going
through. When a deputation arrived in Innsbruck, whither the Court
had by then taken refuge, to ask Ferdinand not to ratify it, it was too
late

The Court was in fact not yet ready to antagonize the Hungarian
Government for the sake of primitive Roumanian shepherds, hardly
more civilized Slovak peasants, or a handful of cautious Saxon
burghers. The Hungarian Serbs and the Croats were in a different
position. Both were organized communities, the former politically,
the latter at least ecclesiastically ; both were virtually nations in arms,
both accustomed to take their orders from the *Hofkriegsrat*, and both
traditional instruments to which Vienna habitually turned when
seeking a counterweight against excessive Hungarian demands. In
the spring of 1848 the Court had particular reason to seek their goodwill because of the importance of their contributions to Radetzky's
armies.

The Court and the Southern Slavs were therefore from the first
potential, and up to a point actual, although surreptitious, allies.
With time the alliance became, as we shall see, open, but this could
not be so at first, since in the spring the Hungarian Government was
still behaving loyally towards the Crown, which could not afford a
breach with it, if only because the number of Hungarian troops in
Italy, although smaller than that of the Frontiersmen (20,000 against
35,000) was still substantial, and Hungary's untapped reserves were
far the larger. For many weeks, therefore, the Crown wavered between law and interest or between one legal case or one argument
of expediency, and another ; it was not until July that the die was cast
irrevocably against the Hungarians.

The alliance between the Crown and the Croats had, however,
been concluded effectively before Batthyány had fairly extracted his
first concessions from Ferdinand. It happened that the dignity of Ban
was vacant in March, and various advisers at the Court suggested

that it should be conferred on a Colonel of one of the Frontier regiments named Josip Jellačić, a romantically-minded man who after a Magyarone past had become a fanatical Croat nationalist with 'Illyrian' sympathies. On 23 March, before Batthyány, on whose recommendation the appointment should have been made, had time to protest, a Rescript countersigned by an official in the Hungarian Court Chancellery appointed Jellačić Ban, also nominating him Privy Councillor and Colonel in Chief of the Croat Frontier regiments. The next week, when he appeared in Vienna, he was promoted again, this time to the rank of Field-Marshal Lieutenant, and made General Commander of the Croat Frontier Districts. Returning to Zagreb, he announced that he regarded the Palatine as his peer, not his superior, forbade Croat officials to communicate with Buda-Pest, and announced the formation of a 'Banal Council' which was to constitute a full-scale administration under his own presidency, competent for Slavonia and Fiume as well as Croatia, and completely autonomous except in respect of foreign affairs and defence. He then announced the 'rupture of relations' between Croatia and Hungary, and published a list of offences triable by Court Martial; these included ascribing the liberation of the peasants in Croatia to the Hungarian law.

After unavailing efforts to reach any agreement with the Ban, the Palatine went to Vienna and extracted from Ferdinand three Rescripts, one addressed to Jellačić which confirmed the constitutional link between Hungary and Croatia and ordered Jellačić to obey orders received from the Palatine or the Hungarian Government, a second authorizing him (the Palatine) to send a Royal Commissioner to Croatia to repress any dangerous separatism, and a third instructing the officers commanding the three Frontier Districts to obey the orders of the Hungarian Minister of Defence. Jellačić ignored the first; the senior Frontier Commander, General Hrabowski, managed to boycott the second; and correspondence between the three generals and Latour produced an instruction to the former so obscure that they could have invoked it in justification of almost any course taken by them. Jellačić then called on 'the inhabitants of the Triune Kingdom' (i.e., of Croatia, Slavonia and Dalmatia) to enrol in a National Guard, and convoked the Diet of Zagreb for 2 June.

Now the threads of the Croat story began to run together with that of the Hungarian Serbs.

They, like the other nationalities, had inaugurated the new era by holding innumerable meetings, which had spoken with various voices; but the most representative of them was a meeting held by the Church Council at Újvidék on 27 March. This, while 'willingly conceding the supremacy of the Magyar language and nationality in the political and social structure of the Hungarian State', asked for legal recognition of their own 'nation', with far-reaching internal autonomy. On 8 April a deputation took these resolutions to Pozsony, where they came into collision with the Hungarians' insistence on the political unity of the Hungarian State. Tempers became frayed, especially in a private interview between one of the Serbs, a young ex-officer named Stratimirović, and Kossuth, both men of fiery temperament, and the Serbs left, having threatened to seek satisfaction elsewhere if they did not find it in Pozsony. The next meeting of the Church Council, on 14 April, went further than its predecessor; it called for the establishment of a Serbian 'Voivody' under its own Voivode (military commander), to comprise Syrmia, the Bánát, Bácska and Baranya, which should form an autonomous unit within the 'Triune Kingdom'. Another 'national Congress', under the Metropolitan, Rajačić, declared the lapsed dignities of Voivode and Patriarch revived, proclaimed Rajačić Patriarch and an officer named Suplyikać, then serving in Italy, Voivode, and announced the constitution of the 'Nation of Hungarian Serbs' as a free and independent nation under the House of Habsburg, in a Voivody which was to be in political alliance with the 'Triune Kingdom'. On 29 May a delegation of Serbs took these resolutions to Zagreb.

By this time the extremists were gaining ground. Serb guerillas, reinforced by volunteers from the Principality, were making life unsafe for the local Magyars. On 16 May Batthyány, who was still in acting charge of Defence, appealed for volunteers for a new force known as the *Honvédség* (Home Defence) for defence against the Serbs. To keep within the letter of the law, this was described, technically, as a civilian body, but pay and ranks within it were equated with those of the regular army, and regular officers and other ranks were invited to transfer into it, so that Vienna regarded it, with reason, as the nucleus of a Hungarian national army. Kossuth, who had been negotiating with the Commercial Bank for a loan, undertook to finance the new force and issued, first Government bonds, then small currency notes, turning the bank, to all intents and purposes, into a bank of issue.

Another series of extraordinary scenes followed. At the end of May, the Palatine, accompanied by Széchenyi and Eötvös, and joined later by Batthyány, went to Innsbruck to invite Ferdinand to come to Hungary to open the Diet, due to open on 2 July, also to instruct Jellačić to cancel the convocation of the Zagreb Diet, which he had not been entitled to order. Ferdinand refused to leave Innsbruck, but the Palatine was authorized to open the Diet in his place, and Jellačić was told to come to Innsbruck and explain his conduct. Batthyány further promised that the Diet would vote 40,000 men and supplies for them if it felt secure from attacks from the Serbs and Croats. In return, he obtained Ferdinand's signature to three Rescripts: one ordering all troops in Hungary, including the Frontier, to take their orders from Buda-Pest, one appointing Hrabowski head of all the Frontier regiments, and the third suspending Jellačić from all his offices, civil and military. The Rescripts were, however, not counter-signed, and were to be used only if Jellačić failed to justify himself. He, meanwhile, took his time. First, disregarding his orders, he convoked the Diet, which approved the Serbs' programme (with a reservation in respect of Syrmia), accepted their alliance and produced a plea for a Great Illyrian province, autonomous except in respect of the central services. Jellačić then led a deputation of Croats and Serbs, bearing these documents, to Innsbruck, where the party arrived only on 18 June, after the Hungarians had left.

The petitions were rejected, but Jellačić himself, when received in audience the next day, won the hearts of those there, especially the ladies. That day Schwarzenberg arrived with Radetzky's encouraging message, and the Court decided to allow Jellačić to carry on as Ban *de facto*, and to ask the Archduke John to mediate between him and Batthyány. But by now fairly severe, although local, fighting had broken out in southern Hungary between Hungarian Home Guards and a Serbian volunteer force commanded by Stratimirović. The Hungarian Government resorted to the desperate expedient of publishing the 'emergency Rescripts' in spite of the absence of a counter-signature to them. Jellačić disregarded them and although he himself had few troops at his disposal (most of the Croat units were down in Italy) he strengthened his hand immensely by reaching a close understanding with Latour and with the other centralists in Vienna, who now sent Buda-Pest two extraordinary Notes, one demanding that Hungary reconcile herself at all costs with Jellačić: 'otherwise we shall be obliged to renounce our neutrality towards Hungary', the other demanding from it 150,000 gulden in silver for Jellačić's forces. A third Note protested against Kossuth's issue of paper money, as infringing the monopoly of the National Bank.

The Diet duly opened on 4 July, and the Palatine read to it satisfactory Rescripts from Ferdinand, expressing his determination to preserve the integrity of the Lands of the Hungarian Crown, and to maintain the April Laws, investing the Palatine himself with unlimited plenipotentiary powers, and enjoining all authorities in Hungary, Transylvania, Croatia and the Frontier to obey him implicitly. When, however, the defence and financial votes came up, Kossuth, putting them to the House for the Government, which, although more than doubtful of his discretion, had felt it necessary, in view of his vast popularity, to make him their spokesman, put them entirely in terms of Hungary's own needs. Saying that 'the Fatherland was in danger from attacks from Serbs, Croats and Slovaks', he asked for 200,000 men, 40,000 of them immediately, and 42 million gulden. Some of the men and money might still have been used to honour Batthyány's promise, but most of them would obviously go to form a national Hungarian army, and a few days later Kossuth proposed making the dispatch of the troops to Italy conditional on Austria's ceding Lombardy-Venetia, or at least – a revision extracted from him by his horrified fellow-ministers – granting them a degree of independence which would fall little short of a Personal Union.

The Diet also approved the dispatch of a mission to Frankfurt to seek an alliance with Germany of mutual defence against attack from 'a Slav element, or other Powers allied with a Slav element'.

This was the situation as between Hungary and the Court when the news arrived of Radetzky's triumph in Italy. Now not only was there no need for more Hungarian troops for Italy, but other units, including Serb and Croat, could be brought back from there and used against Hungary. The prospect was, of course, welcomed most whole-heartedly by the Court and by the three generals, Windisch-Graetz, Latour and Jellačić, but it is important to emphasize the full, and in most cases very willing, support which the trio received from many members of the new Austrian Government. Bach, in particular, was a convinced and even fanatical pan-monarchic centralist, and was firmly turning the Austrian Ministry into an instrument of the Court's Hungarian policy, overriding the doubts of his more hesitant colleagues.

Neither were the ministers' attitudes in this respect at variance with those of Austrian public opinion in general, inside or outside the Reichstag. The convinced and doctrinaire Left, conveniently forgetting their own rejoicings over the Czechs' disaster, still regarded the Hungarians as leading the battle for political and national freedom inside the Monarchy. But these views were now practically confined to the Viennese Left and a handful of Polish radicals. The Czechs were not going to lift a finger to help Hungary, especially in view of the Hungarians' activities in Frankfurt. As for the German middle classes, even those who were still believers in constitutionalism for themselves (Bach himself was this) had become completely unregenerate where other peoples were concerned.

Incidentally, opposition to the Government based on German national feeling had by now gone the same way as Liberal opposition. The Government itself was as German as anyone could wish.

Those who still looked to Frankfurt were the same as those who pinned their hopes on Hungary, and both attitudes were becoming increasingly identified, in the eyes of others, with social radicalism, objectionable on every ground.

The first move in the new *parti* was made by Jellačić. The conversations *à trois* had not taken place, owing to the Archduke's absence in Frankfurt, but Jellačić and Batthyány had met, and the Croat had then spoken as though he had been the Court's own mouthpiece, demanding that Hungary give up her Ministries of Defence and Finance and take over part of the national debt. Batthyány then committed the curious tactical error of asking the Austrian Ministry whether they stood by the Pragmatic Sanction and would support Hungary against Croat separatism. The ministry answered that it was they and the Croats who were standing by the Pragmatic Sanction; but they would send a detailed statement in due course.

On 22 August the Court withdrew the Palatine's powers, which meant that sanction for Hungarian laws had to come from Vienna. When Batthyány and Deák went there to get sanction for putting the defence vote into effect, it was refused – the Court no longer needed a Hungarian army. Neither did it want Buda and Zagreb reconciled. Latour was now sending down arms and supplies to the numerically considerable, if motley, force which Jellačić was assembling on the Drave. A new offer by the Hungarians which would have given the Croats practically everything for which they asked only got as far as Latour, who told its bearers that nothing except cancellation of the April Laws would suffice. Next, they were presented with a letter from Ferdinand to the Palatine enclosing a truly extraordinary memorandum from the Emperor's 'Viennese Ministers' to the effect that the April Laws were themselves illegal since Austria had not consented to them.

The same day Jellačić occupied Fiume and proclaimed its incorporation in Croatia.

The Hungarians took further hurried defensive measures. New *Honvéd* formations were authorized, and officers and men from the regular army urged to transfer into them. The Hungarians decided to make one more appeal to the Crown, and sent a big deputation to Vienna. They were not received at all for some days, and when at last admitted to the Presence, were given only a completely non-committal answer. They read the real answer, with stupefaction, in a Rescript from Ferdinand to Jellačić, published that day in the *Agramer Zeitung*, which reinstated the Ban in all his dignities and offices and expressed the Emperor's confidence in him. Jellačić took this as the official authorization without which he had refused to move, and on 11 September led his troops across the Drave.

The constitutional position in Hungary fluctuated wildly for some days. A flurry of resignations, which included first those of several members of the Government individually, then that of the Government as a whole, and finally of the Palatine (also the lynching by a mob of an unfortunate emissary sent to mediate peace, the news of which was greeted by the Diet with indecent glee), ended in the constitution in Pest of a 'Committee of National Defence', under the presidency of Kossuth, who was given emergency powers which made him in practice dictator.

For a month before Kossuth had been throwing all his superb energy and eloquence into the organization of the national defences. Volunteers for the *Honvédség* had been coming in in fair numbers, and of the regular forces, nearly all the Magyar units, and some others, had opted for the Hungarian side (the confusion of competences and loyalties had by now become so inextricable that a perfectly honourable man could take either side, as his heart prompted him). Even so, Hungary might well have despaired but for two circumstances. One was the conspicuous incompetence in the field of Jellačić, who, when, after an initial, virtually unopposed advance, he for the first time met a considerable Hungarian force, broke off the engagement almost before it had begun and retreated ingloriously to the Austrian frontier, sacrificing his entire rearguard, which surrendered to a Hungarian force half its strength.

The second factor which gave the Hungarians at least the hope of a respite was a renewed outbreak of Left-wing unrest in Vienna.

In spite of the appeasement brought by the Emperor's return, life in Vienna had remained uneasy. Trade and industry continued to stagnate, prices to rise. In the latter part of August the Government cut the rates for the men employed on the public works. They invaded the city, and troops had to be called out, who opened fire; the workers lost 18 dead and nearly 300 wounded. In September there were more demonstrations, this time by artisans who were being forced out of business by lack of demand and the competition of factory labour. Again troops were called out, although this time there was no bloodshed.

Each time the authorities won, and after each victory they gave the screw another turn. After the August troubles they took over control of the National Guard, and forced the Committee of Security to dissolve itself. 30,000 non-Viennese navvies were sent to work on the railways at a safe distance from the capital. In September the university was definitively closed. Many students went home, and the membership of the Academic Legion sank to about 1,500.

The bourgeoisie was now conservative to a man. More and more, the Left was being reduced to a little band of German-Austrian intellectuals, nearly all of them Viennese, and their sympathizers among the students and workers of Vienna, and they were looking more and more to Hungary as their one remaining hope. Threads were spun between Vienna and Pest, and the snubs dealt to Hungary by the conservative majority in the Reichstag were answered by warm demonstrations in the opposite sense from the other side.

On 6 October a regiment ordered to Hungary refused to entrain. The powder-keg exploded. Troops sent to restore order fired on the crowds, and they on them, with considerable loss of life on both sides. Soon the whole city was in uproar. Fanaticized mobs began a hunt for the chief objects of their wrath. Bach escaped, but Latour was bestially murdered. Another mob got possession of the arms stored in the depots of the Innere Stadt.

These excesses, the worst to date, decided Lobkowitz to carry out his orders. On 7 October, the Emperor, with his family, left Vienna for Olmütz, under a heavily-armed escort, leaving behind him a proclamation in which he called on 'all men who loved justice and freedom' to rally round him. Most of the Government and a whole company of other public men, including Schwarzenberg, Hübner, Kübeck and Stadion, took the same road, while the bourgeois of Vienna, where able to do so, left the city. The Czech members of the Reichstag, except two radicals, decamped *en bloc*, the Bohemians assembling in Prague, whence they issued a strongly-worded proclamation denouncing the Left and declaring that 'Vienna was not Austria and was not entitled to impose order on Austria'. The Moravians went to Brünn.

Now Windisch-Graetz set his long-prepared plans in motion. Leaving one third of his command in Bohemia, he gave marching orders to the rest, sent to Moravia and Galicia for reinforcements, and himself set out for Olmütz, where he arranged for the issue of an Imperial manifesto condemning in the sharpest terms what had happened in Vienna and conferring on himself plenipotentiary powers to restore order 'by such means as he thought fit'. He then set his troops in motion, having arranged to effect a juncture outside Vienna with Auersperg, who had withdrawn his troops from the city. On his way he was, to his annoyance, overtaken by a much milder proclamation, dictated by Stadion, in which Ferdinand promised to leave his peoples 'in undisturbed enjoyment of the rights and freedoms conceded to them', and although proroguing the Reichstag, instructed it to reassemble in Kremsier, near Olmütz. Windisch-Graetz nevertheless continued his march, and on the 20th summoned the capital to submit itself to his authority.

In Vienna, meanwhile, the rump Reichstag elected a new President –
the Pole, Smolka – and a Standing Committee which declared itself
in permanence and solely competent to exercise the legislative power.
There were also at first three ministers – Hornbostl, Doblhoff and
Krausz – of whom, however, the two first-named soon resigned
(Krausz stayed on to the last, quietly commuting by train between
Vienna and Olmütz). But both ministers and Reichstag were
operating in a vacuum. Such effective authority as there was in the
city was exercised by the students and by a self-constituted 'Central
Committee of all Democratic Associations', composed, since the
other elements had withdrawn, almost entirely of members of the
extreme Left. They turned their energies to throwing up improvised
fortifications and to organizing a force to man them. This should
have come from the National Guard, but since none of its regular
members would take on the post, the command of its remnants, with
that of the Civic Guard, and the Academic Legion, was eventually
conferred on an ex-regular subaltern named Wenzel Messenhauser,
a curious and innocent enthusiast who maintained to the last that he
had been defending the legitimate order. A paid 'Mobile Guard' was
also established, and a few volunteers came in, including one, the
Polish soldier of fortune, Bem, who proved to be a host in himself.

But Vienna was completely isolated. The whole Austrian country-
side was hostile, and two emissaries from Frankfurt – Blum and
Fröbel – could bring nothing but words, and when they approached
Windisch-Graetz, were curtly sent about their business.

The only hope of the Left lay in the Hungarians, whose advance
guards, following Jellačić, had reached the frontier. But their
regular officers refused to go further unless instructed by lawful
authority, which their Government refused to give, in order not to
give Austria an excuse for further intervention. Messenhauser refused
to invite them to advance, on the ground that he was no rebel and
would not identify the cause of Vienna with that of rebellious
Hungary. Meanwhile, Jellačić's retreat had brought his army,
which was now linked up with that of Auersperg, between the
Hungarian frontier and Vienna.

A deputation from the City Council to Olmütz was simply
referred to Windisch-Graetz, who on the 23rd sent an ultimatum
demanding unconditional surrender within 24 hours. Fighting began
on the 24th, although it became heavy only four days later. On the
29th the defenders sent a message agreeing to open the city gates the
next morning. That morning, unhappily, a detachment of Hungarian
cavalry, advancing after all, on personal orders from Kossuth,
reached the suburbs and the defenders, expecting relief, repudiated
their promise. Windisch-Graetz, announcing that the breach of

faith 'made mercy impossible', turned his guns on the city, while the Hungarians provided Jellačić with the single military success of his career by fleeing before him. The resistance in Vienna soon collapsed; it had cost in all about 2,000 dead. Another 2,000 were arrested, of whom 25 were shot as ring-leaders. These included Blum, whose execution was, it appears, meant as a studied insult to Frankfurt. Fröbel, also condemned to death, was reprieved. Most of the minor offenders were drafted into the army and sent down to Italy. All Left-wing associations were dissolved, and the city placed under strict military control.

The fall of Vienna marked the virtual end of the revolutionary movement in the western half of the Monarchy. It was not only that the counter-revolutionaries were now everywhere in control: their vigilance and their arms were hardly necessary. The Viennese bourgeois were now 99 per cent on the side of 'order', where their counterparts in the other German cities, and the peasants, had long stood. Not only was social revolutionary feeling virtually dead among them, but with it also pan-Germanic enthusiasm. Austria's Germans followed her Czechs into the paths of 'Austrianism', anxious only to secure the best terms for themselves in an Austrian State, which, indeed, most of them (but by no means all) still wanted to be constitutional.

A belated squib of revolt exploded in Lemberg on 2 November, but was easily put down by the officer commanding the local garrison. The hot-heads fled the country, the rest settled down, justifying remarkably an experiment made by Stadion who, when he left the Kingdom, entrusted its affairs to two senior Polish officials, Frh. von Zalewski and Count Agenor Goluchowski.

The centres of political life were now Kremsier, where the Reichstag was gathering, and Olmütz, where preparations were going on for the formation of a new Government. Among the promises that Windisch-Graetz had extracted from the Court had been that he should be consulted on all important business of State, and he insisted that the Wessenberg Government should be replaced by a new one, for the Presidency of which he had nominated his brother-in-law, Prince Schwarzenberg. The names of the ministry were announced on 21 November. Schwarzenberg kept Foreign Affairs for himself, the other ministers were Stadion (Interior), Bach (Justice), Krausz (Finance), Bruck (Commerce and Communications), von Thinnfeld (Agriculture) and F.M.L. von Csorich (War).

It was an able team. Schwarzenberg himself, although entirely without experience of domestic affairs (nearly all his previous career had been abroad) or understanding of the forces moving them, had qualities that served him well; a gambler's hardihood in taking risks and an arrogance so limitless as to make him incapable of imagining that his will would ever be opposed, which, accordingly, it seldom was. He was even – no small asset – not afraid of Windisch-Graetz. The same arrogance lifted him above class prejudice; he regarded his fellow-aristocrats with lofty contempt, and, as his list showed, did not hesitate to go outside their ranks in choosing his assistants. Stadion and Bach were two of the ablest administrators in the country; Bruck, a Protestant Rhinelander whom a curious chance had brought to Austria, both competent and energetic; the others, good in their respective fields.

The cardinal question was what attitude the Government was going to take up on the issue of constitutionalism versus absolutism. Stadion, Bruck and Krausz were all convinced constitutionalists, and strangely, Schwarzenberg seems to have agreed with them. In any case, when presenting his ministry to the 250 members of the Reichstag who had reached Kremsier, he surprised and gratified them by announcing that the ministry 'wanted constitutional Monarchy, strongly and unreservedly, and would place itself at the head of the movement for realizing liberal and popular institutions'. His references to Germany, Italy and Hungary contained, indeed, menacing undertones. The settlement of Austria's relations with Germany would have to await the emergence of 'a rejuvenated Austria and a rejuvenated Germany'. Lombardy was to remain 'organically connected with constitutional Austria'. The war [sic] against Hungary was not against liberty, but against those who would deprive the people of their liberty, and the struggle in support of those peoples would continue until the achievement of the struggle's end, 'the unification of the Lands and races of the Monarchy in one great body politic'.

The next step was to carry through the change of Monarchs. This did not go entirely smoothly, for poor Ferdinand clung with considerable tenacity to the shadow of power that was his, and Franz Karl, too, proved unexpectedly reluctant to stand down in favour of his son. Eventually, however, both were over-persuaded, and on 2 December, in a small gathering attended only by members of the family, ministers, Court dignitaries and the Generals, Windisch-Graetz and Jellačić, Francis Joseph knelt before his uncle who, when the declaration of abdication had been read out, stroked his hair and raised him, saying: 'God bless you, Franzl. Be good. I don't mind.'

The change of dynasty was proclaimed with a fanfare of trumpets outside the city hall of Olmütz and the portals of its Cathedral.

The boy who knelt that day at his uncle's feet was assuming a charge which in the event he bore for nearly seventy years. During this long period of time his conception of the nature of his office, and the qualities of heart and brain which he brought to realization of it, profoundly affected the fortunes of his peoples. Pens far better qualified than the present writer's have described Francis Joseph the man. They are agreed that his intellect was narrow and unimaginative, but not blunt: he was quick enough to size up a situation and draw conclusions from it, and he was blessed with a fabulous memory, and with the family gift of tongues. Many observers have called him cold and unfeeling, a charge hardly borne out by the passionate and enduring devotion which, as his letters to her show, he bore towards his wife. Towards the rest of the world he did, indeed, often show an insensitivity which was probably due partly to a deep inner diffidence, but more, to the feeling that his position set him apart from the rest of the world. This conviction of the unique majesty of kingship bestowed by Providence on himself and his House made him, although his personal tastes were simple and even *kleinbürgerlich*, always insist jealously on punctilious observance of the elaborate Court etiquette, and attach extraordinary importance to the dynastic aspect of any foreign political issue, and it also prevented him from establishing a truly human relationship with any one of his subjects. Furthermore, although not temperamentally autocratic, he conceived the proper relationship between the Prince and his peoples as one of unqualified autocracy. It was his Christian duty not to exploit or oppress them, but theirs to obey his will without question. The limitations on his authority which he was driven in the course of years to concede were wrung from him by sheer necessity: his heart never accepted them. He did not even regard himself as the 'first servant' of his subjects nor as their servant at all: all the 'service' in the relationship was due from them to him – as Monarch, indeed, and embodiment of the dignity of his house, rather than as man. His acts as ruler, and his recorded words, leave the inescapable conclusion that domestic problems as such meant nothing whatever to him. He judged any move in this field exclusively in the light of *raison d'état*. An exception should perhaps be made in respect of his sincere religious feelings, but even in this field he became, as we say elsewhere, pronouncedly more Josephinian as he outgrew early influences. Other predispositions and prejudices of course influenced his conduct of affairs. He inherited all his family's tradition of looking for his immediate helpers to the great aulic families: an observer has recorded that the aristocracy was for him always 'something nearer' than his other subjects. Even the humblest noble ranked for him above any commoner. Another class to which he

certainly felt especially 'near' was that of his officers. This was
partly a matter of temperament, for from his childhood he had shown
a taste, rare in his family, for matters military; and it was certainly
confirmed by the indisputable fact that it was the army that had
saved his throne for him in 1848. To the last he regarded the army as
the most reliable prop of his rule, as witness the extraordinary importance which he attached to his position of 'Supreme War Lord' and
his almost pathological sensitivity towards any attempt to question
or weaken it. It was long before he outgrew a preference for military
solutions to problems, or listened less readily to military advisers,
than to civilians.

German was the language in which he thought, and he could not
help knowing himself to be a 'German' in the personal sense, and
feeling a certain human affinity with his German subjects which did
not exist between him and his subjects of other nationalities. He felt
them to be what they felt themselves, the 'cement' of his Monarchy.
But when they thwarted him he unhesitatingly turned to other
peoples, and if he clung with particular tenacity to the leadership of
Germany, this was out of no 'racialist' feeling, but because it was the
most august of his family's traditional dignities.

His seventy years of rule probably never modified Francis
Joseph's innermost convictions, but they made him less quick to
assert them. He renounced foreign adventure and contented himself
with preserving what could be preserved, as best it could be done.
But the worldly wisdom acquired by him in later years was born of
painful experience. Now, at his accession, his eagerness to restore
the order which alone seemed to be right was equalled by his confidence in his ability to do so. His accession consequently ushered in
a new period of intense activity, although not, immediately, in every
direction.

The Hungarians did not miss the significance of the abdication,
and a party in the Diet favoured abandoning the struggle as hopeless.
But bolder councils prevailed, and on 7 December 1848 the Diet
resolved that Hungary, not having been consulted on the step, was
not bound by it, and would recognize no king but Ferdinand until his
successor had been legally crowned and had taken the oath to the
constitution, as represented by the April Laws, in defence of which
she would continue the struggle.

The gauntlet had been thrown down, and taken up, and both sides
nerved themselves for the decisive contest. Both had been utilizing the
past weeks to speed up their preparations; the Hungarians, who had
discovered in a certain Artur Görgey a soldier of genius, with much
effect. Austrian detachments entering the country from Galicia were
thrown back and an attempted Slovak rising was stamped out,

leaving the Hungarians in secure command of the north and centre of
the country. Their main force, the 'Army of the Upper Danube', had
been welded by its commander, Görgey, into a serviceable force
some 30,000 strong, although while doing this Görgey had unfortunately offended many of the National Guards by simply sending
them home as useless, and had also annoyed Kossuth, although not
yet mortally. Elsewhere the position was obscure. On 18 October
1848, F.M.L. Puchner, commanding the Imperial forces in Transylvania, had assumed 'provisional supreme authority' there, called
on the population to obey him, and formed a sort of local administration. Baron Vay, the Hungarian Government Commissioner,
countered with another proclamation demanding obedience to himself, as the representative of lawful authority. Broadly, the Magyars and Szekels rallied to Vay, the Saxons and Roumanians, to
Puchner. Both men had under them small contingents of regular
troops and much larger forces of irregulars, of which the Roumanian,
commanded by a leader named Avram Jancu, were the largest.
Puchner held most of the fortresses and key positions, but outside
these, each rural district, generally speaking, looked after itself.

In the south, another Serb National Congress proclaimed
Suplyikać, returned from Italy, Voivode on 7 October, and the
Serb forces had been combined with the regular units in the vicin-
ity into an 'Austro-Serb Army Corps', 21,000 strong, under his
command; a considerable force, but still not strong enough to take
the offensive unsupported. Rajačić had meanwhile been besieging
the Court with representations and petitions, but he was not popular
there, and it was only after the Hungarian Diet's Resolution of 7
January that the Court dropped its hesitations. On the 14th and 15th
the Court, in a series of Rescripts, nominated Suplyikać Voivode
and Rajačić Patriarch, and promised the Serbs a 'national internal
organization' when hostilities should have ended. On 16 December
Windisch-Graetz led an army of 52,000 across the Lower Austrian
border, while other detachments advanced from Styria and Galicia.
Puchner and Suplyikać stood ready to repel attacks and another
force of Slovaks, which had assembled in Moravia, re-entered
north-west Hungary.

The Court had expected to carry through, quickly and almost
simultaneously, the military operation of crushing Hungary and the
political one of imposing its own system in Austria, following which
it would turn its attention to Germany. Both operations were delayed, the one by Windisch-Graetz's incompetence, the other by
his obstinacy, Görgey, whose forces were far outnumbered by the
Imperial ones opposite them, withdrew them across the Danube, and
Windisch-Graetz reached Buda almost unopposed on 5 January, the

Diet retiring to Debrecen. He reported back that his military task was accomplished. This was far from accurate. Görgey's army was still intact, and now entirely reliable politically, since those officers who felt that their oath to Ferdinand bound them to obey his successor had left it. That Kossuth gave the supreme command of the Hungarian armies to a somewhat unpopular Polish General, Dembiński, was a retarding factor, but not a fatal one. Bem, who had surfaced in Transylvania, won a series of successes against Puchner's forces, and Damjanić was equally successful against the new commander of the Austro-Serb Corps, Thodorović (Suplyikać had died suddenly). Windisch-Graetz ventured out of Pest, lost heart, and retreated again. It was only on 27/28 February that his armies met the Hungarians in force, at Kápolna, and won a technical victory, since after the encounter the Hungarians withdrew across the Tisza.

In Kremsier, meanwhile, the Reichstag, much heartened by Schwarzenberg's comfortable words, had settled down to the engrossing and psychologically revealing, although, as the event proved, fruitless task for which it had been called together, of framing an Austrian constitution. The Sub-Committee on Fundamental Rights finished its work fairly quickly, and the general debate opened on 4 January 1849. Under horrified protests from Olmütz the plenary session dropped the first clause of the draft, which had laid down that 'all sovereignty proceeds from the people', but many of the other clauses were radical enough: all titles of nobility were abolished, the Roman Catholic Church ceased to be 'ruling', and there was a long list of 'guaranteed' popular liberties. The powers of the Crown were left almost unlimited in respect of foreign affairs, except that engagements involving expenditure had to be approved by Parliament, but they were closely restricted in domestic affairs.

The most controversial question, however, was that of the relationship between the nationalities. The Reichstag adopted, without too great difficulty, a declaration of principle which ran: 'All peoples (*Volkstämme*) of the Empire are equal in rights. Each people has an inviolable right to preserve and cultivate its nationality in general, and its language in particular. The equality of rights in the school, administration and public life of every language in local usage (*landesüblich*) is guaranteed by the State.'

But this was only a generality, after which there followed the manœuvring for position, which in practice turned round two questions: what should be the sub-units of the State, and what the relationship between the central authority and the local constituents; for it was the answer to these two questions that would determine the real power-positions of the nationalities.

The differences between those nationalities, or national groups, which wanted the existing Land boundaries maintained and those which wanted them modified or abolished altogether, and between centralists and federalists, were sharp, and for long sharply maintained. The proposals finally adopted kept the Lands unaltered, with minor changes, but no large ones. The Vorarlberg was reattached to the Tirol, the Bukovina promoted to the staus of a Land, and Gorizia, Gradisca, Istria and Trieste amalgamated into one Land, the *Küstenland*, or Littoral, but Galicia remained a unit, as did Bohemia, Styria, and the Tirol, etc. Lands of mixed population were, however, to be divided into *Kreise* ('Circles'), delimited on ethnic lines and enjoying fairly wide autonomy, and courts were to be set up in each such Land to hear inter-nationality disputes. The Parliament was to consist of two Houses, the Upper composed of three representatives for each Land and one for each *Kreis*, the Lower, to be elected by direct franchise, on a fairly low property qualification. The respective competences of the Parliament and the Lands were, strangely, left undefined.

It was a compromise solution which was far from doing equal justice to all, most notably not to the Ruthenes and the Slovenes, but it contained useful ideas. Its merits were, however, never to be put to the test. Long before the proposals were ready, sentence of death had been secretly passed on the Reichstag and all its works.

Many of its actions had given offence to the Court and ministerial circles and the draft constitution itself, even after the offending clause on the source of sovereignty had been dropped, still contained much which no regime of the nature of that established in Olmütz could possibly have accepted. These apart, there were two things in it which ruled it out of court: it was a product of the popular will, and it applied only to the western Lands, not including Lombardy-Venetia, and not to Hungary.

As early as January the secret decision had been taken to dissolve the Reichstag and promulgate a pan-monarchic constitution by *octroi*. Stadion, helped by Bach, had been composing the new document, and the Reichstag had owed its continued survival for another six weeks partly to the absurdity of issuing a constitution for Hungary while Hungary was still unconquered, partly to the opposition of Windisch-Graetz, who wanted to put in a pseudo-feudal system of his own, and had even introduced it into those parts of Hungary which were under his control. It took painful argument before Schwarzenberg and Bach could talk him round, and when he gave way, time was pressing, for the Reichstag's Committee had completed its work and it was planned to call a plenary session to promulgate the result on 15 March, the anniversary of Ferdinand's promise to grant it.

The battle of Kápolna came just in time. It was not much of a victory, for the Hungarians, although retreating, had done so unmolested. But it was announced as heralding the end of the Hungarian resistance, and on the evening of 6 March Stadion appeared in Kremsier and told the leaders of the Reichstag that their labours had become otiose. The next morning a proclamation, dated the 4th, appeared announcing the dissolution of the Reichsrat on the ground that it had been wasting its time on 'dangerous theoretical discussions'. All Stadion could do for its members was to arrange that the most endangered of them should escape before the constables sent by Schwarzenberg to arrest them arrived. At the same time, the new constitution was promulgated.

The '1849' or 'Stadion' constitution, although it never came into force, has its place in history as having served as a basis for the later February Patent and the 'December Constitution'. It took over many ideas from the Kremsier draft, while omitting its more radical clauses. The Monarch's powers in respect of foreign affairs were virtually unlimited, except that the sanction of the Reichstag was required for foreign political commitments involving expenditure. He exercised the executive authority through 'responsible ministers': the legislative, 'jointly' (*im Vereine mit*) with the Reichstag, which consisted of an Upper House composed of representatives elected by the *Landtage* and a Lower House elected by direct suffrage. The consent both of the Monarch and of both houses was necessary for any law. In an emergency, if the Reichsrat was not in session, the Monarch could rule by Order in Council, but such orders had afterwards to be submitted to the Reichstag for retrospective sanction. The Monarch was advised by an 'Imperial Council' (*Reichsrat*) nominated by himself.

Below the Reichstag came the *Landtage*, Circles, Districts (*Bezirke*: an innovation introduced by Stadion) and the communes, each directed by a freely elected council, and each autonomous within its own field.

All citizens were equal before the law. The principle of international and inter-linguistic equality was repeated in the words of the Kremsier draft, except that the word 'guarantee' was omitted. A Patent applicable to the Austrian Lands only guaranteed their inhabitants freedom of conscience and of the private practice of their religions; the enjoyment of civil and political rights was irrespective of Confession. There was a further generous list of civic freedoms.

But the real significance of the constitution, besides its character of an *octroi*, lay in its pan-monarchic scope. The Monarch was to be crowned once only: as Emperor of Austria. There was to be only one citizenship, one legal system, and one central parliament. The

Monarchy was also to constitute a single customs unit; all internal tariffs were to be abolished.

To this unification and centralization there was one real exception, and one nominal one. Lombardy-Venetia was to receive a separate status, to be determined later. The constitution of Hungary was to remain in force provided that anything in it contrary to the new instrument was abolished, and equality of rights assured to every nationality and every local language in all fields of public and private life; a special statute was to regulate these questions.

As the document further reinstated the Military Frontier and divided the rest of Hungary into three 'Crownlands', the Kingdom, Transylvania (to which the *Partium* were reattached) and Croatia-Slavonia (to include Fiume and perhaps Dalmatia), while again promising the 'Serbian Voivody' 'suitable institutions', it might have been simpler to omit that sentence altogether.

There were three quarters from which hostile reactions to the March coup might be expected: the Austrian constitutionalists, Piedmont, and Hungary, and to these Schwarzenberg promptly added a fourth, by informing Frankfurt that he was now ready to negotiate a settlement of the German question, but on his own terms, which excluded any partition of the unitary Austrian State. Unofficially, it was intimated that Austria would consider a 'Directorate' under Austrian Presidency, the division of Germany into six 'Circles' of which Austria would constitute one, Prussia a second, and the smaller German States the other four. There would be a *Staatenhaus* in which each State would be represented proportionately to their populations, giving Austria 38 seats and the other German States, together, 32.

Three of these stories are quickly told. The unfortunate Charles Albert, believing that Napoleon would support him, denounced the armistice of Vigevano on 13 March. But France was not yet ready to help him, and did not do so. On 23 March the Piedmontese army was crushingly defeated by Radetzky at Novara. Charles Albert abdicated in favour of his son, Victor Emmanuel, who signed a fresh armistice on the 26th. The final peace was concluded on 6 August. Schwarzenberg asked for nothing more than confirmation of the change of rulers, and a small indemnity. In Frankfurt the *Bundestag*, its hand forced, decided by a majority to exclude Austria from the new Germany, the hereditary throne of which was to be offered to Prussia. Frederick William refused it, and that was the end of Frankfurt. The other important German States, following Austria's lead, withdrew their representatives, and the 'German question' resumed its familiar form of a competition between Austria and Prussia for the suffrages of the smaller States, most of which did not much want to be led by either of them.

Austria, many parts of which, including Vienna, Bohemia and Galicia, were under military regimes of one kind or another, did not stir at all. But Hungary was a different matter. In March and April the Hungarian armies drove the main Austrian forces, now commanded by General Welden (Schwarzenberg had found the courage to dismiss his brother-in-law) clean back to the Austrian frontier, and also won considerable successes in the south and Transylvania. Meanwhile, on 14 April, the Diet, assembled in the great Calvinist Church of Debrecen, had, on Kossuth's motion, proclaimed Hungary, including all its adjuncts, a completely independent State, deposing 'the perjured House of Habsburg-Lorraine' from its throne for ever. Kossuth was proclaimed 'Regent' pending the settlement of the future form of State, and appointed a new administration, under Szemere.

But the Hungarians had reached the high-watermark of their successes. When the Debrecen proclamation broke down the bridges, both sides looked abroad for help, and the Hungarians in vain. Liberal opinion in western Europe sympathized with them, but governments would not offend Austria for their sake. The Czar, on the other hand, had been assuring Francis Joseph ever since his accession of his willingness 'to help and advise him', and had concentrated a considerable army, under Paskiewicz, Duke of Warsaw, on the frontier of Galicia. He stipulated only that Vienna must ask for the help, and this Schwarzenberg, out of considerations of prestige, long hesitated to do. In April, however, his generals agreed that they could not win the campaign without the help. Schwarzenberg reluctantly withdrew his opposition and the request went off on 1 May. The Czar sent his orders within two hours of receiving it. Plans were quickly co-ordinated and in mid-June Russian armies, led by Paskiewicz, entered Hungary from the north and north-east, while an Austrian army commanded by Haynau, recalled from Italy, began a new advance south of the Danube.

Against the combined Austrian and Russian strength of 280,000 men (176,000 Austrians and 104,000 Russians) and 12,000 guns, the Hungarians could muster only 152,000 men with 450 guns. The end could be only a matter of time, and many Hungarians did not even want it delayed. A considerable number of deputies had disagreed with the deposition of the Habsburgs, and some of them formed themselves into a 'peace party', which would gladly have made terms with the Crown. Many officers, too, felt unable to stretch their oaths to cover obedience to the new regime. Görgey himself was known to have disliked the deposition, and Kossuth now looked on him with a suspicion to which he replied with resentment against the other man's meddling with military affairs. Nevertheless, he swallowed the proclamation, called on the army to fight on against the 'forsworn dynasty', and accepted the post of Minister of War in the new Government.

So Hungary fought on, and even won some successes, thanks to Kossuth's demoniac energy, and the tactical ability shown by Görgey, Bem and some of their lieutenants, notably Klapka, who held out grimly in the fortress of Komárom. But when the Diet reassembled at Szeged on 21 July, only one magnate was there to represent the Upper House, and many members of the Lower were absent, while of those who did attend, many did not conceal their hostility to Kossuth. An appeal for further volunteers brought no response. The armies were driven steadily back into the south-east of the country, where on 4 August the largest of them, Dembiński's, was crushingly defeated by the Russian force outside Temesvár. On the 11th Görgey told Kossuth that further resistance would be useless, and arranged for the transference of the supreme authority to himself. Kossuth, accompanied or followed by 4,000 adherents, fled to Turkey. At Világos, on the 13th, Görgey made both civil and military surrender to the Russian commander. Paskiewicz reported to the Czar: 'Hungary lies at the feet of Your Majesty.'

This was not entirely accurate, for a few fortresses still held out, the last of them, Komárom, until 1 October. But as early as 1 September, Haynau had felt himself justified in proclaiming the 'rebellion' at an end. Francis Joseph's authority was now established everywhere in his dominions, for Venice had capitulated on 22 August.

Reprisals followed against the 'rebellious' nation for the severity of which, although Haynau organized them, Francis Joseph must bear a big share of personal responsibility. Görgey had to be spared, on the Czar's personal intervention, but on 6 October thirteen Imperial officers who had served as generals in the Hungarian army were shot or hanged. Batthyány, who had tried to cut his own throat in prison, was shot on the same day. The Courts pronounced sentence of death on 231 more officers and many civilians. In all, 114 sentences were carried out, and nearly 2,000 persons sent to prison. There were 75 symbolic executions of men who had fled the country, including the later Minister President and Austro-Hungarian Foreign Minister Count Gyula Andrássy, sen. Men who had served in the *Honvédség* as junior officers or other ranks were conscripted into the Imperial army.

Nine

THE DECADE OF ABSOLUTISM

The ending of the fighting in Hungary and Italy left the German question as the Monarchy's only immediate international problem. A prolonged diplomatic duel with Prussia reached a temporary close in April 1851, when, at a conference in Dresden, each Power renounced its more ambitious hopes, Austria, of imposing the inclusion of the entire Monarchy in the new Germany, Prussia, of excluding it therefrom altogether. The *Bund* was, after all, renewed in its old form, while the two Powers signed a secret Treaty of Mutual Defence, initially valid for three years, but renewable.

Although Prussia resented this as a defeat, the real loser was Austria, for Prussia was left free to extend and solidify her leadership of the *Zollverein*, which was far more valuable than Austria's Presidency of the artificial protocol world of the *Bund*. But it gave Austria a breathing-space in which she could pursue the reorganization of her inner structure, as promised in the Stadion constitution.

It would be for the Reichstag to vote the laws implementing the provisions of the constitution, and that body could not be convoked until the return of normal conditions, but many of the ministries prepared 'provisional' enactments, some of which were put into immediate force where the situation allowed. A 'Communal Autonomy Law', drafted by Stadion, which provided for elected 'Communal' and District Councils with wide autonomy, was promulgated as early as 17 March 1849, and Stadion began also the drafting of statutes for the *Landtage*. Much of this work remained at the blue-print stage, for Stadion's reason gave way, and Bach, who took over the Interior in June, produced a revised measure which reduced the autonomy of the Communal Councils to a shadow, and suspended altogether the elections to the higher bodies. Some *Landtag* statutes were promulgated, but no elections were held: existing members were declared to be public servants, and vacancies were filled by appointment. Bach had, however, meanwhile carried through the corresponding reorganization of the judicial system, which confirmed the separation of the executive and the judiciary and established a hierarchy of Courts, the lowest of which, the District Courts, took over all their functions from the Manorial Courts, which were abolished. Schmerling, who took Bach's place as Minister of Justice, introduced many reforms,

including trial by jury for criminal and major civil offences, and
public and interlocutory examination of witnesses. A long series of
enactments introduced interlinguistic equality, as far as seemed
practicable. While German remained the inner language of administration, every citizen was entitled to use his own language in addressing the authorities, who were expected to reply in it, and officials
were enjoined to familiarize themselves with the local language. The
official Gazette was published in all the ten chief languages of the
Monarchy, every version being equally authentic, and other official
communications in the 'locally current' language or languages. The
same ruling applied to the judicial system.

A draft 'Statute of Education' issued in September 1849 by Thun,
since July of that year Minister of Education, and also, on his own
insistence, of Cults (i.e., questions relating to religion) laid down the
principle that primary instruction should be given in the pupil's
mother tongue, secondary and higher in that language 'subject to
need and possibility'. Some new schools in minority languages were
founded.

An important innovation of the period was the creation of a force,
at first consisting of thirteen battalions, of gendarmerie, which was
called into being by Bach, as one of his first acts, originally with the
much-needed purpose of maintaining public security in those areas
into which the short arms of the local police forces were unable to
reach.

Meanwhile, although the official extension of the constitution to
Lombardy-Venetia and Hungary was announced only on 2 December
1849, a 'Provisional Administrative System' for the former area had
been promulgated on 13 October. Radetzky was Military and Civilian Governor, with a civilian *ad latus* to assist him. Vienna reserved
for itself questions of taxation, but the local administrative, judicial
and educational systems were left broadly untouched. In the Hungarian Lands, the dismemberment announced in the constitution was
treated from the first as operative, and each constituent part received
its separate treatment, which in most of them had to be given in
stages. The Kingdom was in the autumn of 1849 still under the rule
of Haynau, whose plenipotentiary powers, conferred on him while he
was in charge of the military operations, had not been withdrawn
when they ended. Before that date, however, Baron Geringer, of the
Hungarian Court Chancellery, had been sent out to take charge of
the civilian side, as the representative of the Ministry of the Interior
in Vienna, and had quietly liquidated Windisch-Graetz's *extratour*,
and while the armies were still advancing, had extended to the hinterland areas behind their lines some of the measures being introduced

in the West. On 13 October, simultaneously with the parallel enactment in Lombardy-Venetia, a 'Provisorium' was issued for the Kingdom, which made Geringer 'Plenipotentiary Imperial Commissioner'
for internal affairs. For nearly a year his attempts to carry out Bach's
instructions made small progress, because Haynau, out of spite
against Bach, sabotaged the implementation of many of them, as
conflicting with his own plenipotentiary powers. In July 1850, however, that difficult man was, after a quarrel of ususual intensity with
his superiors, induced to retire, and on 1 September the first Provisorium, now nicknamed the 'Provisorissimum', was replaced by a
new one, which was much more severe than its predecessor, both in
its terms and the execution of them; for Geringer, himself a Transylvanian, had ridden with a loose rein, sparing his countrymen's susceptibilities as far as he could, and leaving most of the institutions,
and the holders of them, unless they had compromised themselves
hopelessly, untouched. In the second Provisorium, lip-service was
paid to the unity of what was left of the Kingdom by the appointment
of a Governor-General for the whole of it (this post was at first held
provisionally by Geringer, but given in October 1851 to the Archduke Albrecht) with a staff bearing the old name of *Consilium
Locumtenentiale*, but the Kingdom was divided into five Provinces,
the Governors of which corresponded directly with Vienna. German
was made the sole language of inner service, and all officials required
to pass a test in it, and the occasion was taken to dimiss any who
were thought politically unreliable. The gaps were filled, sometimes by
activist Magyar applicants (who, tempted by the good pay, came
forward in larger numbers than their later historians have always
admitted), sometimes by non-Magyar Hungarians – but the qualified
applicants from this quarter were thin on the ground – and for
the rest, by imported non-Hungarians, mostly Czechs or German
Bohemians. These 'Bach Hussars', as Széchenyi nicknamed them
after a pseudo-Hungarian uniform which Bach devised for them,
came to form a big majority in some departments, especially those of
finance.

All education above the primary level, where instruction was still
given in the pupil's mother-tongue, was now in German. The economic and fiscal unification with Austria was carried to completion,
and the assimilation of Hungarian law to Austrian begun. The whole
rule was, of course, purely dictatorial, and any symptoms of revolt
against it were severely repressed.

The system in Transylvania went through a similar evolution.
F.M.L. Wohlgemuth, who had been commanding the Austrian military forces there when hostilities ended, was at first left in charge,
with a civilian *ad latus*. When Wohlgemuth died, in April 1851,

Prince Carlos Schwarzenberg was made Military and Civilian Gover-
nor, and Transylvania was given its Provisorium. This gave the
Grand Principality a *Gubernium* equal in status to an Austrian Land,
and under this, sixteen *Bezirke* replaced the old Counties and Free
Districts. The Saxon 'University' was dissolved, and pleas from the
Roumanians to be given an autonomous territory were rejected.
German was made the sole language of administration, and of edu-
cation above the primary level.

A Patent for the Military Frontier, issued on 7 June 1850, put the
area back where it had belonged before 1848, and restored its internal
institutions with little modification. Otherwise the settlement of the
Southern Slav areas proved to be difficult, partly owing to the rival
territorial claims advanced by Rajačić and Jellačić, partly to the
extreme recalcitrance of both gentlemen even towards Vienna.

A 'Provisorium' issued on 18 November 1849 constituted the
civilian parts of the three Bánátal Counties, with the Hungarian
County of Bács-Bodrog and the two easternmost Districts of Srem, a
unit with the status of a Crownland, under the title of the 'Bánát and
Voivodina'. To mark its dignity Francis Joseph himself assumed the
title of Grand Voivode, but the Governor-Vice-Voivode, who exercised military and civilian authority, was an Austrian General.

The Croat 'Banal Council' delayed matters through the whole of
1849 by refusing to promulgate the constitution, on the grounds that
it violated Croatia's historic rights and ignored its historic claims.
On 7 April 1850, the goaded Government informed the Banal Council that it must accept the constitution and the frontiers given it, and
dissolved, first the Sabor, then the Banal Council, replacing the latter
by a *Gubernium* which had, indeed, no function beyond that of en-
suring the local execution of the orders sent down to it from Vienna.
At that stage, Croatia still enjoyed preferential treatment in that
Croat was still left as the language of official usage and of education,
but its turn came in January 1853, when all the 'Provisoria' in the
Lands of the Hungarian Crown were replaced by 'Definitiva'. These
changed their predecessors in the Kingdom, Transylvania and the
Voivodina only in minor respects, but brought Croatia into line with
the others. It was divided into six *Regierungsbetirke* (Government
Districts), each under a head nominated from Vienna. German replaced Croat as the language of administration and education, officials were examined in their knowledge of it, and those failing
to pass the test were replaced by equivalents, in this case mostly
Slovenes, of the Kingdom's Bach Hussars.

Jellačić had been created a Count, and left as Governor through all
the changes, although his functions had become little more than
decorative. He passed his few remaining years of lucidity (he died in

1859, victim to the disease which had carried off Stadion, and many others) chiefly in the composition of poetry.

By this time the Stadion constitution had ceased to exist. In October 1850 Francis Joseph instructed Kübeck to prepare draft statutes for the Reichsrat for which the constitution provided, and to suggest members for it. Then he told him that he was himself to preside over the body. Kübeck, whose ideas had changed greatly since his progressive youth, seized his opportunity and submitted proposals which attacked the very roots of the constitutional principle. He argued that responsibility belonged to the Monarch alone, and his proposals amounted, broadly, to the reinstatement, throughout the Monarchy, of the Austrian *status quo ante* 1848 under a new nomenclature. The Ministerial Council was to be abolished. All proposals from ministers, who would in effect sink to the position of the old heads of *Hofstellen*, would be sent to the Reichsrat, itself a simple rehash of the old *Staatsrat*, on the basis of whose reports the Monarch would take his own decision.

The Reichsrat was called into being in April 1851, but prolonged and acrid argumentation, in the course of which Schmerling and Bruck resigned,[1] went on over the question of competence between Kübeck and the ministers, some of whom genuinely wanted a parliament to which the ministry would be responsible, while others disliked the breach of faith. On 17 August Francis Joseph, to whom the idea of his own sole personal responsibility appealed strongly, decided in principle in favour of Kübeck, but partly out of consideration for foreign opinion, partly out of personal regard for Schwarzenberg, refrained from taking the logical sequel which Kübeck urged on him of abolishing the post of Minister President and the institution of a Ministerial Council. Consequently, while Philipp Krausz also resigned, although remaining in office provisionally, the other ministers, to Kübeck's malicious enjoyment, did not follow his example, and the Ministerial Council remained in existence.

Then Louis Napoleon's coup in Paris of 2 November removed one of Francis Joseph's hesitations, and on 31 December he promulgated the documents usually known as the 'Sylve ter Patent'. This consisted actually of three Rescripts, the first of which cancelled the March constitution, except that the provisions relating to equality before the law and the abolition of the peasants' servitudes remained in force. The second annulled the 'fundamental rights' guaranteed to the peoples of Austria in the constitution, except that all 'recognized' churches were still guaranteed freedom of worship and the enjoyment and management of their own property. The third cancelled all measures, except those mentioned above, which owed their origin, directly or indirectly, to the revolution (a list of these had been drawn up by a committee, under the presidency of Kübeck, which had laboriously gone through the public law of the Monarchy, dividing the sheep from the goats) and described in outline what was to take their place. The victims of the axe included the principles of 'freedom of national development' and of inter-national and inter-linguistic equality, together with almost all the surviving institutions which still bore any vestige of popular origin or allowed for any trace of popular representation; even almost all of Schmerling's judicial reforms. The *Landtage* were abolished; the entire authority in each Land was vested, under the ministry, in the head of its *Gubernium*, except that the former Estates were allowed to administer some local funds, and that the great landlords and representatives of 'industry' were allowed to supply two 'advisers' each to the Governor. The *Bezirke* were retained, but Stadion's separate administrative and judicial *Bezirke* were replaced by 'Mixed Districts' in charge of both administration and justice on the lowest levels. The only bodies to survive which were not composed entirely of officials were the Communal Councils, and their members, if elected (which was not always the case) had to be approved by officialdom. The large allodial estates could be removed from the authority of the Commune and placed directly under that of the *Bezirk* or the 'Circle'.

The Patent did not sweep the floor quite clean. But on 5 April, Schwarzenberg died suddenly. Francis Joseph appointed a new Foreign Minister, in the person of Count Buol-Schauenstein (to whom, however, he made it clear that the supreme decisions in foreign policy lay with himself), but abolished the post of Minister President, and the institution of the Ministerial Council. His absolute authority was now entirely unrestricted. The ministers continued to meet weekly in 'conference', but only in order to enable them to co-ordinate their policies where some subject fell within the competence of more than one of them. The minutes of their meetings were sent up to the Monarch, as sources of information for him. The Reichsrat was still entitled to offer him 'advice', but he was not bound to take it, and it soon became as much of a fifth wheel as the old *Staatsrat*, whose cumbersome procedure it inherited, had been. While Kübeck lived, Francis Joseph often consulted him, *qua* reputed financial and administrative wizard, but not *qua* President of the Reichsrat. When Kübeck died in 1856, Francis Joseph gave his succession to the Archduke Rainer, *fils*, but this was for the purpose of grooming him for the succession, should his own marriage produce no heir, or deputy in his absence; the Archduke's training consisted chiefly in sitting in on the meetings of the ministerial conference. When Francis Joseph did feel need of advice, he asked it where he thought best. The three persons who influenced him most in these years were probably his mother, his old tutor, Rauscher, and the man who, when he mounted the throne, had been his Head Court Chamberlain, Colonel, as he then was, Count von Grünne, who came to exert over him an influence comparable to that exercised over the young Francis I by Colloredo, and similar in nature; for Grünne, like Colloredo, combined devotion to his young master with extreme conservatism and outstanding intellectual limitations.

In 1853 von Csorich resigned, and Francis Joseph left his portfolio, too, unfilled. There was to be no intermediate instance between himself and 'his' army. He made Grünne first head of his Military Chancellery, then his Adjutant General, and thus competent, under the Monarch himself, for all military questions; Minister of War in everything but name. By this time certain other ministerial changes had been effected. When Philipp Krausz's resignation became effective, on 31 January 1851, Baumgartner took over his portfolio, in addition to his own. In 1852 Külmer's ministry was wound up, as superfluous; and in 1853, von Thinnfeld resigned, and the business of his ministry was divided between those of Bach and Baumgartner. There were thus left four titular ministers: Buol, Bach, Baumgartner and Thun, with two quasi-ministers, Grünne and another, for in January 1852, Francis Joseph had, to Bach's extreme annoyance, taken the control of the gendarmerie from him and given it to F.M.L. von Kempen, then, under the still existing martial law, Military Governor of Vienna. The gendarmerie was then combined with the police in a single organization, under von Kempen, who ranked only as head of a *Hofstelle*, but reported direct to the Monarch.

The results achieved by the various departments during the first years of Francis Joseph's near-absolutist, then absolutist, rule, were, judged by any standard, impressive: for good or ill, they altered the face of the Monarchy more radically than had the whole half-century of Francis's and Ferdinand's reigns.

The biggest transformation of all was on the land. The abolition of the *nexus subditelae* had, as we have seen, ante-dated the Sylvester Patent, and survived its issue. Under the 'land reform' which followed, every holder of any plot, however small, which ranked as 'urbarial' (a minimum of a quarter *sessio* in Austria or an eighth in Hungary) became its owner in freehold, gratis in the Hungarian Lands and Galicia-Bukovina, and elsewhere, against a small payment, spread over twenty years. Compensation to the ex-landlord for his assessed loss in dues and services rendered to him in that capacity, but not for the loss of his other perquisites, was made to him in 4 per cent bonds, paid out of a fund composed partly of the peasants' payments, partly of Land or State taxation. There was no automatic distribution to non-urbarial peasants, but emphyteutical peasants and some other categories received facilities to buy in their holdings on advantageous terms.

No statistics for the total result of this operation, which took many years to complete, were ever published, and those good for one Land are not necessarily true for another, but it can be said, roughly, that it ended in leaving about two thirds of the land cultivated as arable, vineyards or leys in the hands of peasant proprietors, who constituted about the same proportion of the total agricultural population. Most of the other third, with most of the forests and other less accessible areas, remained in the hands of the State or of large private landowners, individual or corporate, and there were also very extensive common lands.

It is not easy to strike the economic balance-sheet of this vast operation. It certainly conferred great benefits on the thrifty and enterprising ex-villein, especially if his holding was situated near a market, and in an area where credit was not too difficult to obtain. But even for such a man, the picture contained shadows. Loss of easements and countervailing benefits enjoyed under the old landlord-peasant relationship – these had been larger than the peasants admitted, or perhaps even realized – inexperience in money economy and difficulty in obtaining credit – almost unobtainable for the small man, except at usurious rates (which were, indeed, illegal, but current) – made existence difficult even for quite intelligent and hard-working men. In the backward parts of the Monarchy the peasants were not money-minded at all. Their reaction to their liberation was simply to grow enough for their own subsistence and then go to sleep, and when the tax-collector came round they had, after all, to hire themselves out to their old masters.

Similarly with the landlords. Some of the Bohemian and Hungarian magnates were able to use their compensation, which was paid promptly and often amounted to very large sums, in developing their estates into efficient and profitable enterprises. For the smaller land-lords, especially in Galicia and Hungary, who had not owned the capital to employ hired labour and had thus really depended on the *robot*, the loss of it was a sheer disaster, especially since they were often made to wait for years for their compensation. Many members of this class were ruined. Their lands were bought up by richer neighbours, either directly or after passing through the hands of Jewish speculators, who operated for some years so extensively that in 1853 a Rescript was issued through the Ministry of Finance forbidding Jews to own real estate, a step which, as we shall see, had important later consequences for the State.

The land reform was an inter-departmental operation. If we turn to the work for which one department was wholly or mainly responsible, it is fitting to begin with that of Bach, who was Francis Joseph's right-hand man for almost all domestic questions: it was not without reason that later generations often described the years 1849–59 as the 'Bach era'. Yet in some respects, his work was more ephemeral than that of any other minister: his political organization of the Hungarian Lands hardly survived the decade, and what he did in the West was afterwards remodelled repeatedly.

Even while it lasted, his regime east of the Leitha probably did not produce results quite so satisfactory as have been claimed for it by most non-Hungarian historians, who do not tire of praising the efficiency and incorruptibility of the Bach Hussars. We have the Archduke Albrecht's own testimony that not all of them constituted any sort of an elite, and they must at best have been heavily handicapped by their ignorance of the local language and *mores*. But the fact that the Hungarian government of 1867 kept on many of them (see p. 212) shows that the encomia cannot have been entirely undeserved, and it is certain that in the Austrian Lands, too, Bach, who was a first-class administrator, did much to raise both the efficiency of the services controlled by him, and their own conditions.

The same is to be said of the new judiciary. Purely authoritarian, as the Patent had left the system, it was noticeably more efficient than the old Manorial Courts, whose proceedings had not always borne any very close resemblance to the law. The large-scale modernization of the Hungarian legal and judicial systems brought improvements recognized even by Hungarian historians.

Von Kempen was at any rate efficient. A very ambitious man, he expanded the force under his command into a great organization, much larger than that which Sedlnitzky had controlled, and more vigilant. The numerous spies whom it employed were paid by results, and flooded both police and gendarmerie posts with denunciations which resulted in many arrests. The censorship of the Press was also very severe, and when it is remembered that on top of this, martial law was not lifted from Vienna and Prague until September 1853, from most of the rest of the Monarchy only in 1854, and from Transylvania not until 1855, it will be appreciated that whatever were the benefits brought by the absolute rule, freedom was not among them.

Bruck's first tasks had been to initiate the fiscal and economic unification of the Monarchy. This was completed by July 1851, when the last remains of the Austro-Hungarian customs line vanished, and the extension to Hungary of the Austrian system of taxation, direct and indirect, had been completed. The unification should have been followed by the creation, of which it was the essential preliminary, of the 'seventy million Reich'. The Dresden

Agreements had put paid to these larger hopes, and economic
negotiations with several German States brought no immediate
results, but in connection with them Bruck began preparations, which
Baumgartner carried on after Bruck's resignation, for a large-scale
liberation of the Monarchy's economy. The import prohibitions
disappeared altogether, except for a few maintained on moral or
medical grounds, and the number and height of tariff duties were
reduced sharply. Further reductions were made in a commercial
treaty concluded in 1853 with Prussia, and thus with the rest of the
Zollverein.

Bruck also created a network of Chambers of Commerce and
Industry (the only form of popular representation to survive the
Sylvester Patent), reorganized the postal services, developed shipping, and pushed on the expansion of the railways, which were
nationalized as far as possible: all new lines were constructed at
State expense and run as State enterprises, and the privately owned
lines were bought out as occasion presented itself.

It was partly thanks to Bruck and Baumgartner that the early
1850s were, on balance, a period of prosperity for the Monarchy's
industry, and as corollary thereof, its trade – although the prosperity was not evenly distributed over its area, or among its classes.
In these a similar polarization took place as on the land. The weak
were driven back against the wall. After the fiscal unification many
of the smaller Hungarian entrepreneurs were driven out of the field
by Austrian competition, and the reduction of tariffs with Germany
even ruined some Austrian industries. But entrepreneurs possessed
of the resources, enterprise and intelligence to take advantage of the
new freedom and wider opportunities benefited substantially. The
stronger Austrian industries gained more from the opening up of the
Hungarian market than they lost from the weak Hungarian competition. Some industries, including the textile, were also at that time
stronger than their counterparts in the *Bund*. Both textiles and
woollens enjoyed a prolonged boom, while heavy industry received a
big stimulus from the expansion of the railways. And while the lion's
share of the gains went to the Bohemian Lands and Lower Austria,
Hungary, too, profited from the better communications and from
the disappearance of the *aviticitas* and other restrictions on credit.
Further, many Austrian capitalists turned their attention to Hungary,
because of its cheap labour; the same years which witnessed the
destruction of some Hungarian industries saw a rapid expansion of
others, such as flour-milling and brewing.

The industrial development would have been still faster had Austria
not been suffering from an acute attack of its chronic shortage of
mobile capital. Threats of mob violence had driven Salomon Roths-

child from Vienna in 1848, and for some years thereafter his house
had boycotted the Monarchy. Its absence left a gap which no one
seemed able to fill. The National Bank, under Kübeck's direction,
confined its operations almost exclusively to Government business,
and it was not until 1855 that it opened a mortgage branch, but even
this made very few advances. In 1853 the Eskeles opened a private
bank, the *Niederösterreichische Eskomptogesellschaft*, which, however, operated only on a relatively small scale. It was only in 1856
that the situation in this field changed, in the fashion described on
page 142.

Among the weak, both the factory workers and the small craftsmen
had to be counted. The former class lost all the gains (which had
never been statutory) made by them in 1848, leaving hours and conditions of work entirely unregulated, and wages dependent on supply
and demand, which, fortunately for them, was usually good. The
guilds, thanks to the protection afforded them by the Church, survived the decade, but the craftsmen were continually on the defensive,
and their complaints of the competition of sweated factory labour
were as bitter as before 1848.

Thun was the odd man out in the ministry. A great aristocrat, a
convinced champion of provincial rights, a strong Czechophile, a
dyed-in-the-wool feudalist, as well as a fanatical clerical, he represented in all these respects except the last—and even there, there
was a difference of degree—the antipole to the absolutist-bureaucratic
spirit of Kübeck and Bach, and even of Stadion, and in so far as
the political philosophies for which he stood were not completely
shouldered aside during the decade, and were able to emerge at the
end of it, not as masters of the field, but as a powerful force in it, this
was due mainly to his tenacious championship of them.

In his own department Thun had the good fortune to find a band
of exceptionally keen and able assistants, who carried through reforms, based on Prussian models, of the secondary and higher educational systems of the Monarchy, on which later ministers, down to
1918, found little to improve. Less was done for primary education,
partly owing to technical difficulties, partly to Thun's lack of enthusiasm for it.

He was more interested in the other side of his portfolio, where,
indeed, the great issue involved, that of Church–State relations, went
beyond the competence of a departmental minister. As early as
January 1849, a group of Austrian ecclesiastics headed by Rauscher
and the Minister President's brother, Cardinal Schwarzenberg, had
begun pressing Francis Joseph to abolish all Joseph II's ecclesiastical
enactments, this to be followed by the conclusion of a Concordat.
Negotiations, which were conducted from the Austrian side chiefly

by Rauscher, proved to be difficult. since some of the Vatican's
demands were more than most of the Austrians, including even
Rauscher (Thun was the exception) could easily accept. But the
Vatican showed itself to be the tougher of the parties, and a Concordat was eventually signed on 2 August 1855, which confirmed
and extended a package of interim concessions made on Francis
Joseph's personal insistence in 1850, and so met the Vatican's wishes
almost *in toto*. The Roman Catholic religion, with all its rights and
prerogatives, was to be 'maintained for ever' in the whole Monarchy
and all its components. Its property was declared sacrosanct and
inviolable, and the funds derived from Maria Theresa's and Joseph's
confiscations were transferred to its keeping. The *Placetum Regium*
was abolished. There was to be complete freedom of communication
between the Holy See and the Austrian bishoprics. The freedom of
the Church in ordering its affairs, including the disciplinary jurisdiction of the bishops over their clergy, was confirmed, as was its
jurisdiction in all questions relating to the faith and its observance,
including questions of marriage law, and it became almost solely
competent for all teaching in Catholic schools, and for instruction
given to Catholic children in any school. The Emperor promised not
to tolerate any utterance derogatory to the Church, or its faith or
institutions. He also promised in a secret annexe not to change any
Confessional or inter-Confessional law without previous consent of
the Holy See. A supplementary Patent on marriage law made the
ecclesiastical Courts competent also in this field where both parties
were Catholics, or one a Catholic and the other a Protestant. A bishop
was empowered to veto a marriage 'if he feared that it would give
rise to serious discussion, offence, or other scandal'.

After Buol, who hardly took a right decision in all his career, the
most mistaken of all Francis Joseph's choices of servants was probably Grünne. It is true that Grünne's hands were always tied by
financial shackles, but the lamentable showing made by the Monarchy's armed forces in 1859 was due largely to his personal limitations. In his eyes, high social rank qualified its possessor for high
military command. The senior posts in the army, which were his
direct responsibility, were, with few exceptions, distributed between
members of great families, lacking alike in professional knowledge,
experience in the field (Grünne himself had never smelt powder) and
capacity. The money squandered on these appointments, the number
of which was doubled, was made up by cutting the allocations for
equipment, and a considerable amount of the sums spent on these
objects went, as afterwards transpired, into the pockets of unscrupulous contractors. The training of the troops consisted almost entirely

of spit and polish; there was little field training, and hardly any
manœuvres at all.

A problem which since 1849 chronically resisted solution was that
of the Monarchy's finances. Expenditure on the new civil services
rose year by year, and military expenditure, although slightly lower
in 1851 than in 1850, was still far above the pre-1848 level. Large
sums were also being spent on the railways. When Baumgartner took
over the portfolio in 1852, the downward curve seemed to be flat-
tening out, and he hoped that the National Bank would be able to
resume convertibility if the State paper money was withdrawn. Early
in 1854 he reached an agreement with the Bank that it should take
over all State-issued paper money and exchange it gradually for its
own notes, the Government promising to repay the debt (of 155
million gulden) by instalments, and once again pledging itself to issue
no more paper: but as we shall see, this promise soon proved as
worthless as its predecessors.

One more event of this first lustrum calls for recording. In 1853
the Emperor's mother invited her sister, Ludovica, wife of Duke
Maximilian of Bavaria, to stay with the family at Ischl. She was to
bring with her her elder daughter, Helena, who, as the sisters planned,
was to become Francis Joseph's bride. But Helena's younger sister,
Elisabeth, a young girl of only sixteen, came with the party. Francis
Joseph lost his heart to her on sight, and insisted that she, and she
alone, should be his bride. They were married on 24 April 1854, the
pompous ceremony inaugurating a tragic human relationship in
which Francis Joseph's love, deep, enduring and suprisingly romantic
in such a pedestrian nature, was constantly thwarted by his preoccupation with his duties, Elisabeth's inexperience, and above all,
the jealous bossiness of her intolerable mother-in-law.

The ultimate question for the Monarchy was whether its peoples
could be brought to accept sincerely absolutist rule and—more fundamental still—the ideology of the a-national State. During these first
years the prospects in the Hereditary and Bohemian Lands seemed
to be not unfavourable. The bourgeoisie of Vienna were, on the whole,
too happy to see the spectre of red revolution banished to mind anything else. A few initial grumblings from Liberal circles against the
authoritarian character of the Stadion constitution soon died away
and the Sylvester Patent evoked hardly a murmur. Easily the most
unpopular innovation in these circles, and beyond them, was the
Concordat. To the German-Austrian provincials, on the other hand,
the linked domination of Church and State was as congenial as it was
familiar. The workers were silent, the peasants everywhere occupied
in consolidating their gains.

The open reactions among the non-Germans of the Alpine and

Bohemian Lands to disappointed national hopes were astonishingly
weak. We hear of no national unrest at all among the Slovenes. The
Czech leaders protested against the dissolution of the Reichstag, but
it was not long before they, too, had accepted the inevitable. Palacký
withdrew from active politics for a decade. Rieger went into voluntary
exile. The nationalists were defeated in the local elections of 1850 by
moderates who favoured collaboration with the regime. Altogether,
once the initial unrest had passed, Bohemia became one of the
quietest areas of the Monarchy. For this, economic factors were
largely responsible. Bohemia enjoyed the full benefits of the boom,
which brought its business classes prosperity and its workers at least
full employment, and there were outlets in plenty for the aspiring
men, for any of whom, if he could find no place at home, a job was
waiting in Hungary, or in the gendarmerie, which was largely composed of Czechs. There is no indication that the youth of Bohemia
showed any reluctance during these years to learn enough German to
qualify for these jobs. When Havlíček, the most single-minded of
them all, returned from the exile in Brixen to which a court had
sentenced him, his most painful impression was that 'the reaction is
in ourselves, and chiefly in ourselves'.

In Galicia, economic conditions were less favourable and discontent longer-lived, but Goluchowski gradually gathered round him
adherents to his policy of activism. Most important of all, he persuaded considerable numbers of his fellow-countrymen to enter the
Government service, finding places for them by evicting the former
German or Czech officials, so that the administration of Galicia was
becoming mainly Polish. The bill for this was, as usual, paid by the
Ruthenes, who had had to lay aside all hopes of administrative
concessions: even their *Rada* (council) was made to dissolve itself
in 1851, whereupon the Old Ruthenes retired into 'passivity'. The
other Ruthene factions were too weak and too disunited to constitute
even a serious nuisance value.

This acceptance of the ruling orders did not, however, extend
either to Lombardy-Venetia or to Hungary. It is true that there was
only one really serious outbreak in the former province – a rising in
Milan in 1853, which was put down with great severity. The country
was too full of soldiers and spies for disaffection – for which, moreover, the stimulus of official foreign encouragement was lacking – to
organize or manifest itself on a large scale. But the great bulk of the
population, at least above the peasant level, regarded the Austrian
regime as one of foreign domination, and hateful at that.

The shades of opinion in Hungary were innumerable. Irrecon-
cilables *a limine* still looked to the exiled Kossuth, who had himself not given up the struggle. Released in October 1851, through

the good offices of western sympathizers, from the internment in Anatolia that had been his previous lot since his escape from Hungary, he had toured England and the United States, and had received in both countries enormous personal ovations which showed that his country's cause enjoyed wide sympathy in the world. He had, however, been unable to persuade either Government to take it up officially. Now settled in London, he was continuing untiringly his efforts to keep the spirit of resistance alive in his homeland, and commanded enough devoted adherents there to cause the authorities constant anxiety, besides very many more who would have obeyed his call had it promised success. But his following was not nation-wide. As we have said, the extreme course taken by him in 1849, especially the dethronement of the dynasty, had not been universally popular, and after Világos many good Hungarians had hoped and even expected the ending of the hostilities to be followed by a new reconciliation between the nation and the Crown. This hope had not been extinguished by Haynau's reign of terror – generals are, after all, expected to be bloody-minded – and had been kept alive during the 'Provisorissimum' by the lenient character of that dispensation, as administered by Geringer, and by its admittedly provisional character. The Old Conservatives, encouraged as they were by Windisch-Graetz's flirtation with them, had been quite optimistic of persuading Francis Joseph to their prescription of a 'return to '47'. A great disillusionment set in after the issue of the second Pro-visorium, which was rightly taken as signifying the Crown's inten-tion of making the subjection and the dismemberment of Hungary permanent. Thereafter there were few Hungarians, active time-servers and place-seekers apart, who regarded the position as truly tolerable. There seemed, however, no immediate course but to wait for time to bring about a change.

The mass of middle opinion, which would have welcomed an honourable compromise, had in these years no leader, for Deák, who was afterwards to point the way, was sitting silent in his country-home and no one had taken his place. Neither did they receive any encouragement from the other side. Francis Joseph made an extended tour of the Hungarian Lands in 1852. An amnesty was enacted, and honours and decorations were distributed lavishly. The Monarch's marriage in 1854 was celebrated similarly, and martial law lifted. But while these were gestures that did something to al-leviate the national hostility, they did nothing to remedy the causes of it.

The biggest disappointment to the Crown was that this hostility was not confined to the ruling Magyar classes, from whom it had been expected. The peasants persisted in attributing their liberation to Kossuth, while seeing the hand of Vienna in the higher price of tobacco. The Slovak nationalists found that they had after all got little more out of Vienna than out of Pest, and their Lutherans shared the religious grievances of the Magyar Calvinists. The Serbs, who instead of the anticipated self-governing Province, had been given a Department ruled absolutely, in which there were actually more Germans and Roumanians than Serbs, whereas half the Serbs of Hungary were left outside its frontiers, were soon wondering whether they would not have done better to make terms with Hungary after all. In Transylvania the Saxons and the Roumanians were solid in opposing reunion with Hungary, but both communities were bitterly disappointed with their new condition: the Saxons at the abolition of their autonomy, the Roumanians at refusals to grant them recognition as a 'nation'. The Croats found the yoke of the imported foreign officials as heavy as the Hungarians did: all the books quote the remark of a Croat to a Hungarian friend: 'We have got as reward what you have been given as punishment.' Francis Joseph's reception in Croatia during his tour was so cold that it had to be cut short on grounds of security.

Meanwhile the international scene had become threatening again. In 1853 the Czar began to hint to Francis Joseph his intention of renewing Russia's advance into the Balkans. He persisted in his intentions, in spite of Francis Joseph's warnings and remonstrances, and in July sent his armies into Moldavia and Wallachia. The Porte declared war in October, and England and France followed suit in March 1854. The situation thus created was most painful and difficult for Francis Joseph, caught between his obligation of gratitude to the Czar and the obvious threat to the Monarchy's vital interests presented by his actions. In 1853 and 1854 Austria sent considerable forces to the southern and eastern frontiers, and after Russia had evacuated the Danubian Principalities, herself sent an occupation force into them. In December Francis Joseph actually concluded an alliance with the western belligerents (in return for a promise from Louis Napoleon to respect the *status quo* in Italy), but refused to take the final step of war, although Austria participated in the Paris Conference of March 1856, which excluded Russia from the Danube, but left her own frontiers unchanged.

The meagreness of this result disappointed the 'forward party' in Austria itself (which included Buol), who had wanted Austria to take the Danubian Provinces for herself, and both belligerents were angry with her for not having actively taken their side. Hindsight may well find excuse, and even justification, for the vacillations and half-heartedness of Austria's policy, but the fact remained that the end of the war left her international position considerably worse than before. The new Czar of Russia was bitterly disappointed with and hostile to his father's protégé. Never again could Francis Joseph hope for such help as Nicholas had given him in Hungary in 1849, or against Prussia in 1850. Prussia had taken offence at a diplomatic error made by Buol in negotiating the alliance with the Western Powers. Napoleon was vexed at Austria's refusal to declare war, and Piedmont had gained the confidence and prestige which marked her out as the future nucleus of a united Italy. An alliance between her and France could now only be a matter of time.

The crisis also put paid to Austria's hopes of early financial recovery. That she had kept out of war at all in 1854, and had remained mobilized only for a few months, had been due mostly to Baumgartner's insistence that she could not afford a campaign. Even so the costs of arming and mobilization and of the occupation had sent her military budget rocketing up again, and the premium on silver rose further. The Government attached extreme importance to wiping the premium out, but it would clearly not vanish until the National Bank had recovered at least part of the Government's debt to it. The big foreign financial houses refused to help, partly out of resentment against the enactment forbidding Jews to buy real property in Austria; in particular the Rothschilds refused any further help to Baumgartner, whom they held responsible for the measure. In June 1854, accordingly, a great internal loan of five hundred million gulden, the largest in Austrian history, was floated for the express purpose of paying off the debt to the bank. The money was brought in, with the help of heavy official pressure, but almost all of it was promptly swallowed up by the army, so that the debt to the bank was left undiminished.

Now the State changed its policy over the railways, first renouncing the construction of new lines in favour of concessionnaires, then offering its own lines for sale. A few of these had been bought by the Paris House of Pereire, when, in 1855, Baumgartner resigned in despair. Bruck, brought back, attacked the problem with his usual energy. Military expenditure was cut down, taxation raised and the sale of the railways pressed on until nearly all the most important of them, including the Lombardy-Venetian line and the (still incomplete) Südbahn linking Vienna with Trieste, had passed into private hands. The price received for them was far below the costs of construction, but nonetheless made it possible for the State to repay its debt to the Bank, which was now able to bring the discount on silver down to a figure which enabled it to resume convertibility on 28 September 1858. The budgetary deficits, although not wiped out, sank to a less alarming figure.

In connection with the sale of the railways, Bruck had meanwhile achieved the memorable feat of reconciling Austria with the Rothschilds, who were nervous of being cut out by the Pereires, both over the railways and in wider fields (their rivals were planning to open a branch of the Credit Mobilier in Vienna). To carry through this operation the Rothschilds themselves, under Bruck's patronage, and with the co-operation of a group of high Bohemian magnates, who were seeking investments for the sums received by them under the land reform, opened a 'Privileged' bank, the *Creditanstalt*, a grandiose institution which thereafter, to the end of our story and beyond it, occupied in the Monarchy a position analogous to that of England's 'Big Five' together. The immediate effect of the opening of the *Creditanstalt* was the gratifying one of a hectic boom; its long-term effects were less pleasing, but politically very important. For the boom soon ended; in 1857 the great Stock Exchange crisis, travelling eastward from New York via London and Paris, reached Vienna, ruining many small speculators and forcing the Rothschilds themselves to draw in their horns. And by now the financiers, domestic and foreign, were such heavy creditors, direct or indirect, of the State that their interest in its solvency was vital. Thus, as in the *Vormärz*, a powerful movement arose which demanded, for economic-financial reasons, constitutional control over governmental expenditure. Its chief representatives were, indeed, no longer quite the same as the leaders of the *Leseverein;* it was no accident that the first promises made by the Government after 1859 included 'regulation of the position of the Israelites along modern lines'. But it was an opposition which found itself in natural alliance with the other forces fretting against the absolutist system.

The chief foci of these forces were, as before, Hungary and Italy, and in both of them, hostility to the regime grew rather than diminished after 1856. Kossuth was indeed, slipping down into the ranks of the professional émigré. There had been quarrels among his followers, and many of these had accepted the amnesty and returned to Hungary. But the potential rebels were still strong enough to necessitate the stationing there of a large garrison (which spent much of its time collecting unpaid taxation) and the moderate opposition was now drawing heart from the inflexible courage of Deák, who in 1854 had emerged from his geographical and political retirement, moved to Pest, and become the centre of a rapidly increasing circle. Deák's political philosophy was one of elemental simplicity: that law duly enacted was law, and binding. Both the Pragmatic Sanction and the April Laws came under that definition: the existing regime did not, and could not legally command obedience.

At this juncture he was not making this a programme, nor even

enunciating it outside a circle of close friends, but he steadfastly
refused to associate himself with any compromise solution incompatible with his philosophy, and persisted as steadfastly that it would
be unnecessary to do so, since time would bring the victory to
Hungary. Francis Joseph, on his side, was not yet ready to listen to
any voice whatever from Hungary. In 1857 he made another tour
of the country, accompanied in its first stages by his wife, enacted
another amnesty, and restored some confiscated estates. But, still
convinced that his cause was winning, he refused to depart by a
hair's breadth from his principles, and to make his position clear,
appeared in the uniform of.an Austrian field-marshal, and ordered
that the streamers hung out to welcome him should be black and
gold. The trip did more harm than good, and matters were aggravated when his entourage found ways of preventing the presentation
to him of a Memorandum, signed by 227 leaders of Hungarian
society, asking again, in the most loyal terms, for the restoration of
the *status quo ante* 1848. The snub further discredited the petitioners,
who felt that there was no point in compromising on 1848 when the
Crown was unwilling to concede anything at all. The gainer was
Deák, who had refused to associate himself with the move.

A tour which Francis Joseph had made with Elisabeth in
Lombardy-Venetia had been less positively disastrous, but again full
of unpleasantness: projected balls, for instance, had had to be cancelled because the Italian ladies had refused to dance with Austrian
officers. Here, too, there had been concessions: another amnesty,
and Radetzky, now in his ninety-second year, had been replaced
as Governor by Francis Joseph's brother, the mild and affable
Maximilian. But it was not the feelings of the Emperor's Italian
subjects that mattered. Mazzini, now in exile in Paris, said frankly:
'We do not want Austria to mend her ways in Italy; we want her to
get out of it.' It is recorded that Cavour actually asked his friends 'if
they could, to force Austria to reimpose the state of siege'.

And by a very short time after Mazzini spoke, the preparations to
achieve the end desired by him were well under way. In July 1858
Cavour and Napoleon reached secret agreement that Cavour was to
devise a 'respectable' pretext for war against Austria, after which
Italy was to be constituted as a Federation of four States: North
Italy, under the House of Savoy, the Papal States, the Kingdom of
the Two Sicilies and a new Kingdom of Central Italy. A calculated
indiscretion by Napoleon on New Year's Eve gave advance notifi-
cation of the new allies' intentions, and Piedmont began to arm
ostentatiously.

Austria was in no state to meet the challenge. Her armies were
under strength, and above all, ill-equipped. The former deficiency

could be made good after a fashion, but to remedy the latter, money
was required, and it was not there. There was widespread resistance
to the tax-collectors at home, especially in Hungary, and efforts by
Bruck to raise the wind abroad brought in only nugatory sums, while
sending the course of Austrian State papers plunging down again.
The domestic holders of the money-bags, who disapproved of the
war, were equally close-fisted. Bruck insisted that there was hardly
money for a large-scale mobilization, let alone a prolonged campaign. It seemed probable that Napoleon would intervene, and it was
known that he and Cavour were in touch with Kossuth and Klapka;
Hungary might rise. The attitudes of Britain and Russia were
uncertain.

Francis Joseph however, while, unlike Buol, he expected Napoleon
to intervene, thought that it would be possible to contain an attack on
the Rhine (where it was expected) with an Austrian army reinforced
by contingents from the Reich, on which he proposed to call under
Bund law. A Crown Council early in April decided that it might be
possible to crush Piedmont by a swift, and thus relatively inexpen-
sive, attack; for this four of Austria's twelve army corps would be
needed (the number was later raised to five); one would have to be
left behind in Hungary, and the rest would be held in reserve for use
on the Rhine. In the next days, an envoy from Berlin brought the
news that Prussia would not move except on conditions which would
have meant another long retreat by Austria from the leadership of
Germany. Francis Joseph was not deterred by this, nor by the dis-
appointing attitudes of Britain and Russia. He sent the Archduke
Albrecht to Berlin to try to talk the Prince Regent over, and even
before the Archduke's return, another Crown Council, on the 19th,
decided to delay no longer. An ultimatum was dispatched to Piedmont to reverse her military preparations within three days. If she
refused, Austria would attack. F.M.L. Gyulai, the senior Austrian
officer serving in Italy, was put in charge of the operation.

Everything went wrong. Prussia repeated her refusal. Napoleon
announced that he would regard the crossing of the Ticino by
Austrian armies as an act of war against France, and even before
Piedmont's expected rejection of the ultimatum had been sent, set his
troops in motion, not towards the Rhine, but southward. When
Piedmont's answer did arrive, Gyulai, who was a friend and creature
of Grünne's, proved as incompetent and as inexperienced as his
patron. He first delayed for some days before crossing the Ticino,
which was in flood, then shilly-shallied until the news reached him
that French troops were arriving in force, then on 2 June recrossed
the Ticino eastward, ignominiously. The armies first met in force at
Magenta two days later, and then, although the Austrians had not

had the worst of the fighting. Gyulai retreated further, leaving Napoleon and Victor Emmanuel to enter Milan in triumph.

By now Francis Joseph had seen the light. He replaced Buol by Count Rechberg, a competent career diplomat of Bavarian origin, who stipulated he be given also the position of Minister President. While Rechberg engaged in negotiations, which proved fruitless, in London, Berlin and Petersourg, Francis Joseph went down and took personal command of his armies. On 24 June the two armies met again, at Solferino. Again the Austrians did not have the worst of the fighting, but their casualties were so heavy as to draw tears from the young Emperor's eyes, and from his lips the words: 'Rather lose a province than undergo again so terrible an experience!'

He had further cause for despondency. A French detachment had actually landed at Lussin Piccolo near Fiume, awaiting the signal for Hungary to rise, and Klapka was forming a Hungarian Legion to lead the rising. Loyal Hungarians sent urgent warnings to Vienna that some concession was necessary to allay the discontent in their country. In Vienna, too, when the war began to go badly, the murmurings in Liberal circles grew so formidable that on 9 June the Ministerial Council, meeting under the Archduke Rainer, decided that it was their 'sacred duty' to warn the Emperor. Rechberg carried the warning down to Francis Joseph, to whom he repeated it in the strongest terms. After Solferino Rainer himself went down and even warned Francis Joseph not to show himself in Vienna until the impressions of the fighting had grown less vivid.

These warnings convinced Francis Joseph of the necessity of cutting his losses if he could do so on at all reasonable terms. Fortunately for him, Napoleon was ready to offer them. He was not confident that a battle for the Quadrilateral would turn out favourably for him, and the international situation, too, was taking a turn unfavourable to his ambitions. The Italian Principalities had risen against the Austrian domination, but they were looking, not to Paris, but to Turin. There had been a great upsurge of pro-Austrian feeling in the smaller German States, and even Prussia had announced that it would mobilize six army corps, although they would not act unless France attacked *Bund* territory. Mentally depressed and physically exhausted, Napoleon sent Francis Joseph an offer of an armistice, and of relatively favourable terms for a preliminary peace. Austria was to retain Venetia and the Quadrilateral, ceding only the rest of Lombardy. The rest of Italy was to be constituted as a federation.

The idea of a federation appealed to Francis Joseph, who flattered himself that Austria would be able to dominate it through Venetia, her alliance with Naples and her influence in Rome, and perhaps her secundogenitures, if they could be restored. He accepted the offer of

an armistice, which was signed on 5 July, and on the 11th the two
Monarchs met at Villafranca. Francis Joseph agreed to Napoleon's
terms, subject to certain face-saving stipulations: Lombardy was not
to be ceded direct to Piedmont, but to Napoleon, who would recede
it to Piedmont; Francis Joseph was to retain for his own lifetime the
right of conferring the Lombard Order of the Iron Crown. Napoleon
agreed to the restoration of the secondo-genitures, provided it was
not effected by force. We can infer only *ex silentio* what was agreed
about Hungary, but the French detachment was withdrawn from
Lussin Piccolo, and the idea of a rising in Hungary was obviously
dropped. On this point, Napoleon seems to have done no more than
extract from Francis Joseph a promise, which was none too scrupu-
lously kept, of an amnesty for the Hungarian soldiers who had
deserted to join Klapka's Legion. The preliminary peace embodying
these terms was signed on July 12. Immediately thereafter, Francis
Joseph took train for home. Arrived there, he issued, on 15 July, a
proclamation, known from its place of origin as the 'Laxenburg
Manifesto', in which he communicated to his peoples the signature
of the preliminary peace, and promised to use the 'leisure' which
peace would give him to place their welfare 'on a solid basis . . .
by the appropriate development of the Monarchy's rich spiritual
and material resources and by modernizing and improving its legislature and administration'.[2]

It may be noted that the definitive peace, signed at Zürich on
10 November, was less favourable to Austria than the preliminary
peace. The territorial provisions were not altered; but meanwhile,
it had proved impossible to secure the restoration of the secondo-
genitures, whose territories, with Emilia, were annexed by Piedmont
in the following spring. It had also been found impossible to give
Venetia a dual status, as part of the Monarchy and simultaneously,
member of an Italian federation. The idea of a federation faded away,
leaving Austria with no foothold in Italy except her possession of
Venetia.

Ten

EIGHT YEARS OF EXPERIMENT

In issuing the Laxenburg Manifesto Francis Joseph took his first step along the road which was to lead eight years later to the great constitutional settlements of 1867. He took it with extreme reluctance, and its course, the end of which by no means represented his heart's desire, was long and tortuous. His only immediate further step was to throw sops to the popular wrath by dismissing Bach and Kempen (the turn of the third popular scapegoat, Grünne, came a little later), but it was nearly a month before the nature of the promised reforms, and the names of the men who were to carry them out, were announced. The month had been spent in consultations, which were conducted chiefly by Rechberg, although the Emperor himself sometimes took a hand in them. Their openings were dominated by pertinacious endeavours by Thun to secure the establishment of an ultra-conservative and highly decentralized regime, resting on the feudal magnates, with Thun's brother-in-law, Count Heinrich Jaroslav Clam-Martinic, Minister President. Bruck, meanwhile, had been advocating a totally different prescription: a 'far-reaching liberalization of the social, economic and intellectual life of the Monarchy', with concessions to the non-Catholic Christians and the Jews, and a remodelling of its structure to promote the interests and the influence of the middle classes. The Reichsrat should be enlarged by adding to it members elected by the *Landtage*. This programme, he argued, would dispel the misgivings of the foreign financiers whose help was essential for the restoration of Austria's finances, and would also impress favourably the German Princes.

Francis Joseph's final decision amounted to a cautious and limited acceptance of Bruck's proposals. In the ministerial list, which was announced on 21 August, Thun retained his previous portfolio, and Rechberg kept his, as did Bruck, who took over also the agenda of the Ministry of Trade and Communications, which was wound up. Bach's ministry was given, to the general surprise, to Goluchowski. There was a new Minister of Justice, Freiherr von Lasser, and Hübner was given charge of the police, with ministerial status. The programme, published two days later, studiously avoided the word 'Constitution' and offered the *Landtage* no representative functions, but included many of Bruck's other recommendations. It promised autonomy and the free exercise of their religions to the non-Catholic Christian Churches, and 'regulation along modern lines of the position of the Israelites'. The Communal Autonomy Law was to be revised, and 'bodies representing the Estates' to be set up in each Land. There was to be 'effective control of expenditure, both civilian and military'.

The Government, however, showed itself in no haste to put these promises into effect. A Committee to study the reform of taxation was set up in September, and in December, a quasi-independent State Debt Committee. A few, very minor, concessions to the Jews were announced. These half-measures generally met with the contempt that they deserved. Efforts to borrow abroad on anything like acceptable terms still foundered on the mistrust of the quarters approached, which was enhanced when the news leaked out that the 1854 loan had been secretly overspent, presumably with Francis Joseph's connivance. The Government covered its immediate requirements by fresh borrowings from the National Bank, and the bank was forced to issue new notes, which were immediately quoted at a discount.

At last Francis Joseph nerved himself to follow up Bruck's most radical suggestion, and to reinforce the Reichsrat and give it a quasi-representative status by adding to its previous membership, besides ten new members nominated by himself, thirty-eight elected by the *Landtage*. This body was to consider and advise on 'the determination of the Budget, examination of the closed accounts, and of the data of the State Debt Committee'. A Rescript to this effect was issued on 5 March 1860.

It was this Rescript that brought Hungary back into the picture. The frequently made statement that Solferino was followed immediately by concessions to that country is incorrect. The Hungarian Old Conservatives had indeed approached Vienna with assurances that they could render their country completely loyal in return for concessions which were in fact less far-reaching than those extracted from Francis Joseph seven years later.[1] Both Rechberg and Hübner were in favour of meeting at least some of their conditions. But the passing of the immediate danger from Hungary had only hardened Francis Joseph's heart against what he regarded as a nation of inveterate rebels, none of them any better than the others. He refused absolutely to consider any concessions to any Hungarians; Hübner even paid for his intervention with his post.[2] Meanwhile, Thun had made things worse by issuing, on 14 September, a 'Protestant Patent' which violated the autonomy of the Hungarian Protestant Churches, drawing them together with the Catholics in a united front of mood so dangerous that the police reported that it might any day erupt into rebellion.

Then came the Rescript establishing the Reinforced Reichsrat, and this raised a difficulty of the first order. To give separate representation in it to each of Hungary's five Provinces would probably have raised a storm so elemental that Francis Joseph dared not face it. Instead, he made several large concessions. The Provinces were abolished and the Counties reinstated as Hungary's second constitutional instance. The Archduke Albrecht, who disagreed with this line, was replaced as Governor General by General Benedek, a Hungarian citizen and, incidentally, a Protestant. Thun's Protestant Patent was withdrawn. Venice received some analogous concessions.

The Reinforced Reichsrat met on 31 May 1860. Pending the constitution of the *Landtage*, the statutes for which had not yet been drafted, those of its members who should have been elected by them were nominated by the Crown, and while there were among them a few representatives of the middle classes, all the six from Hungary were Old Conservatives, and of the three from Bohemia, two (Clam and another) belonged to a similar group of high aristocrats whom Clam had been gathering round him.

They met in an atmosphere heavily overshadowed by financial apprehensions, for a month before Bruck had taken his own life, probably out of mortification at undeserved calumnies that had been circulating regarding his financial probity, and his suicide had let loose a new flood of rumours. The Reichsrat really produced a report on the financial situation, and elicited from Francis Joseph the notable promise that no new taxes should be imposed, nor existing ones heightened, and no new loans floated, without its consent. But its members did not content themselves with this achievement. The Hungarians combined with Clam and some sympathizers from other Lands in a 'Party of the United Nobility', and in effect turned the proceedings into a sort of Constituent Assembly, producing a 'report' which was actually a draft constitution. This, while admitting, in an obscure phrase, the need for some central, pan-Monarchic institutions, would have left the Lands solely competent outside this very restricted field.

The German bourgeois members, and some others, replied with a minority report which recommended a much larger legislature, which should assure 'the complete maintenance of the unity of the Monarchy and the legislative and executive authority of the Government'. The two documents were presented to the Emperor, who would probably have preferred not to accept either of them, but assured by the Hungarians that their country would accept their draft, but would revolt if it was rejected, he opted for it. On 20 October he promulgated what was announced to be 'a permanent and irrevocable instrument'.

This so-called 'October Diploma' was a collection of several documents. The central one comprised the real constitution. While assuming *ex silentio* the continued control by the Crown of foreign policy and defence, it made not inconsiderable concessions in other fields. For questions of taxation the 'consent' of the Reichsrat was to be necessary; for other questions, its 'co-operation', and that of the *Landtage*. Its membership was to be raised to a hundred. It was to be competent for questions affecting the whole Monarchy, but questions of interest to the western half of the Monarchy only could be discussed by their representatives alone. The *Landtage* were competent for questions not reserved to the Reichsrat.

Another Rescript made further concessions to Hungary which amounted, broadly, to the restoration of the *status quo ante* 1848, modified by acceptance of the emancipation of the non-nobles. The Hungarian Court Chancellery was restored, and the Chancellor, with a second Hungarian Minister, taken into the central Government. A Diet was to meet in 1861 to submit further proposals for redefining the relationship between the Crown and the nation. The Transylvanian Chancellery was restored and instructed to submit proposals for the future Transylvanian constitution to a genuinely representative Diet. The Ban of Croatia, which was given a sub-Court Chancellery (later promoted to a full Chancellery), was to consult the Sabor, and then submit proposals for the relationship between Croatia and Hungary. The Voivodina was incorporated administratively into Hungary, with immediate effect, but a Commissioner was to be sent down to ascertain the wishes of its inhabitants.

In Cis-Leithania the Government was to work out new *Landtag* Statutes. The pan-Monarchic Ministries of the Interior, Justice and Cults were abolished, the first-named being replaced, in Cis-Leithania, by a Ministry of State, still under Goluchowski. Cis-Leithania also received its own Minister of Justice (Baron Mecséry), while Cults and Education were demoted to departments of the Ministry of State, so that the super-barnacle, Thun, was at last prised loose. Rechberg retained Foreign Affairs, and von Plener Finance, which he had taken over after Bruck's suicide. As the defence budget would now have to be submitted to Parliament, the Ministry of War was resuscitated, under the charge of a senior officer, F.M.L. Count von Degenfeld.

Unhappily for its authors, and for Francis Joseph, the Diploma satisfied no one. The Poles sent a deputation to Vienna demanding the same status for themselves as Hungary had received. The Czech bourgeois politicians, emerged from their long hibernation, were aggrieved that the Diploma had not recognized the *Böhmisches Staatsrecht*. The Germans saw the Sudetenlande delivered over to Czech control, while their bureaucrats *à la* Bach saw the control over

Hungary slipping out of their hands, and the Liberals saw landlords and clerics installed as the masters of Austria, and genuine control by the tax-payer over the public purse still not assured. Their dissatisfaction was increased when in December Goluchowski at last began publishing the *Landtag* statutes in what were little more than re-editions of the pre-1848 Estates. The German Liberals and nationalists formed a loose common front under the device that 'Austria must be treated as favourably as Hungary'; if the one got a constitutional Parliament, so must the other.

The worst disappointment of all came from Hungary, where the reactions proved that the Old Conservatives had totally misjudged the feeling of the country. No Hungarian except themselves would accept any *octroied* settlement at all, nor any pan-Monarchic body with the right of voting taxation. Another grievance was the continued separation of Transylvania. Deák, consulted by Francis Joseph, conceded that the April Laws could be revised, but only by agreement with a legally constituted Parliament. The reincorporation of Transylvania was a *sine qua non*. Uninhibited spirits demonstrated noisily and offensively.

Hindsight can perceive that, fundamentally, the most dangerous feature of all these reactions was that all of them were national. The hope that it would be possible to depoliticize national feeling, never realized in Hungary or Galicia, had now proved to be vain in respect of the Czechs and Slovenes, and also, if less universally, of the Germans. But Francis Joseph had first to deal with the immediate situation. His retort to the Hungarians was simply to reinforce the garrisons in their country, and to the Czechs and Slovenes, to ignore them. But these were no answers to the problems of which the German and German-minded bourgeoisie were the mouthpieces. Von Plener, when he took over Bruck's heritage, had found the cupboard bare, and when in September Garibaldi took Naples, and Piedmont, which had already annexed the secondo-genitures, sent troops into Umbria and the Marches, he had to tell the Emperor that there was no money for countering these moves: it was impossible to raise it by increased taxation, and foreign credit was unobtainable. Francis Joseph, who only a few months before had flattered himself that he would soon be back in Lombardy, now had to watch the unification of Italy taking place under his nose, for lack of funds to prevent it.

So the goodwill of the holders of the purse-strings had still to be gained, and there was also another consideration. After his eviction from Italy, the foreign objective nearest to Francis Joseph's heart was the affirmation and consolidation of his dynasty's leadership in Germany, and there was no denying that, as poor Bruck had argued, a German-minded and relatively liberal Austria would command

more sympathies in the *Bund* than a near-autocratic and strongly
federalist one, with Czech, Polish and Hungarian aristocrats calling
the tune in it.

So Francis Joseph switched his policy again. On 14 December
Goluchowski was ungraciously dismissed, to be succeeded by
Schmerling, now commonly regarded as the white hope of the German Liberals. The Monarch still could not bring himself to see the
1849 constitution brought back, but after a long struggle behind the
scenes consented to the halfway house of an enactment issued by
himself that granted some representative institutions. This, after some
further ministerial readjustments had been made, chief of them the
appointment of the Archduke Rainer to be 'Head of the Ministerial
Conference' (Rechberg remained Foreign Minister), and the creation
of a new Ministry of Administration, to leave Schmerling more time
to deal with the Reichsrat and *Landtage*, saw the light on 4 February
1861 in the shape of a series of Rescripts collectively known as the
'February Patent'. These set out provisions for putting into force the
'permanent and irrevocable' October Diploma, large parts of which
were in fact left unchanged. But the composition of the Reichsrat and
its relationship to the *Landtage* were altered radically. The Reichsrat
was to consist of an Upper House of notabilities and a Lower House
with a membership of 343, sent to it by the *Landtage* in proportions
reflecting the numbers, taxable capacities, and some other factors, of
the populations of the Lands, and ranging in numbers from eighty-
five for Hungary and fifty-four for Bohemia to two each for the
smallest Lands. Questions affecting the whole Monarchy came before
it, but as in the Diploma, if a question did not concern Hungary, it
came only before a 'narrower' (*engerer*) Reichsrat, in which the
Lands of the Hungarian Crown were not represented. The *Landtage*
were competent only for questions specifically assigned to them, and
the definition of these was relatively narrow. The composition of this
House was made dependent on that of the *Landtage*. For electoral
purposes each of these was divided into 'Curias', in most Lands four
in number, representing respectively the great landed proprietors, the
Chambers of Commerce, the urban, and the rural communes. Each
Curia was allotted a fixed proportion of seats in the *Landtage*, and
filled these by the direct votes of its own constituents. The *Landtage*
sent delegations to the Reichsrat in which each Curia was represented
proportionately to the number of its seats in the *Landtag*.

The idea of electoral Curias was nothing new, but the Patent
altered the effect of it on the composition of the *Landtage*, and thus
of the Reichsrat, by enlarging the quotas allocated to the Chambers
of Commerce and the urban communes, in which the German element was strong. In Lands of mixed population the German con-

stituencies were also generally smaller than the non-German, and the franchise in them was more liberal than in the rural districts. To describe the Patent, as some writers have done, as 'enshrining the domination of the German *haute bourgeoisie*' is something of an exaggeration, for the representatives of the second and third Curias together still numbered less than one-third of the Narrower Reichsrat (65 out of 203), while the class which by modern standards was heavily overrepresented was still that of the big landlords. But the German and the German-speaking *haute bourgeoisie* did undoubtedly now become a factor of major importance in the political life of Austria.

In 1861 the *Weltanschauung* of this class was still, as it had been in 1848, compounded (often in the same individual) of various, often mutually contradictory, elements, and the manner in which they exercised their power-position was correspondingly ambivalent. *Qua* Liberals, they stood for limitations on the Monarch's authority, especially in financial matters—he who paid the piper should call the tune—and also, more generally, for liberty of the citizen *vis-à-vis* the State in such respects as freedom of the Press and of association. The economic interests which they represented were those of industry versus agriculture, town versus country, capital versus labour; in the last-named respect they were unblushingly Mancunian: no class had less feeling for the workers than they. In the 1860s and 1870s they had two special Guy Fawkeses. One was the Catholic Church, whose position, as enshrined in the Concordat, they regarded with a positively obsessive hatred which was not at all confined to their Jewish members. The other was the army. Their unremitting attacks on every Defence budget were obviously prompted in part by financial considerations—it was, as we have seen, true that the Monarchy's chronic financial troubles had been due to expenditure on the army and on military operations—but largely, one must think, by a psychological fixation. Since the dynasty had made the Church and the army the chief props of its absolutist rule, those institutions were, in that capacity, the principal targets of the opponents of absolutism.

At the same time their mentality also contained a strong Josephinian element, and on the structural issue, including that of the position of Hungary, they tended to be partisans of an unbending centralism, showing themselves in this respect the staunchest supporters of that Monarchic authority which they strove so hard, *qua* Liberals, to undermine.

The issue of the Patent promptly produced another crisis in Hungary, where opinion reacted violently against it. The Reinforced Reichsrat could still appear at a pinch as an assemblage of notables advising the Monarch; the Reichsrat of the Patent was undisguisedly

a pan-Monarchic Parliament. A large party in Hungary was for boy-
cotting the elections, but Deák, who had now become a sort of one-
man Court of Appeal on constitutional questions, advised that the
order to hold them was legal, and held they were (on the 1848 franchise, in default of any other). Not a single deputy, however, was
returned who supported the Patent, and almost exactly half of those
elected argued that since Francis Joseph, not having been crowned,
was not the legal King of Hungary, the Diet should not open its proceedings with the customary Address to the Crown, but express its
feelings in the form of a Resolution of the House. It was only by a
bare and largely fortuitous majority that the House agreed to use the
customary form, but the Address, which was drafted by Deák, when
it did go forward, expressed in courteous but quite categorical terms
Hungary's refusal to attend any assemblage convoked by Patent or
pan-Monarchic in composition, and reminded the Crown of its obligation to restore the integrity of the country, and to honour the April
Laws. A reply from Vienna, arguing the contrary case, was answered
by a second Address by Deák, to which the Crown replied on 21
August by a Rescript which retracted almost all its recent concessions, dissolved the Diet and reintroduced 'provisionally' many
features of the pre-1860 regime. The Hungarians fell back on passive
resistance, one form of which was expressed in non-payment of taxes.

The Sabor, too, decided, although only by a single vote, not to
attend the Reichsrat. Here, too, the Crown's reply was to dissolve
the assemblage, reintroduce an absolutist regime and dismiss some
recalcitrant officials. Of the Hungarian Lands, only Transylvania
proved more complaisant. Elections were held under a revised franchise, and the resultant Diet sent to Vienna its quota of representatives, consisting of thirteen Roumanians, ten Saxons and three Magyars, of whom, indeed, the three Magyars and thirteen of the other
twenty-three were all Regalists nominated by the Government.

Schmerling himself had not expected Hungary to accept the Patent,
and confident that the resistance there would collapse in due course,
he set the Narrower Reichsrat cheerfully to work. Only the Venetians
had boycotted the elections to that body. The Czech bourgeois representatives first thought of doing so, but changed their minds and
allied themselves with Clam-Martinic's group of magnates with a
programme demanding the restoration of the *Böhmisches Staatsrecht*. They, with a rival group of magnates who formed a 'Party of
Constitutional Great Landlords', joined other federalists and clericals to form an opposition, which, however, mustered only ninety
deputies, so that the three groups of the German 'Left' – the 'Great
Austrians', whose strength lay in Vienna, the 'Unionists' (largely
Bohemian) and the Autonomists (Styrian) – who held between them

119 seats, and were supported by twelve Ruthenes and some splinter parties, commanded a reasonably comfortable majority.

The Reichsrat, which assembled on 29 May 1861, began well enough, by extracting from Francis Joseph (with extreme difficulty) a declaration given on 2 July that the ministry should be regarded as responsible *also* to the Reichsrat for the maintenance of the constitution and the execution of laws, and they also got through a number of useful administrative reforms. But its German members were so consistently offensive to their non-German colleagues that first the Poles, then the Czechs, walked out of the 'Schmerling Theatre' (as the improvised premises in which the sessions were held were popularly known), and the Germans themselves attacked Schmerling so venomously for not being Liberal enough (and he was in fact more of a Josephinian than a Liberal) that he had to resort to the emergency paragraph to put through much of the essential legislation. Meanwhile von Plener has succeeded in putting the currency back on par, but only by following a rigidly deflationary policy which created a monetary stringency so acute as to make these years, economically, some of the most difficult in Austrian history, and he was unable to balance the budget, which closed each year with a deficit. The Liberals' only remedy was to insist on economies on army expenditure, which again reduced the defences of the Monarchy to below safety level, should another conflict occur.

And the seeds of such a conflict were already being sown. Francis Joseph was now embarking on an active propagandist campaign to make manifest Austria's leadership of Germany, while Prussia, where Bismarck became Foreign Minister in 1862, was countering it as vigorously. A meeting of the German Princes (*Fürstentag*) in August 1863, at which it had been hoped that Francis Joseph would be offered the Imperial Crown, began and ended in speechifying, because Bismarck has persuaded his king not to attend it.

In the tedious Schleswig-Holstein imbroglio that began that autumn Austria and Prussia still managed to act as partners, but the real advantage in the solution lay with Prussia, and in August 1864, after a meeting with the King of Prussia and Bismarck, Francis Joseph became convinced that Prussia could be checked only by force. He replaced Rechberg, who still favoured conciliation, by Mensdorf-Pouilly, who was for a 'forward' policy, and prepared his mind for war. His mood was still anything but defeatist. Twice in 1865 he rejected offers, one from Bismarck to buy Austria out of Holstein, the other from La Marmora, the Minister President of Piedmont, to buy Venetia as far as the Isonzo, which would indeed have cost him territory, but the losses would have been bloodless, and have enabled Austria to recoup her finances. He does not seem even to have been discouraged by the weakness of Austria's armaments, although in 1862 Degenfeld had drawn attention in the Reichsrat to the mounting expenditure on armaments of Austria's neighbours. But Von Plener replied airily that 'he had his own sources of information: the Press, the House of Rothschild, and other bankers. Austria could safely go on disarming.' And in fact in 1864, and even in 1865, the defence estimates were cut yet again. Francis Joseph actually persuaded himself that the war would not be expensive, since it would end in speedy victory, after which Austria would receive an indemnity, and be able to disarm.

He did, however, think it worth while attempting a new policy towards Hungary. Here he was in conflict with his ministers, for although one group of the Austrian Germans, Kaiserfeld's Autonomists, were beginning to play with the idea, on which the 1867 Compromise was ultimately based, of an alliance between the Liberals in the two halves of the Monarchy, and in 1863 actually reached an understanding with Deák's followers, the two other groups were, like Schmerling himself, unrepentantly and unconcernedly centralist. Hungary would come round.

But it seems that Francis Joseph, whose formerly implacable hostility towards all things Hungarian was weakening, perhaps under the influence of his wife, who had fallen in love with the country, was now not satisfied with the effectiveness of the policy of unbending repression. As early as December 1862, he had asked the ex-Chancellor, Apponyi, for suggestions for a possible settlement. Apponyi had replied with a Memorandum which dropped the Old Conservatives' attitude of 'back to 1847', and instead proposed a solution which contained all the essential features of the 1867 Compromise: common Ministers for Foreign Affairs, Defence, and 'common' finance, responsible to delegations from the two Parliaments, and a ministry, responsible to its own Parliament, for Hungary's *interna*. At the time this had been too advanced for Francis Joseph, who had simply laid it *ad acta*, but as the certainty of war grew, he became uneasy at the prospect of waging it with an unreconciled Hungary in his rear. The Old Hungarians, for their part, realizing their own unpopularity in the country, approached Deák; to whom, finding him open to the view that certain common institutions were compatible with Hungary's position under the Pragmatic Sanction, they left the running. A cautious exchange of ideas, often expressed in the form of articles in the Press, so encouraged Francis Joseph that in June 1865 he suddenly made a series of concessions that amounted in sum to the abandonment of neo-absolutism. A new Chancellor was appointed, and the Hungarian and the Croat Diets convoked for the coming December for negotiations on modifications of the February Patent, and the Transylvanian Diet for November, with the single item on its agenda of 'revising the Union of 1848' (a form of words which recognized that some form of Union would be re-enacted). Francis Joseph had done all this without informing either the Archduke or Schmerling of his intentions. Both resigned on 27 June. The new Minister of State, who took over a month later, Count Richard Belcredi, 'suspended the operation' of the Reichsrat pending the outcome of the negotiations in Pest and Zagreb. The *Landtage*, which were due to meet in November, were promised that the results should be submitted to them 'for the hearing and appreciation of their views, which should be given equal weight' (*um ihren gleichgewichtigen Ausspruch zu vernehmen und zu würdigen*).

When the negotiations did open, a packed Transylvanian Diet voted that the Union of 1848 was still legally valid. Elections for Transylvania's representatives in the Pest Diet were then held on the 1848 franchise. These resulted in the return of thirty-seven Magyars, twenty-two Saxons and fourteen Roumanians. The Sabor, meanwhile, simply reiterated its old maximum demands, from which neither pressure nor allurement from either Vienna or Pest could move it for the next eighteen months. In Pest the negotiations soon reached a deadlock, for Francis Joseph still demanded 'common parliamentary treatment' for all central questions, and the Diet still refused to accept it. But it was clear that a majority, although only a small one, was anxious to find an acceptable compromise, so that Francis Joseph did not this time preclude the chances of agreement by dissolving the Diet, but invited it to submit counterproposals. The Diet accordingly appointed a Committee of sixty-seven, which in its turn appointed a Sub-Committee of fifteen under the Presidency of Count Gyula Andrássy, once a fiery rebel who had been symbolically executed *in absentia* in 1849, but had later returned to Hungary under an amnesty and become Deák's right-hand man. This body produced a report which in substance reproduced Apponyi's ideas as modified by Deák and need not be described at this stage, since it re-appeared almost verbatim in the final settlement as Law XII of 1867. It had just completed its work when, in mid-June, the accumulated powder of Austro-Prussian relations exploded in war.

In this Austria was facing two enemies, herself single-handed, for after Francis Joseph had rejected Prussia's and Piedmont's offers in 1865, the two countries had, on 8 April 1866, concluded an offensive and defensive alliance. In a treaty signed on 12 June Austria obtained a promise of neutrality from France. But in return, she had to promise to cede Venetia, even if she were to win the war.

The task was beyond the powers of the ill-equipped Austrian

armies. The Archduke Albrecht, commanding on the Italian Front, defeated the Italians at Custozza on 24 June, and on 20 July Admiral Tegethoff won a naval victory against the same easy opposition at Lissa. But on 3 July Benedek, commanding the northern armies, was crushingly defeated at Königgrätz (Sadowa) by the Prussians, who proved to be far superior to the Austrians in both generalship and armaments. This disaster could not be retrieved, and a preliminary peace was signed at Nikolsburg on 6 August, followed by the definitive Treaty of Prague on the 23rd. Austria had to consent to 'a new formation of Germany from which the Austrian Empire should be excluded' and to pay Prussia an indemnity of twenty million thaler. She ceded Venetia to Napoleon, who re-ceded it to Piedmont.

The terms were mild, and might have been even milder, since Bismarck would have been willing to renounce any indemnity if Austria left the *Bund* immediately; but Francis Joseph delayed, suspecting a trap, and his final acceptance of the offer arrived half an hour too late.

Particularly unsavoury was the treatment of Benedek, who was first asked for a pledge, which he kept most honourably, to say nothing in his own defence, then viciously attacked in the *officieux* Press for his failure in a post which he had accepted only under pressure, protesting his own unfitness for it.

After the débâcle far-reaching changes were made in the central departments of State. The Archduke Albrecht was given the post (created for him) of Head of the Army High Command (later, Inspector General of the Armed Forces), while under him F.M.L. John became Minister of War, with orders to carry through a complete reorganization of the armed forces. F.M.L. Friedrich (later Count) Beck-Rzikowsky became head of the Emperor's Military Chancellery, *vice* Von Crenneville, who had belonged to the 'forward party'. On 30 October Baron von Beust, until shortly before Foreign Minister of Saxony, replaced Mensdorff at the Ballhausplatz. In January 1867, Belcredi's Minister of Finance, Count Larisch, gave way to Karl von Becke.

Austria's exclusion from Germany obviously altered fundamentally the balance of power between her own component nationalities. Her Germans could no longer command that intangible but still very real reinforcement of their position which derived from her quality of a 'German State'. They still, of course, easily led all the peoples of the Monarchy, not only in respect of numbers, but also of social, cultural and economic development, and they still enjoyed that leading role in her public services which they had acquired in early days. But a centralized German-dominated Monarchy *à la* Bach or Schmerling was no longer a practical possibility. At the best the Germans would have to share their pride of place with one or another partner.

Curiously few of them realized this fully at the time. Only one group in Graz, the same that had already been advocating partnership with Hungary, began almost at once advocating the idea, which was formulated afterwards in the 'Aussee Programme' described on pages 199–200, that the Germans of Austria should withdraw to an inner line. Outside these, most of the Germans who were genuinely grieved at their country's misfortunes told themselves comfortably that they would soon be reversed. Not all even grieved. Many Liberals believed that Austria's defeat had strengthened their position by discrediting the military party, 'whom it just served right'. There was no need to make concessions to anybody : rather the reverse.

But the other nationalities had seen things more clearly. The Poles, no longer believing in the possibility of an early restoration of Polish independence, decided that their best immediate hope lay in a strong Austria, since that could no longer threaten Polish independence. They also saw that their support would be worth paying for, and intimated as much to Belcredi, who in September duly reappointed Goluchowski Governor of Galicia, and allowed him to put through several measures favourable to his compatriots.

But the Poles would, in the end, given their price, help either side to final victory. The immediate issue lay between the other Slavs on the one hand, and the Hungarians on the other ; in political terms, between federalism and dualism. The Czech politicians, who led the former army, now played their hands very badly. They convoked a 'Slav Conference' which produced a plan for reorganizing the Monarchy in a 'Pentarchy' of five federal units, but this satisfied neither the Poles, the Croats, nor least of all, the Slovenes, who had not even been invited to the meeting. Further, the demonstrations of hostility towards the Germans in which both Czechs and Slovenes indulged, hardened the determination of their victims to retain their hold on the west, even if this meant letting Hungary go.

The Hungarians, by contrast, played their cards very well. Among them, too, voices had been raised that Austria's difficulties were Hungary's opportunity, but Deák, more far-sighted, took, and expressed strongly, the opposite view. Hungary, he argued, could remain secure only as a part of a larger unit, and that unit could only be the Monarchy. Further, the enfeeblement of the Monarchy had made it a safe haven for Hungary, to which it could no longer refuse her proper place in it. Consequently, when Francis Joseph asked him, in a famous interview after Sadowa, what Hungary's terms were after Austria's defeat, he answered : 'Exactly the same as before it'. The negotiations, not entirely broken off even during the hostilities, were therefore resumed after Prague with full vigour, on the understood basis that both sides wanted an agreement.

The Hungarians soon received a valuable ally in the person of
Beust, who, while taking it as axiomatic that Austria's policy must
rest primarily on its Germans, saw also that the Germans would need
partners; and to him, a Liberal, a Protestant and something of an
anti-Slav, it was clear that only the Magyars, although he did not personally much like their leaders, could fill that role. It was only slowly
that Francis Joseph renounced the idea of a single Parliament, but
Beust's representations, the diplomatic skill of Andrássy, who acted
as negotiator-in-chief for Hungary, and Deák's polite but adamant
unyieldingness, gradually wore him down. In February 1867, near-
complete agreement between the Monarch and the Hungarians was
reached at a series of meetings in Vienna arranged by Beust. The
chief outstanding difficulty now lay in Belcredi's promise to the Austrian *Landtage*, several of which had, with Belcredi's encouragement
and help – he was himself a member of Clam's group, a federalist and
an opponent of Dualism – shown their intention of opposing any
Dualist settlement. Belcredi now announced elections for an 'Extraordinary' Reichsrat, to which the results of the negotiations with
Hungary were to be submitted, and it seemed certain that the resultant Reichsrat would reject the settlement. Then, however, Beust demanded a confrontation. At the crucial meeting on 1 February
Francis Joseph decided reluctantly against Belcredi, who resigned.
Beust, who took his place, 'made' new elections in three of the most
recalcitrant *Landtage* – those of Bohemia, Moravia and Carniola –
and these, under pressure equal and opposite to that which Belcredi
had exerted, changed the majorities in Bohemia and Moravia, giving
a prospective Reichsrat majority for the Hungarian Compromise.

Now it was safe to go ahead in Hungary. On 17 Febuary Andrássy was appointed Minister President (Deák having refused the
post for himself), and formed an administration, composed of his
own followers, which was sworn in on 18 March. The Diet tied up
some loose ends, and although the enthusiasm was by no means universal, ended, on 29 May, by voting the result as 'Law XII of 1867'
by the comfortable majority of 257 to 117. On 8 June Francis Joseph
was crowned with the traditional pompous ceremony. On 28 July he
gave his royal sanction to the work accomplished up to that date by
the Diet, which he then adjourned for its summer recess.

Put in the briefest possible form, Law XII recognized defence and
foreign policy (as a function of defence) as constituting questions
common to Hungary and the Monarch's other dominions. Since the
Monarch's handling of these subjects was now to be subject to constitutional control in both halves of the Monarchy (an important provision of the Law, on which it insisted, was that the system in Austria,
as well as Hungary, must be 'completely constitutional') each of

these two questions was to be in charge of a common minister, and the financing of them, of a third. The diplomatic and commercial representation of the Monarchy, and dispositions relating to international treaties, fell within the competence of the common Foreign Minister, 'acting in understanding with the ministries of both parts, and with their consent'. Each ministry communicated international agreements to its own legislature. In respect of defence the Law recognized that 'all questions relating to the unitary command, control and internal organization of the whole army, and consequently of the Hungarian army, as a complementary part of the whole army' fell within the competence of the Crown, but Hungary reserved for herself the right of voting the contingent supplied by her to the armed forces, the length of service, and certain other questions. The contingent had to be voted each year by Parliament, even though, under the Army Act described below, the size of it had been agreed decennially in advance.

The three common ministers reported annually to equal 'Delegations' from the two Parliaments, meeting alternately in the two capitals. The Delegations voiced to the ministers the views of their countries, and also determined the budgets for the coming year of the three ministries; these were then passed to the two Parliaments, to be voted by them. The 'quota' of these sums to be paid by each country was agreed every ten years for the coming decade by 'Deputations' from the two Parliaments, who also agreed what was to be the tariff and commercial relationship between Austria and Hungary for the coming decade, and dealt further with certain points 'which could be treated usefully by common agreement and on identical principles'. These so-called 'pragmatic' subjects included credit and currency, weights and measures, indirect taxation and communications of interest to both halves.

Hungary consented as an act of grace to pay a share towards the service and amortization of the State debt. In all other respects Hungary was bound exclusively by her own laws, as agreed between her King and her own Parliament.

Meanwhile, the Reichsrat had assembled in May. The effect of the various manipulations of the *Landtage* had been to give the German fractions, who now styled themselves the 'Party of the Constitution', or 'Constitutional Left', 118 seats out of the 203, and since the Poles had, in return for privy assurances given them by Beust, promised to support the Government on central issues, and the eight Slovenes, who had organized themselves loosely into a 'National Party', took a similar 'opportunist' line, in return for minor concessions, not all of them for strictly public purposes, while the fourteen Czech nationalists had boycotted the elections, preferring to undertake, under the leadership of Palacký and Rieger, a 'pilgrimage' to Moscow, at which they made extravagant speeches hailing Russia as 'the rising sun of the Slavs' – thanks to all this, Beust would have had a comfortable majority for the Compromise, had it come to the vote. As it was, Francis Joseph simply informed the Reichsrat that the Compromise had been concluded, and invited its approval. All he still asked the deputies to do in this connection was to agree with the Hungarians on the details of the 'Economic Compromise'.

The Reichsrat kissed the rod, and drew up a counterpart to Law XII, which contained a few, probably accidental, variants, the most important of which was that the obligation of the Foreign Minister to consult with the ministries of the two halves of the Monarchy was omitted.[3] The consent of the Reichsrat was, however, declared necessary for all foreign transactions involving expenditure, and the defence estimates and the intake of recruits were added to the list of measures for which this consent was required. The economic relationship with Hungary was fixed for the first ten years at that of a Customs and Commercial Union. The first 'quota' was fixed at 70:30.

The Reichsrat spent the rest of its time working out constitutional laws for Cis-Leithania. These left the Crown with most of its powers in internal affairs, including its veto on legislation and its free hand in the appointment of the Minister President, whose 'responsibility' was to the Crown, not to the Reichsrat. The emergency paragraph, now Paragraph 14, was retained, although made subject to some further restrictions (which were habitually ignored).

No substantial changes were made in the division of competences between Reichsrat and *Landtage*, and none in the electoral system. But this time the Reichsrat was not to be done out of safeguarding the 'rights of the citizens', and passed a large number of measures in this field. The Austrian citizen was assured all modern civic liberties, such as freedom of belief and religious practice, of speech, of the Press, and of learning and instruction. The judiciary was separated again from the executive, and the judicial code and procedure modernized. All citizens were declared equal before the law, and all public offices were open to any of them. The word 'Jew' was not mentioned, but the enjoyment of all civil and political rights was expressly declared to be independent of religious Confession. The Liberals would have liked to see the Concordat abolished. This did not prove yet possible, but the Reichsrat adopted, for submission to the Upper House, two Laws which directly contradicted two of its provisions: one, to restore the Josephinian marriage law, the other to put the control of education in the hands of the lay arm.

The old 'Nationalities Law' reappeared, as Article XIX of Law 42, in the wording:

1. 'All peoples (*Volksstämme*) of the State are equal in rights, and every people has an inviolable right to the preservation and cultivation of its nationality and language.

2. 'The equality of rights of all locally current (*landesüblich*) languages in schools, offices and public life is recognized.

3. 'In Lands inhabited by several nationalities, the public educational establishments are to be so organized that each of those nationalities receives the necessary means of instruction in its own language, without compulsion to learn a second provincial language (*Landessprache*).'

The Reichsrat adopted the four Laws containing these provisions, together with its version of the Compromise, on 21 December 1867. The five Laws, which were afterwards known collectively as the 'December Constitution', were declared 'fundamental', that is a parliamentary majority of two-thirds was necessary to change them.

For Hungary, the April Laws and subsequent modifications of them have been described, and the description need not be repeated here; but we should mention a 'Punctuation' agreed on 17 March 1867 between the Monarch and his newly-appointed ministers, which was always thereafter treated as binding. This gave the Monarch very extensive further powers. Besides the ordinary Crown prerogatives such as Acts of Grace, it made the assent of the Crown necessary for public expenditure in many fields, for a wide range of ecclesiastical and educational appointments, and for appointments, promotions and retirements in the upper ranks of the civil service. Under its most important clause of all, all proposed legislation and provisional enactments, etc., had to receive the Monarch's 'preliminary sanction' before being introduced in Parliament.

Neither the Austrian nor the Hungarian laws answered the question of what would happen if a Parliament failed to vote the budget, or the contingent of recruits, before the expiration of the budgetary year. In Austria the gap could be bridged, not quite legally, but nearly enough so for practical purposes, by using Paragraph 14. But Hungarian law contained no emergency paragraph, and a law of 1848 declared specifically that demands for taxes or recruits ceased to be valid after the expiration of the year for which they were voted. During the ensuing '*vacuum juris*' the Counties were legally entitled to refuse to implement them.

The new Military Services Law, or Laws (to meet legal objections from Hungary each Parliament voted a separate law for its own territory, mutating the necessary *mutanda*) provided for a regular army and navy, raised by conscription from the entire able-bodied population with very few occupational exemptions, and two second-line formations, the *Landwehr* and the *Honvédség*. Recruits in the regular army served three years with the colours, seven with the reserves, and two with the *Landwehr* or *Honvédség*, but men surplus to the need of the regular force could serve all their term with a second-line formation. Persons possessing certain academic qualifications might, after serving a year with the colours, do a second as a 'volunteer cadet', and then, if they passed an examination, become officers of reserve. The numbers required were agreed decennially in advance by the two Parliaments; they were apportioned between the the countries proportionately to their populations. For the first decennial period the total was to be that necessary to give a war strength of 800,000 (470,368 from Austria and 329,632 from Hungary) for the regular army, plus 100,000 each for the second-line formations. (This was considered to be the figure appropriate to the Great Power status of the Monarchy, and within its means.) The annual contingents were fixed at 95,174 (54,541 and 40,933) for the regular army, 10,000, plus a contingent of Schützen (sharpshooters) from the Tirol for the *Landwehr*, and 12,500 for the *Honvédség*.

The Military Frontier was abolished.

Law XII should have been accompanied by a new Hungaro-Croat 'Compromise', but this could be concluded only in 1868, after the Sabor of that year had been dissolved and elections held on a new franchise, and under strong official pressure, had returned a less recalcitrant successor. The resultant *Nagodba* restored the historical relationship between the two Kingdoms: they formed one and the same State community *vis-à-vis* the Monarch's other dominions and all other countries, and within this Croatia constituted an autonomous unit under a 'Ban' appointed on the proposal of the Hungarian Minister President, and responsible to the Sabor. Croatia was represented proportionately to its population on the Delegations and in the Hungarian Parliament when subjects affecting the whole 'State community' were under discussion: its representatives might then address it in Croat. Subjects left to Hungary under Law XII as its 'interna' were divided again under the *Nagodba* into 'common' Hungaro-Croat subjects, and Croat 'interna', the former category comprising, roughly, the questions treated in Law XII as 'pragmatic'; for the others, Croatia was completely autonomous. Croat was the sole official language. Croatia retained 45 per cent of her revenues from taxation for her 'interna', paying the remaining 55 per cent over into the common exchequer.[4]

Another Hungarian law to appear belatedly (only in December 1868) was its 'Nationalities Law' (titularly, 'Law on the equality of rights of the Nationalities'). The authors of the law that eventually saw the light had during its prolonged gestation encountered fierce opposition from two sides: the leaders of some of the Nationalities, especially the Serbs and Transylvanian Roumanians, but also some of the Slovaks, wanted Hungary constituted a genuine multi-national State in which each of its component nationalities enjoyed complete equality on all levels; Magyar chauvinists almost denied a non-Magyar the right to exist in Hungary. The final product was in its first form chiefly the work of Eötvös, but revised by others and finally supplied by Deák with a preamble which ran:

'Whereas, according also to the basic principles of the constitution, all citizens of Hungary form, politically, one nation, the indivisible, unitary Hungarian (*magyar*[5]) nation, of which every citizen of the country, whatever his personal nationality (*nemzetiség*), is a member equal in rights:

'And whereas this equality of rights can be qualified by special provisions only in respect of the official use of the different languages current in the country, and that only so far as is necessitated by the unity of the country, the practical possibilities of government and administration and the claims of the administration of strict justice, while in every other respect the complete equality of rights of all citizens remains intact: the following rules will serve as guidance in respect of the official use of the various languages.'

The language of State, including that of Parliament and the University, was Magyar, but ample provision was made for the use of non-Magyar languages on all levels, from the Counties downward, in administration, justice and education, while the use of them in private life was entirely free.

Eleven

INTERMEZZO

The structural pattern of the Monarchy established in 1867 remained
in the event unaltered until the Monarchy's own end, but in 1868 it
was not yet certain that this would prove to be the case. If considerations of foreign policy, offensive or defensive, had seemed to
Francis Joseph to require it, he would still have been prepared to
carry through in their interest far-reaching structural readjustments,
at least in Cis-Leithania, and in 1868 such considerations were still
not excluded. It was not until he accepted as final the relationship of
Austria to the new Germany that he abandoned the thought of further internal structural changes, and that the definitive establishment
of Dualism was signified by the almost simultaneous appointments
of an Austrian Minister President committed to a unitary structure
for Cis-Leithania and a Foreign Minister recognizably devoted to a
policy of reconciliation with Germany. The years before this happened constitute an intermezzo in the history of the Monarchy.
During them Hungary was, indeed, pursuing its own course, which
can be described separately, but the developments in Cis-Leithania
and those of foreign policy were so closely inter-dependent as to
make separate treatment of them impossible.

Beust had given up his internal charges when the December Laws
were put through, and Francis Joseph, while leaving him 'Chancellor'
and Foreign Minister, had, on 30 December 1867, appointed a new
Austrian Minister President. Characteristically, he could not bear to
give the post to anyone but a high aristocrat, and chose for it Prince
'Carlos' Auersperg, a man who combined blue blood with Liberal
sympathies. Count Taaffe, who had been Beust's deputy and Minister of the Interior, retained those posts, coupling Defence with them,
and Count Potocki, a Pole, was given Agriculture. The other ministers were all members of the German 'Constitutional Left', so that the
ministry deserved the soubriquet of 'burgher' popularly bestowed
on it.

The ministry was naturally concerned to carry on the work of the
Reichsrat that had elected its members, and in its first months of
office it put through several measures agreeable to its ideology. The
most far-reaching of these were in two fields. The last remaining restrictions on *laissez faire* on the land disappeared : the maximum rate

of interest that could be charged on a loan was abolished, although grossly inequitable rates were in theory – often disregarded in practice – prohibited, as were all restrictions on the parcellization of holdings. The holder was left completely free disposition, testamentary or otherwise, over his land. Secondly, the Government pressed its Confessional legislation very strongly, and although it was only with extreme reluctance that Francis Joseph gave way in this field, he allowed the Reichsrat's two bills for the control of education by the lay arm, and the laicization of the marriage law, to reach the statute book. These laws once through, the abolition of the Concordat could be only a matter of time, although it was not actually effected until 30 July 1870, after the pronouncement by the Oecumenical Council of the doctrine of papal infallibility had provided a pretext.

The Confessional legislation, in particular, was strongly resented even in the German-Austrian Lands by the Clericals and their peasant followings, and meanwhile, the non-Germans were renewing their campaigns against the German-dominated centralism of the Reichsrat. On 24 September 1868, the *Landtag* of Galicia adopted a resolution which demanded, in effect, complete Home Rule for the Kingdom. The Slovenes asked for a Land of 'Slovenia', with its own *Landtag*, Slovene to be the language of administration and education. The Italians of the Trentino called for their own Land. The Czechs, who were furious at having failed where the Hungarians had succeeded, boycotted a visit by Francis Joseph to Prague in July 1868, and a month later eighty-one members of the Bohemian *Landtag* signed a declaration that the only constitutional bases of the Czech Lands' position in the Monarchy were the settlement accepted by Ferdinand I at his coronation in 1527 and the *Majestätsbrief* of April 1848. They demanded a new settlement based on the '*Böhmisches Staatsrecht*'. They also renewed their efforts to enlist foreign help, this time from France, to which they represented the identity of interests between France and a Bohemian 'State'.

At the outset of its term of office, the Government had honoured certain promises made by Beust to the Poles in the previous summer. In January 1868, it had allowed virtually all education in Galicia above the primary level to be Polonized. A month later it withdrew the provisions allowing the use of German in administration and justice. In June 1869, it made Polish the 'inner language' of service in most instances. But it rejected the 'Galician Resolution', and its reply to the Czechs was to place Prague and its suburbs under martial law. The discontent was, however, so serious as to split the ministry itself. Auersperg had already resigned in connection with the negotiations with the Czechs, and now Taaffe, who had succeeded him, Potocki, and Berger, advised the Emperor to take a more conciliatory line

towards the nationalities. The other five ministers were against re-
laxing the iron hand, and when the Reichsrat voted in their favour,
the three dissidents resigned. Francis Joseph replaced them with
German Liberals, Hasner taking over as Minister President. But the
Poles now put in their Resolution again, and when it was again rejected, resigned their mandates *en bloc*. Most of the rest of the Opposition followed suit, reducing the membership of the Reichsrat to the
German Liberals and a handful of Ruthenes. The Emperor turned,
after all, to Potocki, who dissolved the Reichsrat and the *Landtage*,
which were to meet in the summer to elect a new Reichsrat for the
autumn. But before this could be done, the obvious imminence of war
between France and Prussia, which actually broke out in July, faced
Austria with the necessity of taking a crucial decision on its foreign
policy.

We know now that the view long current that Beust had been
appointed 'to organize a war of *revanche* against Prussia' is an over-
simplification. Francis Joseph had not yet brought himself to accept
the idea of a German Reich dominated by Prussia, and one task
which he assigned Beust in September 1866, had been 'to strengthen
Austria's ties with the South German States and to keep them out of
Prussia's grasp'. But he had also told the minister that he was giving
up the idea of war 'for a long time'. The tangled diplomatic negotiations in which Beust had afterwards engaged had therefore aimed
only at the peaceful containment of Prussia, and he had received with
great caution the overtures that had come to him from Napoleon,
including one made as early as April 1867, for an offensive and
defensive alliance, out of which Austria was to have got Silesia as her
share of the spoils of victory. By the end of 1869 the only agreement
between the two States was an understanding reached in September
of that year between the Monarchs which pledged Austria to benevolent neutrality in case of war between France and Prussia and
active intervention if a third Power (under which Russia was understood) came to the help of Prussia. France promised to support Austria if she was attacked. Conversations that might have made the
understanding binding broke down, and Austria's hands were thus
technically free when, in July 1870, war between France and Prussia
became obviously and inescapably imminent. On the 18th a Crown
Council met to decide how Austria should act. The 'war party', represented by the Archduke Albrecht and the Minister of Defence,
Kuhn (John had resigned in 1868, driven to despair by the Archduke's interferences) wanted Austria to mobilize quickly and intervene in the decisive battle, but Andrássy argued strongly that it was
necessary at all costs to avoid provoking Russia (whence warnings
had already been received), or at least to conserve the Monarchy's

strength against the eventuality, and both John, before his resignation, and Beck had said that the army was in no state, either materially or psychologically, to face another war. The Emperor therefore decided, regretfully, on neutrality, to be accompanied by cautious long-term preparations against any eventuality, and the course of the war later excluded any thought of entering it.

It was the situation created by Prussia's overwhelming military success that led, a little later, to the adoption by Austria of the foreign political alignment described in the next chapter, but not until the culmination and collapse of the remarkable episode with which the 'intermezzo' ended. The immediate effect of Prussia's triumphs was rather to give an impetus to Francis Joseph's search for an accommodation with his Slav subjects. For the foundation of the later Austro-German friendship was the renunciation by Germany of *grossdeutsch* policy directed against Austria, and although Bismarck had soon begun dropping hints of his good intentions, few people in Vienna had at first felt assured of their sincerity, and meanwhile Prussia's victories had sent a wave of *grossdeutsch* enthusiasm sweeping over the Germans of Austria so near-hysterical as to send the Court into a positive panic. A serious Austrian historian has written that 'almost all the members of the Imperial House, except the Empress Elisabeth, were convinced that the existence of Austria, and the rule of the dynasty, depended on dividing the Germans of Austria . . . into two halves, and entrusting the Sudetic branch to the safe-keeping of a Bohemian-Czech State'.[1]

This may be an exaggeration; but Francis Joseph's mind was already brimming over with resentment over the Liberals' attacks on the Church, and over their budgetary parsimony, which was what, in the last instance, had forced John and Beck to their admissions. If the Germans of Austria were not going to be even politically reliable, the Czechs' argument that Austria had entered on a 'false path' by sacrificing its Slavs to its Germans and Magyars, read reasonably enough.

In any case, the German Liberals had emerged from the summer elections with only a small minority, and themselves divided into two mutually hostile fractions, the 'Olds' and the 'Youngs'. Francis Joseph decided to change his course. On 7 February 1871, after top-secret negotiations, he replaced Potocki, who had remained in office *ad interim*, by Count Karl Sigmund Hohenwart, a moderate and conciliatory man, but a strong enemy of centralism, at the head of a ministry in which, from its predecessor, only the Minister of Finance, Holzgethan, stayed on (at Francis Joseph's special request); the rest were all new men: they included two Czechs and the brains and *spiritus rector* of the whole transaction, Professor Schäffle, a Protestant from Württemberg.

The Poles got their sop first. Goluchowski, who had been replaced when Auersperg resigned, was reappointed, and another Pole, Ritter von Grocholski, taken into the cabinet as Minister without Portfolio. In May Hohenwart further introduced in the Reichsrat a Bill which would have given the Poles less than they asked for, but enough for most appetites. Meanwhile the Czechs had been working out with Schäffle proposals for reconstructing Cis-Leithania as a set of federal units, each to enjoy very extensive autonomy. One of these was to be the Lands of the Bohemian Crown, which were to have their own Court Chancellery. The details were set out in eighteen 'Fundamental Articles', to which was appended a sensible and moderate language law for Bohemia, chiefly the work of Adolf Fischhof. Francis Joseph was to take the oath to the Articles at his coronation in Prague.

When the Articles had been agreed with Vienna, the Reichsrat and the centralist *Landtage* were dissolved. The elections, held under strong pressure, gave the Government a majority of two to one. An Imperial Rescript addressed to the Bohemian *Landtag* announced that Francis Joseph accepted the 'Fundamental Articles', 'gladly recognized' the rights of the Kingdom of Bohemia, and was prepared to have himself crowned in Prague and confirm his acceptance in his Coronation oath.

But now a shattering political crisis followed. There were riotous demonstrations in the German-Austrian Lands. The military feared that the unity of the defence forces would be impaired. Holzgethan said that the Articles were 'tantamount to State bankruptcy'. The Poles disliked anything which might blur the distinction between Galicia and other Lands. Andrássy, whom Francis Joseph invited to give his views, said that the Articles, in spite of their careful wording, were incompatible with the Compromise as it stood. Beust, who for a year past had been maintaining that friendship with Prussia was the best prophylactic against aggression by her, feared complications if the Germans of Austria felt aggrieved, and discreet warnings came from Bismarck and even from the German Emperor. Invited to modify their terms, the Czechs refused to do so. On 25 October, the Hohenwart Ministry resigned. Reluctant as he was to turn again to the German Liberals, Francis Joseph found no alternative. He sugared the pill by appointing another aristocrat Minister President in the person of 'Carlos' Auersperg's brother, Adolf, but the other ministers, except one Moravian and a soldier in charge of defence, were all German Liberals. The ministry took over on 25 November, after Andrássy had succeeded Beust at the Ballhausplatz on the 14th. The intermezzo was over.

Twelve

FOREIGN POLICY
1871–1903

It is difficult to find words strong enough to express the importance for the history of the Monarchy of the increased mellowness, or resignation, which, coming over Francis Joseph's spirit as he left youth behind him, made it possible for him to accept as final, first the eviction of his dynasty from Italy, then the impossibility of its recovering its leadership of Germany. From 1871 to 1918 the Monarchy was, for the first time in its history, facing east, sincerely and without *arrière pensée*. During these years it also, again almost for the first time, followed an unambitious foreign policy which, with rare exceptions, aimed only at maintaining, as far as it could, the territorial *status quo*. For its only possible directions of expansion would now have been southward or eastward, into areas inhabited chiefly by Southern Slavs or Roùmanians. Psychologically Francis Joseph seems to have inherited Maria Theresa's indifference towards prizes of undeveloped territories and backward peoples; and this apart, any acquisitions in those areas would have raised grave domestic problems. Neither half of the Monarchy wanted inside its own frontiers populations alien from and presumptively hostile to its own dominant people, but neither did it want the balance between itself and the other half tilted against it by the enlargement of its partner, while to give the acquisitions a separate status would have upset the balance of the Dualist system. If it was from Hungary that these objections came most often, and most effectively, this was because it was on Hungary's frontiers that the areas in question lay; but the German-Austrians showed themselves equally alive to the consideration when occasion arose. The great difficulties in maintaining the *status quo* were the frequent inability of the Porte, and the unwillingness of Russia, to collaborate in preserving it. As the national feelings of the Balkan peoples awoke, they became increasingly unwilling to remain under the Turkish yoke. But if the Serbs and Roumanians achieved independence, they would exercise a dangerous attraction on their kinsfolk in the Monarchy. They might also become satellites of Russia. Russia had already carried her advance south-westward a step further in 1870, when she had unilaterally denounced the clauses of the Treaty of Paris relating to the Black Sea and to navigation on the Danube. Her further wishes, as officially communicated, had not then gone beyond the revision of the rest of the treaty, but she had obviously made no spiritual renunciation of her wider ambitions, and a Balkans dominated by Russia would be even more dangerous to the Monarchy than one composed of really independent small national States.

The most genuinely defensive policy could not be indifferent towards such possibilities. Considerations of sheer self-defence might well lead to actively interventionist moves, which in special cases might even involve departure from territorial abnegation. Outstanding among such cases, and always so treated in Austrian foreign policy, was that of the provinces of Bosnia-Herzegovina, the annexation of which was also strongly urged by a group of highly-placed ex-Frontier officers who possessed the ear of the Archduke Albrecht, as making possible the acquisition of the considerable Croat population in the Provinces. This was an additional, special argument in favour of the annexation. But it could be truly argued that a hostile Power ensconced on the Dinaric Alps would constitute a threat, not only to Dalmatia, but the Monarchy's whole positions on the Adriatic. Finally, it was represented, perhaps not without justice, that even a small acquisition would be a gratifying change to the Monarch after his hitherto unbroken series of losses.

The chief aims which Andrássy set himself on entering on his office were the containment of Russia, and partly as the most effective means to that end, partly for its own sake, the consolidation of friendship with Berlin, always subject to the reservation that Austria must not be drawn by Germany into a conflict with the Western Powers. It was fortunate for him that he and Bismarck, whom he had already met, had liked one another. As early as 1870 Bismarck had given the Austrian ambassador an assurance that he would not allow Russia to attack Austria, but he was not prepared to give Andrássy the full defensive alliance that the Hungarian wanted: his aim, and that of his Emperor, was to bring about solidarity between Germany, Austria and Russia, and interchanges of visits between the three Emperors in fact culminated in the establishment, in October 1873, of a 'Three Emperors' League' (*Dreikaiserbund*) in which the three august signatories pledged one another to consultation should disputes arise between them, and to joint resistance against revolutionary socialism. A lull followed, which was broken by the Balkan peoples themselves. There were stirrings, with which Russian circles showed demonstrative sympathy, among the Bulgarians, and unrest in the Herzegovina which was stimulated by hopes, to which the 'forward' circles in Vienna had given some encouragement, that Austria was going to march into the Province. In 1875 full-scale revolt broke out there.

In the three years' crisis that followed, Andrássy's policy was essentially defensive. He first tried to save the integrity of the Sultan's dominions by organizing pressure on him to introduce adequate reforms. These efforts proved unavailing, and Serbia and Montenegro declared war in May 1876. Their armies were driven back by the Turks, who also repressed atrociously a rising in Bulgaria. The Czar prepared to go to the help of his co-religionists, and Andrássy's problem was then to ensure that if Russia emerged victorious from a war, the consequent redrawing of the Balkan map should not tilt the balance dangerously against Austria. Under the Budapest Conventions of January/March 1877, which developed an earlier understanding reached between Andrássy and Gorchakov at Reichstadt in July 1876, Russia agreed to limit her own European spoils of war to Bessarabia, and not to set up a Great Slav State in the Balkans. Austria was to remain neutral, and if she wished, to annex Bosnia-Herzegovina. The Treaty of San Stefano, imposed by Russia on Turkey in March 1878, ignored these undertakings completely, but other Powers, headed by Britain, joined Austria in insisting on its revision, and it was modified substantially in the Treaty of Berlin (13 July 1878). The European clauses of this recognized the independence of Roumania, Serbia and Montenegro, and modified their frontiers to the advantage of the two Slav States, while a big Bulgaria created at San Stefano, which would have covered much of the continental Balkans, was reduced to a vassal Principality north of the Balkans and an 'Autonomous Province of Eastern Roumelia' in the Maritsa valley, Macedonia remaining under direct Turkish sovereignty. Austria-Hungary received a 'European mandate' to occupy and administer Bosnia-Herzegovina, and the right to station garrisons in the Sanjak of Novi-Bazar, south of Bosnia.

The treaty brought Austria more than Bosnia. Russia's resentment at it led Bismarck to offer Andrássy the full alliance which he had thitherto refused. The Germans still refused to undertake any engagement inconsistent with their friendship with Russia, while Andrássy would sign no text which might conceivably involve him in a conflict with a Western Power. Finally, a text was agreed which pledged the two signatories to mutual support if either was attacked by Russia, and to benevolent neutrality if the attacker was another Power, unless it was supported by Russia, when the *casus foederis* would arise. The treaty was signed on 7 October, to run initially for five years, but renewable. It was to be kept secret, but Russia was to be warned if she made threatening preparations.

This instrument did not free Austria's hands, for to insure himself against getting drawn into war through an Austro-Russian conflict, Bismarck brought those Empires into a new 'Three Emperors'

Alliance' (*Dreikaiserbündnis*) to replace the League, which had disintegrated in 1878. In this instrument, signed on 18 June 1881 by
Andrássy's successor, Baron Haymerle (Andrássy had resigned after
the conclusion of the treaty with Germany), the signatories pledged
themselves to benevolent neutrality if one of them found itself at war
with a fourth Great Power. Any modification of the territorial status
of Turkey in Europe was to be made only by common agreement
between the signatories, but the annexation by Austria of Bosnia-
Herzegovina (but not of the Sanjak) would not count as a modification.

The Alliance, however, fared no better than the League. Again the
first blow was struck by a Balkan State. In 1885 the Principality of
Bulgaria and Eastern Roumelia proclaimed their unification under un-
foreseen circumstances which led to bizarre developments. Russia's
attempt to utilize the situation to bring Bulgaria under her political
control brought her and Austria, at one point, to the verge of war.
The parties eventually simmered down, thanks largely to Bismarck's
intervention. But the Alliance could not be renewed, or replaced.
Austria and Russia were never again allies.

This did not mean that their relations were always hostile. Neither
wanted war, and in 1894 Austria's new Foreign Minister, Count
Gustav Kálnoky (Haymerle had died suddenly in 1881), reached a
sort of standstill agreement with Giers, the Russian Foreign Minister,
that Austria would refrain from meddling in the affairs of Bulgaria
(whose new Prince, Ferdinand of Saxe-Coburg-Gotha, incidentally
showed himself extraordinarily adroit in evading commitments to
either side) if Russia did the same in Serbia. Agenor Goluchowski,
jun., who succeeded Kálnoky in May 1895, was a man of peace, and
when he accompanied Francis Joseph to St Petersburg in 1897 he
agreed with Giers's successor, Muraviev, on a policy of maintenance
of the Balkan *status quo* if possible, and failing that, collaboration to
secure an equitable settlement, under which no Balkan State should
become disproportionately strong. They did in fact honour the pact,
combining under the Mürzsteg Agreements of October 1903 to press
the Sultan to introduce reforms when unrest broke out in Macedonia.
But a closer contractual relationship between them was by this time
hardly possible. When in 1890 Bismarck's successor, Caprivi, had
refused to renew the 'Reinsurance Treaty' with which Bismarck had
sought to make good the collapse of the Three Emperors' Alliance,
and Russia had turned to France, the division of continental Europe
into two blocs had begun to take shape. Austria was still anxious to
keep on good terms with Britain, and in 1897 actually joined her and
Italy in a 'Mediterranean Entente', which survived ten years, to
maintain the *status quo* in the Near East. But in the last resort, Aus-

tria's place could only be in the bloc which contained Germany.

The Austro-German Treaty was a curiously sketchy instrument. It contained no provisions for consultation or co-ordination of policies, or for military dispositions in case of war (a few, not very detailed arrangements between the two general staffs were scrapped by Germany when the Schlieffen Plan was adopted). It did not prevent mutual irritations, jealousies and rivalries. Nevertheless, Germany's and Austria's need for each other did not disappear: it rather increased after the Franco-Russian *rapprochement*, and as time went on, it somehow developed into a relationship of special indissolubility, as between brothers who may fret against their blood-tie, but have to accept the fact of its existence. To the ageing Emperor, in particular, it became as much a fact of life as his relationship with his own German subjects, with which it was interrelated. For them it was at once a symbol and a reinforcement of their claim to be still the leading element in Austria, and any attempt to denounce it would have provoked a storm which Francis Joseph would not have dared conjure up, had he wished. Conversely, the Reich regarded the maintenance of Austria's basic 'Germandom', as essential to its own security, and more than once intervened when it seemed endangered.

By this time Germany was no longer the Monarchy's only ally. In 1881 Kálnoky had concluded with Prince Milan of Serbia a secret treaty which, in return for certain concessions, largely personal to the Prince, made Serbia virtually an economic satellite of the Monarchy. In the same year Italy, alarmed by France's occupation of Tunis, had approached the Monarchy. The eventual result had been the conclusion of an alliance (the 'Dreibund' or 'Triplice') under which Germany and Austria promised to come to the help of Italy if she were attacked without provocation by France, while Italy undertook the corresponding obligation if France attacked Germany; Austria contented herself with a promise of benevolent neutrality by Italy in the event of a war in the East. In October 1883, Austria concluded a treaty with Roumania, to which Germany then adhered. It provided that if Roumania was attacked without provocation, Austria would bring to her, 'in ample time', help and assistance against the aggressor. Roumania undertook the reciprocal obligation if the attack on Austria came on 'a portion of the State bordering on Roumania'.

In 1895 Austria let the treaty with Serbia lapse in return for a promise of good behaviour from the regents for Milan's son and successor. The two other treaties were still in force, but neither stood on solid foundations. That with Roumania had been concluded with the King personally; its very existence was known only to a handful of men, and it could not be prophesied how the Roumanian people would react should it be invoked in a situation in which strongly-

felt national aspirations called for a different orientation. The treaty
with Italy was bitterly resented by Italy's irredentists, and the Italian
Government itself lost enthusiasm for it when Italy's relations with
France improved after 1900. In 1887, however, Kálnoky, under
pressure of the crisis of that year and harried by Bismarck, had
signed a bilateral agreement with Italy under which the two parties
pledged one another to use all their influence to prevent any territorial change 'in the East' detrimental to either of them. Should, however, either of them find itself forced 'to undertake a long-term or
permanent occupation' of any part of the area, it would do so only
after consultation with the other, and on a basis of satisfactory compensation to it. This agreement, which was written into the Triplice
as its Article IX when it was renewed in 1891, proved a veritable
cuckoo's egg, for Kálnoky assumed that it would not imply the granting of compensation to Italy from territory of the Monarchy, but
failed to get any confirmation of this beyond a verbal assurance.

Thirteen

AUSTRIA UNDER DUALISM
1871–1903

Political History: Auersperg-Taaffe

When in October 1871, Francis Joseph dismissed Hohenwart, he also dismissed from his own mind any thought of substituting a different structural arrangement of his Monarchy for the Dualist system; when plans to that effect came to be mooted again, it was only as projects for the future, to be realized after his death, by his successor. He also refused to consider any suggestion for changing the structural pattern of Cis-Leithania, as established under the 'December Constitution'.

Nevertheless, the result which the Hungarians and their Austrian opposite numbers had intended to emerge from the Compromise, and what many writers to this day describe as having been its actual effect – a parliamentary system resting in Cis-Leithania on its Germans, and in Hungary on its Magyars – in fact survived in the West only for a few years. After this, Austria still possessed an elected assemblage, composed from political parties, and those constituting the majority of the day were able, up to a point, to get their wishes satisfied. But it was little more in fact than it was in name, an advisory body to the Crown. Where fundamentals were concerned, the Monarch enforced his will, if necessary, over its head, and if it persisted in opposing his wishes, he replaced it by another. The system was a purely Austrian one, an adaptation of theory to the facts of Austrian life. No analysis can reach the heart of it; all the historian can do is to record the facts as they occurred.

Neither, after the first years, were those majorities exclusively, or even preponderantly, German. In so far as the Germans continued mainly to administer the country (under the Crown) it was from outside Parliament. The few years during which parliamentary government, and that by Germans, was a near-reality were those which followed the appointment of Auersperg in 1871. He and his men really regarded themselves as the rulers, through Parliament, of Austria, and Auersperg put through two measures designed to consolidate their position. One was a new Franchise Act which, while not extending the franchise, and retaining the Curia system, raised the total number of deputies to 353, and increased the proportion in it of

the Government's own supporters. The Great Landlords' Curia was
now to send 85 deputies, the Chambers of Commerce 51, the urban communes 116 and the rural 131. Secondly, an agreement was
reached with the Poles, who, in return for virtual autonomy for Galicia, exercised through a *Landesmannminister*, agreed to support the
Government in power in Vienna. This was a move of extraordinary
importance for the parliamentary history of Cis-Leithania, for it was
often the Polish vote alone that enabled governments to get essential
legislation through. It proved less advantageous than they had expected to the Germans, for the Poles' support was given to all Governments, not to German ones only. When the Germans awoke to this
fact, with a shock, it was too late to undo the work, although they
were trying to do so up to 1918.

Meanwhile, their path when they took office was still being eased
by the extraordinary economic boom described elsewhere. This was
ended abruptly by the gigantic stock exchange '*Krach*' of 'Black
Friday', 9 May 1873, the political effect of which was to deal a shattering blow to popular faith in the blessings of economic liberalism,
and also in the personal integrity of many of its practitioners in high
places. Herbst, who was the leader of the party, was one of the few
who had kept their hands clean, but his dictatorial manners had
estranged many of his followers, and when, in the autumn, new elections were held, the Liberals split into three parties, 88 'Old Liberals',
57 'Progressives' (most of them old 'Autonomists') and 5 'Viennese
Radicals'. They still, however, sat as a 'club', and of the other parties,
the 49 Poles were prepared to support them, as were, for considerations, the 14 Ruthenes and 13 members of 'splinter Parties', while
the 33 Bohemian Czechs still absented themselves from the Reichsrat. The only real opposition in that body thus consisted of the 44
'Constitutional Great Landlords' and 43 members of a federalist
'Party of the Right' organized by Hohenwart. Francis Joseph had no
choice but to reappoint Auersperg, who made only minor changes in
his team.

The reappointed Government returned to its attacks on the
Church, but their campaign no longer went easily. One measure
proposed by them was rejected by the Upper House, another vetoed
by the Emperor. Others they put through, but at the cost of making
implacable enemies, including the Emperor, and when they had completed this side of their programme, as far as they were able, they
found little more to do except to exercise a financial domination,
which had shown its feet of clay. Their last two or three years of office
were practically barren, and in them they incurred further unpopularity by their handling of the negotiations with Hungary on the 'Economic Compromise'; this not quite justly, for Hungarians, too,

thought themselves overreached (see p. 209) and the settlement was not unfavourable to Cis-Leithania: it gained an adjustment of 1.4 per cent of the quota and yielded only a very little ground over the Hungarians' demand for more control over the National (now called the Austro-Hungarian) Bank.

The end for them came with the outbreak of the Eastern Crisis. As soon as the idea of Austria's either annexing or occupying Bosnia became known, it was vigorously opposed by Herbst's followers, who disliked either course, partly on grounds of economy, partly as adding to the number of Slavs in the Monarchy. They claimed that no foreign political enterprise involving expenditure, as either course must do, could constitutionally be undertaken without the consent of the Reichsrat. They threatened to refuse to vote either the occupation, the credits for it, or the defence estimates, which were just coming up for their decennial renewal, and even threatened to vote a reduction of the armed forces.

Herbst had the wording of the law on his side, but it seems clear that Francis Joseph had never understood it to bear this interpretation, and the cup of his resentment against the Liberals was filled. Instead of abandoning the occupation, he set about finding an administration which would vote it. Auersperg, who had tendered his resignation, was kept in office until he had found enough pliable Liberals to vote acceptance of the Treaty of Berlin, a credit to cover the costs of occupation, and a 'provisional' quota of recruits. Then, while a stop-gap administration under Dr Stremayr held the fort, Francis Joseph commissioned his boyhood's friend and old henchman, Count Eduard Taaffe, to collect enough followers to form a stable administration.

This, in the event, proved to be the end of the German Liberals' political hegemony, for although Francis Joseph would have allowed them to continue in office if they had met him on the points which he regarded as touching his own prerogatives, they refused to do so, whereas Taaffe was able to get promises of support from the Poles, the Clericals and most of the feudals. He also performed the important feat of securing from the newly-formed party of 'Young Czechs' their consent to return to Vienna, subject to certain administrative and cultural concessions. When the terms had been agreed, although not published, elections were held (July 1879) which gave the Right a majority, although a small one,[1] and the Emperor appointed Taaffe Minister President.

Even so, Francis Joseph and Taaffe did not want to drive the Liberals entirely into opposition, and three of the six departmental ministers in Taaffe's first list came from that camp. But between

1880 and 1882 the Czechs' bill was honoured in the form of three enactments. The first, drawn up by Stremayr, and known accordingly as 'the Stremayr ordinances', laid down that all State administrative and judicial officials, in any part of Bohemia or Moravia, were bound to use the language of the 'party' with whom they were dealing. The second enabled the Czechs to get more representation in the First Curia, the third divided the University of Prague into two distinct foundations, one Czech and the other German.

Reasonable as were at least the second and third of these concessions (and even the first kept German as the 'inner' official language) the Germans protested furiously against them and abused their three representatives in the Government so furiously as 'traitors' that all three resigned their portfolios, which were filled by a Pole and two non-party men.[2] The Liberals now declared themselves officially 'Oppositional', leaving as 'Government Parties' what came to be known as the 'Iron Ring' of feudalists, Clericals and Slavs.

Taaffe's Minister Presidency lasted for fourteen years. As parliamentary history, these were an off-period, except that in 1882 another franchise reform was enacted, which enlarged the number of voters in the rural communes by 34 per cent, in the urban by 26 per cent, thus enfranchising large numbers of peasants and *petits bourgeois*, both classes sworn enemies of big business and financial interests. In consequence, the elections of 1885 brought a further swing to the Right, bringing its voting strength up to 190,[3] against 163 of the Left. For the rest, the legislative enactments of Taaffe's term of office, the most important of which related to tariff policy, social legislation, and education, are described under their subject headings. He himself did not aim at doing more than keep the machine ticking over, by what one of his opponents called 'muddling through', while he himself described it as 'keeping all the nationalities in a condition of equal and well-modulated discontent'.

He did so with considerable adroitness and success, largely because his regime was, at bottom, not parliamentary. He paid deference, within limits, to the wishes of the parties of the 'Iron Ring', favouring agrarian interests rather than industrial, those of handicrafts rather than factory industry, clerical rather than free-thinking, Slav rather than German. But he was not their servant, but the Emperor's. The 'equal' in his epigram was not meaningless. He seldom insisted on a demand by his supporters which was very strongly resisted by the Opposition, nor rejected absolutely a strongly-felt Oppositional demand. He nearly always tried to find a compromise, and this often contained a good deal of equity. The relative peace which prevailed in Cis-Leithanian domestic politics during his regime was a tribute to this.

Taaffe's fall came over the German-Czech question. The Germans had not ceased to protest against the Stremayr ordinances, which had also brought the Czechs less than their full wishes, but every attempt to reach agreement had broken down on the intransigence of one side or the other. In 1890, the Emperor having become seriously alarmed over the Germans' discontent, Taaffe invited the leaders of the two nationalities to meet in Vienna.

The settlement which the delegations agreed to propose was exceptionally sensible and equitable, but the reckoning had been made in the absence of one of the hosts. By whoever's fault, the Young Czechs, although by now the strongest Czech party, had not been invited to the negotiating table. In revenge, they denounced the aged Rieger, who had led their national delegation, as a traitor, and staged such rowdy scenes that even those who approved the proposals were afraid to say so. In the event, only one of them, the division of the Bohemian 'Cultural' and 'School' Councils into two, ever came into effect.

This would have been just another failure to square the circle, but the elections were due. These took place in February–March 1891, bringing little change in the numbers of the Conservative parties, the Poles, or the representatives of the smaller nationalities, and although the German Liberals lost seventeen mandates to Steinwender's 'German National Party' and fourteen to the newly-formed Christian Socials, this did not upset the national balance. But the Young Czechs emerged with thirty-seven mandates, against only twelve to the Old Czechs, and this shook the foundations of Taaffe's majority, for there was clearly no hope of making the Young Czechs into a governmental party. His only hope was to reconcile the Germans, but some minor concessions which he made to them only further infuriated the Czechs, who initiated the practice, which soon became general, of frustrating the work of the Reichsrat by organized obstruction, and there was such disorder in Bohemia that the Government proclaimed a state of emergency in Prague and arrested seventy members of a subversive organization, the *Omladina*. There were also workers' demonstrations in favour of franchise reform.

Curiously enough, it was these which determined the next move. One of the gestures made by Taaffe to placate the Germans had been to dismiss his Finance Minister, Dunajaweski, one of their *bêtes noires*. His successor, Emil Steinbach, a highly intelligent and progressive man whose sympathies, in spite of his origin (he was a Hungarian Jew by birth), were strongly with the Christian Socials, represented to the Emperor and to Taaffe that 'the lower, politically uncorrupted classes' were 'sound'; 'they would make social, not national politics; they were 'dynastically minded, reliable, appreci-

ative and easy to rule'. He convinced Francis Joseph; Taaffe was
already of the same mind. Steinbach drafted a Bill which, while keeping the Curia system intact, extended the suffrage for the third and
fourth Curias to include virtually every literate male tax-payer who
had reached his 25th year. The electorate was increased from about
1,725,000 to nearly three times that number.

Prepared in deep secrecy, and introduced, without previous an-
nouncement, in October 1893, the Bill had a disastrous reception.
Of all the major parties, only the Young Czechs approved it. The
Poles, Clericals and Liberals all saw their voters going elsewhere,
and united to oppose it so vehemently that on 10 November Francis
Joseph relieved Taaffe of the Minister Presidency.

It seems safe to say that by this time Francis Joseph had quite satisfied himself that 'parliamentary' government, in the sense of a government committed to carrying out the wishes of the parties composing
the parliamentary majority of the day, was not a political form applicable to Austrian conditions. His own wish would have been to
install 'an administration standing above the parties', that is, an
essentially bureaucratic regime, and he had already selected his
preferred successor to Taaffe in the person of the Governor of Galicia,
Count Badeni, who agreed with this conception of a Minister President's office. But the parties which had brought about Taaffe's fall
insisted so vehemently on their right to his succession that Francis
Joseph consented, reluctantly, to allow the next ministry to be a
coalition of the Poles, the Clericals and the German Liberals, giving
the Presidency to Prince Alfred Windisch-Graetz, the grandson of
the hero (or evil genius) of 1848. The three parties agreed between
themselves to introduce no measures which would 'alter the national
status quo'. The experiment, however, was a dismal failure. The
parties not represented in the Government frustrated its work by
obstruction and other sabotage; those in it quarrelled between themselves and after two years the Liberals used a pretext of absurd triviality to bring it down.[4]

After a stop-gap government of officials had bridged the gap from
June to September, Francis Joseph now appointed Badeni, who
formed an administration composed mainly of officials and described
by him as 'standing above the parties', which it was 'to lead and not
follow'. His first moves, which included the lifting of the state of
emergency in Prague, were well received, and in June 1896, he piloted
through the Reichsrat a franchise reform which left the new voters
enfranchised in Steinbach's Bill with the vote, but assigned only a
relatively small minority of them to the existing (third and fourth)
Curias; for the rest, a new 'general' fifth Curia, sending 72 deputies

to the Reichsrat, was created. He then dissolved the Reichsrat, and in March 1897, held elections on the new basis.

These did not alter the picture in essentials. The German Liberals collapsed, but their former followers simply went over to other German parties (the Christian Socials may fairly be counted as such) leaving the national balance unchanged. And by ill-fortune a moment was drawing near at which a parliamentary majority would be a legal necessity: for the decennial revision of the Economic Compromise would then be due and Deák's idealism in 1867 had produced the embarrassing but incontrovertible stipulation that to be valid in Hungary, this had to be voted by both Parliaments.

It would obviously not be possible to get laws to this effect voted by Parliament, but both Badeni and Francis Joseph believed that if the reforms were enacted by Order in Council, the Germans, although they would be angry at first, would simmer down. In this faith Badeni, on 5th April, issued Orders in Council for Bohemia and Moravia, the effect of which was to put Czech on a footing of complete equality with German in both the inner and the outer services of those Lands. As from 1 July 1901 no person should be employed in the State public services of either Land who was not conversant with both languages.

The event, however, proved that Badeni and the Emperor had misjudged the feelings of the Germans, who reacted with unprecedented fury. They made work in the Reichsrat impossible until its Standing Orders were amended by a trick. But no such operation was possible against the disorder in the streets, which reached near-revolutionary dimensions. On 28 November Francis Joseph accepted the luckless Pole's resignation.

He gave Badeni's post to the Pole's Minister of Education, F.M. von Gautsch, who composed an administration all the members of which, including Gautsch himself, were civil servants. Gautsch put through (by Paragraph 14) a six-months' budget and a short-term prolongation of the Economic Compromise, and also, while leaving Badeni's ordinances on the statute book, modified them considerably: the 'language of service', outer and inner, was to be that of the District concerned (German, Czech or mixed) and officials were required only to possess such linguistic knowledge as their service 'really required'. This done, Gautsch gave way to Count Franz Anton Thun, who formed another Government of civil servants, plus three ministers representing respectively the Poles, the Czechs and the Germans.

Thun was no fanatical Czech, but his name associated him with the Czech cause (Count Leo Thun was his uncle), and the Germans chose to regard him in that light. They opened a furious campaign for the repeal of the Badeni-Gautsch ordinances, coupled with vicious attacks on Thun. This was supported from the Reich, which also chose to take exception to Austria's foreign policy (this was the juncture at which Goluchowski was seeking a *rapprochement* with Russia, and the Czechs in the Delegations were indiscreetly advocating a reversal of Austria's international alignments). The German ambassador in Vienna, Count Eulenburg, told Francis Joseph that German opinion, even the Kaiser himself, 'would be unable to ignore, with the best will in the world, the effects of a Czech majority as Government Party (in Austria)'.

At first Thun, and Francis Joseph himself, annoyed at the Germans' interference, and especially at support which was coming from Germany for the '*Los von Rom*' movement (see p. 202), gave as good as they got. But various factors, among which the Germans' warnings must have been one, tipped the scales in Francis Joseph's mind, and he decided, as he told Eulenburg, 'to turn towards *Deutschtum*'. On 2 October 1899, after various attempts to form another parliamentary or pseudo-parliamentary government on a coalition basis had failed, he dismissed Thun and appointed Count Clary-Aldringen, Governor of Styria, with the avowed mission of repealing the Badeni-Gautsch ordinances, which he duly did on 14 October.

Clary's tenure of office was short: the repeal of the ordinances had infuriated the Czechs, while leaving the Germans unsatisfied. In view of the complaints against his predecessors' abuses of Paragraph 14 (Thun had used this fourteen times) he had promised not to use it, but found it impossible to carry on without it, and being an honest man, resigned after six months. After an interim administration headed by Ritter von Wittek had carried on for a few weeks, during which it put through essential business by using Paragraph 14, Francis Joseph, on 18 January 1900, appointed Dr Ernst von Koerber, another civil servant with ministerial experience, who composed his administration on what was now becoming the regular pattern: civil servants, with a Polish and Czech *Landsmannminister* (the Germans could not agree on a man to represent them), both without portfolios.

Koeber began his administration with an attempt to work with the Reichsrat. He invited representatives of the Germans and Czechs to work out their own solution of their problem, promising to accept it. Meanwhile, the economy had run into difficulties. He prepared a grandiose programme of public works to meet the crisis, and then dissolved the Reichsrat, adjuring the electorate to choose a successor which would pay attention to the real problems of the country.

The move failed to achieve its purpose. Everywhere, the extremists, national and also social, gained ground at the expense of the moder-

ates, and the results offered no hope of a stable parliamentary majority. The Germans had the largest single national contingent, but
not an absolute majority. They could frustrate the wishes of others,
but not impose their own. The parties did for a brief while renounce
obstruction while they scrambled for pickings from the public works
programme, but soon relapsed. The Czech-German conversations
produced no result whatever. Koerber had to fall back on methods
which were rather a prostitution of parliamentary government than a
legitimate use of it. Where the quirk conventions of Austrian parliamentary life demanded it, he got together a majority by more or less
undisguised corruption of parties and individuals; otherwise, he resorted to Paragraph 14.

By these devices, in which he developed a great expertise, Koerber
got budgets voted, reached the agreement described elsewhere with
his Hungarian counterpart on the renewal of the Economic Compromise, and got the upward revision of the standing army through the
Reichsrat. A very able man, he was the author also of much valuable
work in other fields. Only a part of the public works programme was
realized (the estimates of the cost of it had been over-ambitious) but
so far as it went, it produced beneficial results, as did many of his
other reforms. But while the record showed that Francis Joseph could
still find able and devoted servants to govern Cis-Leithania for him,
it did not show that they were able to govern themselves.

Economic and Social Developments

In the thirty years 1870–1900 the population of Cis-Leithania rose
from about 20 million to 27 million, and the increase would have
been even greater but for large-scale emigration which, setting in
after 1880, was running at over 100,000 a year by 1900. The accompanying development of the economy was irregular. Paradoxically,
the war of 1866 had given it a remarkable stimulus, since extra currency had, perforce, been printed to finance it, and had remained in
circulation, thereby relieving the near-intolerable stringency which
had prevailed. The Treaty of Prague, then the Hungarian Compromise, had been widely taken as marking the opening of a new era of
peace, international and domestic, and they had been followed by a
series of bumper harvests in Hungary, coinciding with shortages elsewhere in Europe. The growth in domestic capital had attracted
foreign speculators and an extraordinary boom had set in, during
which new railway lines were laid down, new industries founded, and
credit institutions, many of them, indeed, the merest bucket-shops, pro-
liferated. The boom collapsed abruptly in the great *Krach* of 1873, after
which the foreign capital retreated as precipitately as it had come,

leaving behind it a trail of ruin. Several years of depression followed, but after 1879, when the Monarchy adopted an autonomous tariff, a gradual recovery set in, and in spite of a couple of further, less severe, set-backs, the general trend became upward. Industrialization set in again and work on the railways recommenced. The 1900 census showed 13,700,000 persons – 52 per cent of the population – still deriving their livelihoods from agriculture, forestry and fisheries, but these occupational groups were now barely holding their own, while just over seven million persons (25.9 per cent) were deriving their livelihoods from industry and mining, 10 per cent from finance, commerce and communications, and 3.4 per cent from the public services. Except in Galicia-Bukovina the towns were now taking up nearly the whole increase of the population: Vienna had a population of 1,675,000, Prague, 201,000, Trieste, 178,000, Lemberg, 160,000, Graz, 138,000, Brünn, 109,000. There were 44 towns with populations of 20,000, 74 of 10–20,000, 198 of 5–10,000 and 344 of 2–5,000.

These developments had brought with them shifts in the social and political importance of the different occupational and vocational groups which were sometimes considerable, although smaller than would have occurred in a framework less resistant to innovation.

The great landlords, who, as we have said in an earlier chapter, had survived the land reform with relatively small economic losses – sometimes even with profit – had continued to hold their own, economically, not too ill. In 1896 over 29 per cent of the area of Cis-Leithania fell into the category of 'large estates' (200 + hectares), of which about two-thirds were owned by a few hundred *hochadelig* families. 1,200,000 hectares (4.5 per cent of the whole area) were protected by *fideicommissa*, of which there were 292.

As a class the great feudal magnates had naturally lost some of their old political weight: the relatively centralized bureaucratic system of the late nineteenth century had no place for the provincial kinglets of the early eighteenth. But their voices still carried enormous weight in the affairs of State: not only were they still very largely represented in the Lower House, and more largely still, in the Upper; even more important was the fact that Francis Joseph, to the end of his days, had never truly rid himself of the Habsburg family habit of using the highest aristocrats as his viceroys. Almost all the Ministers President appointed by him up to 1900 were taken from this class, and all the Foreign ministers. All the Court posts went to them automatically, and nearly all the senior administrative positions such as that of Governor of a Land. On their own ancestral acres they were still near-omnipotent: it would have been a bold minor representative of the State who would have dared oppose the will of the local lord. How far, as their enemies maintained, the *Hochadel* used their power simply to defend their own interests is a question which it is difficult to answer. They were probably neither more nor less selfish than any other class which earlier history had placed in a position that now carried with it more advantage than responsibility.

The economic developments of the period had naturally brought a big increase in the numbers of the upper and middle bourgeoisie, and also a change in its composition which it would be a falsification of history to leave unmentioned. This was the increase of the Jewish element in it. Even up to the 1850s the Austrian Jews had not emerged in large numbers from Galicia; in the Alpine Lands they were still almost unknown, and in Vienna they consisted mainly of two groups, neither of them numerically large: a small, although immensely powerful, coterie of financiers, whose importance derived chiefly from their international connections, and some representatives of certain professions, especially that of medicine, to which they were admitted freely. They had been still subject to inequalities before the law from the last of which they were relieved only in 1867 and 1868. But even before that date their numbers had been growing rapidly, chiefly by immigration from Galicia. While only 6,200 of them had been counted in Vienna in 1860, the number had risen by 1870 to 40,200; by 1880 to 72,600 and by 1890 to118,500. By this time they virtually dominated the entire central credit system of Austria and owned a big part of its industry, most of its wholesale and much of its retail trade. The central Press was almost entirely in their hands and they were very strong in most of the professions and in the arts.

On national issues, it may be added, all of them in the Hereditary and Bohemian Lands counted themselves, and were counted by others, as Germans. They tended to remain behind the scenes in politics, but they supplied much of their brains (and sinews) to the Liberal parties. They also influenced Austrian politics very strongly in another way, in that from the 1880s onward the programmes of almost all the newer German parties, including the Christian Socials (but excepting the Social Democrats) contained an ingredient, sometimes a large one, of anti-Semitism.

With this reinforcement, the *haute* and *moyenne bourgeoisie* of Austria, particularly of Vienna, had come to constitute a very powerful factor in the State. Their role in its cultural life apart – and it is fair to say also that the imposing, if sometimes slightly indigestible, cultural life of the period, much as it always owed to the patronage of the Court and the aristocracy, was bourgeois in its inspiration – the economic and financial interests represented by them had to be taken into account by every government. Yet it was only during a dozen or so years in all – five under Schmerling, two under 'Carlos' Auersperg and six under his brother – that the bourgeoisie as a class could be said to be politically 'in power' in Austria. And the interests which they represented even during those years were only in part those of their class; in part (during the Schmerling era) those of the centralist State; in part those of the German nationality to which most of them claimed adherence. Later it was not class interests at all that dominated the Reichsrat, but national.

The 1860s and 1870s had been hard years for that very characteristic element of Austrian society, the *petite bourgeoisie*. The *Gewerbeordnung* introduced by Bruck in 1859 had swept away many of the safeguards of their position which, thanks largely to the influence of the Church, had survived the earlier onslaughts of the fashionable Liberalism, leaving them exposed to the full blast of capitalism. Their plight, however, and particularly the fact that the forces against them were so largely Jewish, had in time brought friends to their help. Taaffe's reform of 1882 had enfranchised large numbers of these. Many of the new voters had at first been attracted to Schönerer's movement described on page 200 but 'Ritter Georg's' hostility to the dynasty and the Church repelled the mass of this eminently God-fearing and loyal class; more of them were attracted by a crusade for social reform on Christian Social lines preached in these years by Freiherr von Vogelsang (himself by origin a Protestant from Prussia) and then taken up by a group of Austrian aristocrats headed by Prince Alois Liechtenstein. The several fractions accepting Vogelsang's doctrines were united and formed into a Christian Social Party by Dr Karl Lueger, a young man of humble origin and a golden tongue, who had made a name for himself on the municipal council of Vienna by his attacks on corruption and vested interests – attacks which seldom failed to stress the Jewish element in their objects. Formed just in time to take part in the 1891 elections, the party secured in them twelve mandates, seven of them in Vienna. Its declared policy was protection for the 'little man' against exploitation which did not need to be Jewish, but was often assumed to be so. For the rest it was strongly and demonstratively dynastic and 'Great Austrian', in spite of which the Christian Socials were for some years something of outcasts: their social radicalism not only antagonized their die-hard enemies, the Jewish capitalists, but made them suspect in the eyes of the Court, the aristocracy and the higher ranks of the Church. Francis Joseph repeatedly refused to confirm the election of Lueger as Burgomaster of Vienna. His popularity was, however, so enormous that eventually the Emperor gave way and Lueger became Burgomaster. The Christian Socials won twenty-eight seats in the Reichsrat elections of 1893, and almost every seat in Vienna in the 1902 elections for the Lower Austrian *Landtag*. The party had by

now also a considerable following outside Vienna, gaining many
rural seats from the 'Bishops' Party', as the Catholic People's Party
was often known.[5] Lueger was, moreover, an administrator of
genius: under his direction the municipal services of Vienna became
among the most progressive in Europe.

The condition of the peasants in the 1870s and 1880s was one of
general, although not universal, deterioration. The Liberal legislation
of 1868 had produced the same dichotomy as the land reform. Some
thrifty and enterprising farmers had been able to take advantage of
the new freedom to re-equip, consolidate and even enlarge their holdings: success stories among this class were not unknown, especially
in the more fertile Alpine valleys where the population was economically mature and credit comparatively easy to obtain. But even efficient Alpine farmers often found it impossible to overcome the
handicap of bad local communications. To others, the impact of
1868 had been even more severe than that of 1848/9, which had
been followed by years during which the price of peasants' produce
had been high and the trade in it still largely carried on in the local
markets. Now the importation from Hungary was organized and that
from overseas on the threshold, and outside the favoured areas, the
peasants were in no state to meet it. The removal of restrictions on
borrowing often had disastrous effects. The 'Rustical Bank of Galicia',
a Jewish enterprise which operated from 1868 to 1884, and to which
one Galician peasant in twenty was indebted, charged 40 per cent,
and this was much lower than the rate charged by the local money-
lenders: this, we are told, ranged from 50 per cent to 150 per cent,
and cases of 500 per cent were not unknown. The peasant here,
moreover, seldom borrowed for productive purposes, more usually to
help himself out after a bad harvest, to pay the tax-collector, or to
finance a wedding, which it was a point of prestige to celebrate on the
most extravagant scale. An enormous number of peasants were sold
up, either turned into tenant farmers working for rentals which were
far more exorbitant than their old obligations when they were not free
men, or driven off the land altogether.

Their holdings were taken over, sometimes by a neighbour (in the
Alpine lands, a valley farmer often added an upland farm to his
holding) or by a big landowner, who might let them simply revert
to deer forests. Not infrequently an ignorant peasant, unused to the
sight of money in any but the smallest quantities, was dazzled into
sale by a large bank-note dangled before his eyes. There were districts in which the number of farms and even the total populations
actually went down.

These, as a rule, were areas in which the peasants could find an
alternative livelihood off the land. Elsewhere, holdings were sub-

divided until they fell below subsistence level. In these, the surplus populations helped themselves out by working on neighbouring large estates, or as seasonal labourers, often organized in gangs, some of which travelled as far afield as Germany, France or Belgium. The remuneration was usually paid directly in the form of a quota, traditionally a ninth of the crop harvested, and on this they subsisted from the end of one harvest year to the opening of the next.

The safety-valve of emigration, when it opened towards the end of the century, relieved the congestion perceptibly, and by this time conditions were improving a little also in other respects. The weakest members had been eliminated altogether and the survivors were organizing their defences. Various technical improvements had brought about a considerable rise in the yield of most main crops and the spreading co-operative movement was enabling the peasant cultivators to get a more decent share of the fruits of their labours, while a recovery in world prices from the nadir of 1895 made that share worth more.

As for the farm labourers, one may quote the comment of one observer that 'it was a wonder that there were grown people who would give a whole day's work for such pay'. They were, indeed, beginning to refuse to do so, and the landlords were complaining that the wages asked were higher than they could afford.

The greatly enlarged numbers of the factory workers and miners long failed to bring them any improvement either in their material conditions or in any other direction. The policy of the Liberals towards them was one of unrelieved harshness. Their single gain during these years was that the right of association, inserted by the Liberals in the December constitution for their own benefit, could not be denied to others, and after its enactment, a number of workers' associations, including the important *Arbeiterbildungsverein*, came into being. Following this, various political movements were founded, but none of them could make much headway against the hostility of the Government, which pursued their leaders with ruthless hostility. A slight relaxation of the persecution came during the Hohenwart-Schäffle interlude: some imprisoned leaders were released, and the Government was preparing to introduce some social reforms. But it fell before the measures were ready, and the returning Liberals left the drafts lying. Meanwhile conditions had got worse than ever. The boom of 1868–74 produced an influx into the factories, causing great housing shortages in the industrial centres, which were exploited by unscrupulous landlords; then the *Krach* caused unemployment on an unprecedented scale. This weakened further the labour movement. The workers dared not complain for fear of dismissal, and they were disillusioned with their leaders. In any case they had no money to pay subscriptions. Trade Union membership sank to a low level. In the 1880s 'anarchistic' tendencies developed. There was violence, against which the authorities reacted very strongly. A state of emergency was proclaimed in Vienna and its environs, including Wiener Neustadt. In 1886 an 'anarchist law' was passed which suspended trial by jury for offences which had 'anarchist or subversive tendencies'.

Social reform was, however, now being urged both by the 'Viennese radicals' and by the leaders of the nascent Christian Social movement. In 1885/7 a series of reforms based on German models was introduced. Hours of work were limited to eleven daily in factories, ten in mines, with compulsory Sunday rest. The working day for women and young persons was limited to eight hours and the employment of children under twelve prohibited. Factory inspectors were appointed, and accident insurance introduced for factories and mines, with sickness insurance for some workers. Incomplete as these measures were (and often evaded), they yet brought a big improvement on earlier conditions.

Now Social Democracy as a political movement, after touching a nadir in 1886, began a recovery which it owed almost entirely to the efforts of one man, Dr Viktor Adler, a well-to-do ex-Liberal who had taken up the cause of the workers out of sheer compassion. After years of effort he succeeded in uniting the various rival factions on a programme of orthodox Social Democracy, the final aim of which was the dictatorship of the proletariat, but its immediate programme called for universal suffrage, the separation of Church and State, the abolition of the standing army and an advanced system of social reform. This programme was adopted at the 'Hainfeld Conference' of December 1888–January 1889. On it the Social Democrats got fifteen deputies into the 1897 Reichsrat, and ten into that of 1901. The party now constituted a considerable political force. It maintained intimate relations with the Trade Unions, whose membership, although still modest – in Vienna, where they were much the strongest, only 25 per cent of the workers belonged to them, while in outlying districts the figures were 5 per cent, 2 per cent or even 1 per cent – was now rising rapidly. The last years of the period saw a large number of strikes, which brought further improvements in working conditions.

Of the other social factors, the Church had lost its overwhelming power-position with the abolition of the Concordat, and subsequently, with a certain perceptible turn in Francis Joseph's mind towards Josephinianism as the influence of his mother and Rauscher faded from it,[6] but it still retained and even extended its material possessions and still possessed great political influence. Its representation in the

Herrenhaus apart, its hold over the minds of the rural populations, especially in the Alpine Lands, was still so strong that a high proportion of the deputies sent by them to the Reichsrat were always Clericals. The peasants still took their political cues largely from the parish priest's Sunday sermon, and most of the schools, even after the 1878 Act, were still staffed by products of the seminaries. In 1883 the Catholics secured the concession that the 'responsible head of a school' must be a person qualified to give religious instruction in the Confession of the majority of its pupils, and Lands were empowered to reduce the pupils' hours of instruction in their last two years. Even this, however, was only a sop thrown to them after their more far-reaching demands had been rejected, and repeated efforts made by them thereafter to get the Act repealed, or even modified, failed to bring them more.

Meanwhile, the very virulence and vulgarity of the Liberals' attacks had awakened in Catholic circles a combative spirit which made *croyant* Catholicism a more living force than it had been for many years. The new movement contained an element of revolt against the extreme hierarchical spirit of the traditional Church, and it was none the weaker for its tinge of democratic appeal, which, indeed, ultimately led to the desertion of many of the Clericals' voters to the Christian Social camp. One way and another Catholicism still came nearer than any other political force in Austria, except perhaps Social Democracy, to transcending nationalism, and as Liberalism withered, it challenged German nationalism longer than any other force.

The real government of Cis-Leithania, under and for the Monarch, had by now passed to its civil service. In this, the very senior posts, which were in the gift of the Crown, were still usually held by members of the aristocracy, and the holders of the posts next below them were very often titled; but this should not mislead us. The Governors were often figure-heads, and their lieutenants were *Beamtenadel*, either themselves ennobled as reward for their services, or the sons or grandsons of men so promoted. If they were generally conservative, this was because the structure of the State was conservative. Within these limits, they were not concerned with defending either class or local interests, nor, indeed, with national interests. If most of them were 'Germans', linguistically and by personal sympathy, this was because the machine of the State which they served was linguistically German. They were there to make the machine work, and they did so loyally, and on the whole, efficiently.

Much the same is to be said of the officers of the new army organized by F.M.L. John. The parentage of nearly all of them was, unlike that of their predecessors, middle class, or humbler still: they were products of the military academies and cadet schools who were making their occupation their life's career. Like their counterparts the civil servants, they were taught to regard themselves as simply and solely the servants of the Crown. Not only was any kind of 'national' activity forbidden them, but they were not supposed to entertain any sympathies in these fields. And exacting as this requirement was, it was very generally met. The officers who, in the Monarchy's death-agony, took sides with the centrifugal political and national forces, were almost all war-time reservists.

While renouncing all national partiality for themselves, the officers were, however, not encouraged to show equal impartiality towards all the peoples of the Monarchy. They were taught, especially by the Archduke Albrecht, to regard every Hungarian as a rebel, and particularly the Germans, who made up three quarters of the Corps of Officers, imbibed this doctrine, and when stationed in Hungary, often behaved accordingly, as a patriotic duty. Often, indeed, they overshot the mark by provocative behaviour, which itself bred ill-feeling against the regime and the dynasty.

The Nationality Question

The 1860s had, as we have seen, shown that the attempt to depoliticize national feeling among the peoples of Austria had failed, and the decades that followed proved the failure to have been final. There were, of course, circles (chiefly among the higher servants of the Crown) who were still able to accept the old a-national basis of the State; and at the other end, there were plenty of men and women to whom their bread and butter was more important than the language in which they had to buy their postage stamps. But increasingly with every year, the political life of Cis-Leithania, and of every Land in it, was dominated by the struggle for position between the nationalities. It was true, as an Austrian historian has pointed out, that for most of the nationalities it was still a struggle 'about Austria'—that is, for position within it—not 'against Austria', but it was reaching a pitch at which the more comforting preposition would cease to apply unless a way was found of adjusting the rival claims on a basis acceptable to them all, and in 1903 the magic formula had still evaded discovery.

The development took a different form, and reached a different result, in almost every case.

The Czechs were the strongest numerically of all the non-German peoples of Cis-Leithania, and in most respects the most advanced. They could thus legitimately demand, and effectively compel, full attention to their demands. The fatality was that each one of their ambitions—the long-term one of seeing the Monarchy made to rest on its Slav elements, with the Czechs calling the tune, the intermediate aim (with which the Czechs of Moravia did not always agree) of the restoration of the *Böhmisches Staatsrecht*, and the immediate one of establishing their own national supremacy in Bohemia-Moravia, within their historic frontiers—each conflicted directly with the wishes and interests of the Germans; and not, even in the case of the last-named, those of the local Germans alone, for the inter-dependence of the three was obvious. Consequently, each aspect of the Czech problem was also an aspect of the German, and even the most apparently local issue was so regarded by all the Germans of Austria, sometimes even by those of the Reich, and contested with corresponding bitterness.

In the years now under review, the international alignment established after 1871 clearly put the long-term objective, for the time, out of the field of practical politics. The intermediate, after having, as we have seen, come within measurable distance of realization in 1871, had perforce had to be shelved (although not abandoned) after the fall of the Hohenwart government. The immediate struggle during the period was therefore waged within the arena of the innermost ring. The Czechs carried it on with an astonishing purposefulness and a success that increased, rather than diminished, when the Old Czechs were replaced by the Young Czechs as their dominant political party, for if the change lost them the support of the feudal landowners and the favour sometimes shown to the latter by the Crown, it gained them a much wider support from the 'little man'. As we have seen, the parliamentary battle turned chiefly round the official use of the two languages. The Czechs claimed that the *Majestätsbrief* of 1848 and Paragraph 3 of Article XIX of 1867 obligated any official in any part of the Kingdom to answer in the same language any person addressing him, orally or in writing, in either Czech or German (these were admitted to be the two *Landessprachen* of Bohemia), while the Germans claimed that under Paragraph 2 of Article XIX he need do so if the language was *landesüblich*, that is, the language of a sizeable fraction of the local population. So long as the fact of life held good that every Czech with an education above the primary level spoke German, while hardly any Bohemian German spoke Czech, or was willing to learn it, the effect of the Czech interpretation would be that the administration throughout Bohemia, even in purely German Districts, would be staffed almost entirely by Czechs.

The question raised innumerable side-issues. What proportion of a nationality in any District entitled its language to rank as *landes-üblich*? Were persons not regularly and legally domiciled in a District to be counted as belonging to its population? If so, were they entitled to schools for their children? And so on, and so on. It would be impossible to list all the solutions suggested for the problem. Purely chauvinistic, as some, from both sides, were, reasonable as were others, all met with the same fate. If one side accepted them, the other rejected them. The problem had not been finally solved by 1919, when the Peace Conference accepted the Czech claim that Bohemia was indivisible, and rejected the desperate remedy on which the Germans had fallen back, of partitioning the Kingdom. Meanwhile, the Stremayr ordinances had in fact given the Czechs a large part of their case, with the remarkable result that by the turn of the century there were more Czech officials than German in many purely German Districts, and the equally noteworthy one that this had not shifted perceptibly the balance of power between the two nationalities. The Czech officials in the German Districts seem to have carried out their functions in a perfectly correct and neutral spirit, and they were far too few to alter the ethnic composition of the areas concerned.

The proportion of the two nationalities remained almost unchanged, with a fractional gain to the Czechs, and in their distribution there was only one major change, although that was major indeed: Prague, once an almost purely German city, had become, chiefly through immigration, a preponderantly Czech one. The immigration of Czech workers into the industrial Districts had changed the population of a few of them from German to mixed, but frontiers of ethnic settlement on the land had hardly shifted at all. But politically, socially and economically, the Czechs had made enormous advances. Besides controlling the administration of Prague, they were actually over-represented, even proportionately to their numbers, on the *Landesausschuss* (executive committee of the Diet), through which they dominated the provincial administration of Bohemia. High finance and big business were still chiefly in the hands of Germans or German-minded Jews, but the Czechs were beginning to penetrate into this world through various institutions, notably the important Živnostenská Banka, which, founded in 1868 originally to finance the Czech co-operatives, was used afterwards for wider purposes. There was a great network of co-operatives, in which the Czechs led the peoples of the Monarchy, and savings-banks. The Czechs now possessed a skilled industrial class and a small and medium bourgeoisie of artisans, shopkeepers and petty officials (they showed a special aptitude for the career of *rond de cuir*). They had long possessed an adequate elementary and secondary school system, and now the university allowed to them in 1882, with a Technical High School already opened in 1869, were turning out an annual crop of young men educated nationally up to the highest level available. They had their own national theatre and an ample supply of public libraries and reading-rooms. There was even a great gymnastic organization, the *Sokol* (Falcon), founded in 1863 with objectives which were by no means purely physical.

The Slovene 'National Party' split in 1870 into two: the 'Young Slovenes', who were a party of lawyer-led urban intellectuals, and a stronger party officially entitled the 'People's Party', but habitually termed, by themselves as well as others, the 'Slovene Clericals'. The appellation was just, for the peasant masses on which it rested followed the guidance of their parish priests, who in turn took their orders from their ecclesiastical superiors. On social issues the party stood near the Christian Socials; on national, it was particularist Slovene, Austro-Slav and impeccably *kaisertreu*. The Young Slovenes continued to organize meetings and submit resolutions (which were regularly rejected) to the local *Landtage* demanding a Great Slovene Crownland. This was the final ideal of most, although not all, of the Clericals, but they took the line of the 'Opportunists' of 1867 that it would pay them better to collaborate with the regime than to put forward claims which would only irritate the authorities.

On the whole, these tactics paid them well enough. Starting from further behind than the Czechs, and possessed of fewer resources, they long enjoyed the advantage that Vienna, regarding them as harmless, treated them with some benevolence. Owing to the jealous opposition of the local Germans, they never obtained a university, and even their secondary schools were thin on the ground, but they came to possess an extensive system of primary schools – in Carniola, nearly sixteen times as many as a generation before – with cultural and political associations, co-operatives, etc. on the Czech model, although less highly developed. They evolved a substantial *petite bourgeoisie*, and by 1903 controlled almost all the rural districts of Carniola, and most of the towns there, including Laibach itself. Since 1873 they had held the majority in its *Landtag*, in which the only Germans were now the representatives of the Great Landlords' Curia. Demographically, they were on the retreat in Carinthia, but holding their own in Styria and gaining ground in the Littoral, including Trieste.

After Cilli the Slovene political leaders had to renounce their collaboration with the German parties and began to flirt with the idea of finding a common platform with the Dalmatian Croats. This thought found some echoes among the latter people, who, however, were still more interested in realizing political unification with their kinsfolk in Croatia and the Herzegovina, and in consolidating the economic, social and political progress that they were making in their own province. This was considerable: by 1870 they had gained the majority in the *Landtag*, and by a few years later, that in all the municipalities except Zara.

The Dalmatian Serbs usually allied themselves with the local Italians; it was not until after 1903 that they changed sides in the fashion described below.

The cultural standards of the Roumanians of the Bukovina rose rapidly after the removal of the Polish control. It is true that the university founded in Czernowitz in 1875 was German, as were many of the secondary schools, but the Roumanians received enough elementary and secondary establishments to permit the emergence of a perceptible intelligentsia. The local Roumanian nationalism was for long extraordinarily pacific. There was practically no irredentism, and no trace of such hostility to the Monarchy, or to the local Germans, as prevailed among the Roumanians of Transylvania towards the Hungarian State and the Magyar people. Their chief quarrel was with the Ruthenes, who outnumbered the Roumanians in the Duchy and demanded a share in its public affairs which the Roumanians, who treated them as recent interlopers, steadily refused to give them. The landowners, who, with the higher Orthodox clergy, dominated the Duchy politically, made loyalty to the Monarchy a fixed principle of policy, ordinarily associating themselves with whatever party was in power.

Only after 1892, when the two main traditional parties, the 'Autonomists' or 'Federalists' and the 'Centralists', fused, with smaller groups, under the slogan of 'solidarity of all Roumanians on political, national and ecclesiastical questions', did they take a more independent attitude.

The Italians of the Monarchy had few causes for complaint of their treatment at the hands of authority. They never succeeded in getting the Trentino made into a separate Crownland, nor in getting a university of their own – this a real hardship, for after the Monarchy lost Lombardy-Venetia they could no longer attend the universities of Pavia and Padua with material profit, since the Austrian Government did not recognize degrees from foreign universities as qualifying for admission to the State services or professions. The same event brought Austria's Italian middle classes a perceptible loss of income, since before it, the administrative services in Lombardy-Venetia had been largely staffed with Italians from the Trentino.

But the Italians controlled the municipality of Trieste, they were fully represented, proportionately to their numbers, in the Innsbruck *Landtag*, and administration, justice and education, primary and secondary, in the Trentino were purely Italian. The heart of the problem of the Monarchy's Italians lay in the geographical location of their homes, just across the frontiers of the new Italy, and in that State's ambition to annex them. It is very certain that by no means all Austria's Italian subjects wanted to be annexed. Precisely in the

Trentino, the Catholic Church long threw its weight into the Austrian scale, and its party, the *Partito Populare*, contained many *Austria-cante*. The local nobility was divided, the peasants largely indifferent, or loyal out of tradition. In Trieste the business interests, many of which were, indeed, German or Jewish, were pro-Austrian, as were the Social Democrats there (although not in the Trentino). But the 'intellectuals' nearly everywhere, and especially in Trieste, were Italian nationalists, often turbulently so. Trieste was the scene of many rowdy demonstrations and it was there that in 1882 a fanatic (incidentally a German Austrian by origin) achieved the distinction of being the only man during this period to attempt the life of the Monarch as a purely national gesture.

The Polish Party which had concluded the deal of 1873 with the Auersperg Government had been that of the 'Cracow Conservatives'. The political leadership in Galicia then naturally fell to them, al-most unchallenged until the extension of the franchise in 1897. This brought into being a number of smaller parties, some of which even refused to join the *Polenklub*; but the Cracow Conservatives were still the strongest party in 1903. They kept their side of the bargain, and remained impeccably loyal to the Monarchy. They had no im-mediate national ambitions, except to keep the Ruthenes in their place, and found in the respite from the once all-absorbing national struggle an opportunity to employ their large talents in other direc-tions, money-making and the arts. In the latter field they were notably successful. Cracow and Lemberg developed into centres of learning and the arts which gave birth to many brilliant products, some of them the work of Poles from Russian or Prussian Poland who found in Galicia a freedom lacking in their own homes.

The Ruthenes had emerged from their passivity when parliamen-tary life returned to Austria, and in the 1861 elections had secured 49 out of the 150 seats in the Galician *Landtag*, and 14 mandates to the Reichstag. All of these had fallen to the Old Ruthenes. But after 1867 the Poles had had a freer hand, while the impossibility of persuading the local peasants to speak 'Jasice' had become incontrovertible. The party split. One wing, who kept the name of Old Ruthenes, went over to the thesis of Russo-Ruthene ethnic and linguistic identity, but this, too, was glaringly at variance with the patent fact that the language spoken by the masses in East Galicia was indistinguishable from that of the population of the Russian Ukraine. This identity, and the right of the speech to rank as a true language, were put beyond doubt when the persecution to which the Ukrainian national culture was subjected by the Russian Government, drove many of its leaders to take refuge in Lemberg, which became the cultural centre for both fractions of the people. The linguistic identity brought with it a consciousness of national identity, which was, indeed, at first confined to the sparse intelligentsia; the masses as yet hardly thought in such wide terms. The intellectuals themselves hardly thought of themselves as Ukrainians *sans phrase*, but they knew that they were not either Poles or Russians.

In 1882 some of the Old Ruthene leaders received prison sentences, which were fully deserved, for the movement was in fact a quite artificial one (it had to issue its own propaganda in the local dialect). The Young Ruthenes had the political field to themselves for some years, but their party disintegrated in its turn when an ill-kept truce with the Poles, which had been negotiated by Vienna, broke down after bringing them little advantage. The franchise reform of 1897 produced in their stead a host of small parties, generally led by lawyers or peasant tribunes. The deplorable social conditions led most of these parties to give the chief place in their programmes to social issues, but the circumstance that the Ruthenes were the local social underdogs, suffering under the dual exploitation of Polish landlords and Jewish gombeen men, had the effect that these programmes were also nationally coloured. Both the big groups which eventually emerged, a relatively conservative one called after its strongest component the 'Ukrainian National Democratic Party' and a smaller aggregation of radicals, put in their programmes an agreed common declaration that 'the final aim of their policy was the achievement of cultural, economic and political independence for the entire Ruthene-Ukrainian nation and its future unification in one body politic'. The declaration was, however, worded to avoid any suspicion of irredentism: the Ruthenes remained, as always, stoutly *kaisertreu*, if only because Vienna was still their strongest shield against the Poles.

Towards the turn of the century, meanwhile, they had begun to make sudden and rapid advances, which gathered speed in the next decade in many fields, not only cultural, but also economic.

Their high degree of social, economic and cultural differentiation, making them prone to think in terms of class or Confessional interest, their geographical distribution over so many Lands, each with its special traditions and problems, and above all, their historically deep-rooted habit of regarding themselves not as one nationality among many, but as *the Staatsvolk* of the Monarchy—all these factors combined to produce the results that the Germans of Austria were the last of its peoples to evolve a specifically 'national' outlook and policy, and that to the last, a considerable proportion of them denied the necessity, or even the propriety, of any such thing. The first step along the road was, as we have seen, taken in the autumn of 1866 by a group of Styrian Germans, who in 1868 at a conference in Aussee, produced a programme which approved the Compromise with Hungary and went on to advocate that the link with Galicia-Bukovina should be reduced to a Personal Union and Dalmatia attached to Hungary. This would leave a unit, consisting of the Hereditary and Bohemian Lands, in which the Germans would be in a safe majority. Ultimately, history would bring about the break-up of the Monarchy and this unit would become part of Germany.

But these were still voices in the wilderness. In 1870 the 'Constitutional Left' included in its programme a phrase that Austria was 'a German State', but no more. The Hohenwart experiment aroused transitory passions, but when the Liberals returned to office, they put away their fears. With the Poles appeased, the Slovenes hardly yet awakened and the Czechs, as they thought, decisively defeated, all, they told themselves, was safe. The Progressives of the 1870s still sat with the Old Liberals in one parliamentary club, and accepted the thesis that the party was concerned with the interests of the State, not with those of one national group in it. The only Reichsrat deputy in the decade to call for a German National Party was Georg von Schönerer, a doughty eccentric, who left the Progressives because they were 'insufficiently national-minded'. But Schönerer was at this stage primarily a social revolutionary, who identified social injustice with Jewish exploitation. It was the Jewish question that drove him out of the Liberal camp, and at that time, he failed to take a single colleague with him.

Even their defeat in 1879 did not move the Liberals to change their principles, while German Clericals continued cheerfully to combine with Slavs against Viennese Liberalism, and the German feudalists with the Czechs against Viennese centralism.

Public feeling, however, was less immobile than the Liberal leaders. The 1870s had seen a considerable upsurge of national feeling in the Lands of mixed nationality, especially Bohemia. In 1881 Schönerer joined a group of intellectuals which included the historian Friedjung, and the later Socialists Engelbert Pernerstorfer and Viktor Adler, to produce on 1 September 1882 the so-called Linz Programme for a 'German People's Party' — a rehash of the 'Aussee Programme' spiced with a series of advanced social and political postulates.

Opposition from 'high quarters' prevented the People's Party from coming into being. Schönerer, undeterred, took over its social items, added a pinch of his own anti-Semitism, and founded his own *Deutschnationaler Verein*. This was frankly extremist. Schönerer wanted the Monarchy to disappear, and declared war on anything in it that separated or even distinguished it from the Reich, including the Catholic Church and the dynasty itself. As we have said, some features in this programme at first appealed to the newly-enfranchised 'little men', but its radicalism scared them off, and in the 1880s

Schönerer never had more than three followers in the Reichsrat, while in 1888 his enemies (including the Emperor) took advantage of one of his numerous indiscretions to have him publicly disgraced. This did not, however, mean that German nationalism was on the decline. A great number of self-help organizations were coming into being, some, like the *Alldeutscher Verein*, receiving help from Germany. In Austria, the German Clericals sat apart from their Slav colleagues after 1882. The German Constitutional Landowners were already a specifically German party, and the Liberals half-way towards becoming so. After the 1885 elections, even the old faithfuls, now led by Ignaz von Plener's son, Ernst, consented to call themselves 'German Austrian', but they now commanded only 87 followers, while 32 other deputies formed a separate 'German Club', which laid down as the first point of its programme that 'our supreme principle, which must determine our attitude on all questions, must be the welfare of the German people in Austria'. Then, in 1887, one of the three dissident groups, led by Dr Steinwender, broke away to form a *Deutsch-nationale Vereinigung*, with a programme which was, in the main, another rehash of that of Linz, but included a declaration of disbelief in parliamentary government and a call for 'a neutral government standing above the nationalities'.

Steinwender had taken only 17 followers with him, the other dissidents having rejoined the orthodox Liberals to form a '*Vereinigte Linke*' which still emerged from the elections of 1891 with 108 mandates against 16 for Steinwender and 4 for Schönerer. Most of the Germans were still reluctant on principle to step down from their position of *Staatsvolk* to that of a national group, and both the new parties now emerging, the Christian Socials and the Social Democrats, began, in theory, as supra-national. But the 'Cilli episode' shattered the Liberals' credit, reducing the number of their followers, in the 1891 elections, to 14, while Steinwender's adherents, who now called themselves the German People's Party, numbered 41, and a 'Progressive Party', 33. Then came the Badeni ordinances, following which the German People's Party, the Progressives, Constitutional Landowners, Old Liberals and Christian Socials—thus, if we exclude the Social Democrats as being still theoretically supra-national, all the German parties except the Catholic People's Party, who refused to make their programme specifically national, and the *Alldeutsche* (as Schönerer had rebaptized his followers), but including the Christian Socials, agreed on a programme which was, in substance, a slightly modified version of that of the German People's Party. It contained the now familiar demands for a retreat to the inner ring of the Hereditary and Bohemian Lands (although the references to Galicia were ambiguous) and for fidelity to the German alliance, but went further than its predecessors in its other demands. The national struggle in Austria could be eliminated only 'by recognition of the position of the Germans won by them many centuries ago, the maintenance of which was a central necessity for the future of the State'. The name of the new unit was to be 'Austria'. German was to be the 'general language of communication' as was the language of the Reichsrat and of all ministries and central organs dealing with its affairs as a whole. All State officials must have a thorough knowledge of the language, and 'educational establishments which prepared pupils for the State services' must instruct them adequately in that language.

There followed detailed proposals for the regulation of linguistic usage in each Land, some moderate, others (especially those for Lands with Slovene populations) highly chauvinistic.

It was obvious that these were demands to which the non-German peoples of Austria could never submit in 1899, and if these were the Germans' terms for Austria, then Austria was lost indeed.

Schönerer had stood aside from all this: it was too moderate for him. His own contribution to the period was to organize a *Los von Rom* movement for secession from the Catholic Church. Estimates of the number of converts range from 50,000 to 100,000.

These pages will have shown how lamentably mistaken had been Steinbach's belief that the poorer classes would prove any less nationalist than their betters. Where the extended franchise produced new parties, with social platforms, each habitually prefaced its name with an ethnic adjective, and stood solid with its nationality's traditional parties on national questions. The original Christian Social Party formed an exception as regards nomenclature, but in no other respect: in membership and ideology it was a German party like any other.

At the Hainfeld Conference the Social Democrats, in duty bound, adopted the Marxist slogan that the national struggle was 'a means by which the ruling classes assured their domination', and at their Brünn Conference in 1899 they called for a sensible regulation of the national question on the basis of international equality (interesting blueprints for such a reorganization were afterwards worked out by two of the party's thinkers, Karl Renner and Otto Bauer). But most of the German Austrian workers themselves accepted the Brünn Programme only as a *pis aller*; what they really wanted was a socialized version of the Liberals' programme – a centralized Austria run by its German workers – and most of their non-German colleagues did not want any German leadership at all. Their revolt was headed by the Czech workers, to meet whom the Brünn Conference converted the party into seven national sections, each largely autonomous, although there was to be a federal executive and the party was to act in the Reichsrat as a united whole. But even this, while going too far for the Germans, did not go far enough for the Czechs, and renewed trouble soon broke out.

The Monarch

Francis Joseph's domestic life during these years was not happy. Left, perforce, much to herself by her husband's necessary preoccupations and goaded by her intolerable mother-in-law, Elisabeth had soon taken refuge in other pursuits, especially riding, on which she spent more and more time, and less and less on ceremonial functions. Later, more serious difficulties developed. Although genuinely and deeply devoted to his wife, Francis Joseph was not faithful. Her health suffered, and she took to spending long periods abroad, in Madeira, in Corfu, where she built herself an extraordinary fantasy palace, or in the huntingfields of England and Ireland.

The estrangement was not the worst blow which fell on Francis Joseph's family life. The couple had, besides three daughters, of whom the eldest died in infancy, one son, Rudolph, born on 21 August 1858. Rudolph had in him more of his mother than his father. He was gifted but unstable. Like Elisabeth, he rebelled against the stiff Court ceremonial and sought friends in artistic circles, among Liberals and even Jews. The Liberals pinned high hopes on him, although it may be doubted whether, had he come to wear the crown, he would have fulfilled them: in politics, as in other respects, he was essentially a dilettante, a Prince Hal playing at opposition to his father, with whom he got on only moderately well.

The direct cause of his tragedy seems to have lain in his love-life. He was married, in 1881, to the Belgian Princess, Stephanie, a singularly plain young woman who soon failed to satisfy his imagination. He consoled himself with many mistresses, and on the morning of 30 January 1889, his body, disfigured with severe head wounds, was discovered with that of one of them, a young girl named Baroness Marie Vetsera, in his hunting-lodge at Mayerling. The exact circumstances of the tragedy have never been completely cleared up.

The tragedy brought his mother's distraction to overflowing. After it, she was seldom seen in Vienna. Always dressed in black, she wandered over Europe like an unquiet ghost, until, on 10 September 1898, she met an equally tragic and senseless end, assassinated by an Italian anarchist on a quay in Geneva.

Now Francis Joseph was really alone. He was fond of his youngest daughter, Maria Valerie, and a reasonably affectionate grandfather to her children. But he had little use for the rest of his family, hardly caring for the new heir presumptive, his nephew, Francis Ferdinand, and his pride of birth prevented him from having real men friends not of royal blood; perhaps his only true friend was Albert of Saxony, who, however, died in 1902. The only true intimate human contacts which he had in his later years were with an actress, Katherina Schratt, whom Elisabeth herself introduced to him, and even with her, he remained the Monarch. He still took great pleasure in his shooting expeditions, principally after chamois. Otherwise, outside the ceremonial functions which he still performed punctiliously, but without gusto, he took little time off from his desk, rising at an unconscionable hour and spending long hours over his papers. By now he was leaving minutiae to his ministers, reserving to himself only final decisions, but the impotence of the Austrian Parliament placed on his shoulders an enormous number of these, and the cases were innumerable in which he had to intervene and decide because everyone else had reached a deadlock.

The end of his statecraft was still the simple one of keeping his Monarchy from disintegrating, and he followed it with considerable skill, the fruit of an experience which by now had become unique.

Fourteen

HUNGARY
1867–1903

Political History: The Question of Public Law

The parliamentary history of Hungary under Dualism presented quite a different picture from that of Cis-Leithania during the same period. The Hungarian parliament spared itself the tempestuous conflicts over national and social issues that convulsed the Reichsrat by the simple device of denying *de facto*, where not *de jure*, admission to its membership of representatives of the national and social oppositions. On the other hand, it allowed its energies to be absorbed by something from which the Reichsrat was exempt: the so-called 'Issue of Public Law' (*a közjogi kérdés*) that is, the relationship between Hungary on the one hand, and on the other, the Crown and the Crown's other dominions. Was the Compromise to be maintained intact, or should it be amended or repealed altogether?

For the whole period with which this chapter is concerned, and indeed, up to 1918, this question dominated Hungarian parliamentary life near-completely. With a single exception, which did not long maintain its distinctive quality, no major nation-wide political party made any other question the central plank of its political programme.[1] No election was fought on any other issue. Again with a single exception,[2] no other problem was ever treated in Parliament entirely on its own merits, but always with at least an eye on its bearings on the Issue, and these often played the decisive part in determining the solution given to the problem, as they ended by dictating the outcome of the one problem which had threatened to take a different course.

Even contemporaries deplored that so many precious energies, which might have been spent more constructively, should have been wasted on barren wrangling and legalistic minutiae. But it must be remembered that the *közjogi* Issue – the national defence against the Crown's encroachments – had been for centuries almost the sole business of every Diet. That the psychological reactions produced by centuries of history should have lived on now was understandable enough, especially when it is remembered that the Parliament which reassembled in the autumn of 1867 was simply the Diet of 1865 in continued session; and that that body had been convoked with the single task of reaching agreement with the Crown on the *közjogi* issue. It was natural that the minds of its members should still be preoccupied by the Issue, and also natural that the opponents of the Compromise should be unwilling to accept their defeat as final. Many even of the members of the Diet who had voted to accept Law XII had done so with inner reluctance, and the Diet itself had been far from representing all Magyar national opinion. To the small country nobles, and above all, to the sturdy Protestant farmers of the Alföld, among whom anti-Habsburg feeling was traditional, it was easy to represent the Compromise as the return of 'Austria', and 'Austria' as synonymous with Haynau's punitive squads, rapacious tax-collectors and unsympathetic Czech officials. On these masses, who knew nothing of the balance of European forces the consideration of which was what had ultimately governed the minds of Deák and Andrássy, a 'Cassandra letter', published in a newspaper on the eve of the conclusion of the Compromise and subsequently reprinted in pamphlet form and widely circulated, from Kossuth to Deák, in which the exiled leader prophesied woe to the Compromise and accused its author of having sacrificed the honour and vital interests of the country to a short-lived and illusory expediency, fell like a spark on tinder.

In 1867 and 1868 many circles styling themselves 'Honvéd' sprang into existence with the avowed purpose of overthrowing the 'accursed settlements'; the movement was sometimes accompanied by social unrest already in places so threatening that troops had to be sent to 'restore order'. The obvious popularity of the feeling behind the agitation encouraged the deputies of the Left Centre in the belief that their best chance of obtaining the sweets of office lay in identifying themselves with it. In February 1868 they drew up a programme (known from its place of origin as the 'Bihar Points') the essence of which was the demand for the abolition of the 'Common institutions' established under Law XII. It contained, indeed, also social demands, but these were hardly less *közjogi*, since the authors of the programme adopted the old Kossuthist attitude that real progress on domestic issues was impossible without near-total national independence. In face of this, the Government had no practical alternative but to follow suit, and to make the defence of the Compromise the central plank of its own programme for the forthcoming elections. That programme also included some promises on social issues, but these differed so little from those of the Opposition (the representatives of the two parties were drawn largely from the same social classes) that the voters could reasonably feel that all they were asked to say was whether they were for or against Law XII.

So the pattern was fixed, hardly to change before 1918, and if, until that date, the ''67' held office continually, except for a brief and unrealistic interval between 1906 and 1910, this did not mean that they had the country behind them. They were enabled to retain the power by two factors. One was the will of the Crown. That a challenge to the Compromise was a challenge to the Crown was a fact well appreciated by all. The other lay in the provisions of the Hungarian electoral law. The government in office during any elections enjoyed many means of influencing their results; and the "67ers', being in office when the period opened, in any case got off to a flying start; but the provisions of the law also worked out to the curious and surely unintended effect that a deputy from the Magyar constituencies of the centre needed more votes to return him than one from the periphery. The Magyar constituencies were not easy to dragoon, but a pro-Compromise Government could keep them in a minority by 'influencing' the more malleable voters from the peripheral constituencies.

At the outset the Government's position was still relatively strong. The glamour of the coronation had not yet faded: Deák's personal prestige was enormous, and Andrássy's almost as high, and the economic prospects were rosy: phenomenal wheat harvests in 1868 and 1869 had brought a great influx of money which had started a boom even more spectacular than its counterpart in Austria. This apart, the real achievements of the Government in many fields (many of the reforms described on later pages date from these first years) earned it widespread respect.

Even so, when elections were held in 1869, the Government, although applying considerable pressure, lost 48 seats to the Left Centre, and 12 to the Extreme Left, which had meanwhile organized itself under the name of 'party of 1848'. And by 1870 things were already changing for the worse. The run of good harvests ended. The railway programme proved to have been over-ambitious and to involve the State in heavy losses. In industry, a severe slump succeeded the boom. The new administrative system was expensive. Deák retired into private life. Eötvös died, Andrássy moved to the Ballhausplatz, and Lónyay, whom Francis Joseph appointed to succeed him, was not popular, even in his own party.

So much had the Government's self-confidence dwindled that before the 1872 elections Lónyay tried to get the Parliament to accept a revised franchise, directed in effect against the Left Centre. The Opposition succeeded in talking the Bill out, so that the Government had to hold the elections on the old franchise. By exerting heavy pressure, it slightly increased its majority, securing 245 seats against 116 of the Left Centre and 38 of the Party of 1848. But then Lónyay was forced to resign by attacks on his financial probity, and under his successor, Slávy, the effect of the great Austrian *Krach* reached Hungary, with disastrous consequences.

Immediately after 1867, Hungarian finance ministers had begun copying the Austrian example of budgetary deficits covered by borrowing abroad. Their original belief that the 'virginity' of Hungary's credit would enable her to obtain favourable terms had remained unshaken by repeated proof to the contrary, and the Exchequer was now quite empty. In November 1871 the Finance Minister, Kerkápoly, succeeded in obtaining an emergency loan from the Rothschilds, but on terms for which 'exorbitant' would be far too weak a word. The situation was one with which the Government was quite unable to cope, but the logical conclusion, that it should give way to an administration formed by the Opposition, on its programme as announced, was ruled out by the attitude of the Crown. Francis Joseph would never appoint a Government sincerely pledged to carry out the Bihar programme; his only imaginable reply to a refusal by Hungary to honour Law XII would be to scrap that document himself and resort to abolutism.

It is also a reasonable guess that the House of Rothschild expressed its objections to concessions to the 'Left'.

The situation was saved by the fact that the Left Centre was itself perfectly well aware of the realities of the position. Its opposition had, in reality, not been sincere: it had been shadow-boxing – for prize money. Now it adapted its attitude to the facts of life. Negotiations, too complex to be described here, set in which ended, in effect, with the conclusion of an armistice. Kálmán Tisza, now the leader of the Left Centre, announced his readiness, not to renounce his party's *közjogi* programme, but to put it in cold storage until altered conditions should render realization of it possible. Francis Joseph, in return, tacitly renounced his support of the Nationalities. On 2 March 1875, the two big parties fused under the name of 'Liberal Party'. Slávy's successor, Bittó, gave way to a caretaker government under Baron Wenkheim, who appointed Tisza his Minister of the Interior. Elections held in June gave the Liberals the enormous majority of 336 seats to 35 of the Party of Independence, 18 Conservatives, 24 Saxons and 2 Serbs. On 26 October Tisza took over the Minister Presidency.

This was the opening of the reign of the Liberal Party, which lasted, under one name or another, with the brief intermission mentioned above, virtually to the end of the Monarchy, the first 15 years of it under Tisza's personal Presidency. It was, in substance, another partnership between the Crown and those forces in Hungary which were prepared to work with it. Tisza was not, indeed, the complete renegade as which his enemies described him. He remained to the end very much a Hungarian, and in the first years probably felt the need to press the national elements in his programme with two-fold vigour, to rebut his enemy's charges, and perhaps those of his own conscience, and to placate that considerable fraction of the new party which was composed of his own old followers and had not wholly jettisoned their old ideas. When the Economic Compromise came up for revision in 1877 Tisza pressed Hungary's wishes, particularly her claim for an independent Bank of Issue, very strongly, and when they were refused, he offered his resignation.

This brought back the old dilemma, Francis Joseph tried to get a Conservative to take on the Minister Presidency, but could find none willing to do so. He was forced, after all, to fall back on Tisza, who eventually agreed to accept a compromise on the Bank issue which was in reality a second surrender. On this basis he took office again. This seems to have marked a turning-point in his own outlook. The maintenance of the Compromise became for him ever less of a temporary and pragmatic expedient, ever more an end in itself. Naturally, his regime was not uncontested. Tacit agreement between all the major Hungarian parties still kept the active representatives of the Nationalities, and those of the lower-income groups, out of the field, so that the opposition to it was still exclusively *közjogi*, and came exclusively from the Left, for the Conservatives now gave up the hopeless struggle. But the Extreme Left, which reunited in 1888 as the 'Party of Independence and 1848', returned about 20 per cent of deputies at each election, and among Tisza's own followers, his second surrender had gone less smoothly than his first. Various groups of dissidents combined with the remnants of the Conservatives to form a 'Party of the United Opposition' (later, 'Moderate Opposition'), the leadership of which eventually passed to Count Albert Apponyi. This also counted a respectable number of adherents; although owing to its lack of any real programme, a less stable one than the Extreme Left.

To deal with these opponents, Tisza organized a machine as efficient as it was unscrupulous, the agents of which, popularly known as the 'Mamelukes', saw to it that his party was returned at each election with a sufficient majority. Neither was this result achieved exclusively by pressure. The Compromise suited many important interests, especially the big agrarians and the financiers, and these expanded and became vested. Even outside them, the system acquired the unpositive acceptance of the accustomed. Further, while Tisza's system shared the defect of that of his near-contemporary, Taaffe, in being essentially unconstructive, it also shared its virtue of being unprovocative. Where he could, Tisza avoided thin ice and more than once withdrew a proposal which had evoked strong protests. There was probably no period in its history in which the Compromise was so widely accepted as the decade after 1878.

Even the 1887 revision of the Economic Compromise went through smoothly. Such storms as ruffled the surface arose chiefly over the army. The military circles in Vienna never made even the motions of accepting the Dualist system with any sort of good will. There were many incidents, nearly all provoked by Vienna, which aroused justified resentment in Hungary. It was a conflict over army questions that brought the end of Tisza's personal rule. An army Bill, passed to his Government for introduction in January 1889, contained provisions which the national opposition regarded as objectionable, and it unleashed a tumultuous demand for an independent army. Apponyi's 'Moderate Opposition', ganged up with them, shouting louder than they. On Andrássy's advice, Francis Joseph withdrew the most objectionable clauses of the Bill and granted some of the Opposition's reasonable demands, but the attacks on Tisza had been so venomous that he sickened of office, and in March 1890, when a more popular pretext presented itself, he resigned.

The remaining thirteen years covered by this chapter saw the Liberal Party still in office, under a rapid succession of Ministers President, Count Gyula Szapáry (1890–2), S. Wekerle (1892–5), Baron Dezsö Bánffy (1895–9), Kálmán Széll (1899–1903). During the earlier of these years the Issue was, for the first and last time during the Dualist era, displaced from its position of dominance by that of Church-State and inter-Confessional relations, which, before it found the solution described elsewhere (see p. 212),[3] had brought about the resignations (one of them given twice) of two Ministers President, one because he disapproved of the proposed changes, the other because he approved of them, and one Imperial and Royal Foreign Minister, had split alike the Liberals and the Opposition from top to bottom, and even produced the unique phenomenon of a nation-wide political party (the People's Party) with a programme the central plank of which was not *közjogi* (it soon, indeed, lost this character and became, apart from minor nuances, a *közjogi* party like any other). Yet even here, it was the Issue that determined the outcome. When, in order to avert a head-on collision, Francis Joseph intervened to get the crucial Bill on mixed marriages through the Upper House, he did so only because Wekerle represented to him that if the Bill did not go through, so many members of the Liberal Party would revolt that the Compromise would be jeopardized. And once the Confessional question had been got out of the way, the pattern reverted to the normal one.

It was not, however, a full psychological return to the *status quo ante* 1889. The Compromise, while still intact, had lost its aura of permanency. If Francis Joseph had yielded twice, once over the army Bill and once over the Confessional, he had done so only *à contre cœur*. By now he was too set in his ways to consider seriously another reshaping of the Monarchy. But he probably never again trusted Hungary, and only rarely, a Hungarian.

On the other side, the concessions had only whetted appetites. The death of Lajos Kossuth, in 1894, deprived the Extreme Left of its rallying point. The party elected the old rebel's son, Ferenc, to be its leader, but he was unable to inspire it, or even to hold it together: one fraction of it, led by Gábor Ugron, left it. Against this, Apponyi, whose followers now called themselves the 'National Party', evolved an interpretation of his party's programme which claimed that the Monarch possessed no rights whatever in Hungary, except those exercised through the Hungarian Parliament; and the eloquence with which he expounded this theory won him many disciples.

Consequently, when the struggle reopened in 1896, after a pause during which the nation was celebrating the thousandth anniversary of its arrival in what was now its home, it was marked by a new impatience and venom. In the negotiations for the renewal of the Economic Compromise the Hungarians demanded protection for their industry, and also the replacement of the Customs Union by an autonomous tariff. Bánffy reached a reasonable compromise agreement with Thun, in Austria, but when the news leaked out that he and his Finance Minister, Lukács, had secretly agreed that the agreement should continue in force after 1907, unless denounced, the Opposition, which hated him for the brutality with which he had conducted the elections, prevented him, by obstruction, from getting his budget through within the legal time, and refused him an 'indemnity' for a period of grace. Francis Joseph solved the problem by replacing Bánffy by the conciliatory Széll, and provisional agreement on the last outstanding issue of the new Compromise was reached literally at the twelfth hour (midnight on 31 December 1902). Meanwhile, Széll had persuaded the National Party to fuse with the Liberals (some of its members, indeed, demurred and went over to the Independence Party) and the elections of October 1901, gave the United Party another big majority (267 to 137). But the downward trend was unmistakable, and a new crisis soon followed.

Economic and Social Developments

The Governments in Budapest after 1867 had to deal with a wide range of tasks which their Austrian colleagues were spared. Where the latter were able to build on existing foundations, the Hungarians had often not only to lay the foundations, but where they could do so, to clear the debris left by a sequence of revolutions and counter-revolutions, followed by a series of regimes each of which had been principally concerned with undoing the work of its predecessor.

Much of this was successfully accomplished, often in the first years after 1867. Transylvania, the Partium and the Bánátal Frontier districts were brought into the normal administrative pattern, the first-named at the cost of the destruction, except for purely cultural purposes, of the old autonomy of the Saxons, with its territorial basis, the *Sachsenboden*. Later, the number of the 'Jurisdictions' was brought down through rationalization of boundaries and abolition of dwarf units to 63 Counties and 24 Boroughs of County status. The administrative structures of these surviving bodies were, after embittered struggles between modernizers and traditionalists, reorganized. The autonomous rights of the Jurisdictions were left intact, but the field of their competence was reduced by nationalization of various services, and the powers of the Föispans were strengthened.

Justice was separated from administration on all levels, and the whole judicial system recast and modernized.

The Government services, including the new judiciary, were enlarged to meet the new requirements. This itself was a big task, which could be accomplished only gradually, since the training of the new men took time, and pending its completion, nearly all the old Bach Hussars had to be left in their posts, unless they refused to serve on under their new masters. This, indeed, happened only rarely; most of them stayed on happily until they reached the age limit.

In 1885 the membership of the Upper House was revised. The members of some empoverished magnate families lost their seats in it, as did persons possessing Hungarian *indigenat* but not residing in the country. The Crown was, however, empowered to appoint, on the proposal of the Minister President, a maximum of fifty life members whose distinguished services in public life made them valuable members of the legislature.

In 1869 the Roumanian Orthodox church received its Statute of Autonomy. Two years before, the Israelites had been admitted to full equality of civil and political rights with other Hungarian citizens. Later, the great Confessional struggles of the 1890s ended in the adoption of legislation on inter-Confessional questions, and on the relationship between Church and State, including marriage law, approximately the same as the Austrian. The Israelite Confession was then made 'received'.

In 1868 the Parliament adopted a law making primary education compulsory from the age of 6 to that of 12. If a parish did not already contain a Confessional or other school, it had to provide one. Instruction had to be in the pupil's mother tongue.

The period brought with it many other changes to the 'Face of Hungary'. Exceptionally, the economic development of the period had not been preceded by any preliminary work of demolition. The Compromise had, as we have said, laid down that the Customs Union with Austria should remain in being for the next ten years, and in the subsequent decennial reconsiderations of the economic relationship between Hungary and Austria, this cardinal feature of it was never, in practice, altered: the changes made in this respect were either purely verbal, or consisted of minor devices which partially got round the Customs Union without, technically, repealing it. The economic development of Hungary after 1867 therefore followed in a straight line the course that had been set for it in 1851, which had made Hungary, economically, a part of the larger economic unit of the Monarchy.

The relationship had, as we have said, been favourable to the agricultural producers, whose stronger members, the big landlords, had been able to use their political strength to preserve their advantage by influencing in their own favour the tariff policy of the Monarchy, and at home, by obstructing developments of nature to draw off the land the supply of labour, which until the 1880s was regularly below the demand for it, or to compete with their requirements of credit. Hungarian agriculture, like that of most European countries, suffered severely from the slump in world wheat prices of the 1880s, but by 1900 it had recouped most of its losses. Improved strains and techniques, including larger use of fertilisers, had greatly improved yields per acre of almost all arable crops, and since the cultivated area, too, had been enlarged, total yields had risen even more – that of wheat had almost doubled. There had been similar progress in animal farming. In 1900 agriculture was still easily the leading branch of the national economy. Two-thirds of the population derived their living from it, and the net value of its production was still 63 per cent of the total national income.

Other branches of the economy were, however, gaining on it. Industrialization after 1851 had been an affair of spurts and standstills. A first few years of rapid development, carried through almost entirely with Austrian capital, had been checked in 1857 by the drying-up of the Austrian capital market. The boom years 1867–73 had brought a second spurt, ended still more abruptly by the *Krach* of the latter year, which had hit Hungary even more severely than Austria, and by the withdrawal of the foreign capital which had played a major part in the boom. Several lean years followed. The ruin had, however, not been complete: the stronger banks and industries had survived it, and the railways laid during the boom years were still there. After some years, some foreign capital ventured back, and a considerable amount of native capital had by now been accumulated. With Government assistance (national pride was also a factor) a third advance set in in 1890. This, again, was extremely rapid. The number of persons gainfully employed in factory industry rose between 1890 and 1900 from 165,000 to 320,000, and the total listed in the 1900 census as deriving their livelihoods from industry and mining was 2,400,000 (14.2 per cent of the total). The figure was rising rapidly. The pattern of Hungary's industry was not, indeed, that which would have evolved under an autarkic economy. The big industries were those based on local agricultural raw materials, such as flour-milling, breweries and brick-making, with a smaller heavy industry based on the local deposits of coal and iron. The third spurt, however, was bringing more diversification.

Urbanization had followed a similar course. In 1900 Hungary contained only one really large town, Budapest, with a population of something over 700,000. 80 per cent of the population still lived in small towns, villages, or scattered farms, and the homes of a fair proportion of the remaining 20 per cent were the huge conurbations of the Alföld, which in all but name were simply over-grown villages of peasants. But here, too, the position was changing. The population of Budapest had grown by 45 per cent in a single decade. National pride had been lavished on making it a peer of Vienna, and it now contained many imposing buildings: the vast new Royal Palace (not yet complete), the neo-Gothic parliament, a national theatre and opera, a new university building, galleries, museums and libraries, besides hotels and luxury shops. Besides the original suspension bridge which had been the child of Széchenyi's inspiration, four more bridges for road traffic and one for rail now joined the twin cities.

Compared with Austria – and that was the yard-stick by which Hungarians usually measured their achievements – Hungary was still materially an underdeveloped country, and a poor one. While the ratio of the populations of the two countries was 3:4, that of their national incomes derived from production was still little over 1:2 and of their expendable incomes, less, since Hungary was paying abroad in dividends and interest on loans about 7 per cent of her income derived from production, while Austria had now a considerable invisible income, much of it coming from Hungary. But the gap, although not yet filled, had narrowed appreciably. Hungary's national income is estimated to have nearly doubled between 1867 and 1902, a much faster rate of increase than Austria's, and the increase in her national wealth, counting in buildings, bridges, railways, etc. (the main railway network had by now been virtually completed) must have been much larger still.

The implementation of the primary education act had been retarded, both by material difficulties, and by disputes between the State and the Churches. It had also become involved, in the fashion described below, with the national issue. Nevertheless, the number of primary schools had increased largely, and that of secondary establishments, nearly all of which, like most of the primary, were Confessional, almost as fast. New higher establishments included, besides the University of Zagreb, one in Kolozsvár, and the Technical High School of Budapest had been promoted to university status. The Széchenyi Academy had got down to serious business: many valuable works in both the humanities and the natural sciences saw the light under its auspices. In music, literature and painting the period produced many works which, if lacking something of the freshness of its predecessor, and the distilled but often bitter refinement of its successor, were yet imposing in quantity, and in quality, often up to the highest European standards of the day.

In 1900 3.1 per cent of the population were deriving their livelihood from the public services (exclusive of the armed forces), or the professions, the same number from commerce and finance, and 2.4 per cent from communications; 1.5 per cent were rentiers or pensioners, and 2.4 per cent domestic servants. These figures show a large rise in the numbers of the Hungarian bourgeoisie; but this had not brought with it the same effects as had accompanied the parallel, although larger, growth that had taken place in Austria. There the bourgeois and intellectual classes had been able to combine with their country cousins of the same stock to produce a class which constituted a distinct, and important, element in the political and social life of the country. The Hungarian bourgeoisie had in the old days been precluded from playing such a role, not only by its numerical insignificance, but also by the circumstance that its members, too, were largely of German stock, and therefore different, not only in respect of their economic interests, but also ethnically, from the Magyars, who had treated them almost as enemy aliens. The new Hungarian bourgeoisie was numerically not inconsiderable, but the recruits which had swollen its numbers were still not Magyars (these had maintained their obstinate refusal to enter commerce or industry), but members of another non-Magyar people, the Jews.

The number of these had been increasing very rapidly, chiefly through immigration from Galicia, since Joseph II's reign. From 87,000 (1 per cent of the total population) in 1787, they had risen to 343,000 (2.65 per cent) in 1850 and 830,000 (8.49 per cent) in 1900. They were still thickest on the ground in the North-Eastern Counties, which formed the first stage on their journeys, but by the end of the century few towns, and not even many villages, in Hungary were entirely without them, and in Budapest itself they numbered over 167,000, almost a quarter of the population. By now they had achieved a position in many fields of the national life even far more command-

ing than that of their Austrian confrères. The capitalist development
of modern Hungary, in so far as it was carried out at all by domestic
forces, was almost entirely of their doing, and the fruits of it almost
entirely in their hands. They had a virtual monopoly of finance, and
their domination of industry and trade, above the artisan and village
shop level, was hardly less complete, and they were very strongly
represented in most of the free professions, especially medicine, the
bar, and the Press, their hold over which, in the capital, was near-
complete. Jews, or Jewish-owned corporations, even owned or rented
nearly 20 per cent of the landed estates of 1,000 *hold* + and as high
a proportion of those of 200 – 1,000.[4] What proportion of the rent-
rolls of properties still standing in the names of others actually flowed
into Jewish pockets, the statistics do not reveal, but it was certainly
large, for acreage did not always represent real wealth; many of the
largest estates were mortgaged to the hilt.

Some wealthy Jews notoriously exercised a very large political influence, but this was mainly behind the scenes and exercised through
personal connections; few of them sat in Parliament, and hardly any
in the *congregationes* (more indeed – this was through personal connections – or the Councils of the Royal Free Boroughs). Their own
tradition, or that of others, debarred them from entering the regular
armed forces, or the national administrative services. They were also
denied admission to the more select clubs and associations.

In 1900 Hungary was, therefore, still socially, and at least on the
surface, politically, the domain of its landowners, large and near-
large. Among these, the magnates still held pride of place. The compensation promptly paid to them for such parts of their estates as
they had had to yield to their peasants under the land reform, which
was relatively small – since the proportion of allodial land on many
of their estates had been large – had enabled them not only to keep
their existing estates, but often even to extend them by buying up the
properties of less fortunate neighbours. Consequently, the proportion
of the soil of Hungary held in very large estates, vast as it had been
before 1848, had actually increased after that date. An agrarian census taken in 1895 showed that 12 of the 41.7 million *hold* which then
comprised the cultivable area of the country, or, if forests and rough
grazing were reckoned in, 20 out of 56.5, were held by just over
4,000 proprietors, and about one quarter of this consisted of the great
latifundia of 10,000 *hold* +. As in Austria, a proportion of these
were Crown lands, and others belonged to corporations such as the
Roman Catholic Church, or the 'village towns', which had inherited
the lands of neighbouring villages destroyed by the Turks, but most
of them were still in private hands. Some of these were enormous: the
Princes Esterházy owned 516,000 *hold*, the Counts Schönborn,

241,000, the Counts Károlyi, 174,000, Prince Festetich, 161,000, the Archduke Friedrich, 145,000, the Princes Coburg-Gotha, 141,000. Most of these big family estates were entailed: between 1867 and 1900 Francis Joseph sanctioned the formation of 60 new *fideicommissa*, bringing the number to 92 in all, with a total acreage of nearly 3,000,000 *hold*.

The medium-large landowners of 500–1,000 *hold* were the *bene possessionati* who before 1848 had led the national opposition to the Habsburgs. In and after 1849 they had been punished for this role so severely that many historians describe the subsequent years as having brought the ruin of the class. Many of them in fact found the struggle against the new conditions too hard for them, sold their estates and moved into the towns; it was from them or their sons that the new State employees were chiefly recruited. In 1900 the landed members of the class, whom it had become fashionable to call the 'gentry', were largely new men. But the newcomers to the class adopted its traditional *mores* and political outlook so completely that only a genealogist could have distinguished them from the survivors of an older day. The numerical membership of the class, if we add to the 3,000 owners of 500–1,000 *hold* the 6,500 owners of 200–500, made up a substantial figure, and the Compromise made one section of them the strongest political force in Hungary. For the Crown's partners under that instrument were not, as is so often written, the magnates, but the pro-'67 section of the gentry. It was they who under it took over from the magnates the task of keeping in check the national opposition, the leaders of which were the ''48 minded' members of the same class. The good will of his gentry supporters was far more important to Francis Joseph than that of the magnates, whose unpopularity in the country made their friendship more of a debit to the Monarch, than an asset. It was true that he usually, although not so regularly as in Austria, chose a magnate for his Minister President: but that was his personal idiosyncrasy. He bowed to the fact that the political weight of the legislature had shifted to the Lower House, which was largely an assemblage of representatives of the gentry (the County *congregationes*, virtually exclusively so). On the one occasion on which the Upper House opposed the will of the Lower, although his personal sympathies on the issue, which was a Confessional one, were with the magnates, he overruled them, rather than endanger the '67 majority in the other body.

It was symptomatic that young sprigs of the high aristocracy desirous of making a name in politics usually chose for their ladder to fame membership of the Lower House, where their snob value, perhaps their class's biggest surviving asset, quickly procured them the leadership or near-leadership of a political party. The programme of these parties was, indeed, not class, but *közjogi*.

It has been said with truth that in the Compromise Era Hungary was dominated socially by its magnates, financially by its Jews, politically by its upper middle classes.

Next down the scale came the urban middle and small bourgeoisies, and on the land, a considerable class, numbering some 700,000, of farmers cultivating between 200 and 10 *hold*. Then came 400,000 smallholders with 5–10 *hold* each, then the industrial proletariat, and on the land, 700,000 dwarf-holders with 1–5 *hold* each, and two and a quarter million with less than one *hold* apiece, or totally landless.

The dwarf-holders included some vintners, market-gardeners, etc., for whom even a few acres supplied a comfortable living, and the condition even of the landless men was not always intolerable for some years after 1867. The demand for agricultural labour still exceeded the supply, and it was well paid. Further, big public works were going on on the railways and the regulation of the waterways, especially the Tisza and its tributaries; on these, too, wages were high. But in the 1880s the railway progamme was nearly completed, and the regulation of the waterways was wound up. At the same time, the agricultural depression forced the landlords to reduce their wage bills by mechanizing, and by cutting wages, especially by reducing the share in kind of the crops harvested by him which had formed the larger part of a seasonal labourer's remuneration. The destitution which then became chronic among the rural poor was terrifying, and its effects were registered in a decade of harvest strikes, and sometimes, outbreaks of violence. The Government took a few remedial measures, and more repressive ones; more important, the accelerating industrialization and emigration, now setting in on a large scale, drained part of the surplus agrarian population off the land. The curve flattened out, but a frighteningly large proportion of the agricultural population was left still existing on, or below, subsistence level.

Similarly, at the outset of the period skilled industrial workers were in short supply, so much so that many had to be imported from Austria or the Reich. They commanded good wages. But the economic refugees from the congested rural areas who formed the bulk of the expanding labour force held no bargaining cards, and could be, and were, exploited almost at their employers' will. In practice, wages and labour conditions kept approximate pace with the Austrian, or a step behind.

In one respect the industrial workers enjoyed an advantage over the agricultural. The landlords saw to it that the latter got no form of political or vocational organization. The industrial workers were at first allowed to form many craft associations, and in 1868 even to found a 'General Workers' Association'. In 1870, however, this was dissolved, and the restrictions on craft associations tightened up, although association, within prescribed limits, was still lawful, as were strikes, provided that they did not involve breaches of contract with the employers. In 1890 the political movement made a fresh start: a Social Democratic Party was founded with a programme taken bodily from that of the Austrian sister party. It succeeded in remaining in existence, at the price of confining its activities strictly to the industrial workers. Széll allowed the latter to form nationwide associations deserving the name of Trade Unions, and these established an intimate connection with the party by the device of setting up behind each official trade union a 'shadow' or 'free' union which performed the political functions of its official counterpart. In 1903 the membership both of the party and the unions was still very small, but rising rapidly as industrialization proceeded.

The Nationalities Question

The first Compromise Governments genuinely tried to give the Nationalities Law a fair run, at least in essentials. No special pressure was put on nationality candidates at elections, and their representatives spoke freely in Parliament. Eötvös' law on elementary education was absolutely fair, and its principles were not disregarded.

Even then, however, the greater part of Magyar public opinion regarded the Law as ridiculously, and even dangerously, generous. They might conceivably have repressed this feeling had the Law not also been attacked from the other side. In January 1869 the Serbs' 'national' deputies held a great conference at which they adopted a resolution reaffirming their policies previously declared, announcing their hostility to the Law and inviting the other nationalities to form a combined party. The Roumanians of Transylvania, at a mass meeting in March of the same year, resolved by an overwhelming majority to maintain their full demands as formulated in 1866 (thus including the demand for the repeal of the Union) and a majority resolved not to attend the Budapest Parliament until these were satisfied. When Lónyay tried to reach an agreement with them, they insisted on their full demands. Even one party of the Slovaks announced their programme to be that of a memorandum sent by them to Vienna in 1861 which demanded wide territorial autonomy. The Hungarian Independence Left was for accepting some of these demands, but all the other Hungarian politicians only saw in them proof that generosity did not pay. Kossuth had been right: the way to deal with the Nationalities was to assimilate them where this was possible, and where it was not, at least to keep them firmly in their places.

A policy based on this view set in after the party fusion which, as has been mentioned, carried with it the tacit abandonment by Francis Joseph of any support for the Nationalities.

In this policy (which was, indeed, seldom expressed in new legislative enactments; much more often existing machinery was used, or interpreted, in the sense of the policy) it is possible to distinguish three threads: one which treated Hungary as being politically already a Magyar national State; one which made it look as though it were one; and one which aimed at making it into one. The first of these was the earliest taken in hand, the most systematically pressed, and by far the most effective. As we have said elsewhere, a few years passed before the public services could be Magyarized completely, for at the outset there were simply not enough qualified speakers of Magyar to go round. But the requirement that a Hungarian university degree was necessary for a Grade A administrative or judicial post, coupled with the fact that the language of what was then Hungary's only university was Magyar, ensured that virtually all new entrants to those services should be Magyar by birth or adoption. The same principles were applied *mutatis mutandis* to the professions (excluding the Churches and Confessional schools) for which a degree or a diploma was required: the candidate had to be at least conversant with the Magyar language. The attainment was required even from such small fry as engine drivers and postmen.

The chief of the eye-wash measures were the Magyarization, decreed in 1898, of all place-names, even of towns and villages founded, and exclusively inhabited since their foundation, by non-Magyars, and the encouragement, sometimes reinforced by pressure in the case of State employees, given to the adoption of Magyar family names. The principal instrument of direct Magyarization was the educational system. The university, as we have seen, was Magyar by law. On the lower levels, the hands of the Governments were to some extent tied by the autonomy enjoyed by, and guaranteed to, the Churches, which controlled the overwhelming majority of the primary and secondary educational establishments, and only two laws were, in fact, passed restricting that autonomy; one in 1879, which made Magyar a compulsory subject of instruction in all primary schools, State or Confessional, and required all training colleges to make their students competent to give it; and another, in 1883, which laid down that pupils in secondary schools must receive sufficient instruction in that language for them 'to master it adequately'. But the non-Magyar Confessional secondary schools were only a handful, and permission to add to their number was, except in the case of the Saxons, regularly refused. The authorities controlling the Roman Catholic schools, and the Lutheran outside Transylvania, as well as the Calvinists, saw to it that all instruction in the secondary schools controlled by them should be in Magyar, and the same practice was followed in all State secondary schools (except in Fiume). By the end of the period, virtually the entire educational system above the primary level had been Magyarized. The language of instruction in 189 of the 205 *Gymnasia* and *Realschulen* was Magyar; in six, German, in one, Italian, in one Serb, in seven, Roumanian, in one, mixed Magyar and Roumanian; none at all in Slovak or Ruthene. Even in primary schools, the language was Magyar in 12,223 of the 16,618, as it was in virtually all the infant schools established under a law of 1891.

It should not be thought that all these efforts were wasted. The Magyarization of the public services was almost complete; over 90 per cent of the employees in these services were 'Magyars', and Magyar was now, in practice, the sole inner language of administration and justice, and except on the lowest level, and not always there, that of the other services. Almost as high a proportion of the lawyers and physicians were linguistic Magyars, and the same held good of social and business life, outside the remote provincial centres. Even in the arts and sciences, an astonishing proportion of the chief ornaments of the age had begun their lives (or their fathers had done so) with names different from those under which posterity knows them.

Magyarization had made astonishing progress in the towns. Between 1880 and 1900 alone the Magyar-speaking population of Hungary's 25 largest towns had grown by 29 per cent. Budapest, which had been three-quarters German in 1848, was 79 per cent Magyar-speaking in 1900, by which date its population had trebled. In the smaller towns the rise, although less sensational, had still been large. In the rural communes it had been smaller, but in the country as a whole, the percentage of the population giving Magyar as its mother tongue had risen from 40–42 in 1840–50 to 51.4 in 1900 and in absolute numbers, from under 5 million to 8.6.

It should, moreover, be emphasized that contrary to what has so often been written, virtually all this increase was psychologically real, the fruit, where not of enthusiasm, at least of ready acquiescence. The census figures were generally honestly compiled, and in the overwhelming majority of cases the man who put himself down as 'Magyar by mother-tongue' (in fact the criterion used was not mother-tongue but habitual language) regarded himself, or at any rate wished others to regard him, as a Magyar.

Unhappily for Hungary's later fortunes it was in the centre of the country that most of the Magyarization, where it went below the upper middle classes, took place through assimilation of its islets of non-Magyar colonists to the surrounding majorities, its other subjects being the immigrant Jews or workers from the north, whose

children Magyarized automatically and almost imperceptibly. But
central Hungary was Magyar already. It was otherwise on the periphery. The little Slovak boy or girl who had Magyar grammar drilled
into him for a few hours a week in a school which he did not want to
go to anyway, forgot it as soon as he left school, and the Magyar
ethnic islets sank under the surrounding flood just as their non-
Magyar counterparts did on the other side of the main ethnic frontiers. In the north, east and west these remained stationary on almost
the exact lines on which they had been stabilized at the end of the
eighteenth century. If, therefore, those areas were claimed by other
States on ethnic grounds, Hungary's only hope of retaining them
would have been if the criterion adopted had been that of real self-
determination (which it was not) and if she had succeeded in preserving, or creating, a real attachment to herself among the non-Magyar
populations.

The basis of the policy followed by Tisza and his successors was,
of course, a denial of the very possibility of this, and the impatient
intolerance with which it was pursued obviously rendered the possibility more remote. Even so, it was not a total failure; the results of
it varied from one nationality to another, as did, indeed, the details
of its application.

The Jews embraced whole-heartedly the opportunity given them
by the 'system' to merge themselves in it, provided their religion was
respected (as it was). The same could be said of the Germans outside
Transylvania: attempts by pan-German enthusiasts to make them
feel differently had only minimal results. It could also almost be
said of the Ruthenes and the Slovaks, on whom the full weight
of the Magyarization was turned. A very high proportion of their
intelligentsias became Magyar in their national feeling. Those
who did not do so naturally resented the ruthlessness with which
their most legitimate cultural demands were rejected, but even they
were not combative. The 'Memorandists' soon faded out, as did
even some activist movements which appeared round 1868. For
twenty years after this no Slovak nationalist candidate even stood
for Parliament.

These were the only nationalities on whom any serious pressure
was put to Magyarize. For some years relations between the Government and the Transylvanian Saxons were very strained; the Government remembered the attitude which the Saxons had adopted after
1848, while the Saxons resented the loss of their old political autonomy. Then, in 1881, a tacit agreeement was reached: the Saxons
dropped the demand for the restitution of their autonomy, and the
Government replaced the more aggressive Föispans. The Saxons
rolled themselves into a more compact hedgehog than ever, under

the protection of their Church, the autonomy of which the State respected, with its own network of schools, co-operatives, etc. They regularly supported whatever Government was in office, while allying themselves with the Magyars against the Roumanians on local issues. They thus became a *staatserhaltendes Element*, but at the same time a *corpus separatum*, although their hearts' loyalty was with Vienna, rather than Budapest. How little they ranked the interest of the Hungarian State above that of their own community was shown in 1919, when they voted for the attachment of Transylvania to Roumania (having first ascertained in Paris that this had been decided).

The Serbs, rather surprisingly, reached a somewhat similar accommodation. At the outset, when memories of their lost Voivody, gilded with a somewhat deceptive afterglow, were still vivid, and relations with the Principality close, their representatives in the Budapest Parliament were more bellicose than those of any other Nationality (the extremist Roumanians not being present then), and they led the opposition against the Nationalities Law. Relations became further inflamed during the Bosnian crisis. Then, however, the Government intervened. Their leaders, Stratimirović and Miletić, were arrested, and their militant organization, the *Omladina*, dissolved. The Government had already won an important success in 1875 when, the Patriarch Maširevics having died, they secured the election of a conciliatory man, Ivacsković, as his successor. The National Liberal Party itself split in 1884, and the stronger wing, led by Polit, accepted the Compromise and the Nationalities Law.

The Government did not attempt to interfere with the autonomy of the Orthodox Church, and allowed the Matica to function undisturbed. But the national-minded alumni of that institution emigrated to Serbia and the rest accepted their position as a fact of life. They were, incidentally, a prosperous community, and although hardly any of them assimilated, they led a peaceable enough multilingual existence with their German, Roumanian and Magyar neighbours.

Easily the most difficult case was that of the Roumanians. A mass meeting of the Transylvanian Roumanians in 1871 resolved by an overwhelming majority to maintain their full demands, including that for the revocation of the Union, as formulated in 1866, and to continue their boycott of the Budapest Parliament until those demands were fulfilled. A minority, led by the Archbishop Şaguna, dissented from the policy of abstention, but not from the programme, and even this small 'activist' group disintegrated in 1873, when Şaguna died. The Roumanians of the Partium and the Bánát had meanwhile kept their separate organization, and continued to send their representatives to Budapest. But their continued lack of success disheartened them, and in 1881 they agreed with the Transylvanians

to form a 'United Roumanian Party' on a programme which, besides demanding redress for various grievances, undertook 'to fight
by all constitutional means for the restoration of Transylvanian
autonomy'.

The Government vetoed the formation of the party. The leaders
continued, of course, to meet unofficially, but the leader of the Hungarian Roumanians, Mocsonyi, used his influence on the side of reconciliation, and the next years were still inactive; in particular,
Mocsonyi succeeded in blocking periodical proposals to address the
Crown with a new petition. In 1884, however, new life was breathed
into the movement by a brilliant young journalist, Ion Slavici, who
founded a journal, the *Tribuna*, which became the rallying point of
the younger radicals, social and national. He had spent several years
in Bucharest, whither he returned in 1890 and organized the foundation there of a 'League for the Cultural unity of all Roumanians',
which, on his suggestion, produced a memorandum (drafted by him)
on the grievances of their brothers in Hungary. Translated into
several languages and circulated throughout Europe, this attracted
much attention and sympathy. This encouraged the Transylvanians
to compile their own memorandum, which a great deputation carried to Vienna. Francis Joseph refused to receive them and several
people afterwards received prison sentences for their parts in producing it. The ebullience subsided. The *Liga Culturale* exhausted its
funds, and its agitation, discouraged by the Roumanian Government, died away, while the Hungarian Roumanians relapsed into
political passivity under Bánffy's heavy hand.

Meanwhile, they had been anything but passive in other fields. A
network of self-help organizations had done remarkable work in
raising their cultural and even their economic standards. They now
possessed a prosperous peasantry and a considerable intelligentsia;
they were even gaining ground demographically, at the expense of the
local Magyars and Saxons. What proportion of them would really have
welcomed changing their allegiance to Bucharest it is impossible to
say: probably not many, for they were well aware that the conditions
under which they lived were far superior to those in the Regat. But
they were still far the most combatively anti-Budapest of all the
Nationalities.

The turn of the century saw certain indications that the relative
success which Magyarization had achieved in the preceding decades
might not prove lasting. Among the Slovaks, in particular, a real
national revival set in, partly under the influence of Masaryk, who
inspired the foundation of a Czecho-Slovak Society in Prague; partly
in answer to which, the Slovak People's Party reconstituted itself in
Hungary, and got four deputies into Parliament. Roumanian, Serb

and Slovak leaders met and agreed on a joint programme which, while dropping the old demand for 'national' territories and organizations, agreed to press their cultural demands more vigorously. This evoked great rage among the Magyar chauvinists, and its chief immediate effect was an increase in Magyarization, including the foundation of 400 new State schools. But it seemed at least possible that the tide was turning.

Croatia

It had, as we have said, been a packed Diet that voted the *Nagodba*, and the National Party refused to recognize their defeat. For four years they kept up their agitation against it, enforcing, in the course of it, the resignations of both Rauch and his successor,[5] until, in 1873, the Archbishop of Zagreb succeeded in forming a Party of the Centre which, while retaining the name of 'national', dropped its predecessor's obviously unrealizable demands, while the Hungarians conceded some amendments to the original instrument: some restrictions were placed on the powers of the Ban, and the proportion of its revenue retained by Croatia for internal expenses was raised slightly. The acting Ban, Vakanović, was then replaced by the popular Ivan Mazuranić. Mazuranić, who was by profession a civil servant,[6] and a competent one, introduced a number of administrative and judicial reforms. Himself a poet of repute, he presided over the opening of the University of Zagreb. He kept the peace with Hungary. The dark side of his regime was its extreme national chauvinism, which he vented in particular on the Serbian minority in Slavonia, and it was his demonstrative sympathy with the demands made by extremist Croat nationalists during the occupation crisis that eventually led to his resignation in February 1879.

The next Ban, Count Pejačević, was a man of peace, but under his regime there occurred one of those trivial incidents which entail disproportionate consequences. On instructions from Budapest an official in the Joint Finance Office in Zagreb had the escutcheons bearing inscriptions in Croat only taken down from above the doors of his and some other offices and replaced by others bearing inscriptions in Magyar and Croat. An enormous uproar ensued. Rioting mobs tore down the offending escutcheons; 23 deputies left the 'National Party' to form an 'Independent National Party', and Pejačević resigned.

After order had been restored by a Royal Commissioner, Tisza nominated for the new Ban his own cousin, Count Károly Khuen-Héderváry, then a young man of only 30, who was technically qualified for the position, being domiciled in Slavonia, but a true

Tisza man in spirit. He combined the Unionists with the remnants of the old National Party[7] in a new 'National Party', which had little in common with its predecessor except the name: it now consisted of a clique of men dependent on the Ban, who were given by the people the same name of 'Mamelukes' as had been bestowed on Tisza's followers in Hungary. As reinforcements he used the local Serbs, to whom, in return for their support, he granted many political, cultural and economic favours – a device for which he was attacked most bitterly by the Croats and their partisans, but with less than justice, for the Serbs now numbered one quarter of the population of Croatia-Slavonia and it was no more than the duty of any man in authority to protect them against the tyranny to which they would otherwise have been (and had been) subjected by their Croat fellow-citizens. Thanks to this expedient, and to his unscrupulous use of pressure and corruption at elections, Khuen was able to secure a majority at all elections during his reign, which ended only with his translation to higher spheres in 1903, and a revision of the Sabor's Standing Orders in 1884 made it possible for it to put through the business entrusted to it. The more extreme national opposition to him was further weakened by another split in its own ranks, which ended, after Starčević's death in 1896, with its division into two parties: a 'Party of Right', composed of the more moderate of Starčević's old followers and survivors of the 'Independent Nationals', with a programme which asked for little more than a revision of the *Nagodba* to place Croatia on a footing of complete national equality with Hungary, and a 'Party of Pure Right', organized and led by Dr Josef Frank (a Jew), which demanded the unification of all Southern Slavs in the Monarchy, including Bosnia-Herzegovina, in a jumbo Great Croatia as a partner-State in the Monarchy.

It should, however, be recorded that if the methods employed by Khuen to keep the power in his hands were often dubious, the uses to which he put it were, on balance, good. His regime was neither oppressive nor unenlightened. Less richly endowed by nature than the Kingdom of Hungary, and less favourably situated geographically, Croatia lagged behind it in respect of industrialization and urbanization; a symptom of the consequent rural congestion was an even higher rate of emigration (assisted, indeed, by the fact that since the Croats were a maritime people, the number of them emigrating for short periods, and then returning, was abnormally high). Even in these fields, however, and in that of communications, and still more, in the modernization of agriculture, progress was made which, considering the limited resources available, was far from despicable. In other fields, Khuen made no attempt to stifle the Croat national culture; under him the University and Academy of Zagreb prospered, and Croat literature enjoyed something of a *floraison*. Even politically, his methods met with some success. When his enemies complained that he 'corrupted the soul of a whole generation' what they meant was that he induced a considerable number of Croats to accept the relationship with Hungary in principle, if not in every detail.

Fifteen

BOSNIA-HERZEGOVINA
1878–1903

Contrary to expectation, the Austrian armies entering Bosnia in 1878 met with strong resistance from the local Mohammedans and even from some of the Serbs. Military rule had to be maintained for several months, and then further time elapsed before the Austrian and Hungarian Governments, neither of which was prepared to let the other have the job, agreed to entrust the administration of the provinces to the Common Minister of Finance, operating through an office which contained departments dealing respectively with internal affairs, justice, and finance and economics.[1] The Governor on the spot was the officer commanding the local garrisons, assisted by a civilian *ad latus*.

The next three years were still experimental, and the real history of the Monarchy's rule dates from the appointment to the post of Common Minister of Benjamin Kállay, a Hungarian who had been Consul for the Monarchy in Belgrade, and possessed a sympathetic understanding of the South Slav problem. Kállay held the post until his death in harness in 1903. His regime was one of benevolent despotism. It was not until 1897 that a small measure of self-government was allowed to the towns, and then the concession was limited to the towns, and native Bosnians were admitted only grudgingly to the administrative services, which were staffed mainly with Slavs from the interior of the Monarchy, Croats providing the largest contingent. A large force of police, open and secret, was maintained, and the Press 'influenced' in both positive and negative directions.

The Monarchy's general policy towards the provinces was unfortunate in several respects. They were made subject to the Austrian military service law,[2] – a measure deeply resented by the local population – and it was further decided that they were to be financially self-supporting, except insofar as the Ministry of War made a grant towards the maintenance of the local garrisons. Devices were found for getting round this law, for example, by counting some railway lines as 'military', while loans were advanced for the construction of others, but expenditure on the public services, and on the most desirable public works, had to be cut to the bone. Even so, taxation, both direct and indirect, had to be raised sharply: it rose some fivefold under Kállay's regime. This was deeply unpopular among a

people many members of which saw no necessity for, nor even advantage in, the improved sanitation, education, and security (all
things probably non-existent before 1878) which they now enjoyed.
One problem which Kállay shrank from attacking was that of the
landlord-peasant relationship. In 1878 perhaps two-thirds of the
cultivated area of the provinces was owned by six to seven thousand
large landlords, almost exclusively Mohammedan 'begs'. The rest was
owned by free peasants, a few of them Christian, but the majority,
said to number 77,000 families, Mohammedans, while the majority
of the 100,000 families of 'Serbs' and 25,000 of 'Croats' were 'kmets'
or tenants on begs' estates. The rentals which they paid were largely
in kind, and usually amounted to about one-third of their produce.
Not only had the system grown more onerous in the course of time,
but many *begs* had also extended their estates, by usurpation. The
Christian population had confidently expected the Austrians to correct the usurpations, perhaps to introduce a general land reform. The
Austrians, however, found the task of disentangling legitimate titles
from usurpations too difficult for them, and simply recognized the
status quo, except that they introduced facilities, of which advantage
was rarely taken, for a *kmet* to buy in his holding on terms which
were not particularly easy.

These, however, were the dark – if sometimes undeservedly deni-
grated – sides of a picture which could show many bright ones. The
general standard of the administration, although below that of the
Monarchy proper, was far more efficient and less corrupt than that of
the old Ottoman Empire or of the neighbouring Balkan States. Security now in fact became almost absolute, and justice even-handed, and
much was done for the improvement of public health. Communications, again almost non-existent before 1878, improved vastly. Better
agricultural methods were introduced, and courageous attempts were
made to introduce more industries and to develop the natural resources of the provinces – in some cases, it is true, this was done
through the grant of concessions to entrepreneurs whose operations
proved more profitable to themselves and their shareholders than to
the local population. By and large, however, the Government's economic policies can be described as eminently successful.

The national problem was closely bound up with the Confessional.
In this respect Kállay tried genuinely to maintain strict inter-Confessional equality and freedom of worship. The religious susceptibilities of the Moslems were meticulously observed, and the appointment of their clergy was left in the hands of the Sheik-ul-Islam. The
Catholics came under the general rules governing the relations between the Catholic Church and the Monarchy. Kállay did introduce
a measure of indirect control over the Orthodox Church in that he

bought the episcopal advowsons from the Patriarch of Constantinople, abolished the fund, known as the 'Vladicharina', out of which
they had been paid, and paid them out of general taxation. The parish
priests were still, as before, elected by their parishioners, but no priest
could now be given a cure of souls unless he possessed a certificate of
suitability from his seminary. This measure raised substantially both
the intellectual and the moral levels of the priests. But it is clear that
the certificates took account of the aspirant's political views as well
as his morals, and that these considerations weighed also in cases of
candidacy for episcopates.

Of the three Confessions, the Catholics prospered most. The Pope
created a new Province of Bosnia-Herzegovina, with an archbishop
and three suffragans, and soon a network of parish churches came
into being, some of them in villages in which there was hardly a
Catholic to be found. The Catholics were also admitted into the State
services in far larger numbers than the Moslems or Orthodox. This
was their due reward for the superior educational qualifications
attained by them through their own efforts, but it gave colour to the
widespread belief that the Government was favouring the Catholics,
or Croats, at the expense of the Serbs. This was not at all Kállay's
wish. He had originally hoped to call into being a distinct 'Bosnian'
national feeling, transcending other loyalties, but this proved beyond his powers. The Moslems came nearest to feeling themselves
'Bosnians', but after the 1880s the Catholics, under the influence of
their combative Archbishop, Mgr Stadler, flung themselves into the
Great Croat movement, and Serbian national feeling, too, weak at
the outset, grew apace with the years, parallel with its growth across
the frontier. The Serbian 'intellectuals'' chief complaint was against
the lack of self-government, and as meanwhile their own agitation
had made Kállay feel that it would be unsafe to introduce institutions
which gave them any influence over the country, a vicious circle was
created and his regime developed more and more into one of opposition to the Serb element, with the result that the other grievances of
the population – the military service, the high taxation, the *kmet*
system, and the rest – came to be represented, and felt, as national
injustices.

Sixteen

THE LAST YEARS OF PEACE

The last decade of the Monarchy's peacetime existence forms a distinct chapter in its history. In 1903 the long-accustomed cavilling of the Hungarian 'National Opposition' against the Compromise developed into a storm so intense and widespread as to call into question the very existence of the Compromise and thus the whole internal structure of the Monarchy. In the same year events occurred in Serbia out of which there emerged a new and obviously dangerous international situation. In the same year again, the death of Kállay ended the long period of stability in Bosnia. Thus in three fields, two of them of the first importance, the prospect opened of a future the nature of which no one could prophesy except that it would be different from the past. And it was to be anticipated that the same position would arise shortly in respect of a wider field still.

So long as the last word rested with Francis Joseph, it could be assumed that there would be no radical alterations in either the foreign or the domestic policies of the Monarchy. By now he had long since given up all thoughts of conquest, content to keep what he had, and looking to the German alliance to enable him to do so. In respect of the central internal problem of the Monarchy, that of its structure, he had also come to accept as final the settlements reached in 1867. He demanded, indeed, an equally punctilious observance of them from others, but so long as he could compel this, as with his authority he was able in the main to do, they were safe.

But in 1903 Francis Joseph had passed the Psalmist's statutory tale of years, and his Crown, with all the immense powers vested in the wearer of it, must by all human reckoning soon pass to another. His Heir Presumptive, the Archduke Francis Ferdinand, had hitherto come before the public eye chiefly in connection with his insistence on marrying the bride of his choice, and ironically, his constancy to his love, the one redeeming quality in a character otherwise of unrelieved nastiness, had been the cause of a bitter conflict with his uncle: for although the family of the lady, a Countess Chotek, was indisputedly *hochadelig*, it was still not one of the tiny innermost ring membership of which would have allowed marriage into it to rank as *ebenbürtig*; on contracting it in 1900 Francis Ferdinand had been compelled solemnly to renounce the right of any issue of the union to succeed to the throne. He had not, however, renounced his own right to the succession, so that his political views would presumably, in a few years, be of prime importance for the future of the Monarchy.

They were unlikely to bring any fundamental change in foreign political alignment. Francis Ferdinand attached great importance to re-establishing friendship between the Monarchy and Russia, but not at the expense of Austria's alliance with Germany, which he regarded as the kingpin of its international relations, and the German element in its population as its 'cement'. His ideal was a revival of the Three Emperors' Alliance. Italy he would gladly have let go. He disliked and despised the people and regarded war with the State as inevitable – nor did he mind the prospect. If he felt differently about Roumania, this was partly out of political considerations, and partly because King Carol, like the German Emperor, but unlike some other Heads of States, treated his wife with full Royal honours. For the rest, he did not want war for war's sake, and would have been glad to see Austria on good terms with the Western Powers, or at least, Britain.

His outlook on domestic problems was largely governed by his emotions. One strong element in it was a very bigotted Catholicism. He was profoundly anti-democratic, wholly uninterested in social questions. Although without any ambition to be a personal dictator *à la* Joseph II, he was quick to resent any questioning of his will. Very notorious was the prejudice felt by him and ostentatiously expressed against some of the peoples over which he seemed destined to rule. He strongly disliked the Poles, whom he regarded as an arrogant and subversive lot and also an obstacle to good relations with Russia, and had little sympathy either with the Czechs, partly because their super-magnates sneered at his wife for being less loftily born than they. But these feelings paled beside those with which he regarded the Magyars. Towards them he had, partly for political and partly for personal reasons, early conceived a veritably pathological hatred which became perhaps, after his love for his wife, the strongest element in all his emotional make-up. It seemed almost certain that when given the opportunity, he would seek to give this obsession some form of political satisfaction, although just what form, could not be said.

Francis Joseph had been slow to admit his nephew to any share in the business of State, or even to take him into his confidence. The younger man had represented his uncle on a few ceremonial visits, and in 1898 had been given a sort of roving commission to interest himself in all aspects of the defence of the Monarchy. At home, he was President of the 'Catholic Schools Association' (in which capacity he had contrived to give deep offence to wide circles) but had been given no *locus standi* to intervene in top-level political questions. It was, however, obvious that if he chose to do so, his voice would carry much weight, for few public men could be quite indifferent to the wishes of a man who would presently have such power to enforce them. There already existed a 'Belvedere Party' to which an ever-increasing number of holders of, or aspirants to, key posts belonged. From as early as 1904 onwards, many appointments to top-level positions, political as well as military, were made on his suggestion, or out of deference to his known wishes.

The uncertainty about the Archduke's intentions was one of the factors which invested life in the Monarchy during these years with a curious atmosphere of impermanence. Change, for better or worse, was in the air. Not everyone felt that it would necessarily be for the worse. There were many who felt that the stability of the preceding thirty-five years had degenerated into fossilization, and that what the future would bring would be rejuvenation, salutary reform, consolidation on a new and firmer basis.

And in some fields, there were grounds enough for optimism. Many aspects of the economic picture were extraordinarily bright. In Hungary, in particular, legislation, more generous than its predecessors, had led on to an industrialization almost dizzy in its tempo. The number of industrial plants rose between 1898 and 1913 by 84 per cent, that of workers employed by 76 per cent, the net output of machines by 188 per cent and the value of goods produced by 126 per cent. The share of industry in the nation's income was now 27 per cent, about three-quarters of this coming from the so-called factory industry, in which the light industries, especially the textile, were now producing 20.6 per cent of the national income from industry, while the share of the food industries had shrunk to 39 per cent (heavy industry remained nearly constant at 41 per cent). In Cis-Leithania the growth was a little less rapid, but still big: the number of factories rose by over 40 per cent, that of workers in industry by 49 per cent, the output of industry and building by over 90 per cent. In agriculture, the yield of all the main crops continued the rise that had set in ten years previously and total production rose even more with reclamation of marginal land and diminution of fallow. The value of the net output of agriculture doubled in Hungary, and its share in the national income actually rose, although only fractionally, in both halves of the Monarchy. Trade, communications and the professions were all earning larger sums, and the total national income of the Monarchy, measured in money terms, rose in ten years by 86 per cent in Austria and 105 per cent in Hungary. The real increase in the individual's standard of living was smaller, for we must allow for the larger population, up again by 1910, in spite of continued emigration, which in 1907, its peak year, topped 200,000, to 51.3 million, including 1.8 million in Bosnia-Herzegovina, and also for a sharp rise

in prices which followed when Austria retaliated to the agricultural
duties imposed by Germany in 1902 by herself introducing a provisional regime with relatively high duties on imports, both industrial
and agricultural, which enabled her own producers in both fields to
raise their prices by an average of about 25 per cent. The *per capita*
increase in real incomes was probably about 40 per cent in both
halves of the Monarchy.

This was, of course, not equally shared out between all classes
of the population, especially since industry, commerce, and even
agriculture, were passing increasingly under the control of an ever-
diminishing number of ever-larger concerns, themselves owned or
controlled by a handful of holding-banks, which kept prices high, to
the very great profit of themselves and their share-holders, but not of
the workers. Industrial wages, with an average rise of 40 per cent, did
little more than keep pace with prices. In agriculture the social scis-
sors opened perhaps less wide. The small producers, as well as the
large, profited from the high prices, and thanks partly to the emigration,[1] partly to the movement of workers into industry, the agrarian
population of Austria increased only fractionally, and the rate of
increase in Hungary slowed down. There still remained black spots,
but it seemed reasonable to hope that if things went on as they were
going, the scourge of rural over-population that had so long afflicted
the Monarchy would disappear from all parts of it, as it had already
from some.

Even the national finances did well. In 1907 the Austrian budget
closed with a record surplus, and Hungary's too, was regularly active.
The capital national debts of both countries rose further, but thanks
to successful conversion operations, the servicing of them did not rise
proportionately, and the general increase in both revenue and expenditure made this item relatively tolerable. The trade balance of the
Monarchy was active until 1906, and Austria's invisible balance
continued active after that date. Hungary's was still passive, but
there, too, the tide was beginning to turn.

In the arts, the robust but sometimes crude productivity of the
Monarchy's Victorian age was giving way to new fashions as the
eternally indispensable task of leavening the Teutonic lump, performed in earlier days by Italians, was taken over by the sons and
grandsons of the Jews who had established themselves in Vienna and
Budapest half a century before. There was indeed a good deal of self-
pitying *Weltschmerz* in some of the products of this new cross-
fertilization, but at their best they achieved a heartbreaking loveliness
which was not the less beautiful for the occasional touch of over-
ripeness. Few capitals in any age could show such a variety of genius,
native or imported, as Vienna, with its Hofmannsthal, Rilke, Schnitz-

ler and Richard Strauss, or Budapest with its Ady, Bartók and Kodály.

The crisis between the Crown and Hungary broke out over the old question of the army. Owing to the chaotic parliamentary conditions in Austria, it had been impossible in 1899 to fix the new ten-years' figure for the annual intake of recruits. The Ministry of War had carried on in Austria by calling up the annual contingent, at the old figure, by Paragraph 14, and in Hungary by not releasing the men already with the colours. In 1902 the results of the 1900 census had been published, and the Ministry asked the two Parliaments for enlarged contingents, to take account of the increased population. The Reichsrat, after prolonged objections, eventually accepted its figure conditionally on Hungary's doing the same. But the Hungarian Independent Party seized the occasion to demand a number of 'national' concessions: the language of command and the regimental language in all Hungarian units to be Magyar (Croat in Croatia),[2] the oath of loyalty to be taken to the Hungarian constitution, the Hungarian coat of arms to be given a place in the insignia of the Common Army, and others. Apponyi, although a member of the Government party and President of the Lower House, produced a list of demands only a little less far-reaching. Obstruction set in and on 1st May the country passed into the 'ex lex'. Széll resigned in despair. Francis Joseph first offered the succession to Kálmán Tisza's son, Count István Tisza, leader of the most reliable fraction of the Liberal Party, and a known advocate of the strong hand. Tisza's rivals refused to serve under him, and Francis Joseph appointed instead Count Héderváry, who had kept Croatia in order for so long. But Héderváry found his own countrymen tougher than the Croats. The agitation assumed such dimensions that the Ministry of War prepared plans to occupy Hungary with units from other parts of the Monarchy. On 17 September Francis Joseph issued an Army Order, known from its place of origin as the 'Chlopy Order'[3], declaring that he would allow no tampering with his own supreme rights or with the unity of the army. Couched in very wounding terms, the Order poured oil on the flames (as its authors probably intended it to do[4]). Khuen got the Monarch to write a letter which filed the rough edges off the original Order, then resigned his commission. Meanwhile, however, the Liberals had taken fright at the violence of the Left, and a Committee of them drew up a modified list of demands which Francis Joseph agreed to accept. He now after all appointed Tisza, who formed an administration on 31 October.

There followed a brief lull, during which Parliament got through some essential legislation. But Tisza's personal rivals combined with his enemies against him. Apponyi went back into opposition at the head of a refounded 'National Party', which later joined the Party of Independence. Bánffy founded a 'New Party' of his own. Then, after Tisza had, like Falkenhayn before him, used dubious methods to put through an absolutely necessary reform of the Standing Orders of the House, Andrássy jumped on the waggon with a 'Constitutional Party' of dissident Liberals. The People's Party jumped with him. The Party of Independence was, of course, already seated on the waggon. In January 1905 Tisza got the House dissolved, and new elections held, with which, believing that the country would repudiate the obstructionists, he told the Föispáns not to interfere. He had overestimated his countrymen's good sense. They returned only 159 Liberals (a number reduced by later desertions to 102), against more than twice that number of representatives of the four main Opposition Parties, who then formed a 'Coalition of National Parties'.

Francis Joseph first invited Andrássy to form an administration. He refused to do so without further 'national' concessions over the army. The spring passed in fruitless negotiations, with Tisza, although he had resigned, remaining, reluctantly, in charge. Then on 18 June Francis Joseph nominated Baron Géza Fejérváry, formerly commander of the Royal Hungarian Bodyguard, to carry on *ad interim*, at the head of a Cabinet of officials. The Coalition denounced Fejérváry's regime as unconstitutional, and called on the Counties not to obey its orders. Fejérváry's Minister of the Interior, Kristóffy, countered with a memorandum to the Crown in which, like Steinbach before him, he argued that there was no doing anything with the 'historic classes'; it was necessary to find a counterweight to them in the other classes of the population. He proposed enlarging the electorate from its then figure of about 1 million (6.9 per cent of the population) to something over 2.5 million (15.74 per cent). Many of the new voters would have been non-Magyars, and of the Magyars, a substantial proportion would have been Social Democrats, with whose leaders Kristóffy had been in touch.

This reform would by no means necessarily have strengthened the hands of the supporters of the Austrian connection. Tisza was bitterly opposed to it, believing that it would strike the death-blow to that Hungary which, as he saw it, was the only kind of Hungary that could exist at all. The leaders of the '67 Parties in the Coalition, Apponyi and Andrássy, took the same view. Only Justh and, surprisingly, Bánffy, really welcomed the proposal, while Kossuth wavered. Francis Joseph himself was far from enraptured with the idea, and at first allowed Kristóffy only to ventilate it as a personal suggestion, and after Parliament had reassembled in September, he invited the Coalition leaders to meet him, having cleared the ground by letting Fejérváry resign. But the audience, which took place on 23 September, and lasted exactly five minutes, did nothing to resolve the deadlock. Francis Joseph simply read out to his auditors the conditions on which he would entrust them with office: no tampering with the unity of the armed forces, or of the foreign services: the Economic Compromise to be negotiated and agreed with representatives of Cis-Leithania: guarantees that essential legislation, budgetary and military, would be voted. They were to discuss details with Goluchowski. When the discussions led to no agreement, he reappointed Fejérváry, this time with instructions to form a parliamentary Government in the programme of which he was to include franchise reform.

Fejérváry tried to form his own parliamentary party, but only three deputies volunteered for it, and when the Parliament reassembled in December, the scenes in it were so rowdy, that a Crown Council decided that the only course would be to dissolve it. On 19 February 1906 the edict to this effect was read out, and the premises cleared by the military.

The Coalition's hope was in the Counties, but that reed broke. New Föispáns put in in the autumn had already brought most of the Counties to heel, and the Government put an end to the remaining resistance by stopping the salaries of recalcitrant officials. The Coalition leaders found themselves lacking in the heart to carry on a struggle which seemed hopeless, while Kossuth was not even convinced of its rightness. They put out feelers. Francis Joseph now added two more conditions: they must agree to introduce a franchise reform, not necessarily Kristóffy's, and they must accept Wekerle as Minister President. Kossuth was brought in a very curious way (through a prophecy by a sooth-sayer) to agree to the franchise reform, and Apponyi and Andrássy swallowed their misgivings rather than be left out in the cold. The bargain having been struck in deep secrecy, the new Government was appointed on 8 April. The elections were held in May. Since Tisza had dissolved the Liberal Party, which did not contest the elections, the Coalition won an overwhelming victory, the only real opposition to it coming from twenty-six representatives of the Roumanians, Slovaks and Serbs (the Saxons voted with the Constitutional Party).

It is hardly surprising that the years that followed this transaction were among the most ignominious in Hungarian parliamentary history. Their secret promise to the Crown prevented the Coalition from fulfilling virtually any of the promises in faith whereof their constituents had voted for them. The Austrians organized a grand counter-offensive against Hungary's allegedly exorbitant demands in connection with the Economic Compromise, and all that Hungary achieved here was the barren change in nomenclature that the relationship was to be termed a 'Customs Treaty'. Trade was, however, to continue free for at least the next ten years. She paid for this with material concessions which included another change of 2 per cent to her disadvantage in the quota. One or two enlightened ministers produced some valuable social legislation in both industry and agriculture, but politically the regime was as narrow as its predecessor. Andrássy was charged with the franchise reform, and after two years produced a Bill so narrow that Justh refused to accept it, and it was withdrawn. Apponyi's contribution to the nationalities problem was an Education Act which, while it introduced long overdue improvements in the salaries of teachers in the elementary schools, also increased substantially the amount of instruction in Magyar that had to be given in them: some thirteen hours weekly out of thirty were devoted to this in non-Magyar schools, in which, too, several other subjects were usually taught in Magyar.

In general the Coalition showed itself to be even more intolerant than its predecessors towards the Nationalities. Under no previous Government had so many leaders, especially Roumanians and Slovaks, been sent to prison for 'agitation against a nationality' (always construed as agitation against Magyar nationalism).

Remarkable developments, not all of Hungary's making, went on in Croatia. In 1903 a refusal by the Hungarian Government to revise the financial clauses of the *Nagodba* had led to rioting in Croatia, which spread to Istria and Dalmatia. Deputations went to Vienna to beg Francis Joseph to intercede for them, and his refusal led to a widespread feeling that the best hope for the Croats lay in their forming a common front with the Serbs. Simultaneously, but certainly not coincidentally, a parallel movement set in among the Serbs of Croatia, who had just reorganized under a new leader, Svetozar Pribičević.

Yugoslav unity was, however, music of the distant future. For immediate policy the Croat leaders decided to turn first to Budapest in its conflict with Vienna. On 4 October 1905, forty Croat leaders from Croatia, Istria and Dalmatia, meeting in Fiume, adopted a resolution offering Croatia's support to Hungary in its conflict with Vienna in return for Hungary's support for the reattachment of Dalmatia to the Triune Kingdom. These resolutions were endorsed the next month by the Serb deputies from Croatia and Serb and Croat deputies from Dalmatia. The Resolution adopted at the latter meeting contained the affirmation that 'the Serbs and Croats were one people'.

This was also the belief of the chief inspirers of the Fiume Resolutions, a journalist named František Supilo and the ex-Mayor of Spalato, Anton Trumbić, and a 'Coalition' of Serb and Croat deputies from Croatia, who accepted it, secured 28 mandates in the Croat elections of 1906, while the old National Party emerged with only 27,

12 of whom subsequently went over to the Coalition, and the Party of Pure Right, with 23.

The fraternization with Hungary did not last long, for the Hungarian Coalition, which had welcomed the Fiume Resolutions with innocent enthusiasm, soon offended the Croats by issuing a tactless, although perhaps legally defensible, order making knowledge of Magyar compulsory for all employees on the Hungarian State railways, including the lines in Croatia. The Croat deputies denounced this as a violation of the *Nagodba*, and meetings up and down the country called for total separation from Hungary. The Ban resigned, and his successor, Baron Pál Rauch, dissolved the Sabor and held new elections, but in these the Unionist Party disappeared altogether, fifty-seven of the eighty-eight seats going to the Coalition, twenty-two to the Party of the Pure Right and seven to splinter Parties, including Radić's Peasant Party. A new Ban, Professor Tomašić, got the Sabor to accept an enlarged franchise and reorganized the National Party as a 'Party of Progress', but new elections gave only eighteen mandates to this Party, while the Coalition still got thirty-six, and yet another election did not alter these figures substantially. Tomašić resigned. His successor, Čuvaj, again suspended the constitution, whereupon someone threw a bomb at him, wounding him severely.

Meanwhile, the Hungarian Coalition itself became divided on two issues. Justh's wing of the Independence Party was in favour of the suffrage reform: Kossuth's and Apponyi's agreed with the '67 Parties in opposing it. Similarly, Justh's wing insisted that Hungary must be given her own National Bank by the end of 1911, while Kossuth's wing and the '67 Parties thought that an independent bank would be disadvantageous to Hungary, as being financially the weaker half of the Monarchy. The differences proved irreconcilable and the Coalition became unworkable. On 27 April 1909 Wekerle resigned.

After another prolonged deadlock, Khuen-Héderváry volunteered to form an administration resting on the old Liberals. He became Minister President on 17 January 1910. For the new elections, held in May, Tisza reconstituted the Liberals under the name of 'Party of Work'. This time no holds were barred, and the Party of Work secured 258 mandates, against only 110 for the four Coalition Parties together.

The situation was back to the *turbulentia ante quo*, with a Government pledged to support the Compromise and an Opposition against it, with the complication that this Government also was, on Francis Joseph's insistence, pledged to introduce suffrage reform. In fact, Francis Joseph contented himself with a nominal honouring of the obligation in a Bill so cautious that after it the agitation for and against reform went on as though it had never been enacted. Otherwise history repeated itself with uncanny fidelity. Khuen introduced another Bill for raising the strength of the armed forces. The Opposition resorted to such frenzied obstruction that in April 1912 Khuen resigned. He was succeeded by László Lukács, while Tisza took over the Presidency of the House, in which capacity he forced through both the Army Bill and another reform of the Standing Orders which made the Parliament workable.[5] In June 1913, Lukács resigned, and Tisza took over the Minister-Presidency, making the reversion complete in appearance.

Only, however, in appearance. It had not been against the Coalition's programme that its voters had rebelled, but against their leaders' failure to carry it out. The ideas for which they professed to stand were more popular than ever in the ring in which the battle of '67 versus '48 was traditionally fought out. More important still was the increased growth and determination of the factors still excluded from the arena. The Social Democrat Party, which had reorganized in 1903 with a new programme and new statutes, was now an unquestioned factor in the social equation, and the membership of the Trade Unions had multiplied. There were repeated strikes and demonstrations, culminating in 1912 in a General Strike which cost heavy bloodshed. Several peasant parties had appeared, with programmes of land reform, and there had been more harvest strikes. There was even a small but vocal group of radical middle-class intellectuals, centering round the periodical *Huszadik Század* (Twentieth Century), the editor of which, Oszkár Jászi, was regarded as their oracle. The spirit of the Nationalities had only been hardened by the intolerant treatment meted out to them; the age of assimilation was drawing to a close.

When Tisza was firmly in the saddle, the curve of trouble flattened out slightly. In particular, the new Ban in Croatia, Baron Skerlecz, achieved a reasonable *modus vivendi* with the Serbo-Croat Coalition. On the other hand, talks between Tisza and the Roumanian leaders ended in deadlock. Tisza was still able to keep 'his' Hungary in being so long as he enjoyed the support of the Crown, but it was difficult to see how it would survive if its friend there were replaced by an enemy.

On 29 May 1903 the young King of Serbia, Alexander Obrenović, and his wife, were murdered by conspirators belonging to a secret association of officers, who then called to the throne Peter Karageorgević, of the rival dynasty. Very soon relations between the Monarchy and its southern neighbour degenerated disastrously. Peter himself may not have harboured hostile feelings towards the Monarchy, which certainly felt none towards him, but he was the prisoner of the men who had put him on the throne, and of the Serbian Radical

Party, which had developed from a Left-wing peasant party into one dedicated to the aggrandizement of Serbia. Nationalist societies, open and secret, were soon spreading their gospel abroad, at first chiefly in Macedonia and Bosnia.

Immediately thereafter an economic crisis arose between Austria and Serbia. The Commercial treaty between them was due to expire shortly, and Germany's new protective tariff threatened the chief foreign market for Hungary's agricultural exports, for which the Austrian market was now all-important. Her producers maintained that they could no longer allow large quantities of cheap Serbian produce to enter the country when their own exports of the same commodities were blocked. The Austrian industrialists also demanded that Serbia should at least pledge herself not to reduce her imports of Austrian industrial articles. In January 1904 Serbia instead placed a large order for arms, not with Skoda, but with its French rival, Schneider-Creuzot. She also concluded with Bulgaria a secret Treaty of Friendship which envisaged the later conclusion of a Customs Union. This leaked out, and Austria vetoed the treaty as incompatible with her own treaties with both States. As Serbia still refused to accept the Monarchy's conditions, a 'treatyless condition' came into being on 1 March 1906.

The 'Pig War', as it was epigrammatically although somewhat unfairly called, lasted for over three years. Serbia emerged from it almost unscathed economically, having found alternative markets and sources of supply in France and Germany. But she was deeply embittered, and now further raised the cry that she would not be economically secure without a direct outlet to the sea, from which she was cut off by Austrian or Austrian-occupied territory.

Her agitation turned increasingly against the Monarchy, and the path for it in Bosnia was smoothed by Austria's own good intentions. For after Kállay's death in 1903, his successor, Baron Burián, introduced several cultural and other concessions to the local Serbs, in the belief that these would content them and stop them from 'gravitating outwards'. He also relaxed the censorship. The Serbs took advantage of this to stage an unbridled agitation against 'Austrian tyranny' and demand for the Provinces complete autonomy and the right to determine their own international status.

Serbia's agitation inside the Monarchy had to be carried on more discreetly, but it is now well attested that Serbian circles, official as well as unofficial, played a part in bringing about the Fiume Resolutions and their more important accompaniments, the public declarations of Serbo-Croat identity, and that the same circles thereafter largely directed the policies of the Serbo-Croat Coalition. For the time being, the Serb Government thought it safer to play for a *modus*

vivendi with Vienna, or alternatively, with Pest, and framed its immediate activities, and those of its agents, accordingly. But the final aim
was always to further Serbia's national ambitions, whether in Yugoslav or in Great Serbian form, and even where the Serbian Government did counsel discretion, its advice was often disregarded by
hotheads whose passions it had itself fanned.

Meanwhile, another factor had entered the picture. Round the turn
of the century, Russia's attention had centred on the Far East. She
had signed a Military Convention with Bulgaria in 1902, but this had
been only to cover her rear against Roumania. In October 1904, when
her differences with Japan reached the point of war, she had followed
up the agreement of 1903 with Austria with another agreement, valid
for five years, which pledged each party to neutrality if the other became involved in a war not provoked by it with a third Power, other
than a Balkan State.

But her defeat at the hands of Japan altered the situation. The
first effect of it which touched Austria was the emergence during the
short-lived revolutionary era of 1905 of the 'neo-Slav' movement,
which, while repudiating imperialism and professing to aim only at a
close and friendly relationship between all Slav States, was nevertheless basically political in the highest degree in that it counted the
Monarchy as a Slav State, which would have to be transformed politically 'so as to give its Slav peoples the weight in it to which their
numbers entitled them, the Germans and Magyars stepping down into
their proper places'.[6] This doctrine had effects on the Slavs of the
Monarchy which are described elsewhere (see p. 250), and while
neo-Slavism as such was killed by the Russian counter-revolution
which retracted almost all the concessions made in 1905—7 to the
Czar's non-Russian subjects, it left behind it in Russia a new idea
of Slav solidarity, much rather pan-Slav than neo-Slav, which denounced as 'oppressors' all non-Slavonic states which contained
Slav subjects.

Secondly, Russia's interests now turned westward again. When
Izvolski, who was a convinced 'Westerner', became Foreign Minister
in 1906, the international situation was still fluid, but by the end of
1907 the division of Europe into Triple Entente and Triple Alliance
was nearing completion. Russia was still very weak, and very conscious of her weakness, but Izvolski was anxious to go over to a more
active policy, if it could be achieved safely.

By this time there had been changes in some of the key posts of the
Monarchy, the most important being the replacement, in October
1906, of Goluchowski by Baron Lexa von Aehrenthal, Austro-
Hungarian ambassador in Petersburg from 1889 to 1906, and a
month later, of Beck as Chief of the General Staff by Conrad von

Hoetzendorf. Both appointments had been blessed by the Heir Presumptive, and both men played, or aspired to play, a part in determining the Monarchy's foreign policy.

Conrad's prescription for Austria's problems was preventive war against Italy and Serbia before the balance of military preparedness should have turned further against her. He used to advocate this policy with a singular outspokenness which naturally increased the tension between Austria and the designated victims, and caused Aehrenthal many difficulties. Since, however, he never got either Francis Joseph or Francis Ferdinand to adopt his nostrum, he cannot be held responsible for the crisis which broke out soon after his appointment.

Such responsibility does fall on Aehrenthal, and it was a curious irony that he should have succeeded, in a couple of years, in making Russia at last the Monarchy's open enemy, with Serbia as its preferred client. For he had come to the Ballhausplatz from the Neva convinced of the desirability of the closest practicable friendship with Russia and with a record for good work in promoting it (the agreements of 1903 and 1904 were largely of his making). This friendship was to be turned to account. Aehrenthal was a very vain and ambitious man, who fretted greatly against the role of second fiddle in the Triple Alliance which Germany seemed to be assigning to Austria, and he hoped to remedy this, firstly by improving the Monarchy's relations with Italy (in this respect, too, he did some good work, in spite of Conrad), and secondly, by raising its prestige by a forward policy in the Balkans, to be achieved on the basis of a deal with Russia. Russia was to have what she wanted in the Straits, and also the patronage over Bulgaria (there would, he thought, be no danger in this, if Russia were friendly), while Austria was to annex Bosnia-Herzegovina, and beyond this to exercise 'some sort of protectorate, that is, the establishment of overlordship, over the Western Balkans, down to Salonica inclusive, by means of alliances, trade and military conventions, etc.'. There were to be no further annexations, 'unless justified or compelled by the actions of others'.

Some of Aehrenthal's more intimate utterances suggest that he really meant to go much further, finding 'justification or compulsion' to annex or partition Serbia. But the programme as it stood was compatible with correct relations with Serbia, and would have provided a fair basis for the deal with Russia. It was a fact also that the agitation in Bosnia had reached such a pitch as to leave the Monarchy no alternative to annexing the Provinces, if we exclude as humanly impossible the course of handing them back to the Sultan. Aehrenthal, however, set about realizing his plan with a maladroitness extraordinary in a man of his indubitable intelligence. On 27 January

1908, after the barest intimation to Russia of his intentions, he announced in the Delegations that Austria proposed to build a railway through the Sanjak, to join the Turkish line to Salonica; another line was to run from Serbia to the sea, across Bosnia. Izvolski produced a counter-plan for a trans-Balkan line from Roumania to the Adriatic, but wrote secretly to Aehrenthal offering his consent to the annexation in return for support of a Russian request for revision of the Straits regime. Both questions would have to be discussed on a European level, but he was prepared to enter into friendly discussion of them with Austria. Then, however, the Young Turks carried through their revolution in Istanbul, and compelled the Sultan to issue a firman convoking a parliament to which Bosnia-Herzegovina, as well as Roumelia and Crete, were to send elected representatives.

This made the annexation urgent. Aehrenthal arranged to meet Izvolski for conversations. These took place at Buchlau, in Moravia, on 16 September. They left Izvolski under the impression that Austria would, indeed, be carrying through the annexation at some early date, but that there would be a Conference of the Powers at which Russia's demands in the Straits would be considered. Instead, a proclamation appeared on 7 October that Austria had annexed the Provinces, and was withdrawing her garrisons from the Sanjak.[7]

A major diplomatic crisis followed. Serbia made military preparations, demanded compensation and appealed to Russia for support. Montenegro showed equal resentment, while Turkey, too, protested. Izvolski, who protested that Aehrenthal had misled him, began by backing Serbia, and demanding a Conference to discuss both the Bosnian problem and that of the Straits. But the German Emperor decided to back Austria to the limit, and summoned by Germany to make her position clear, Russia, which was neither ready nor anxious for war, advised Serbia to submit. Serbia had even to give Austria a promise of 'good-neighbourly relations', in return for an assurance from Austria that she would not attack her. Turkey was placated by a cash compensation.

So the crisis ended leaving Austria the richer by the two Provinces, while everyone else came out practically empty-handed, since Britain refused to let the Straits question be reopened. The result was celebrated in Austria as glorious proof of the Monarchy's continued vitality. Yet Austria had probably lost, internationally, more than she had gained by the coup. Germany's affirmation of her *Bündnistreue* had been comforting, but even before the crisis Bülow had laid down that 'Germany and Austria must stand together . . . loyal co-operation with Austria shall be and must remain the fundamental basis of German foreign policy',[8] and the closer the co-operation, the greater the converse danger (which Aehrenthal took with extraordinary lightness[9]) that Austria might be dragged into war against the Western Powers. All the signatories to the Treaty of Berlin, Germany not excepted, had been offended by Aehrenthal's unilateral action, and by the insultingly short notice he had given them, and precisely Germany's support had dealt the faith of Britain and France in Austria as a counterweight to Germany, already shaken at Algeciras, another blow, and one from which it never fully recovered. Tittoni in Italy signed an agreement with Russia under which the signatories agreed *inter alia* on a common attitude towards Balkan problems incompatible with a further Austrian advance. Immediately after, indeed, he signed a similar agreement with Austria, this time directed by implication against Russia, and in 1911 Austro-Italian relations improved again, for when Italy, after making slow progress in her invasion of Tripoli, carried her arms into the Aegean, the disapproval of Britain, France and Russia drove her back onto her old alliance, and the Triplice was renewed unaltered in 1912.[10]

There was no comparable improvement in Austria's relations with Serbia, whose promises to mend her ways proved not worth a piecrust. She was fortunate in that two monster political trials staged in Zagreb, one against members of the Serbo-Croat Coalition, the other against a number of Serbs of Croatia, proved to be based on documents all or most of which had been forged, and collapsed ignominiously, grievously discrediting the Ballhausplatz and its tools who had produced them. This did not alter the fact that an active agitation against the Monarchy was being carried on by the nominally cultural 'Narodna Obrana', behind which, and closely connected with it, stood after 1911 another society, the *Ujedinjeje ili Smrt* (Union or death), commonly known as the Black Hand, which was purely terrorist. The head of the Black Hand, Dragutin Dimitrievic, was also head of the Intelligence Department of the Serbian General Staff. Soon, indeed, differences, especially over Serbian policy in Macedonia, led to the foundation, under the patronage of the Crown Prince Alexander, of a rival 'White Hand', which in 1917 liquidated its competitor in the famous 'Salonica Trial'. It may well be that the key to the 'riddle of Sarajevo' lies in the ambivalent relationship between the two Leagues.

Serbia could afford these tones towards Austria because she was now under open Russian protection. The policy of Russia's new Foreign Minister, Sazonov (the annexation had brought with it the fall of Izvolski) was not to seek territorial advances for Russia, but to organize the Balkan States, including Turkey if possible (for if he renounced taking Constantinople for Russia, he did not want to see Greece or Bulgaria installed there) in a league under Russian patronage. In 1912, however, Serbia, Bulgaria, Greece and Montenegro, disregarding his warnings, combined to attack the Porte. There followed the two Balkan Wars of 1912–13, the first between Turkey and the four Balkan allies, the second between Bulgaria and her former allies, reinforced by Turkey and Roumania. Berchtold, who had gone to the Ballhausplatz on Aehrenthal's death in February 1912, refused to take the opportunity repeatedly pressed on him by the 'forward party' of joining in the competition for territorial gains, 'settling accounts' with Serbia in the process. He confined himself to making the redrawn map as innocuous as possible (when necessary, indeed, by the threat of force). He obtained the creation of an independent Albania, but the settlement left Serbia and Montenegro both substantially enlarged, and brimming with self-confidence.

Austria's natural community of interests was now with Bulgaria, but considerations arising out of the personality of King Ferdinand apart, the alliance with Roumania prevented her from establishing close relations with Bulgaria. The Roumanian alliance was, however, growing very hollow. Austria certainly could not rely on her for help against Serbia, and probably not against Russia unless the war had already been three-quarters won without her.

The uncertain international situation alerted the Monarchy to the weakness of its defences. In 1912 the Minister of War, Auffenberg, got the annual intake of recruits for the regular army raised to 159,000, which would bring its peace strength up to 350,000 and its war strength to 1,500,000. A further small increase was voted in 1914. Considerable sums were spent on new artillery, fortifications and strategic railways, and in 1909 a big programme of naval construction was launched. The strength of the Monarchy's armed forces was, however, still very low compared with that of Germany or Russia, and even so the cost of the programmes, added to that of two partial mobilizations in 1912–13, reimported the old uncertainty into the financial position. One consideration behind the decision for war in July 1914, was unwillingness to spend capital, material or moral, on a third mobilization not followed by action.

The question where Bosnia was to belong in the Monarchy was never settled. Provisionally, the Common Finance Minister remained in charge. The Proclamation announcing the annexation promised the provinces representative institutions, and a *Landtag* was in fact called into being, but with limited competences. The most important measure enacted by it, an agrarian law enabling a tenant to buy in his holding, produced only meagre results: by 1915, when it was suspended, only 45,000 tenant farmers out of 145,000 had taken advantage of it, and 85 per cent of these were in arrears with their payments.

The year 1903 marked no hiatus in the domestic politics of Cis-Leithania. Through that year and the next Koerber carried on, cajoling the Reichsrat to vote the essential legislation, presiding over the performance of much useful work in other fields. But he was still unable to find a solution to the crucial Czech-German problem, and many of his activities, and even more his methods and those of his unduly powerful and greatly detested *chef de Cabinet*, Sieghart, made him influential enemies, including the Heir Presumptive. The attacks frayed his nerves. When Kramář offered to call off the obstruction if Koerber were replaced by Gautsch, with whom he was personally friendly, Francis Joseph consented to the bargain. The change was made on 31 December 1904.

Gautsch, an able and reputable civil servant, kept his predecessor's team as far as he could (Koerber had been holding three portfolios) and would probably have aimed at nothing higher than to keep things ticking over, but his hand was forced first by Kristóffy's initiative in Hungary, then by the Czar's action in promising to grant his peoples a constitution and to convoke a Duma. On 3 November 1905 Francis Joseph suddenly informed Gautsch that he had decided 'to introduce the institution of general suffrage in both halves of the Monarchy'. Gautsch deferred, although with personal reluctance. He decided to recognize the priority given by most voters to national issues by re-delimiting the constituencies so as to make them as far as possible uni-national, while weighting them in favour of the more 'advanced' nationalities. The Poles objected so strongly to the first key produced by him that he resigned in April 1906. His successor, Prince Conrad Hohenlohe, who had accepted his appointment only reluctantly, found a pretext to resign after only a few weeks. His successor again, another civil servant, Freiherr von Beck, revised Gautsch's figures, in favour of the Germans and Poles, making the presumptive figure, in a Reichsrat of 516, 241 Germans, 97 Czechs, 80 Poles, 34 Ruthenes, 23 Slovenes, 19 Italians, 13 Croats, 5 Roumanians and 4 Serbs. Parliament was now dissolved, and elections held in May.

These did not work out quite according to plan. Fewer Germans and Poles were elected than had been expected, and more Czechs; there were also four Zionists and one Jewish-Liberal, on whom no one had reckoned. For the rest there was, naturally, a strong swing to the Left. The Christian Socials had allied themselves with the Catholic People's Party, and the combination secured 97 mandates. 87 went to the Social Democrats (50 German, 23 Czech, 14 other), and nearly all the national parties split into fractions, some of them pronouncedly left-wing. For the first time in its history, Austria now possessed a Parliament in which almost all classes of the population were represented. Naturally, however, the result was not a Govern-

ment of the Left. For a while Beck – whom many believe to have
been the best Minister President in Austrian history – did preside
over something like a parliamentary Government. While he gave half
the portfolios in his Cabinet, as was now *de rigueur*, to civil servants,
the other half were parliamentarians from German, Czech and Polish
Conservative parties, who sank their differences in face of the emer-
gent danger from the Left. But this phase did not last for long. Beck
had formerly enjoyed the special regard of the Heir Presumptive,
whom he had instructed in public law, and had helped over his marriage crisis. But that difficult man now found offence in various of
Beck's actions, and turned against his former mentor and friend with
extraordinary fury. Some of the same actions also offended the Clericals, and Beck further annoyed Aehrenthal by lack of enthusiasm for
the annexation. In November 1908, he was intrigued out of office by
a combined manœuvre in which these forces were joined by the
Christian Socials, who were playing for the Archduke's favour. Since
the parties which the Christian Socials had hoped to make their partners proved as greedy as themselves, the idea of a genuine parliamentary coalition had to be given up. The next Government, presided
over by another civil servant, Freiherr von Bienerth, was again one of
civil servants and *Landsmann* Ministers, and the Poles, Czechs,
Christian Socials, and German nationals, whose leading parties, this
time excluding the Christian Socials, had combined in a new association, the *Deutscher Nationalverband*, gave him enough support to
keep a nominally parliamentary regime alive for a couple of years.
But they were lamentably barren years. When Bienerth did try to do
anything constructive, which was not often, for he was not outstanding either in willpower or in brains, it was made impossible by one
or other of the thirty parties and five independent members in the
Reichsrat. Hoping to get a more secure majority, he dissolved the
Reichsrat in May 1911, but in the new elections, while the *Nationalverband* increased their representation to 104, the Christian Socials,
much of whose virtue had gone out of them with their fusion with the
Clericals, and more when Lueger died in March 1910, lost heavily
(down to 76) and the Poles were now hopelessly divided. Bienerth
resigned. The Emperor called again on Gautsch, who again tried to
get the Czechs to support him, but they asked too high a price. He
gave up on 31 August, and the Emperor now turned to Count Karl
Stürgkh, a Styrian landowner who had left the administrative service
in 1891 to enter parliament as a representative of the Conservative
Big Landlords. Stürgkh got together a Cabinet composed almost entirely of officials, with a Pole and a Czech. He at least had no illusions
about the Reichsrat. For two and a half years he got through necessary business by Paragraph 14. Then, in March 1914, obstruction by

Czech radicals led him to adjourn the Reichsrat, and it had not re-assembled when Austria declared war on Serbia four months later.

The increased number of votes cast at the 1907 elections for parties of the Left did not mean the opening of any prospect that Austria would be governed through a Parliament of the left, because, as we have seen, Parliament had ceased to have any effectual voice in the government of the country. But it did reflect a growth in the importance, outside the Reichsrat, of the classes which voted for those parties. The Christian Socials were now essentially a Conservative party resting on the rural electorate of the Alpine Lands. But they still represented the smaller men against the big landlords, as did the 'peasant' Parties in other Lands. Both the Social Democrat Party and the Trade Unions had increased their numbers very largely, and were now, on any reckoning, a force which every Government had to take into account.

If the only issues had been social ones, Austria might have ended by evolving into a parliamentary democracy. The national question, however, remained as intractable as ever. Two Lands, Moravia and the Bukovina, evolved satisfactory *modus vivendi* between their nationalities by registering the electors in national 'catasters' each of which sent an agreed proportion of representatives to the electoral curias and to the various vocational, etc., bodies. But this did not signify any general abatement of national passions. The one nationality whose feelings seemed, so far as their relations with the Government were concerned, to have gone off the boil, were the Germans. The *Nationalverband* supported the Government on all vital issues and refrained from making intolerable nuisances of themselves in the Reichsrat. But this was simply because they had stopped being frightened. The stock claim made by every Government, from Koerber on, of being 'neutral' on national questions, leaving any change in such respects to agreement (which, they could be certain, would never be reached) between the parties concerned, and in practice eliminating Parliament and ruling through the bureaucracy, suited the Germans perfectly, for the administrative *status quo* was still on balance favourable to them, and the senior civil servants who really governed the country were not, at bottom, nationally neutral : they were Josephinian Austro-Germans. The more logically-minded Austro-Germans were advocating making permanent the course to which necessity was increasingly driving the Ministers President to adopt as a pragmatic and theoretically temporary expedient, of dispensing with the Reichsrat altogether and reverting to confessed absolutism, exercised through the bureaucracy.

Where, as in some of the *Landtage*, the Germans found it necessary to defend their interests, they did so quite as ruthlessly and egotistically as any other nationality : it was obstruction by the Germans in the Bohemian *Landtag* that provided the Czechs with their excuse to resume obstruction in the Reichsrat; for they said that if the one body did not work, neither should the other.

The Czechs were perhaps more intransigent than ever before, and they were now looking outside the inner ring of their ambitions. Neo-Slavism found a strong advocate in Austria in Kramář, who claimed, indeed, to be its author. In July 1908 he convoked a great neo-Slav 'Preparatory Conference' in Prague, which drew up an imposing programme of all-Slav solidarity. This was carefully framed to avoid any disloyal wording, but the distinction between a strongly Russophile movement that was non-irredentist and one that was secretly irredentist was one which it would not be easy to preserve in a conflict between Austria and Russia. In December 1908 the Czechs, alone among the peoples of the Monarchy, boycotted the celebrations of Francis Joseph's sixty-year jubilee. A State of Emergency had to be proclaimed in Prague and the *Landtag* adjourned. After further fruitless attempts to make it workable, it was replaced in 1913 by an 'Imperial-Royal Commission'.

The leadership of the Slovene People's Party was taken over by new men, among them Mgr Korošec, who were both socially more radical than their predecessors, and nationally less particularist. Under their influence the party formed an alliance with the Austrian Croats and an understanding with the party of the Pure Right in Croatia.

The agitation among the Italians continued to grow, being directed especially against the Austrian Government's continued refusal to meet their demands for an university. An Italian Law Faculty, opened in Innsbruck in 1904, had to be closed on account of rioting between German and Italian students. In 1914 they were promised a Faculty in Vienna, but it never saw the light.

The Poles clung firmly to their privileged position. As their attitude towards Gautsch's franchise reform showed, they were prepared to overthrow a Government which threatened it, and in other respects also they gave the Austrian Governments anxiety. The concessions made by the 1906 Duma to the Poles in Russia had inspired some of their kinsmen in Galicia with a belief in the possibility of a reconciliation with Russia. This was the view of the National Democrats, after 1907 the strongest Polish party in Austria, and also of another group, the 'Podolian Conservatives', who thought the Ukrainians a greater danger than the Russians. The renewed Russification which set in in 1908 cooled the Poles' enthusiasm, but Austrian Governments admitted that they could not count on their Poles as implicitly as they had between 1870 and 1905.

From about 1900 the Ruthenes had been developing their 'nat-ional' associations, cultural and economic as well as political, with a great rush, and their national feeling had grown correspondingly stronger and more bellicose. The franchise reform had also greatly enlarged the numbers of their voters, although still leaving them most inadequately represented.[11] Under strong pressure from the Crown, the Poles agreed in 1914 to a 'Reform Bill' which gave the Ruthenes more representation in the *Landtag*, and they were promised more secondary schools, and an university, but these concessions did not come near bringing peace between the two peoples. The position was complicated when the Russians rediscovered the Ruthenes and began again sending missionaries to Galicia to convert them to the Ortho-dox faith. The results, although backed by material incitements, were not sensational: only two Russophiles were returned in the 1911 elec-tions against twenty-five 'Ukrainians'. But Berchtold took the move-ment very seriously, although he found it difficult to suggest a remedy.

The most discouraging proof of the inability of other considerations to outweigh those of nationality came from the Social Democrat Party, where in 1905 another quarrel led to its Czech members form-ing what amounted to a separate party (to which almost all the Czech workers adhered), with its own political organization and Trade Unions.

The great majority of the nationalities were still not aspiring to leave the Monarchy, but only manœuvring for position within it. Interesting plans published by two Social Democrat thinkers, Renner and Otto Bauer, both specifically accepted the multinational State, as affording, if properly organized, a better form of coexistence for small nationalities than imperfectly realized national States. Many other proposals for such a reorganization were being mooted, an in-teresting feature of many of them being that they no longer assumed the intangibility of the Dualist system, or of the territorial integrity of the Hungarian Lands. The Christian Social Party, at its 1905 Con-ference, adopted a Resolution condemning the Dualist system. This was because they were bidding for the favour of the Heir Presumpt-ive, as were other planners who hoped to turn to the advantage of their own causes his demonstrative hatred of all things Hungarian. In 1906 the Archduke had set up his own little Chancellery, and in 1911 this became the seat of a regular 'shadow Cabinet' and a centre from which contact was maintained with various circles and movements. Which, if any, of the many solutions proposed to him he would end by adopting when he came to the throne, was still quite uncertain, for he changed his mind on the point many times. His name is most often associated with the idea of replacing the Dualist system with a

'Trialist' one, the third component of which was to be formed out of the Serb and Croat areas of the Monarchy (he does not seem to have heard of the Slovenes), but this did not last long: he was put off it by the Fiume Resolutions and the Serbo-Croat fraternization. Later he took up many other plans, only to lay each aside.

But which of them, if any, he would have attempted to realize on his uncle's death will never be known, for on 28 June 1914 he and his wife were assassinated in Sarajevo, whither he had gone to attend the army manœuvres.

The assassin, a youth named Gavrilo Princip, was a Bosnian Serb, as were all the other persons whom the authorities apprehended in connection with the crime, but the inquiries showed that the conspirators' arms had come from the Serbian State arsenal in Kragujevać, and that they had been trained in their use in Serbia and smuggled across the frontier by a Serbian organization (although strangely enough, the investigators missed the real culprits, the Black Hand, and put the blame on the *Narodna Obrana*). The official sent down from Vienna to take charge of the inquiries, *Hofrat* Wiesner, reported that 'there was no proof, nor even grounds for suspicion that the Serbian Government was privy to the murder, or to the preparations for it', and to this day it has not been possible to prove the contrary quite conclusively. But the suspicion was strong enough to give rise to a general feeling in Vienna that an end had been reached. Not the military alone clamoured that the hornets' nest must be smoked out once and for all by war. When the official discussions began, the only dissident was Tisza, whose chief real objection was the old Hungarian one that even a victorious war would be followed by annexations which would increase the number of Slavs in the Monarchy, but he argued also that the war would not be localized so easily as others maintained: Russia would never allow Serbia to be wiped off the map, and Roumania might invade Transylvania if an action began before arrangements had been made with Bulgaria to hold her in check. He communicated his misgivings to the Emperor, whose dynastic feelings were deeply outraged, but he thought that the Monarchy could not risk war unless fully assured that Germany would stand behind her.

But in the next days the Wilhelmstrasse (and the German Emperor personally) not only sent the fullest assurances of support, but strongly pressed Austria to take action. The Austrians even feared that if they did not do so, the Germans would regard them as not *bündnissfähig*. The encouragement satisfied the Emperor. Out of deference to Tisza's wishes, he agreed that the Monarchy's Note to Serbia must give her an opportunity to accept its demands, but sent an appeal to Tisza not to oppose war if she failed to do so. Tisza submitted, stipulating only that the Joint Ministerial Council must make an unanimous declaration that the Monarchy had no plans of conquest against Serbia and would annex no Serbian territory beyond frontier rectifications.

Berchtold now composed a Note that was deliberately framed to be unacceptable. It went off on 20 July. The Serbian Government accepted almost all its demands, but made minor reservations on two points. Berchtold made these an excuse to describe the reply as insufficient, and the declaration of war went off on the 28th.

Even the Germans had got cold feet by now, but it was too late to stop the avalanche. Inevitably Russia stood by Serbia, France by Russia, Britain by France. Austria and Germany were soon at war with Russia, France, Britain, Belgium, Serbia and Montenegro. Their own allies, Italy and Roumania, took the view that the *casus foederis* had not arisen for them, and stood aside.

It is easy to understand the feelings of the men who took the decision for war. Austria had indeed long been subjected to intolerable provocation, and all minor remedies had proved ineffectual. There were other considerations also, strategic and even financial, that made the decision comprehensible. But Austria's apologists should not overstate their case. The decision between war and peace in July 1914 was hers to make, and she made it for war in full knowledge that the war might prove to be general. No special pleading can alter that fact.

Seventeen

THE END OF THE MONARCHY

At the outset of the war, as at that of most wars in most countries, *Kriegsstimmung* in the Monarchy was fairly general, particularly since no one expected the war to last long. Some of the Monarchy's Serbs associated themselves with their nation rather than their State, and when the Russian armies entered Galicia they were welcomed enthusiastically by an unexpectedly large number of village priests and peasants (many of whom may not have understood fully what was happening). Many members of both these nations were executed, or interned. But these special cases apart, both the leaders and the masses of all the Monarchy's peoples rallied behind their Government. For the non-Socialist German-Austrians this was natural, and the Social Democrats, who had protested and washed their hands of responsibility when the clouds were gathering, changed their attitude when the storm burst, and finding theoretical excuses for human weakness – in their case the threat of Czarist tyranny – became quite remarkably bellicose. In Hungary, the Party of Work naturally stood behind Tisza (who did not reveal his initial misgivings) and the Coalition leaders, now headed by Apponyi,[1] even suggested joining a Cabinet of National Concentration, provided Tisza would stand down (an offer which he refused). Károlyi was abroad, but when he returned he promised that his party would suspend inner political struggles until the war ended in victory. The Social Democrats made a tacit pact of mutual toleration with the Government. In the Sabor, the Coalition deputies sat discreetly silent, while their Croat colleagues, including Radić, poured out objurgations on Serbia.

The Poles, after considerable discussion between themselves, elected an inter-Party Committee (from which, it is true, the National Democrats seceded later) with a programme of reuniting Galicia with Congress Poland under Habsburg sovereignty. It was difficulties not of the Poles' making that, as described later, prevented the Austrian Government from immediately identifying itself with this programme.

Understandably enough, in view of the people's record, the authorities suspected all Czechs of being traitors and arrested numbers of them, including Klofáč. In fact, the inbred hostility to everything German combined with a somewhat nebulous *Schwärmerei* for things Russian, produced among them anti-war feelings which found expression when opportunities occurred; there were more individual or group desertions to the enemy in the first months of the war from Czech units than from those of any other nationality. If the Czar's armies had entered Bohemia, and he had then assumed its Crown, as a group of Czech expatriates in St Petersburg asked him to do, the action would doubtless have been acclaimed enthusiastically. As, however, they did not do so, the Czech leaders preferred to keep more than one iron in the fire, and made protestations of loyalty.

The operations did not, indeed, bring the anticipated quick successes. Conrad's plan, which had been imperfectly co-ordinated with those of the Germans, had been to crush Serbia in a swift offensive, meanwhile holding the line against Russia with relatively small forces. But the Serbs put up an extraordinarily tough resistance, twice throwing back the Austrians with heavy losses, and the Russians, too, proved more efficient than had been expected. They overran East Galicia and the Bukovina in September 1914 and threatened the passes into Hungary. In March 1915 the fortress of Přemysl surrendered and after 26 May, when Italy, after prolonged negotiations with both sides, decided to accept the Allies' bid, and declared war on Austria, another front had to be defended.

1915 nevertheless passed off well enough for the Central Powers. A great Austro-German offensive, which opened on 2 May 1915, drove the Russians back to a line east of Vilna, Pinsk and Luck, leaving only a small corner of Austrian territory in enemy hands. The Italians were held on the Isonzo, and after difficult negotiations had brought Bulgaria into the war on the side of the Central Powers in September (Turkey had already entered it in September 1914) Serbia and Montenegro were overrun and Albania occupied. In 1916 there were again dark months; the Italians won a little ground, the Russians opened an offensive in Volhynia from which the Austrians were saved from complete catastrophe only through an emergency operation mounted by the Germans, and on 28 August Roumania after, like Italy, bargaining at length with both sides, declared war on the Central Powers and invaded Transylvania, which at the time was almost denuded of troops. But the Italian line was stabilized after only a short retreat, the Russian after a retreat which, although larger, still stopped east of Lemberg, and the Roumanian armies thrown back, not only out of Transylvania, but out of Wallachia also, and left holding only a precarious line in Moldavia.

Since the Germans were holding virtually all Belgium and important areas of northern France, the autumn of 1916 found the immediate military position of the Central Powers unquestionably favourable. But the success had been dearly bought. Particularly Austria's best

officers and men had suffered appalling losses in the fierce fighting:
60,000 dead and 90,000 other casualties in Serbia, 250,000 dead or
wounded and 500,000 prisoners on the Russian front in 1914–15,
and as many again in 1916. The rate of sickness and of mortality
from it, owing to inadequate hospital services, was also very high. As
early as November 1914, the 21–31 classes had to be called up, the
32–42 not long after, and the term of service in the *Landsturm* was
extended. Even so the Austrian armies were often outnumbered in
the field, while the new men were physically of secondary quality, and
imperfectly trained. Most of the officers were now reservists. Supply
difficulties had set in early. The bread-grain harvest of 1914 had already been below the average, and after war had broken out little
could be imported. The Russian invasion of Galicia cut off one of
the Monarchy's main domestic granaries, and even where war did
not reach, shortage of man-power and animal labour, and of fertili-
zers and fodder, and deterioration of machinery, further reduced
yields. The 1915 harvest was well below that of 1914, that of 1916
lower still. In 1915 Tisza ordered that Hungary should send Cis-
Leithania only what she had left after supplying her quota towards
the army and satisfying her own needs, which left only a small remainder. The position in the big cities of Cis-Leithania was already
most miserable, with bread rations meagre and unpalatable, and milk,
meat and fats in shorter supply still. The Russian occupation of
Galicia had cut off the Monarchy's chief domestic source of oil, and
ill-considered calling-up took many coal-miners out of the pits. The
fuel shortage affected industry and transport. After the spring of
1915 the British blockade cut off other sources of raw materials,
including a large proportion of those needed by the textile industries.
Inferior substitutes had to be used widely. The cost of living was
rising sharply.

The authorities took Argus-eyed precautions against any possibility of subversive action, national or social. When the war began,
many civil liberties were suspended, restrictions introduced and activities declared punishable. The railways and other essential services,
including factories working for the forces, were put under military
control; offenders could be clapped into uniform and sent to the front,
or alternatively, classed as 'civilians', when they came on lower scales
for pay and rations. Areas near the front—and these came, in time, to
include all Cis-Leithania except Lower and Upper Austria, Bohemia
and parts of Moravia and Silesia – with large parts of Hungary, were
classified as 'military zones', and in the Austrian zones the local
army commanders enjoyed powers equal to those of a Provincial
Governor 'to safeguard military interests within the field of the political administration'. Some commanders interpreted their powers

very widely, carrying through mass arrests of civilians. In the Trentino the commander forbade the use of Italian in official documents and even in place-names. Security in the Austrian hinterlands was in charge of the 'Kriegsüberwachungamt' (K.U.A. – War Supervisory Office), a department of the Ministry of War. Persons accused of offences coming within the purview of this office were tried by military courts, which had to apply the provisions of the civilian code, but enjoyed practically complete freedom in arresting suspects, framing charges and assessing evidence. The K.U.A., again, made very full use of its powers; in May 1915 Kramář himself was arrested. Tisza did not allow the K.U.A. to operate in Hungary, and the military commanders in the Hungarian zones were not empowered to issue orders affecting the civilian population; instead, Government Commissioners were attached to their staffs and transmitted their wishes to the Government. The civilian authorities were, however, given emergency powers in Transylvania and the Southern Slav areas, and the eyes of the Hungarian authorities were little less vigilant, and their hands little less heavy, than those of their Austrian counterparts.

There was little opportunity, even on the highest level, for protesting against the severities of this regime, still less for disagreeing with Government policy. The Parliament in Pest, and even the Croat Sabor, continued to meet, so that opposition to the official course could still be expressed in these two assemblages by those entitled to voice it (it is true that the franchise practically confined the exercise of this licence to the Hungarian Independence politicians); but in Cis-Leithania Stürgkh evaded any embarrassing criticism by the simple device of leaving the Reichsrat unconvoked and governing through Paragraph 14. The premises of the Reichsrat were used as a hospital for officers. It was this denial of any less drastic means of expressing his opposition to the war and its attendant tyrannies that eventually decided Viktor Adler's son, Friedrich, a pure-minded but somewhat unbalanced fanatic who disagreed with his party's policy, to resort to his own desperate remedy: on 21 October 1916, he emptied a revolver into Stürgkh, then surrendered himself to his captors. He had not kept a bullet for himself because he proposed to utilize his trial to air his views.

In the main, however, the regime, while draconian, was effective, and so much severity was not even necessary. Most of the enthusiasm for the war had evaporated, and there was grumbling enough, especially in the urban centres, but the workers' leaders in both halves of the Monarchy held to the attitude that victory for the Central Powers was preferable to defeat at the hands of Russia, and had instructed their followers accordingly. No strikes had been called on either side of the Leitha. The entries of Italy and Roumania into the war had produced some indiscreetly manifested disaffection among the Monarchy's Italian and Roumanian subjects, but not on a dangerous scale. Italy's entry had had the opposite effect on the Monarchy's Croats, for whom, as for the Slovenes, it made the war a truly national one.

Since the Polish question had already assumed the international aspect described below, the only important internal 'national' movement of these years was one that regarded as its purpose not to weaken the Monarchy, but to strengthen it. In the spring of 1915 the *Nationalverband* and circles connected or sympathizing with it decided to press for the realization of changes substantially identical with those of the 'Whitsun Programme', except that Galicia was not to be represented in the Reichsrat at all. These changes, it was said, would place Cis-Leithania firmly in the hands of its Germans; in Hungary the Magyars were already dominant, and the danger would thus be banished of a Slav-dominated Monarchy. These proposals, or a version of them, must have been early made known to the Wilhelmstrasse, which showed knowledge of them at an early stage of the conversations with Austria on the Polish question. Inside the Monarchy the *Nationalverband* at first kept them in reserve, thinking that the time for introducing them would be when the victorious end of the war should have arrived. Meanwhile, the Reichsrat should be left unconvoked. Time passed, however, without bringing the consummation: it seemed impossible to leave the Reichsrat unconvoked indefinitely. In March 1916, accordingly, the *Nationalverband* sent a memorandum to Stürgkh asking that Francis Joseph should take advantage of the fact that he had never taken the oath to respect the December Laws, and enact the programme by *octroi*. Stürgkh, for one reason or another, did not hurry to fulfil the demands, and in the autumn of 1916 they were still accumulating dust in his pigeonholes, and the doors of the Reichsrat were still closed, except to patients and nurses. But a change was to follow shortly. Up to that date the Central Powers had confidently expected to win the war, and the Austrians' chief political preoccupation (apart from the bargaining with Italy and Roumania) had been to see that the victory did not bring with it any dangerous shifting of the Central European balance of power in favour of Germany. Any acquisitions by Germany should be balanced by equivalent gains for themselves. But where were these to be found? Tisza was successfully opposing any large-scale acquisitions of Southern Slavs; Roumania was, until August 1916, still neutral; and nobody wanted more Italians. There remained Poland, and Tisza, again, objected that the Monarchy must not be enlarged in such a way as to destroy its Dualist structure, or

tilt the balance of it against Hungary; this was one of the reasons why
the *Polenklub's* programme had not been taken up.

The other reason was objections from Germany. In August 1914,
and again in 1915, Bethmann Hollweg gave a somewhat vague consent to Austrian suggestions that Congress Poland, when liberated,
should be united with West Galicia in a kingdom attached to the
Monarchy. Then, however, the Germans, who had been reading the
Nationalverband's proposals, or a version of them, had second thoughts
and began demanding guarantees, in the form of long-term treaties,
economic, political and later, military, that 'the supremacy in Cis-
Leithania should remain with the Germans, and in Hungary with the
Magyars'. In April 1916 Bethmann Hollweg said that he could not
accept any 'Austro-Polish' solution at all. Argumentation between
him and Burián, who had succeeded Berchtold on 1 January 1915,
went on for many months until, under pressure from the military, who
hoped (incidentally, vainly) to recruit a million Poles from Congress
Poland for their armies, the two Emperors, on 5 November 1916,
issued a joint proclamation promising to construct ex-Russian Poland
as an independent State linked militarily with the Central Powers. The
proclamation was followed by the appointment of a Council of State
the powers of which were, however, only advisory: the administration
remained in the hands of the occupying Powers, each of which was in
charge of a 'zone', with H.Q.s in Warsaw and Lublin respectively.

The seeds of the Monarchy's subsequent disintegration were, indeed,
sown during these years, but they had not yet sprouted inside its frontiers. But outside them bargains had been struck. The Treaty of
London, which embodied Italy's terms for entering (and remaining in)
the war, promised her, of Austrian territory, the Tirol as far north as
the Brenner Pass, Gorizia-Gradisca, Trieste, Istria as far as the
Quarnero, then, after skipping the Hungarian and Croat Littorals,
Dalmatia as far south as Cape Planka. The treaty with Roumania
promised her, on the same conditions, Transylvania, the Bánát, the
Bukovina and a wide strip of the Hungarian plain. On 16 August
1916, after dealings rendered exceedingly difficult by the opposition
of Italy, Britain, France and Russia (Italy followed suit later) promised Serbia Bosnia-Herzegovina and an outlet to the sea (i.e. South
Dalmatia) and also considerable tracts of South Hungary, conditionally on her ceding a zone of Macedonia to Bulgaria. None of the
Notes mentioned Croatia, but Grey, who had seen the Croat émigré
leader, Supilo, shortly before, had promised Serbia to facilitate her
union with Croatia 'if the latter so desired', and on 1 September he
told Supilo that if Serbia agreed to meet Bulgaria's wishes over Macedonia, she was to get Bosnia, Herzegovina and southern Dalmatia,

while Slavonia and Croatia were to be allowed to determine their own
fate.[2] Since Pašić refused the concessions to Bulgaria, none of the
offers to Serbia were quite firm, while Grey's assurances to Supilo
were treated by his successors as not binding. Their combined effect
was, however, to create a strong presumption that if the Monarchy
lost the war, it would lose its Serbo-Croat areas, as well as the Italian,
Roumanian, and, presumably, the Polish.

The 'principle of nationality' played its part in all these transactions,
inasmuch as the demands made on the one side were represented as
justified, or even necessitated, by that principle (equated, not always
accurately, with that of national self-determination) while the other
side consented more readily when such a justification could be found.
No one, however, had yet reached the stage of holding the assimilation of political to ethnic frontiers to be an over-riding postulate of
international morality, and in 1914 and 1915 Britain and France, and
even Italy, still believed that the Monarchy had a vital role to play as
a factor in the European Balance of Power and a barrier against both
German and Russian expansion. This was a main reason for the slow
start made by the campaign for the creation of an independent
'Czecho-Slovak' State within the frontiers which its advocates asked
for it; for while the Monarchy could conceivably have survived, after
a fashion, without its Polish, Italian, Roumanian and even its Serbo-
Croat areas, it was difficult to see how it could possibly exist when to
these losses were added that of the Bohemian Lands and North
Hungary.

The start had in fact been slow. In the first months of the war the
Russians had played with the idea of using Czech disaffection as a
lever to break up the Monarchy, but they had soon got tired of their
Czech protégés. The Czechs' campaign in the West began later: of
its two *spiritus rectores* Masaryk went abroad only in December
1914 and Beneš joined him later still, and it was only in 1916, after
the latter's arrival, that a 'Czecho-Slovak Committee Abroad', later
renamed 'National Council', came into being in Paris. In February
1916, however, it scored a success of the first importance. Masaryk
obtained an interview with M. Briand, then Minister President and
Foreign Minister of France, to whom he represented that 'the division of Austria into her historical and natural elements', that is the
realization of the Czecho-Slovak programme, was 'a condition of the
reconstruction of Europe and of the real enfeeblement of Germany,
that is, of French security'; and Briand, according to him, 'promised
to carry out' his programme.[3]

Briand's promise was personal to himself, but the importance of
his acceptance of the Czech argument can hardly be exaggerated.
Long-term developments apart – and France's subsequent Central

European policy was really founded on this strategic thesis – the fateful inclusion by the Allies, a year later, of 'the liberation of the Czecho-Slovaks' among their war aims derived directly from it. And the strategic as well as the ideological case for replacing the Monarchy by a chain of national States was by now, partly as an effect of the publication of Friedrich Naumann's *Mitteleuropa*, finding growing support in both Britain and France. It was put with learning and passion in the *New Europe*, a periodical issued in London by a small but influential group of unofficial experts, and found its adherents in the Foreign Office, two members of which, commissioned in the summer of 1916 by Mr Asquith to suggest a basis for a peace settlement, came down in favour of it.[4] The memorandum was never officially adopted as British policy, but the ideas behind it came, as will be seen, to dominate that policy.

Friedrich Adler's protest had big long-term effects in stimulating anti-war feeling in Cis-Leithania, but it had no immediate political consequence except that Francis Joseph had to find a new Minister President; reluctant to work with a man unknown to him, he fell back on Koerber. But it was followed by two other events, each of which profoundly affected the future of the Monarchy. The re-election, on 8 November, of Wilson to the Presidency of the United States both made the eventual entry of the States into the war, on the side of Austria's enemies, a near-certainty, and also raised the hopes of those who deduced (mistakenly) from his speeches that he would favour the break-up of the Monarchy.

Then, on 21 November, Francis Joseph passed peacefully away in the eighty-seventh year of his life and the sixty-eighth of his reign. Even the most convinced advocates of change among his subjects had, by some tacit consent, largely held their hands while he lived, and his death released a whole multitude of pent-up forces, national and social, sufficient to test to the utmost the statecraft of his successor, Charles.

Charles was only 29 years of age, only recently brought by his uncle's morganatic marriage to within measurable distance of the throne, still more recently, by the crime of Sarajevo, to that of Heir Presumptive, and even thereafter he had been employed by his great-uncle almost exclusively on military assignments. The peoples who now became his subjects knew him as an amiable and obviously good-hearted young man, married to a sensationally beautiful wife. They knew nothing of his political ideas, which, however, were interesting and original. He saw that new social and political forces had been growing up in the Monarchy, and that they had demands which could not be eliminated by repression, but ought, where justifiable, to be satisfied through constitutional channels. He also saw that the answer given to the national problem in 1867 was no longer appropriate – still less that of 1849. He believed the solution of this problem to lie in a true federal system, broad enough 'to give all the peoples a chance'. This would, of course, have involved breaking the supremacy of the Magyars in Hungary, but unlike most Austrians, Charles rejected also the domination of Cis-Leithania by the Germans. Alone of his dynasty he has been credited with the (not, indeed, altogether accurate) remark that the majority of his subjects were Slavs.

He may have been led to this heresy by the efforts of the *Nationalverband* to draw Austria into a relationship with the Reich in which the latter would obviously have been the senior partner, and dynastic pride probably played a part in it, for he had his full share of that pride and was very quick to resent any suspicion of being treated as a second fiddle. To him, an over-powerful Germany was a real danger; it was probably this feeling that lay behind his flirtations with the Entente, for he could not rid himself of the feeling that in this respect their interests and Austria's were identical.

The unhappy paradox of his reign was that the compulsive force of circumstances prevented him from realizing almost any of his wishes; indeed, he frequently found himself driven, or over-persuaded, into taking a course the direct opposite of that which he would have preferred. An ironic destiny also forced him, although he was strongly desirous of peace, both out of general humanitarian feelings and because he saw in it the best hope of preserving his Monarchy intact, to spend his entire reign in a struggle which he detested, at the side of partners whom he disliked. Pity for this his destiny must indeed be tempered by recognition of the extreme, and blind, obstinacy with which he refused to pay the price of escape from it.

His opening proclamation duly contained an assurance, included on his personal insistence, and undoubtedly sincere, of his intention to do all in his power to restore to his peoples the blessings of peace; but this was followed by the no less operative qualification 'as soon as the honour of our arms, the vital conditions of My States and of their loyal allies, and the arrogance of our enemies, allow it'. The Monarchy would fight on until a peace was achieved which assured its integrity and 'the firm foundations of its undisturbed development'. Pending this, Charles would 'carry on and complete' his predecessor's work. His next moves did not belie these assurances. In the first weeks of his reign he carried through a great changing of the guard in key positions. To take first those connected most closely with the Monarchy's international position, including its war effort; one of Charles's first acts was to assume for himself the position then held by his cousin, the Archduke Frederick, of Supreme Commander of all the Monarchy's armed forces, then transferring the General Headquarters of the Austrian armies from Teschen to Baden bei Wien. On 21 December Burián was replaced at the Ballhausplatz by Count Ottokar von Czernin, the Monarchy's previous Minister in Bucharest. On 1 March 1917 Conrad was replaced as Chief of the General Staff by General Arz von Straussenberg,[5] and many more changes were made in the personnel of the General Staff and the top level commands in the army and navy.

A search for peace at any price played no part in any of these moves. The main purpose of the first-named was to avoid an awkward question of precedence between Charles and the German Emperor. Considerations of personality contributed to the demotion of Conrad, but the chief reason was that Charles thought Arz the better general, and capable of carrying on the war more efficiently. The consideration which prompted him to appoint Czernin (in so far as Czernin did not impose himself) was, we are told, besides his 'liveliness of mind and self-confidence' the fact that, of all possible candidates, he appeared the most conscious of the need for an Austrian peace initiative.[6] Czernin was, in fact, most firmly convinced that its economic plight alone would make it possible for the Monarchy to survive another year of war. But he also held, no less apodictically, that the Monarchy's only hope of obtaining satisfactory peace terms lay in complete solidarity with Germany, whose military strength alone would enforce moderation on the enemy. His appointment was thus in no sense an anti-German move: it was, in fact, welcomed by the Germans, whose dislike of Burián had been one reason why he was sacrificed.

The purpose behind the changes was thus really to bring about peace, but a peace in the negotiation of which Austria would be leading from strength. They neither implied nor resulted in any relaxation of the war effort. During the next months there was a certain lull on the Austrian fronts, but the armies of the Monarchy played their full part when it was required, and Arz used the lull to retrain and re-equip them, while a still larger proportion of the national production was directed towards supplying their needs.

As to peace, neither group of belligerents was at that stage prepared to offer it on terms acceptable to the other, and before the Central Powers could either themselves make an offer, or consider one from the other side, they had first to agree between themselves. A peace balloon launched by Burián in the previous November had already foundered on the Germans' refusal to offer specific terms (the terms which Burián had suggested would, indeed, in any case have been unacceptable to them). Then, when Wilson had, on 18 December, invited the belligerents to state their peace terms, the Allies' reply had, on its side, listed conditions which they could not have expected either Germany or Austria to accept except after total defeat. As regards Austria, the list, besides taking into account the contractual obligations towards Italy and Roumania, also included among the peoples to be 'liberated from foreign domination' the 'Slavs' and the 'Czecho-Slovaks', words which were taken in both Vienna and Berlin as meaning that the Allies were pledged, not only to the mutilation, but to the dismemberment of the Monarchy.

Confirmed by this in his conviction of the vital necessity for the Monarchy of preserving complete solidarity with Germany, Czernin rejected in January an offer by Wilson to mediate peace between Austria and the Central Powers, and the same fate attended a secret offer to mediate brought to Charles in January 1917, by his brother-in-law, Prince Sixtus of Parma. The attempt would in any case have been doomed to failure, for the list of Austria's peace terms which the two brothers-in-law concocted was inconceivably unrealistic – it treated Italy, not to mention Roumania, completely as *quantités négligeables* – but the Austrians also stipulated that the peace must be a general one. Unfortunately for himself, Charles also promised that he would 'support with all means and by the use of all his personal influence on his allies the just claims of France respecting Alsace-Lorraine', and this phrase was, as we shall see, afterwards resurrected with disastrous effect.

The prospect of peace dwindled further when the Austrians reluctantly endorsed Germany's decision to begin unrestricted submarine warfare. The consequent declaration of war on Germany by the United States clearly lengthened the long-term odds against the Central Powers, unless the new tactics brought speedy results in their favour. The Germans were confident' that they could do so, and although the Austrians, less hopeful, pleaded quite desperately for peace, saying that Austria 'must make an end, at any cost, by the late summer or autumn', the Germans, confident in their strength, saw no need for any concessions – none, at any rate, by themselves (nor can we in fairness deny the justice of their comment that the Austrians, while representing peace to be a necessity for themselves, always asked that Germany should pay the price). Since the Allies were equally confident, the months passed without any new peace offer from either side, nor did either return any constructive reply to the Vatican's peace initiative of August.

Meanwhile the Austrians had drawn up their own peace aims. These were still based on the presumption of victory, and thus envisaged no territorial concessions, but the Austrians still did not want large territorial aggrandizement in the south. The possible prizes thus

still lay in Poland and, after her defeat, in Roumania. At the Kreuz-
nach Conference of May it was agreed that Roumania should, subject to safeguards for Germany's economic interests, fall within the
Austrian sphere of interest. On 8 June the two Emperors agreed that
the organization of Poland's military forces should be entirely in the
hands of Germany. The Poles proved so refractory that on 1 August
Bethmann Hollweg's successor, Michaelis, threatened to revoke the
proclamation of November 1916, and revert to a straightforward
military regime. A fortnight later he suggested that Germany should
annex such areas as she wanted for herself and let the rest go where
they would — if they liked, back to Russia. The prospect of a Russian-
dominated Poland so alarmed Czernin that he threatened to denounce
the alliance, but fortunately for that instrument, the Germans were
coming round to the view that Roumania offered fatter pickings.
They now offered, if Austria agreed to the 'integration programme'
which they had pressed on Burián, and to other demands, which included the direct annexation by Germany of a large strip along the
Western frontier of Congress Poland, to accept the 'Austro-Polish'
solution for the remainder; and further, to the establishment of a
Polish Council of Regency and Ministry. These were really called
into being; the negotiations on the rest of the 'New Deals' were still
going on months later, without bringing any result except frayed
tempers on both sides.

Neither ally, in the event, secured any advantage from Roumania,
which outlived the end of the war. Nor, for that matter, did Austria
make any annexations in the Balkans.

Charles's hopes of introducing domestic reforms were speedily forestalled, as regards Hungary, by Tisza, who threatened to cut off supplies unless Charles submitted himself to immediate coronation.
After the ceremony had taken place — which it did on 30 December
1916 — Charles's coronation oath made it impossible for him to realize his special desire of extending the suffrage, for although he
could constitutionally have appointed a new Minister President and
had a new Parliament elected, the attempt would clearly have been
extremely dangerous, and its success uncertain. In May he did compel Tisza to resign, but did not dare hold elections, so that the Parliament remained the old one, dominated by Tisza's Party of Work. The
man whom Charles selected for his new Minister President, Count
Mór (Maurice) Esterházy, formed a Cabinet drawn chiefly from the
Coalition parties, with a newcomer, Vilmos Vázsonyi (incidentally a
professing Jew), who had good connections with the Left, and agreed
with the Social Democrats on an electoral reform bill, but Esterházy
resigned in August, daunted by the impossibility of realizing his pro-

gramme against Tisza's opposition. Charles fell back on the old utility man, Wekerle, who, after innumerable efforts, and after having
extracted from Charles sundry sops to the Independence parties,
which included a promise to introduce, after the war, concessions
demanded by them in respect of the Common Army, did in July
1918 get Parliament to vote a franchise reform, less extensive than
Vázsonyi's, but still more liberal than that of Lukács.

All this while, however, he was governing without a parliamentary
majority, for although he tried to form his own party, Tisza on the
one hand, and Károlyi on the other, refused to join it. Károlyi's star
was now in the ascendant. In July 1916 he had constituted his followers
as a new 'United Party of Independence and '48' with a programme
of the replacement of the Compromise by a Personal Union with independent Hungarian army, National Bank, etc., democratic reforms,
concessions to the Nationalities, and an early peace without annexations, to be achieved, if necessary, at the price of denouncing the
alliance with Germany. It was his thesis that realization of this programme, besides being desirable in itself, would at a stroke resolve
all Hungary's international difficulties, for her neighbours would
drop their designs on her when they saw their kinsfolk well treated,
and the Entente would have no reason to deal harshly with her. He
soon acquired a considerable following, the backbone of which was,
indeed, still composed of Magyar nationalists, but he was in touch,
although not yet in full agreement, with the Social Democrats. His
contacts with the Nationalities seem not to have begun before
October 1918.

It proved in the end equally impossible to introduce any material
political changes in Cis-Leithania, although there much shifting of
pieces took place before the final stalemate was reached.

Relations between Charles and Koerber were difficult from the
outset, partly owing to differences of temperament, partly to disagreements over policy, particularly in respect of the *Nationalverband's*
demands. Koerber was for carrying on, if necessary with the help of
Paragraph 14. Charles had set his mind against that device, and was
in a hurry to see the Reichsrat convoked, so he let Hohenlohe and
Czernin talk him into accepting the *Verband's* programme and post-
poning his oath to the constitution (which he meant, and had even
promised, to take) until the *octrois* had been issued. On 11 December,
he summoned Koerber to resign, and a tangled fortnight of intrigues
(which saw the appointment of Czernin to the Ballhausplatz) ended
with the Minister Presidency going to Count Heinrich von Clam-
Martinic, another member of the Czernin-Hohenlohe clique, who, in
spite of his family traditions and in contrast to his own early career,
which had been federalist, was now prepared to accept the *Verband's*

programme. The new Government, which contained, besides the obligatory Pole, two German nationalists, the rest being permanent officials, was sworn in on 20 December.

There were some delays while the immediate work on the new settlement with Hungary was got out of the way.[7] Meanwhile, the work on the proposed constitutional changes went on. It was, however, clear that they would not go through easily. The Poles were mistrustful, and an opposition to them was developing among the Czechs. In November 1916 the political leaders of that people had abandoned their policy of 'passivity' and had founded two organizations, a parliamentary 'Czech Union' (*Český Svaz*) which had been joined by almost all their political parties, including the Socialists, and a 'Czech National Committee' (*Národny Vibor*) in Prague. At that stage the Czechs saw the biggest danger to themselves in the *Nationalverband* and its allies, and their best hope in a strong Austria so constructed as to defend them against German pressure. Their first published programme expressed an almost servile devotion to the 'ancient and glorious dynasty' and to the Monarchy's 'great historical mission', and when the Allies' programme of 'liberation of the Czecho-Slovaks' was published, they accepted, not entirely unreluctantly, a request from Czernin to repudiate it. They made it clear, however, that they would oppose strenuously the proposed reorganization. The Southern Slavs' deputies, who similarly combined in a club, took the same attitude.

The Government ignored these representations, and the drafts of an octroied settlement had been finalized when, in March, the Russian revolution broke out. This event, which was followed closely by America's declaration of war on Germany, hardened the attitude of the Poles, who now no longer feared Russia, and now saw in the Central Powers the chief obstacles to the realization of their hopes, for which they looked to the West, whence declarations of sympathy reached them. The Czechs and Slovenes, too, were heartened, and joined in the growing insistence on convocation of the Reichsrat, which the Austrian Social Democrats also made a condition of their participation in the proposed Stockholm Conference. In April Charles, who had been growing increasingly uneasy about the octrois, retracted his consent to them. The *Nationalverband* was induced to accept the inevitable, and on 1 May the opening of the Reichsrat, unreformed, was announced for the 30th of that month.

In preparation for it, the Poles, who had decided that the situation provided no basis for discussions which offered them no more than Clam's proposals, adopted a resolution to the effect that their objective was 'an independent and united Poland with access to the sea': how this should be brought into being would be a matter for inter-

national discussion. The Czechs, who had reknit the broken threads
of their connections with the émigrés in the West, had adopted
a new and more radical policy which was largely dictated to them
· by the émigrés. Their earlier programme had been very moderate : it
had hardly gone beyond realization of the 'Böhmisches Staatsrecht'.
Now, while still accepting the sovereignty of the dynasty, they called
for the transformation of the Monarchy into a 'federation of free and
equal States', one of which, the 'Czecho-Slovak', should both honour
the 'historic rights' of the Czechs (i.e. provide for the restoration of
a State which should include Bohemia, Moravia and Silesia within
their historic frontiers) and also realize the unification in one democratic State of all branches of the Czecho-Slovak people, including
'the Slovak branch living in a unit contiguous to the Czech mother-
land'. The programme of the Southern Slav Club called for 'the unification of all districts of the Monarchy inhabited by Slovenes, Croats
and Serbs in an autonomous State under Habsburg sovereignty'. The
Ruthenes' resolution promised not to give up the struggle until the
great Ukrainian nation was in enjoyment of its full rights on its entire
national territory 'which was to include the Ukrainian areas of Galicia,
as well as Cholm, Podlachia and Volhynia'.

When the Reichsrat met, these declarations were read out. The
effect of all this was to prolong the deadlock, for if the Germans had
renounced their own programme, they were not going to accept those
of the Czechs and Slovenes. Clam resigned, and after a long search
Charles appointed to succeed him – at first provisionally, then definitively – his ex-Minister of Agriculture, Dr Ernst von Seidler, who,
after the Slavs, Social Democrats, and also the Christian Socials had
refused to enter a Coalition Government, perforce fell back on a
Cabinet composed of the usual civil servants, with a Pole, a Czech,
a Slovene and a Ruthene, all of these non-parliamentarians. Since the
Germans and the Poles consented to vote the budgets and war credits,
he was able to carry on on this essentially non-parliamentary basis
for another year.

Meanwhile, Charles had announced an amnesty for all offenders,
except those who had fled abroad, who had been sentenced or arrested
for high treason and similar political offences. Other concessions included the restoration of trial by jury and the abolition of military
jurisdiction over civilians. The effects of this magnanimous gesture
were, unhappily, not what it deserved. The Czechs, who were the
chief beneficiaries of it,[8] simply swallowed the present and asked for
a second helping. Kramář, escorted to his home in triumph, became
again the heart and soul of their national movement. A Young Czech
Congress in October declared that the only programme for the Czechs
could be complete international (*staatsrechtlich*) independence for

the Czecho-Slovak people. Meanwhile, the German nationalists were deeply embittered; this was the first time that a serious rift had opened between them and their Monarch. Graver still was the resentment of the army officers who saw the spirit of their men corrupted by this condonation of treachery.

For the rest, the summer and autumn of 1917 and even the opening months of 1918 presented for the Monarchy a curious mixture of bright and dark colours. The military situation of the Central Powers was still the reverse of unfavourable. Time must still elapse before the United States could put an army into the field. The unrestricted submarine warfare, although proving less effective than the Germans had prophesied, was yet taking a heavy toll of Allied shipping. The British offensive in Flanders was a costly failure; France was nearing exhaustion, and in October, German and Austrian armies inflicted a crushing defeat on the Italians at Caporetto. Above all, Russia's war effort, after a brief revival in July, collapsed. On 8 December the Bolsheviks, who had seized power a month before, sued for an armistice, which was signed a week later; Roumania had already signed an armistice on the 10th. The army leaders, and also the *Nationalverband*, were confident that victory would soon be theirs; they only had to hold out a little longer.

On the other hand, the harvest had been bad again. The farmers were hoarding, and little was reaching the towns, where prices were soaring, and inflation become rampant. It was a time of great hardship for the workers and middle classes. Social unrest, fed by sanguine reports of conditions in Russia spread by returning ex-prisoners of war, and demands for peace, grew apace. In these circumstances the Austrian Social Democrat Party became a potent force. In October 1917, its Congress adopted a resolution based on that of the Independent Socialists of Germany, calling for early peace without annexations or reparations. One wing of the party, led by Otto Bauer, produced a programme which recognized the right to self-determination of the non-Germans of Austria, while claiming the same right for its Germans. In January 1918 a strike of almost revolutionary dimensions broke out in Wiener Neustadt, whence it spread to other centres. The Government had to promise not to let the peace negotiations then proceeding at Brest-Litovsk break down on territorial issues. The January strikes were followed by others elsewhere, and even, on 1 February, by a mutiny of the fleet at Cattaro. This was put down by force, but hardly a week passed thereafter without a strike by the workers in one enterprise or another (including the railways) or mutinous outbreak in some one of the armed units behind the lines. Among the latter the ex-prisoners of war returning from Russia proved a particularly turbulent element.

At this stage the unrest was chiefly the expression of revolt against material hardship, and not even always accompanied by political demands. But these were entering into it, and national demands, too, were increasingly finding expression. Among the Czech politicians, the old 'opportunist' leaders had been largely replaced by radicals. On 6 January Czech members of the Reichsrat, and of the *Landtage* of Bohemia, Moravia and Silesia, had adopted another resolution (known from its date as the 'Epiphany Resolution') which now demanded independence in a fully sovereign independent State, and did not mention the dynasty.

Important movements had been going on among the Yugoslavs. On 2 July 1917, the Serb Government and the 'Yugoslav Committee', who had long been at variance, had signed the 'Pact of Corfu', providing for the union of 'the Serbs, Croats and Slovenes, also known as the Southern Slavs, or Yugoslavs' in a single State under the Karageorgević dynasty. The news of this agreement greatly reinforced the Yugoslav idea inside the Monarchy. A new Ban in Croatia, while maintaining a correct attitude on the surface, allowed a free rein to the Yugoslav movement, to which the Starčević Party and Radić went over. At a Conference in March 1918 nearly all the participants wanted a Yugoslav 'State', although they were not agreed whether this should be inside or outside the Monarchy, or unitary or federal. The old Slovene People's Party disappeared altogether, to be replaced by a new, radically nationalist 'All-Slovene People's Party', led by Korošec, which demanded 'liberation from the Germans and the constitution of an independent Yugoslav State within the Monarchy, comprising all its Yugoslav peoples'. Most of the smaller Slovene parties made similar shifts.

The Poles had remained relatively quiet, for the news of the mutilations which Germany planned to inflict on the future Poland, and the harshness of her rule in the Warsaw zone, had strengthened their sympathies for Austria. In January 1918 the Austrian Poles had persuaded the Regents to offer the throne of Poland to Charles. The formal invitation was to go out on 17 February.

Then, however, came an abrupt change for the worse. The Brest-Litovsk negotiations with Russia had made only slow progress and the treaty was not concluded until 3 March. But while the negotiations dragged on, the Central Powers had, on 9 February, signed a separate peace with Ukrainian delegates present at the Conference, under which the Ukrainians promised to deliver at least a million tons of bread-grain, while Czernin agreed to recognize as Ukrainian the district of Cholm, which was claimed also by the Poles, and to constitute East Galicia, with the Bukovina, as a Crownland. This proved a most unfortunate bargain. When it leaked out, a first-class crisis

ensued among the Poles. The Ministry resigned and in the Reichsrat the *Polenklub* announced that they would impeach Czernin
and oppose the Austrian Government by all means in their power.
The number of Poles genuinely attached to the Monarchy dwindled
to a handful. Virtually all the Poles regarded even autonomy as insufficient, if it did not bring with it the unification of the entire Polish
people; and after France and Britain had followed the United States
in declaring themselves in favour of an independent and united
Poland,[9] most of them were now pinning their hopes on an Allied
victory.

Meanwhile, the Ukrainian Government which had signed the
peace had been overthrown almost immediately by the Bolsheviks.
The Germans and Austrians sent occupation forces into the Ukraine.
But their bayonets were unable to unprise the peasants' stores. Only a
trickle reached Berlin and Vienna.

The boldness of the extremist national leaders in the Monarchy
was largely due to their expectations of help from the Bolsheviks on
the one hand, and President Wilson on the other. In fact, a year
passed before these beliefs came to possess any real justification. The
Bolsheviks concentrated on promoting social, rather than national
revolution, and the Western Allies had still not given up hope of de-
taching the Monarchy from Germany. The half-promise of January
1917 to the Czecho-Slovaks was watered down or explained away,
and when Mr Balfour visited Washington a little later, he told the
Americans that Britain was not bound by treaty to detach the Croat
and adjacent areas from the Monarchy. Wilson's attitude, except for
his promise to the Poles, was not very different, and when he asked
Congress to declare war on the Monarchy on 4 December 1917, he
said that the States 'did not wish in any way to impair or rearrange
the Austro-Hungarian Empire'. Lloyd George, on 5 January 1918,
while including in his speech phrases that made it compatible with
the Treaties of London and Bucharest, and another recognition of
Polish claims, said that 'the break-up of Austria-Hungary is no part
of our war aims', and Wilson again endorsed this in the Tenth of his
Fourteen Points.[10] During these months, in fact, several secret talks,
in some of which Wilson took a keen personal interest, went on with
the object of enticing Austria into a separate peace, and had they
succeeded, it might have emerged with only peripheral losses, which
might not even have been as large as those promised under the Allies'
treaties, by which Wilson refused to be bound. But they all broke
down on the refusal of Charles and Czernin to break with Germany
(or to cede any Austrian territory). The only gains made by any of
the nationalities, other than the Poles, were that Masaryk got permission for the establishment in Russia of a Czecho-Slovak army,

politically under the control of the Czecho-Slovak National Council, and that later, France, and then Italy, agreed to the formation within their borders of Czecho-Slovak military units.

The change came in March 1918, when the German offensive opened in the West and a counterpart to it threatened on the Italian front. Mr Wickham Steed, now in charge of the section dealing with the Monarchy in the recently-established British Ministry of Propaganda, submitted a memorandum to the Foreign Office in which he argued that efforts to detach the Monarchy from Germany had failed; it was necessary to try the alternative policy of 'supporting and encouraging all anti-German and pro-Ally tendencies inside the Monarchy'. He did not get from the Foreign Office the promise that he asked, that the Allies should include Polish, Czecho-Slovak, Yugoslav and Roumanian independence among their declared war aims, but Mr Balfour did authorize him to issue leaflets containing assurances of sympathy to soldiers of those nationalities, and promises that if they came over, they would be treated 'not as prisoners of war, but as friends', and allowed to fight on the side of the Entente. The propaganda to this effect began to go out. Steed and his coadjutor, R. W. Seton-Watson, also brought about exchanges of friendly notes between the Italians and the Yugoslav émigrés, and a 'Congress of Oppressed Nationalities' in Rome welcomed the exchange and proclaimed the right of each of the peoples concerned to full political and economic independence.

The Allied Governments had, meanwhile, been careful not to commit themselves too far. But at this juncture there occurred a singular *contretemps*. On 2 April Czernin, returned from Brest-Litovsk sporting a halo of popularity as bringer of peace and bread, was moved by an extraordinary illusion that he could undermine M. Clemenceau's position to make a foolish and provocative speech in which he said, *inter alia*, that France had made Austria overtures for a separate peace, but the conversations had broken down on France's intransigent attitude over Alsace-Lorraine. He was really alluding, although even so inaccurately, to another set of conversations, but after a heated public exchange of incivilities, Clemenceau published Charles's promise to his brother-in-law to 'support France's just claims in Alsace-Lorraine'. Charles issued an undignified and transparently untruthful *dementi* and tried to make Czernin take the blame. Czernin refused, and after a scene which can seldom have been paralleled between a sovereign and one of his subjects, resigned, and the enraged Germans, whose patience with the Austrians had long been wearing thin, especially since Brest-Litovsk, forced Charles to travel to Spa with Burián, whom he had persuaded to take Czernin's place, there to protest his complete loyalty to the alliance, and to sign, on 12 May,

a promise to implement the complete 'integration programme', political, military and economic.

The Spa 'Agreements' were taken in the West as well-nigh decisive
proof of the futility of attempting to detach the Monarchy as a whole
from Germany, of which, if this could not be done, she would remain
a mere satellite, with Germany dominating Continental Europe. The
logical conclusion, drawn swiftly by Britain and France, and after
more hesitation, by Wilson, was to intensify the Allies' support for
the 'oppressed nationalities', and in the next few weeks all the Western Allies pledged themselves more or less definitely to independence
for Poland. They also made declarations which, on any normal interpretation, committed them to support an independent Czecho-Slovak
State, and less explicitly and more tardily, owing to objections by
Italy and obstruction by the Serb Government (the final answer here
was not given until after the conclusion of hostilities) a Yugoslav one.
Roumania had invalidated the Treaty of Bucharest by concluding
peace with the Central Powers on 7 May, so that no definite promises
were made in respect of her claims, but it was generally assumed that
the Roumanians of the Monarchy would share in the 'liberation' of
the 'oppressed nationalities'.

Meanwhile, Burián was allowing the economic conversations with
Germany to go on, but the political and technical aspects of the proposed alliance had become side-tracked behind the barrier of the
Polish question, on which wrangling was still going on as late as
September 1918, although a succession of other events was rendering
them more meaningless almost every day. The German offensive in
the West was now in full swing, and on 15 June the Austrians, anxious
not to lag behind-hand and confident that their rested and re-equipped
army would win an easy and popular victory over the despised enemy, opened an offensive against Italy. It proved a disastrous failure
and had to be called off on 24 June, after having cost casualties which
drained dry the Monarchy's last reserves of manpower and stocks of
ammunition. All this encouraged the Czechs in Bohemia to transform
their 'National Committee' into a 'Czecho-Slovak National Committee' and to make another declaration demanding complete independence. In Hungary, too, both anti-German and anti-Austrian feeling
were stimulated by a widespread belief that the country's men and
resources were being sacrificed for causes that were none of hers. The
Austrian Social Democrats were now taking the line that nothing
mattered but that the war should end quickly, and rather welcomed
any symptoms of approaching disintegration in the Monarchy. Disaffection was growing also among the non-Socialist Germans, for a
different reason. More and more of them were reversing their priorities: instead of feeling that their function was to act as the Mon-

archy's servants in chief, and pre-eminence among his peoples their reward for doing so, they were claiming that that pre-eminence was their due, and the Monarch was there to safeguard it; and their faith in his ability, or even his willingness to carry out his duty, already shaken by his gestures of conciliation towards so many traitors, had been dealt further traumatic blows, first by the Sixtus revelations, then by a widespread, although erroneous, belief that the Empress had betrayed the plans of the offensive to the enemy.[11] They renewed with insistence their demands that the Monarchy should follow a 'German course', particularly in Bohemia, and their nervous agress-iveness presently brought about the fall of Seidler. When the Reichsrat reassembled in July, he tried to meet the pressure from them, and from the Reich, by tabling a Bill for the administrative division of Bohemia. The Czechs raged, but Seidler might yet have survived the storm had the *Polenklub* not announced its intention of refusing to vote a budget presented by 'an accomplice in the treachery of Brest-Litovsk'. Seidler resigned, flinging behind him an affirmation of faith in the 'German course', which doubtless relieved his feelings, but was grist to the mills of the other side.

His Minister of Education, Fhr. von Hussarek, a civil servant of Christian Social sympathies, whom Charles appointed to succeed him, scraped together, from a remarkable variety of sources, a major-ity to vote another 'provisional' budget before the Reichsrat adjourned for its summer recess, but this proved his only success. He and Charles worked out plans the essence of which was that the Poles were to be persuaded, by inducements which included the sacrifice to them of the Ruthenes, to accept the 'Austro-Polish solution', and the Southern Slavs placated somehow. It should then be possible to impose in Bohemia a solution which the Germans would accept, and the Czechs be unable to resist. But they made no progress with the Poles, and every proposed answer to the Yugoslav problem was op-posed either by the Hungarians, who would consent only to a 'sub-Dualist' solution, which should include Bosnia and Dalmatia in the proposed unit, but still leave it under the Hungarian Crown, by the *Nationalverband*, which refused to allow any concession whatever to the Slovenes, or by the Slovenes, who announced they would accept nothing short of full Trialism.

Meanwhile, general conditions continued to deteriorate. Conditions of living in the urban centres of Cis-Leithania were reaching the limit of human endurance. The peasants were only a little better off, and Hungary not very much. Disaffection was rife among the civilians, and in the army depots behind the lines, whence men slipped away and went into hiding: 'green cadres' composed of such fugitives de-fied the authorities. So many troops had to be kept in the hinterland to repress unrest there as gravely to weaken the combatant strength of the army. The forces at the Front were themselves short, not only of rations, but of ammunition and even uniforms and after the failure of the summer offensive, a rot set in here too. Desertions to the enemy multiplied. On top of all this, both the front and the hinterland were ravaged by influenza.

Charles and Burián again warned their allies that Austria could not face another winter of war, but it was not until 14 August, a week after the 'black day' which made clear that the offensive in France had failed, that the Germans even consented to discuss peace, and then they wanted to wait until their front was stabilized, so another month passed. On 14 September Burián, acting without them, sent a Note to the enemy proposing peace talks: it elicited unhelpful or offensive answers from its recipients, and a rebuke to Charles from the Kaiser.

Then, on 19 September, the Bulgarian front cracked and on the 26th Bulgaria sued for an armistice. Now the Germans themselves decided that the Central Powers should ask President Wilson to mediate an armistice on all fronts, and initiate peace talks on the basis of his Fourteen Points. The Note went off on the night of October 3/4.

Wilson deliberately delayed his answer, and while waiting for it the Austrians, besides making further attempts to contact the Allies, pursued their search for a formula which would satisfy Wilson, while leaving the Monarchy near-intact. On 1 October, when the Reichsrat met, Hussarek told the Poles that they might choose their own form of State, although he hoped that this would be realized in close connection with the Monarchy. Bosnia and Dalmatia might go to Hungary. But for the other peoples of Cis-Leithania he offered no more than as much free activity as would not preclude the same possibility for any other people. The speech fell completely flat. On the 6th a 'National Council' representative of all Southern Slav peoples and deputies of the Monarchy announced its intention of preparing the union of all those peoples in 'a national, free and independent State'. On the 9th the *Polenklub* called into being a 'National Committee' representative of all Polish Parties, and on the 15th announced that 'the independent, free, united Poland is beginning to conduct its own sovereign life'. On the 14th Beneš announced the constitution of a 'Czecho-Slovak Government' in Paris, under the Presidency of Masaryk.

In view of this the German Austrians began to draw together. On the 3rd the Social Democrat Party adopted a Resolution recognizing the right of the other peoples of Austria to self-determination and demanding the same right for its Germans. All its German-speaking areas, including the Sudetenlande, should join to form a German-Austrian State, which would regulate its own relations with the other nations of Austria and with the Reich. The *Nationalverband* agreed to take this as a 'basis for negotiation', and the Christian Socials followed suit after some hesitation, and subject to the reservation that this 'State' was to be a member of a 'federation of free national communities' into which Austria was to be transformed.

When it became clear that no one was going to accept Hussarek's offers, Charles jettisoned them, and opened new consultations in various quarters with the object of finding a formula which should meet Wilson's conditions, as known, without going beyond them, and without sacrificing the position of the Austro-Germans. The outcome was the appearance, on 16 October, of a Manifesto addressed by Charles himself to the peoples of Cis-Leithania. The Poles were to go their own way; the other peoples to form a federal State, in which each of them was to constitute its own 'State-community' (*staatliches Gemeinwesen*) on its own ethnic territory (*auf seinem Siedlungs-gebiet*). This fared no better than its predecessor. Wekerle had insisted that it should contain an assurance that the proposed changes 'in no way infringed the integrity of the Lands of the Hungarian Crown', and the Czechs and Slovenes used this as a pretext for rejecting it; (the Poles explained that they had already left the Monarchy). But at least for the Czechs there was another and overriding objection: the limitation of their 'State' to their 'ethnic territory' would have excluded German Bohemia from it (this, of course, was precisely the reason why the *Nationalverband*, the main authors of the formula, had chosen it).

In any case, the Czechs were by now taking their instructions from Paris, and the Southern Slavs from Zagreb, so that the chief move of the next days (apart from the formation in Lemberg, on the 19th, of a Ukrainian National Council) was that on the 21st the German-Austrian deputies of the Reichsrat met and resolved that the German-speaking districts of Cis-Leithania should form an 'independent national state', the constitution of which was to be determined by an elected Constituent Assembly. Pending the election, the deputies of the existing Reichsrat would act as a 'Provisional National Assembly', while immediate business was transacted by a 'Provisional Executive Committee', composed of representatives of the three big parties.

The 21st was the day on which Wilson's reply to the Central Powers' Note of the 3/4 was officially delivered (although it had been communicated to the Allies, and to the Press, two days earlier). It ran that the President could no longer be bound by the Tenth of his Fourteen Points: the Czecho-Slovaks and the Yugoslavs must be their own judges of what would satisfy them. Strangely enough, an Austrian Ministerial Conference on the 22nd believed that this was not an irrevocable death sentence, and Burián set himself to compose an argumentative answer to it, and continued the search for friendly hearts in Paris and London. These were now being conducted under the shadow of a grave military danger, newly emerged. As soon as the Bulgarian armistice came into effect (30 September), General Franchet d'Esperey, commanding the Allied forces in the Balkans, prepared to move the French and Serbian units of them[12] northward. The German and Austrian commanders tried to plug the gap with such forces as they could scrape together; but the German units were few, and many of the Austrian commanders refused to fight against the new enemy. After a little initial resistance had been overcome, the advance of the Allied armies was almost unopposed. By the latter half of the month they were approaching the frontiers of Hungary and Croatia.

These were almost undefended, since nearly all the combatant Hungarian and Croat units were in the Tirol. They now clamoured to be sent East to defend their own homes. Assurances designed to placate them only encouraged the demand, since they were interpreted as implying official agreement with it. When, on the 24th, the Allies opened an offensive on the Italian Front, many of the units refused to obey orders to go up the line. The infection spread, and soon the military hinterland simply disintegrated. Not only Hungarian and Croat units, but those of almost every nationality, were simply leaving their stations and making their ways home, as best they could.

Meanwhile, the political situation in Hungary itself had become critical.

The symptoms of disintegration had been slower to appear in Hungary, than in Austria. Up to the middle of the month, the non-Magyars, except the Croats, had not given tongue at all, and although on the 3rd, Károlyi had announced his intention of setting up a 'National Council' composed of representatives of his own party, the Social Democrats, and a recently-constituted midget party calling themselves the 'Bourgeois Radicals' 'to form the nucleus of a future assemblage' which should preside over the coming changes, he had taken no steps to give effect to his intentions. Things had warmed up only on the 16th, when Wekerle told Parliament of the manifesto, and said that it reduced the link between Hungary and the Monarch's other dominions to a Personal Union, and that the Government would introduce the necessary legislation. The Károlyists shouted: 'That is not enough! We want total independence.' On the 18th the Roumanian leader, Vaida-Voevode, read out a declaration demanding self-determination for the Roumanians of Hungary, and the right of Bucharest to speak for them, and on the 20th the Slovak, Juriga, followed with a similar declaration in the name of a newly-constituted Slovak National Committee. On the 22nd, when Wekerle introduced the promised legislation, Károlyi read out his party programme, which demanded for Hungary an independent army and economic system, although not yet total separation. But now Charles's ill-luck pursued him. On the 23rd he went down to Debrecen to open the new university there, and the military band welcomed him with the hated strains of the 'Gott erhalte'. There was another storm in Parliament, of which Wekerle took advantage to resign. Burián followed suit the next day. Charles now had to find both a new Foreign Minister and a new Hungarian Minister President; also a new Austrian Minister President, for he had decided to replace Hussarek, and had already decided on his successor, Professor Lammasch, a distinguished international lawyer, *bien vu* in the West.

Andrássy accepted the Foreign Ministry. His one act in his new capacity was to send a Note to Wilson, saying that Austria accepted all his conditions, and asking him to initiate negotiations for an armistice with her 'without awaiting the result of other negotiations' (i.e. independently of Germany). No one took the slightest notice of this.

On the 27th Lammasch succeeded in forming a so-called administration, but round it, the disintegration of Cis-Leithania was now going on apace. On the 28th the National Council in Prague proclaimed a Czecho-Slovak Republic, and took over the authority in the main centres of Bohemia, except where prevented by the resistance of the local Germans (the history of the Czechs' dealings with the Sudeten Germans falls outside the scope of this volume), and a little later, in Moravia. On the 29th the Sabor in Zagreb proclaimed 'Croatia, with Dalmatia and Fiume', an independent State, 'part of the national and sovereign State of the Serbs, Croats and Slovenes'. The *Landtag* of Laibach issued a similar declaration on the 31st, Sarajevo on 1 November. The Poles set up a 'Liquidation Committee, to wind up relations between the already existent Polish State and Vienna. On the 30th the German-Austrian deputies of the Reichsrat met again and declared themselves authorized to speak for the German-Austrian people in matters of foreign policy. A Council of State, to be elected immediately by the Reichsrat, was to take over the executive authority. On 31 October the Roumanians of the Bukovina declared for union of the Land, within its historic frontiers, with Roumania. On 1 November, the Ruthenes proclaimed their independence. Last of the peoples of Austria to be out of one war, they were the first to be in the next, for they promptly opened hostilities against the Poles on one flank, and the Roumanians on the other. The process of disintegration could not be arrested, and the Lammasch Government confined its activities to seeing that it went through with the minimum of bloodshed and dislocation. Since Charles ordered the old authorities to vacate their desks quietly, and the commanders of local garrisons to withdraw peacefully, the transfer of authority from the old hands to the new in fact went through quietly : such bloodshed as occurred was between rival grabbers for the spoils.

By the 24th Croatia was in practice lost to Hungary, and the leaders of some of the Nationalities were making further dispositions against future contingencies.[13] But it was still possible to think in terms of a central Hungarian Government, even one which still acknowledged the dynasty. Charles first promised the Minister Presidency to Count Hadik, but the next day Károlyi called his National Council into being and agreed with it a programme which called for complete independence for Hungary, both foreign-political and military, and also the return to Hungary of all its combatant forces, but did not repudiate the connection with the dynasty. The popular clamour for Károlyi was by now so tumultuous that on the 26th Charles called him to him, and when Károlyi said that, if appointed he could save for Charles his Hungarian throne – otherwise inevitably lost – Charles took him to Vienna as a second Minister President designate. But the next day he changed his mind again, and instead of formally appointing either Hadik or Károlyi sent the Archduke Joseph, then in Vienna,[14] down to Budapest to hold further consultations. These convinced the Archduke that the dynasty's only hope of retaining at any rate one Crown in fact lay in Károlyi and an administration which he had formed out of members of the National Council. This was at 6 p.m. on the 31st, almost the exact hour at which assassins broke into Tisza's house and murdered him.

Károlyi's new Minister of War, Col. Béla Lindner, at once telegraphed ordering all Hungarian units to return and not to resist the armies of the Entente, with which Hungary was not at war.[15]

The next day Károlyi himself found his position, as it then stood, untenable, and on his request, Charles unbound him and his ministers from their oath. They then took a new one, to the National Council, announcing themselves to be representatives of an independent State, unconnected with any of the Habsburgs' other dominions.

Meanwhile, the Monarchy's troops still in the line had resisted the attacks of the Allies bravely. But heavily out-numbered and out-gunned, they were driven back remorsely. On the 28th the army commanders reported that further resistance was useless. Emissaries were sent across the lines to sue for an armistice. The terms of the Allies, hurriedly drafted in Paris, were handed to the emissaries only late on

1 November. They obligated Austria to evacuate areas roughly the same as those promised to Italy under the Treaty of London, and further to allow the Allies to occupy 'strategic points' behind the lines. This last clause would have enabled Allied forces to attack Germany from the rear, and at first Charles refused to accept the terms, as dishonourable; he further insisted that the new Austrian Council of State must be consulted. But everyone agreed that the terms had to be accepted, and at 3 a.m. on the 3rd the order to cease hostilities went out. This was, indeed, anticipating the understanding with the enemy, for the armistice was signed only that afternoon, to take effect 24 hours later, and in the intervening 36 hours the Italians advanced further, capturing large quantities of stores and over 30,000 unresisting prisoners. Those who escaped this fate joined the rush for their homes. The fleet escaped this fate for a while, because on the 31st Charles had ordered its Commander in Chief, Admiral Horthy, to hand it over to representatives of the new Serb-Croat-Slovene State, in the hope, which proved, indeed, vain, of saving it from falling into Italian hands.

Hungary had already stopped resistance. General Franchet d'Esperey regarded the Padua armistice as not applying to the Eastern Front. His troops advanced into the south of the country, and Czech units moved into the north, under the pretext that they were Allies, and that Northern Hungary constituted a 'strategic point' under the armistice of Padua. On 9 November, Roumania redeclared war and prepared to invade Transylvania.

At home, once the Padua armistice had been signed, only one top-level question remained to be decided. Neither Austria nor Hungary had yet declared on its future form of State, but in both Vienna and Budapest mobs were clamouring for republics. After the German Emperor had abdicated on the 9th, Charles's advisers warned him that his own person was no longer safe. He refused to make a formal abdication, but consented to a compromise form of words, in which a proclamation signed by him was posted up in Vienna on the 10th. 'Filled', it ran, 'now as ever with unshakeable love for My peoples, I will no longer set My person as a barrier to their free development. I recognize in advance the decision which German-Austria will take on its future form of State. The people has now taken over the government through its representatives. I renounce any participation in the business of the State. At the same time, I relieve My Austrian Government of its office.'

The next day the Austrian Provisional Parliament met. The Christain Socials had given up their previous position as hopeless, and the assemblage now proclaimed unanimously the constitution of German-Austria as a 'democratic Republic and a component of the German

Republic', On the 15th, Charles, who had retired to his near-by estate
of Eckartsau, handed a declaration in similar terms to three emissaries from the Hungarian Parliament, which on the 16th in its turn
proclaimed Hungary a republic. The old Monarchy had ceased to
exist.

NOTES AND REFERENCES

Chapter One
The Turning-Point of 1790

1. The term 'Hereditary Lands' was long used to denote those Lands —
broadly, the Alpine bloc and its southern outliers — to which the
Habsburgs succeeded automatically, by contrast with the Bohemian
and Hungarian blocs, to which the succession was at first by election.
After 1626/7 the Bohemian Crown, too, became hereditary, and later,
the Hungarian also, but the old term continued to be widely used,
and is convenient. In these pages I also use, again for convenience's
sake, the word 'Land' to denote any of the Kingdoms, Duchies,
Counties and so on, the aggregate of which made up the Habsburgs'
dominions.

2. The Military Frontier was that strip of territory which ran behind
whatever at the time constituted the frontier between the Monarchy
and Turkey. It was administered from Vienna by the *Hofkriegsrat*,
or for certain purposes by the Camera. Its male inhabitants were organized militarily in regiments, etc., and did a term of service, first
with the colours, then with the reserves. They were not subject to any
other obligations. They could be called on to serve anywhere, and
some of them were regularly employed to guard the frontier against
smugglers, bandits and persons infected with the plague. Most of the
rank and file were Serbs or Croats, with a few Germans and Roumanians. The officers above the rank of Colonel were usually Germans.
An analogous institution, the Bánát of Temesvár, was in process of
liquidation in 1780.

3. The Littoral (Gorizia-Gradisca, Istria, Trieste) had no Estates, and
the Military Frontier, no institutions of self-government at all. In 1780
Estates were still in process of formation in Galicia.

4. Nominally three: the Hungarian, the Transylvanian, and the Unified
Bohemian-Austrian Court Chancellery, which was competent for the
Lands named in its title, and in 1780, also for Galicia. The correspondence with the Netherlands and the Milanese went through sections
of the *Haus- Hof- und Staatskanzlei*. The Hungarian and Transylvanian Chancelleries were distinct only in name; their personnel was
the same and they sat as one or the other according to the agenda.

5. The appellations both of the offices and their presidents varied. The
commonest, and generic, title of the office was *Gubernium*; that
of its President, *Landeshauptmann*. In these pages, for simplicity's
sake, I call the offices, *Gubernia*, and the heads of all of them, Governors.

6. Transylvania's Three Nations were the nobles of those areas of it organized on the County system, and the Free Communities of Saxons and Szekels. The Szekels were a people of uncertain ethnic origin, but certainly cousins, near or remote, of the Magyars. Their ancestors had been settled, probably in the twelfth century, in Eastern Transylvania to guard its passes against invaders from the East. They were governed for the Monarch by a 'Count' appointed by him. The ancestors of the 'Saxons', most of whom really came from Luxembourg or the Rhineland, had been brought to South and North-eastern Transylvania for the same purpose. In 1224 they had been granted a 'Privilege' which allowed them extensive self-government.

7. The theoretical justification for this privilege was that the military service for which the Hungarian nobles were still liable, if the *insurrectio* was called out, constituted their obligations towards the State, discharged in the form of taxation by the unfree population, which did not perform such service.

8. The labour service for his lord paid to him by his peasants as part of the rental of their holdings.

Chapter Two
Leopold II

1. This obligation did not apply to the Austrian Netherlands, nor to Prussian Westphalia or East Prussia.

Chapter Three
Francis II (1)

1. I. Beidtel, *Geschichte der oesterreichischen Staatsverwaltung* (Innsbruck 1896) 2 vols; vol. II, p. 45.

2. The *Staatsrat* was an advisory body which had been set up in 1760 on the initiative of Kaunitz, largely in order to strengthen his own position against his rival, Haugwitz. It then consisted of the Chancellor (presiding) and of three members of the higher nobility and three of the lower; none of these might hold any official position. Their duty was to give impartial opinions on all questions submitted to them.

3. Joseph had become Palatine in 1796 after his predecessor and brother, the Archduke Alexander, had been killed by the explosion of a firework.

4. A Diet's proceedings opened with the presentation to it by the Crown of its *propositiones*, the consideration of which formed its first, and technically, its only business. When these were out of the way, the nation in its turn presented its *postulata* and *gravamina*. Since each party knew in advance what the other was going to say, the Crown often bought in advance the Diet's consent to its own *propositiones* by agreeing in advance to some of its wishes, so that much of the real bargaining went on during, or even before the discussion of the *propositiones*. The Crown was entitled to close the Diet when it would, but it could not exact the *contributio* until the Diet had given assent to it in the form of a law.

5.   Odessa wheat in fact came chiefly from the Danubian Principalities,
      in which costs of production were even lower than in Hungary.
6.   His first wife, Elizabeth of Württemberg, had been married to him
      in January 1789; she had died in February 1790, when bearing him
      a child, who survived only a few months. In September of the same
      year he had married Maria Theresa of Bourbon-Parma, who bore him
      twelve children, and died in April 1807 of the effects of a thirteenth
      confinement.

Chapter 4
The System at its Zenith

1.   I use this wording out of deference to the fact that of the six names
      listed below, three (Dobrovský, Kollár and Šafařik) were Slovaks by
      birth and one (Jungmann) a German, while Palacký, although born
      in Moravia, had been educated in Pozsony. But they all made Prague
      their homes and wrote in Czech.
2.   It is interesting that Palacký wrote the first volume of this work in
      German, in order to reach a wider public among his own compatriots.

Chapter Five
The System on the Wane

1.   This was a system under which all land was entailed in the male line
      of the owner's family, collaterals, however remote, succeeding in
      default of direct heirs. If the line had died out completely, the estate
      would have reverted to the Crown.
2.   The chief of these related to the position of the peasants, which was
      brought roughly into line with the western Lands: they could commute
      their dues and services for cash, and the powers of the Manorial
      Courts were restricted.
3.   It was a frequent practice of deputies to bring with them young univer-
      sity graduates to act as their secretaries, or simply to learn their trade.
      They were allowed to sit in on sessions of the Diet, and should have
      done so as silent spectators, but often turned the proceedings into
      bear-gardens by the applause, or cat-calls, with which they accom-
      panied the speeches. The *jurati* present at the Long Diet were Liberals
      almost to a youth. Many of them played large parts in the Diets and
      ministries of later years.

Chapter Six
The *Vormärz*

1.   The prescription for Hungary of the 'Centralists' (alternatively known,
      in derision, as the 'Doctrinaires') was a strong central government
      responsible to an efficient and representative parliament. Their mem-
      bers included Baron József Eötvös, László Szalay, and others who
      played important parts in the political life of the ensuing years.
2.   A corruption of 'Magyaromanes'.
3.   This had been organized in preparation for the 1830 Diet under the
      name of the 'Party of Considered Reform' by Count Aurel Dessewffy,

who had since died. The Party had then elected Apponyi to lead it, and had changed its name.

Chapter Eight
The Year of Revolution: 1848

1. The Partium were certain areas which had never been legally transferred from Hungary to Transylvania, but were administered as if belonging to the latter.

Chapter Nine
The Decade of Absolutism

1. Schmerling's portfolio went to Philipp Krausz's brother, Karl, Bruck's, to A. von Baumgartner.

2. This document had been drafted for his signature, presumably on the instructions of the Archduke and Rechberg. An ill-humoured dig at Prussia which it contained may have been Francis Joseph's own addition.

Chapter Ten
Eight Years of Experiment

1. Their programme, as it then stood, was set out in detail in a memorandum by Count Emil Dessewffy, which contained many of the proposals in the 'Apponyi Memorandum' described below (p. 136).

2. It was given to Baron Thierry.

3. In practice, this omission was disregarded, and the Ministers President of both halves of the Monarchy were consulted equally.

4. All of these figures were revised on various later occasions.

5. The Hungarian language uses the same word, *magyar*, as an ethnic term and also as a political one with no ethnic or linguistic significance whatever. When used in the former sense the correct equivalent is 'Magyar': in the latter, as here, it should be translated as 'Hungarian'.

Chapter Eleven
Intermezzo

1. A. Friedjung, *Historische Aufsätze* (Stuttgart-Berlin 1919) p. 468.

Chapter Thirteen
Austria under Dualism, 1871–1903

1. The main parties were: of the Right, Poles, 57 (including 5 Ruthenes); Hohenwart Club, 57; Czechs, 54; of the Left, 91 Liberals, 54 'Progressives', 15 other Germans; smaller parties, which divided their votes, 25. The Right were generally reckoned to have 179 members, and the Left, 174.

2. The Czech, Pražak, who had already been in the Cabinet, without a portfolio, now took over the portfolio of justice.

3. These included 19 German Clericals, who had broken away from the Hohenwart Club to form a new party led by the brothers Alfred and Alois Liechtenstein.

4. The Slovenes had asked for an *Untergymnasium* of their own in the little town of Cilli, a German outpost in a Slovene countryside, or alternatively, Slovene classes in the German Gymnasium there. The Germans, while not denying the justice of the Slovenes' wish for more education in their own language, insisted that this must not be given in Cilli, whose *Deutschtum* it would endanger. Von Plener, as Minister of Finance, sanctioned a budgetary appropriation for the parallel classes, whereupon his own party disavowed him and withdrew from the coalition on the pretext that the inter-party agreement had been broken. Under the next Government the appropriation was passed without difficulty, and Cilli remained a German town until its inhabitants were expelled or slaughtered in 1945.

5. Most of the German Clericals had organized themselves under that name in 1895.

6. The Archduchess died in 1872, Rauscher in 1873.

Chapter Fourteen
Hungary, 1867–1903

1. The Christian People's Party (see below, p. 210). The Conservatives also refused to adopt a strictly *közjogi* basis, but they were always a group rather than a party and disappeared altogether after a few years. I use the word 'nation-wide' because a reader would naturally associate the word 'national' with the nationalities' issue. Under 'nation-wide' I mean the exact opposite: a party which claimed to concern itself with the country as a whole.

2. The Confessional issue of the 1890s (see below, p. 210).

3. The question of the 'Jurisdictions' (below p. 212) also played a considerable part in the conflicts of these years.

4. One *hold* = 0.576 hectares, = 1.43 English acres.

5. Rauch in 1871, Bedeković in 1872.

6. He was the first untitled man ever to hold the office of Ban, and was consequently nicknamed 'the peasant Ban': but he had in fact been head of the Croat Chancellery in Vienna.

7. In 1880, 23 members of the party had seceded from it to form an 'Independent National Party' against the introduction of compulsory courses in Magyar for the staff of the Financial Ministry in Zagreb.

Chapter Fifteen
Bosnia-Herzegovina, 1878–1903

1. A fourth department, for forestry and mines, was added later.

2. Some alterations were later introduced in the terms of service.

Chapter Sixteen
The Last Years of Peace

1. The emigration was doubly beneficial, for many émigrés sent back substantial remittances to their families, or themselves returned, bringing with them savings out of which they bought small-holdings from

indebted landowners. Whole prosperous villages of 'Americans' were to be found in Galicia, parts of Hungary, and Dalmatia.

2. There were three 'official languages' in the Austrian army. The 'language of service' (*Dienstsprache*) was used for written communications between the ministry and 'units'. It was German. All officers had to know it. The 'language of command' (*Kommandosprache*) consisted of only about seventy words, which every recruit had to know by heart. It was German except in the *Honvédség*, in which it was Magyar (Croat in Croatia). Each regiment had also one or more 'regimental language' (*Regimentssprache*) which was that, or those, of the district from which the regiment was recruited. Instruction to the rank and file was given in it, and other purely internal business transacted in it. It was obligatory on every officer to know the regimental language of his regiment, and such knowledge was a condition for his promotion in it.

3. Chlopy was the village from which Francis Joseph had been watching the manœuvres in Galicia.

4. According to R. Sieghart, *Die letzten Jahre einer Grossmacht* (Berlin 1932) p. 117, the Order had been 'influenced' by Koerber.

5. The Coalition had repealed his previous reform.

6. In fact, the non-Slavs of the Monarchy slightly outnumbered its Slavs in 1900, and fractionally, even after the annexation of Bosnia-Herzegovina, in 1908.

7. This was meant as a token of reassurance to the Porte that Austria was harbouring no further designs on it.

8. A. Mendelssohn-Bartholdy *et al.* (ed.) *Die grosse Politik der europäischen Kabinette* (Berlin 1922–6) 38 vols; vol. 30, pp. 474ff.

9. See his self-briefing for his conversation with Sir Charles Hardinge, 19 August 1908 (*Oesterreich-Ungarns Aussenpolitik* (Vienna 1930) 9 vols; vol. I, p. 27). This version omits the devastating last sentence quoted by E. Crankshaw, *The Fall of the House of Habsburg* (London 1963) p. 37.

10. Conrad was forced to resign, on Aehrenthal's insistence, in November 1911, but the Archduke secured his reinstatement in December 1912.

11. The Ruthenes came off the worst of all the nationalities in 1907 with only one Reichsrat deputy to each 102,000 voters, while the Poles had one to 64,000. The best situated were the Italians, with 1:38,000, then the Germans with 1:40,000, third, strangely, the Roumanians with 1:46,000.

Chapter Seventeen
The End of the Monarchy

1. Kossuth had died on 5 May.

2. Some words have obviously fallen out of the text of the version of this conversation given in Grey's memoirs. But this must have been what he said.

3. T. G. Masaryk, *The Making of a State* (London 1927) p. 105.

4. The text of the memorandum was published by D. Lloyd George in

his *The Truth about the Peace Treaties* (London 1938) 2 vols; vol. 1, pp. 31ff.

5. Conrad was given the command of the Army Group of the Tirol. The Archduke retired into private life.

6. G. Brook-Shepherd, *The Last Habsburg* (London 1968) p. 58. The witness is the Empress Zita. Czernin's candidature was urged also by Prince Conrad Hohenlohe, the ephemeral Minister President of 1905, whom Charles had made his Marshal, and on whose advice he made many of his first appointments.

7. In the event, agreement was, largely thanks to considerable concessions by Tisza, reached on a new settlement which was scheduled to last for 20 years. It had not come into operation when the Monarchy broke up.

8. The only prominent non-Czech beneficiary was Schönerer.

9. M. Pichon on 27 December 1917; Mr Lloyd George on 5 January 1918; President Wilson repeated his earlier pronouncement in his Fourteen Points Speech of 8 January 1918.

10. The words were: 'The peoples of Austria-Hungary, whose place among the nations we wish to see safeguarded and assured, should be accorded the fullest opportunity of autonomous development.' Later Wilson was so contemptibly dishonest as to allow the 'safeguarding and assurance' to be interpreted as referring to the peoples, not the Monarchy.

11. It appears that in fact the warning had been given by Yugoslav deserters.

12. The British units were diverted East to the Straits.

13. On the 27th another meeting of Roumanian leaders demanded self-determination for their people. On the 28/29 a meeting of Slovak politicians at Turóczszentmárton adopted a Resolution claiming the right of self-determination for the Slovaks 'as part of the single Czecho-Slovak people'. Later, indeed, acute controversy arose over exactly what the meeting meant to say on the future relationship between the Slovaks and the Czechs, what it did say, and who said it. But this, again, falls outside the scope of this volume.

14. Joseph, who had been born and brought up in Hungary (he was the grandson of the old Palatine) was a relatively popular figure there. Charles had given him the command of the South Western Army Group after the failure of the June offensive, but when the direct military danger seemed to be that threatening Hungary, had asked him to take over the defence of that country. On the 26th he was in Vienna *en route* to take over the new appointment.

15. Lindner's message, on which much ink had been spilt, had in nact little effect on the situation in the Tirol. Some commanders there at first refused to pass it on, and in any case, many of the units were already on their way home.

APPENDIX

Approximate population in 1780, *by nationality,*
of the Habsburg Monarchy

Thousands have been omitted throughout. The following abbreviations are used: Cr Croats; Cz Czechs; G Germans; Gy gypsies; I Italians; J Jews; M Magyars; P Poles; Rou Roumanians; Ru Ruthenes (Ukrainians); S Serbs; Sk Slovaks; Sl Slovenes.

Hereditary Lands
Carinthia: G 190; Sl 80.
Carniola: G 20; Sl 370; others (mainly Cr) 10.
Littoral (Gorizia-Gradisca, Istria, Trieste); G 10; Sl 130; I 55;[1] others (incl. Jews) 5.
Lower Austria: G 1,200.
Styria: G 480; Sl 265.
Tirol-Vorarlberg: G 310; I 240.[2]
Upper Austria: G 600.
   Total: G 2,810; I 295; Sl 845; others 15.

Lands of the Bohemian Crown
Bohemia: G 1,050; Cz 1,600; J 40; others 10.
Moravia: G 400; Cz 910.
Silesia: G 150; Cz 60; P 90.
   TOTAL for Hereditary Lands and Lands of the Bohemian Crown: G 4,410; Cr 10; Cz 2,570; I 295; Sl 845; P 90; J 45; others 10.

Lands of the Hungarian Crown
Kingdom of Hungary: G 775; M 2,960; Ru 290; Rou 635; Sk 1,220; Cr 65; S 250; Sl 40; other South Slavs[3] 40; J 80; Gy 75; others 5.
Civilian Croatia: G 5; I 15; Cr 460; S 165.
Military Frontier: G 30; Rou 80; Cr 360; S 240.
Transylvania: G 135; M 400: Rou 850: J 5; Gy 40; others 10.[4]
   Total: G 945; M 3,360; Ru 290; Rou 1,565; I 15; Cr 885; Sl 40; S 655; Sk 1,220; other South Slavs 40; J 85; Gy 115; others 10.

   Galicia-Bukovina: G 10; P 1,000; Ru 1,500; Rou 50; J 210; others 30.[5]
   TOTAL for Central Monarchy: G 5,365; M 3,360; Cz 2,570; P 1,090; I 310; Ru 1,790; Sl 885; Cr 910; S 655; other Southern Slavs 40; Sk 1,220; J 340; Gy 115; Armenians 15; others 15.
   For total population of Monarchy add: G 250 (Vorlande); I 1,500 (Milanese); Flamands and Walloons: 2,000 (Netherlands).

1. In some Austrian statistics 'Friulians'. 2. Including 20 Ladins. 3. Sokci, Bunyevci, Bulgars.
4. Including 5 Armenians. 5. Including 10 Armenians and 10 Gypsies.

INDEX

absolutism: of Francis II, 27-8, 29,
31, 32, 48, 54; of Francis Joseph,
126-37; of Joseph II, 1-2, 4, 18, 19;
of Leopold II, 24; reactions to, 54,
137-40, 142, 153
Academic Legion, 91, 97, 111, 113
Adler, Friedrich, 257, 261
Adler, Viktor, 191, 200, 257
administration: aristocratic, 14-15,
31, 48; bureaucratic, 5, 14-15;
centralist outlook of, 15, 31, 36;
Dienstrèglement, 31-2; in 1848,
86-7; in 1849-59, 132-5; in 1871-
1903, 192-3, 211-12; in the
Vormärz, 63-4; of Hereditary
Lands, 2-3, 8, 13; of Transylvania,
3, 13; policy of Francis II, 30-2, 40,
47-8, 56; policy of Francis Joseph,
132-5; policy of Joseph II, 13-15;
policy of Maria Theresa, 5, 8, 14-15
Adriatic, the, 172
Ady, E., 235
Aehrenthal, Baron Lexa von, 242-5,
246, 248
agriculture, 6, 37, 43, 45-6, 64, 66,
68-9, 80, 185, 186, 190, 207, 213,
218, 229, 233-4
Albania, 246, 255
Albrecht, Archduke, 85, 127, 133,
144, 149, 157, 158, 168, 172, 193
Alexander, Archduke, 283n3
Alexander, Czar, 45, 47
alispán, 4, 13
Alldeutscher Verein, 201
Alpine Lands, 6, 8, 47, 64, 91-2,
137-8, 189
Alsace-Lorraine, 264, 272
Andrássy, Count Gyula, sen., 124,
157, 160, 168, 170, 172-3, 174,
206, 207

Andrássy, Count Gyula, jun., 236,
237, 238, 278
Anticipationsscheine, 44
anti-Semitism, 187, 200
Apponyi, Count Albert, 209, 210,
211, 235, 236, 237, 238, 239,
254
Apponyi, Count György, 76, 81, 83,
86, 88, 156, 157
April Laws, 88-90, 103, 104, 108,
110, 117, 142, 151, 154, 163
Arbeiterbildungsverein, 190
army, armed forces: Army Act, 161,
163-4; conscription, 2, 18, 36, 38,
39, 163; controversy over, (1859-
67), 153, (1880s), 210, (1903-13),
235, 236, 237, 240, 266; Monarchy
and, 2, 15, 18, 23, 25, 37-8, 136-7,
153; organization of, 36, 38, 192-3;
second-line formations, 2, 39-40,
163-4; strength of, 2, 38, 41, 46-7,
78, 164, 246; under Law XII,
160-1; *see also contributio, Honvédség, insurrectio*
Asquith, H. H., 261
Auersperg, Count Karl, 97, 112
Auersperg, Prince Adolf, 170, 177-9,
188
Auersperg, Prince 'Carlos', 166, 167,
187-8
Auffenberg, F.M.L. M. von, 246
Aussee Programme, 159, 199-200
Austria (Cis-Leithania) under
Dualism: December Constitution,
161-3, 177; 1871-1903, 177-204;
1903-13, 247-9, 251-2
Austrian Lands, 13
Austro-Slavism, 95, 99
Autonomists, 154, 156, 178
aviticitas, 58, 59, 81, 89, 134, 284nl

296
Index

MAPS

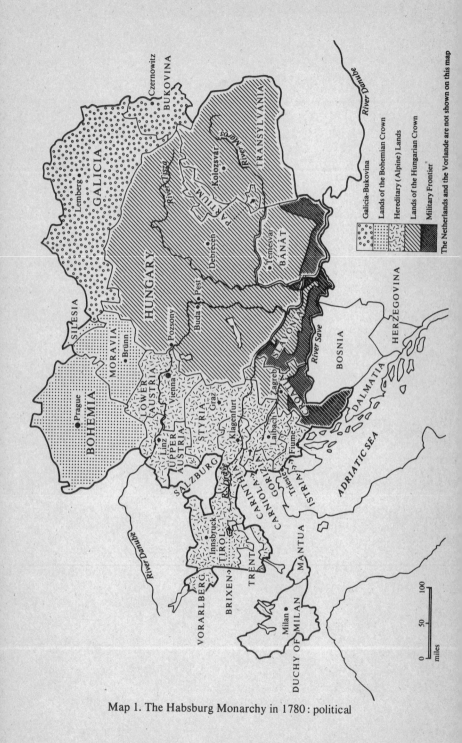

Map 1. The Habsburg Monarchy in 1780: political

Legend:
- Galicia-Bukovina
- Lands of the Bohemian Crown
- Hereditary (Alpine) Lands
- Lands of the Hungarian Crown
- Military Frontier

The Netherlands and the Vorlände are not shown on this map

GALICIA
Lemberg
Czernowitz
BUKOVINA
SILESIA
MORAVIA
Brünn
BOHEMIA
Prague
HUNGARY
River Tisza
River Maros
Kolozsvár
TRANSYLVANIA
Debrecen
Pest
Buda
Pozsony
Temesvár
BANAT
LOWER AUSTRIA
Vienna
STYRIA
Graz
Klagenfurt
Laibach
Zagreb
SLAVONIA
CROATIA
River Save
BOSNIA
HERZEGOVINA
DALMATIA
Trieste
Fiume
GORIZIA
CARNIOLA
CARINTHIA
UPPER AUSTRIA
Linz
SALZBURG
River Drave
TIROL
Innsbruck
BRIXEN
TRENT
VORARLBERG
MANTUA
Milan
DUCHY OF MILAN
ISTRIA
ADRIATIC SEA
River Danube

0   50   100
miles

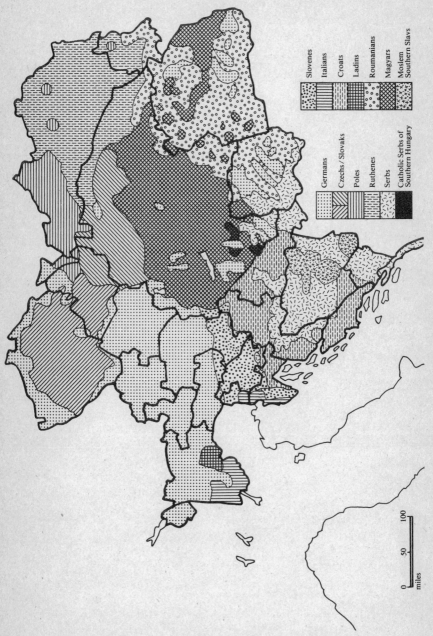

Map 2. The Habsburg Monarchy in 1910: ethnic and linguistic

Slovenes
Italians
Croats
Ladins
Roumanians
Magyars
Moslem
Southern Slavs

Germans
Czechs / Slovaks
Poles
Ruthenes
Serbs
Catholic Serbs of
Southern Hungary

0 50 100
miles